Strategic Human Capital Development and Management in Emerging Economies

Anshuman Bhattacharya
Sunbeam College for Women, India

A volume in the Advances in Human Resources Management and Organizational Development (AHRMOD) Book Series

IGI GLOBAL
DISSEMINATOR OF KNOWLEDGE

www.igi-global.com

Published in the United States of America by
IGI Global
Business Science Reference (an imprint of IGI Global)
701 E. Chocolate Avenue
Hershey PA 17033
Tel: 717-533-8845
Fax: 717-533-8661
E-mail: cust@igi-global.com
Web site: http://www.igi-global.com

Library of Congress Cataloging-in-Publication Data

Library of Congress Cataloging-in-Publication Data

Names: Bhattacharya, Anshuman, 1981- editor.
Title: Strategic human capital development and management in emerging economies / Anshuman Bhattacharya, editor.
Description: Hershey : Business Science Reference, [2017]
Identifiers: LCCN 2016049582| ISBN 9781522519744 (hardcover) | ISBN 9781522519751 (ebook)
Subjects: LCSH: Human capital--Developing countries--Management. | Strategic planning--Developing countries. | Organizational behavior--Developing countries.
Classification: LCC HD4904.7 .S775 2017 | DDC 658.3/01091724--dc23 LC record available at https://lccn.loc.gov/2016049582

This book is published in the IGI Global book series Advances in Human Resources Management and Organizational Development (AHRMOD) (ISSN: 2327-3372; eISSN: 2327-3380)

British Cataloguing in Publication Data
A Cataloguing in Publication record for this book is available from the British Library.

Advances in Human Resources Management and Organizational Development (AHRMOD) Book Series

ISSN:2327-3372
EISSN:2327-3380

Mission

A solid foundation is essential to the development and success of any organization and can be accomplished through the effective and careful management of an organization's human capital. Research in human resources management and organizational development is necessary in providing business leaders with the tools and methodologies which will assist in the development and maintenance of their organizational structure.

The **Advances in Human Resources Management and Organizational Development (AHRMOD) Book Series** aims to publish the latest research on all aspects of human resources as well as the latest methodologies, tools, and theories regarding organizational development and sustainability. The **AHRMOD Book Series** intends to provide business professionals, managers, researchers, and students with the necessary resources to effectively develop and implement organizational strategies.

Coverage

- Corporate Governance
- Organizational Behavior
- Job Enrichment
- Executive Compensation
- Personnel Retention
- Human Resources Development
- Skills Management
- Employment and Labor Laws
- Organizational Learning
- Coaching and Mentoring

IGI Global is currently accepting manuscripts for publication within this series. To submit a proposal for a volume in this series, please contact our Acquisition Editors at Acquisitions@igi-global.com or visit: http://www.igi-global.com/publish/.

The Advances in Human Resources Management and Organizational Development (AHRMOD) Book Series (ISSN 2327-3372) is published by IGI Global, 701 E. Chocolate Avenue, Hershey, PA 17033-1240, USA, www.igi-global.com. This series is composed of titles available for purchase individually; each title is edited to be contextually exclusive from any other title within the series. For pricing and ordering information please visit http://www.igi-global.com/book-series/advances-human-resources-management-organizational/73670. Postmaster: Send all address changes to above address.

Titles in this Series

For a list of additional titles in this series, please visit: www.igi-global.com

Handbook of Research on Human Resources Strategies for the New Millennial Workforce
Patricia Ordoñez de Pablos (University of Oviedo, Spain) and Robert D. Tennyson (University of Minnesota, USA)
Business Science Reference • copyright 2017 • 523pp • H/C (ISBN: 9781522509486) • US $310.00 (our price)

Management Education for Global Leadership
Neeta Baporikar (HP-GSB, Namibia University of Science and Technology, Namibia)
Business Science Reference • copyright 2017 • 321pp • H/C (ISBN: 9781522510130) • US $185.00 (our price)

Innovation and Shifting Perspectives in Management Education
Neeta Baporikar (HP-GSB, Namibia University of Science and Technology, Namibia)
Business Science Reference • copyright 2017 • 352pp • H/C (ISBN: 9781522510192) • US $190.00 (our price)

Strategic Labor Relations Management in Modern Organizations
Ana María Lucia Casademunt (Universidad Loyola Andalucía, Spain)
Business Science Reference • copyright 2016 • 313pp • H/C (ISBN: 9781522503569) • US $205.00 (our price)

Bridging the Scholar-Practitioner Gap in Human Resources Development
Claretha Hughes (University of Arkansas, USA) and Matthew W. Gosney (Hillcrest Health-Care Systems, USA)
Business Science Reference • copyright 2016 • 267pp • H/C (ISBN: 9781466699984) • US $185.00 (our price)

Quantitative Multidisciplinary Approaches in Human Capital and Asset Management
Meir Russ (University of Wisconsin-Green Bay, USA)
Business Science Reference • copyright 2016 • 317pp • H/C (ISBN: 9781466696525) • US $205.00 (our price)

Strategic Information Technology Governance and Organizational Politics in Modern Business
Tiko Iyamu (Cape Peninsula University of Technology, South Africa)
Business Science Reference • copyright 2015 • 326pp • H/C (ISBN: 9781466685246) • US $210.00 (our price)

IGI GLOBAL
DISSEMINATOR OF KNOWLEDGE
www.igi-global.com

701 E. Chocolate Ave., Hershey, PA 17033
Order online at www.igi-global.com or call 717-533-8845 x100
To place a standing order for titles released in this series,
contact: cust@igi-global.com
Mon-Fri 8:00 am - 5:00 pm (est) or fax 24 hours a day 717-533-8661

Editorial Advisory Board

Table of Contents

Detailed Table of Contents

Nowadays, finding qualified labor force among the job applicants is one of the main problems in organizations and companies, so employee selection is one of the main challenges in human resource management. In this case, the variety of methods and tests has been represented and used in order to evaluate the employees' abilities up to now. However, determining the best selection methods according to the job requirements is one of the basic challenges in organizations and companies. In this chapter, different selection methods and their capabilities have been studied in order to assess various job abilities. The results, of this research, showed that the methods such as Assessment centers have significantly assessed a persons' job abilities, however we should pay attention to some parameters such as time, cost, the method's validity, and moral and legal aspects for an appropriate selection method.

This chapter analyzes the effects of macroergonomic compatibility of organizational elements on the performance of manufacturing systems in terms of Clients, Manufacturing Process, and Organizational Performance. As methods, a macroergonomic compatibility questionnaire is developed, statistically validated, and administered to middle and senior managers of manufacturing companies. Also, a hypothetical causal model is proposed and tested to find relationships among the constructs by using a Structural Equation Modeling. Direct, indirect, and total effects are determined, and results show that macroergonomic organizational elements have significant direct effects among themselves. Likewise, it is found that Organizational Culture and Organizational Communication have significant direct

Preface

Definition of human being rapidly changed after 1760. Initially after industrial revolution, human was the facilitator for machines. Gradually, human-machine difference was blurred by greed of industrialists in European and American continents. Men were turned into half machines; human factor was lost in management. Third phase of industrialisation is characterised by automation of industries, when human rights are uplifted by international bodies and most of the industrialists. Human being has been turned into the 'capital' by now, which generates some added-values through inputting this element of production; so, development of this resource is taken good care of. The labour factor in production was almost substituted by automatic machines in this phase of industrialisation; the definition of human capital, hence, transformed into "the creator who frames knowledge skills competence and experience originated by persistent interactions between self and environment" (Dae-bong, 2009).

Any organization is a unique composition of positional hierarchy and human interactions. One is obvious static structure and the other is intangible (sometimes spiritual) aspect of the same organization. These two aspects collectively form the most valuable intangible asset of any organization – Human Capital. Maximum return from this asset at present and to prepare this for managing contingencies depends upon its effective management and development. Human Capital Management is concerned with entire structure of stakeholders, shared services and centres of expertise. Managing and developing human capital from different parts of the sphere is no more possible through trial and error techniques. The amount of investment in this intangible asset is growing up; hence more realistic and precisely applicable models are required for developing human capital. One should be able to measure the development in absolute quantitative norms.

Although models are considered to be ready to apply tools for specific situations, it is a myth. Models are subject to paradoxes; positivity of results is dependent upon appropriate strategic choice and expertise of the applier or manager who has to set equilibrium amongst these complexities and paradoxes including performance plan of the organization, budgetary constraints, and internal and external drivers impacting human capital need. Development of a contemporary and practical measure of Human Capital Development is imperative in such circumstances. The first step towards construction of such a refined measuring technique is developing a vision of future workforce need. The gap between present and future key themes of core human capital functions can be identified by review of strategic documents and workforce information.

Comprehension of strategic direction and goals is the first step of strategic human capital management. It is followed by change management and implementation of the strategic plan; further, development of a sound accountability system. Human capital development index identifies 46 indicators in two broad categories, namely education and employment grouped in eight parameters. Although strategically sound human capital development is essential for emerging economies, normally these economies lag behind in any one or more of these aspects. The present edition is an attempt to develop holistic perspective of human capital development.

In the present global scenario when previous standards have radically changed and unrecognized economies are emerging in the world's economic canvass, it is essential to review current management techniques, especially in reference to these emerging economies. These economies have great potentials for production as well as for market, as enormous man power on one hand and on the other huge consumer base is present there in these economies. Unfortunately most of the man-power is unorganised in these economies, the little part of organised and productive man-power lacks vision to capitalise on their competence. The proposed book is to examine the existing variability in development of human capital in emerging economies and thereby to identify the indicators responsible for the disparity in development in the capital. The book tends to focus especially on human behaviour in organizations, and development of skills initiated by behavioural remedies that reflects in enhanced productivity. Present effort is to discuss infrastructural parameters in business organizations to achieve substantial development in human capital in developed, developing and under developed countries in Eurasia, Africa and Latin America with special reference to globalized economies.

The proposed edition on human capital development aims at assessment of impact of globalization on human capital development. It further tends to analyse different measures to improve production per-man-hour and per-unit of money, say productivity of human resources and capital. Globalization is observed not only in respect of market for output, but also in respect to inputs including human resources. It has, therefore, become a necessity of the hour to review the principles being applied to manage human behaviour in organizations. The collection, however, is not confined to the pure economic perspectives rather includes all derivatives of socio-economic and socio-psychological concerns.

The present book contributes to a great extent to the scholarly world; especially policy makers, academicians including researchers, entrepreneurs and intrapreneurs, and all globalized institutions as the book is a conglomerate of intellectual empirical contemplation on the issue from diversified perspectives. It is divided into eleven chapters each representing different perspective of human capital.

Ergonomics is traditionally believed a science to study human efficiency and designing the work place accordingly. Although it has been significantly contributing in improving productivity of workforce, but the branch of knowledge considers only physical aspect not mental aspect of the task. First chapter of the book contributes towards identification and assessment of mental tasks through the development of task flowcharts.

Second chapter concerns with influence of organizational climate on organizational-role stress. Aggregate of psychological climate, comprising of individual perception of physical structure, organizational policies and interpersonal relations, forms work climate in an organization. The climate plays key role in degree of organizational-role stress and eventually job satisfaction of an employee. The perception of organizational elements contributes to value addition in organizational rewards and its characteristics. Finally, the research concludes that healthy combination of the elements of organizational climate increases human capital formation rate.

We cannot ignore existence of criminals in any society. A significant share of human resources in any country happens to be involved in crime, say organized crime; so organized crime has now become a serious issue claiming intense research on how these organizations are managed inter se as well as protected from external threats. Chapter three focuses on structure and operation of organization crime networks, contributing factors for management of such organizations, role of organised crime in legitimate businesses and how to defeat or dismantle these organizations.

The fourth chapter in the sequence is an overview of human capital. It is a study of interrelationship between human capital and economic growth, innovation and knowledge management. The study also focuses on research and development (R&D), political regime and foreign direct investment (FDI). Further, the chapter deals in employment, labour markets, measure of human capital, and the challenges and implications of human capital in the digital age. Creating an organization that relies on human capital for competitive advantage involves designing every organizational system with an essential approach to attracting, developing, motivating and retaining the highly qualified people. The chapter argues that developing human capital has the potential to enhance organizational performance and gain sustainable competitive advantage in the digital age.

The fifth chapter analyses the selection tests based on their capabilities to evaluate various jobs proficiencies and abilities. Nowadays, employee selection is one of the main challenges in human resource management. In this case, the variety of methods and tests has been represented and used in order to evaluate the employees' abilities up to now. However, determining the best selection methods according to the job requirements is one of the basic challenges for organizations. The present chapter assesses affectivity of different selection tests for weighing various job abilities.

In the modern era of cosmopolitan industries designing of individual tasks and processes is not sufficient rather, harmonization of overall task systems comprising of a top-down socio-technical systems is necessity. Sixth chapter in the book analyses characteristics of work system designs of human-job, human-machine and human-software interfaces to ensure complete harmony in the entire work system in terms of clients, manufacturing process and organizational performance.

When we discuss human resource capital condition in one of the most prominent emerging countries, that is India, we find a major part of the resource is either idle or not being optimally capitalised on. Even today Indian rural women are marginalized by depriving them from education, employment and productive resources. The seventh chapter is a case study of an NGO, Mann Deshi Foundation, which endeavours to bring rural women of a province back to main stream through creating them micro-entrepreneurs, educating them business tactics, providing them easy-finance and supporting them by experienced business leaders.

Next chapter deals with banking industries in Iran where industrial activities have recently been more competitive than last decade perhaps because of presence of private companies in competition. The research aims at provide banker's emerging strategy using blue ocean solution within Pasargad Bank of Iran. The current study is accomplished based on descriptive – analytical method and collection of required data has been implemented through designed questionnaire. Then, utilizing QSPM matrix, most attractive strategies prioritized (such as creation variety of services providing travelling banking services and enhance productivity, as well as to offer CCDM (Check/Cash Deposit Module), increase in security and reduce misuse of related information, implement of updated software, establish a system to update expiration date of credit cards, and online payment of other currencies.

The ninth chapter emphasizes corporate social responsibility (CSR). The study establishes connections between CSR and human values; CSR in mining operations; CSR in sports tourism industry; CSR in emerging economies; and the perspectives of CSR in the digital age. The chapter assesses significance of strategic approach to CSR to a company's success. CSR can bring various benefits in terms of risk management, cost savings, access to capital, customer relationships, human resource management, and innovation capacity. CSR encourages more social and environmental responsibility from the corporate sector at a time when the crisis has damaged consumer confidence and the levels of trust in business. Socially responsible companies can improve their brand reputation, attract more customers, and increase stakeholder engagement. The chapter argues that promoting CSR has the potential to enhance organizational performance and reach strategic goals in the digital age.

Growing complexities and competitiveness has significant contribution to enhance burnout of middle and senior management. The research report presented in tenth chapter presents a descriptive study of both conditions among middle and senior managers in the maquiladora industry of Ciudad Juarez. Burnout was surveyed and obesity was studied in these managers. The result was shocking, nearly 70% of the sample was suffering from burnout syndrome and 35% of them were suffering from obesity. Work psychosocial aspects and their effects on human capital development in the industrial sector are not sufficiently studied in developing countries so as to develop strategies for the prevention and effective handling of both burnout syndrome and obesity.

Recent demonetisation in India has given a fresh thrust to cash-less transactions and mobile banking. Mobile banking in India has witnessed a lot of changes with respect to technological and architectural changes. A significant surge in mobile banking users is due to technological advancements and establishment of faith on the mobile banking. However, the growth is still not as it was expected; in a developing economy like India the number of mobile users is expected to grow exponentially. The probable reasons for slow adoption rate may be non-parity of fulfilment of users' expectations (fast, convenient and most importantly, more secure) with growing complexities. There is a scope of improvement with the already existing resources and mobile banking is not an exception in this direction. The National Payments Corporation of India has initiated a system called Unified Payments Interface (UPI) that further eases the process of money transfer through smart phones and feature phones, thereby bringing this technology within everybody's reach. This eleventh chapter further puts insights into the implementation and feasibility aspects of UPI and how it is better than the systems prevailing today.

The holistic approach of the edition is a committed attempt for identifying and removing the loop wholes in development of human capital in emerging economies. There are two approaches to achieve dominance – quantitative supremacy or qualitative supremacy. Former approach can certainly dominate the environment, but it does not positively contribute anything towards development. However, the second approach to achieve supremacy is of course contributing to sustainable development. This is why no positive relations have been observed in population and strategic development of a nation. It is higher human capital index that contribute towards economic and overall development of a country. All round development of human capital entails best management of constraints through identification and removal of the same; most suitable investments in human capital in form of applied education and health facilities; and optimum utilization of the resource by way of women employability and maintaining productivity of both men and women by keeping a sound work culture.

The present edition covers scanning of organizational climate, identification of mental tasks and scientific assessment of proficiencies and abilities. On one hand banking strategy in Iran has been analysed, on the other mobile banking prospects in India has also been discussed in this compilation. The publication recognises essentiality of macro ergonomics concepts including psychological aspect of job design and effect of burnout in employees and on their productivity. Further, the collection also considers role of women empowerment and responsibility of corporate houses in human capital development. The philosophical base for including all possible aspects of human capital is to ensure best possible tapping of human capital potential in emerging economies.

REFERENCES

Kwon, D.-B. (2009). Human capital and its measurement. Retrieved November 30, 2016, from http://www.oecd.org/site/progresskorea/44109779.pdf

Chapter 1
Identification and Assessment of Mental Tasks Using Task Flowcharts

Juan Luis Hernández-Arellano
Autonomous University of Ciudad Juarez, Mexico

J. Nieves Serratos-Perez
Universidad de Guanajuato, Mexico

Aide Aracely Maldonado Macias
Universidad Autonoma de Ciudad Juarez, Mexico

ABSTRACT

Traditional methods for ergonomic evaluation do not consider the identification and assessment of mental tasks. This chapter proposes a method for the Identification and Assessment of Mental Tasks (IAMT) through the development of task flowcharts. Using a semi structured interview and a task flowchart, the mental tasks are identified and described. Applying the Cognitive Task Load Model (CTLM), a cognitive effect is assigned to every mental task identified. A theoretical/common example and a study case were developed to exemplify the proposed method. IAMT method was developed to be useful mainly in industrial environments; however, IAMT should be applied in different work contexts and environments.

DOI: 10.4018/978-1-5225-1974-4.ch001

INTRODUCTION

Over the last few decades, the way many human beings perform their work has changed significantly. Factors such as huge production increments, the use of new and more sophisticated machinery, among others, have modified the traditional ways to work (Hernandez-Arellano, Ibarra-Mejía, Serratos-Pérez, Garcia-Alcaraz, & Brunette, 2012; Salmon, Stanton, Walker, & Green, 2006). The physical component of the labor and the jobs has diminished, whilst the cognitive component has increased significantly. Nowadays it is common to find jobs where the mental component is much higher than the physical one. This has been reported, for example in the work performed by a secretary in an office environment (Sonne, Villalta, & Andrews, 2012), or the work done by a control room operator (N. A. Stanton, Ashleigh, & Cale, 2006). In these cases, workers are asked mainly to stay in front of a computer screen, developing mental tasks.

The traditional methods for ergonomic task analysis and ergonomic evaluation, do not consider the mental evaluation as a component of the analysis. Thus, today exist methods used to develop ergonomic diagnoses, which include physical evaluation or Physical Task Analysis (PTA), along the cognitive evaluation or cognitive task analysis (CTA). However, these methods do not involve the clear identification of mental tasks. The main goal of this chapter is to present a method developed purposefully for the Identification and Assessment of Mental Tasks (IAMT), using task flowcharts.

BACKGROUND

As things stand today, ergonomic evaluation covers two main areas: physical and cognitive, and usually they are considered separately. So, methodologies have been developed in principle for Physical Task Analysis (PTA) and Cognitive Task Analysis (CTA); there are however methods that combine the evaluation of physical and mental tasks. This section presents a review of the most common and most used methods in ergonomic evaluation.

Methods for Ergonomic Evaluation

Methods for physical evaluation are aimed at postural demands, lifting operations, repetitive movements, environmental, and biomechanical stressors. All of them focus on the determination of a risk level during a specific task. Table 1 summarizes the most widely used among these methods.

Table 1. Methods for physical evaluation

Area	Method	Objective	Author
Postural	Rapid Upper Limb Assessment (RULA)	Determine a risk level	Mcatamney & Corlett (1993)
	Rapid Entire Body Assessment (REBA	Determine a risk level	Hignett & McAtamney (2000)
	Ovako Working Analysis System (OWAS)	Determine a risk level	Karhu, Kansi, & Kuorinka (1977)
	Muscle Fatigue Assessment (MFA)	Determine a risk level and priority of change	Rodgers (2005)
	Rapid Office Strain Assessment (ROSA)	Determine a risk level	Sonne et al (2012)
Lifting	NIOSH equation	Determine a risk level and lifting index	Waters, Putz-Anderson, & Garg (1994)
	Snook and Ciriello tables	Determine a risk level and lifting index	Snook & Ciriello (1991)
Repetitive movements	Job Strain Index (JSI)	Determine a risk level	Steven Moore & Garg (1995)
	Occupational Repetitive Action (OCRA)	Determine a risk level	Colombini, Occhipinti, Álvarez-Casado, Hernández-Soto, & Tello Sandoval (2012)
Environmental evaluation	FANGER	Determine the level of thermal comfort	Fanger (1973)
Biomechanics	3DSSPP Biomechanics software	Determine a risk level	University of Michigan (2012)

Cognitive evaluation methods cover the areas of mental workload and human error, focusing mainly on the determination of the workload levels during a specific task. Table 2 shows the most important methods used in cognitive evaluation.

Diagnostic methods have been developed in order to perform an overall evaluation in a given context, for example, in industrial settings. Table 3 shows the most important among these methods.

Combined methods were created to assess a situation where a worker in a specific context performs both physical and mental tasks. Although some methods were developed more than 15 years ago, its application in occupational activities remains limited. Table 4 shows the most important methods used in combined evaluation.

Another kind of methods used in ergonomics are the task analysis methods. For example, methods such as Hierarchical Task Analysis (HTA) (N. A. Stanton, 2006) allow identifying the tasks (physical and mental) before evaluating. The methodology for physical task analysis proposed by Gómez-Bull, Hernández-Arellano & Ibarra-Mejía (2015) focuses on the identification of physical tasks to be evaluated by postural methods.

Table 2. Methods for cognitive evaluation

Area	Method	Objective	Author
Human error	Systematic Human Error Reduction and Prediction Approach (SHERPA)	Human error assessment	Embrey (1986)
Mental workload	NASA-Task Load Index (TLX)	Determine the level of workload	Hart & Staveland (1988)
	Subjective Workload Assessment Technique (SWAT)	Determine the level of workload	Luximon & Goonetilleke (2001)
Cognitive Task Analysis	Cognitive Task Load Model	Determine the cognitive effects	Neerincx (2003)
	Applied Cognitive Task Analysis (ACTA)	Identify cognitive skills, or mental demands, needed to perform a task proficiently	Militello & Hutton (1998)
	Analytic Cognitive Task Allocation (Analytic CTA)	Decision model for task allocation	Papantonopoulos & Salvendy (2008)

Table 3. Methods for ergonomic diagnoses

Method	Objective	Author
LEST	Industrial diagnoses	Guelaud, Beauchense, Gautrat, & Roustrang (1977)

Table 4. Methods for combined evaluations

Method	Objective	Author
Overall Workload Index (OWI)	Physical and mental evaluation	Jung & Jung (2001)
Multivariate Workload Evaluation (MWE)	Physical and mental evaluation	Miyake (2001)
Multivariate Evaluation of Workload using Analytic Hierarchical Process (AHP)	Physical and mental evaluation	de la Torre-Caldera, Hernandez-Arellano, García-Alcaraz, & Ibarra-Mejia (2014)
Combined Evaluation of Cognitive and Physical Ergonomics (CCPE)	Physical and mental evaluation	Bligard & Osvalder (2014)

In general, the methods mentioned so far focus on identifying the risk level or the level of demands (physical and/or mental) during the performance of a specific task, or group of tasks. However, physical, cognitive, diagnostic, and combined methods are not clear in the identification and classification of the cognitive tasks. Considering the actual work conditions where mental and physical efforts/demands are present in many industrial jobs, it is necessary to develop a method to identify, characterize, and evaluate the cognitive tasks during the occupational performance.

The Cognitive Task Load Model (CTLM)

Most of the methods for Cognitive Task Analysis (CTA) have been developed in recent years. CTA is a methodological proposal born from the need to address two problem areas: a) work has become more cognitively demanding and b) the analysis methods available do not consider explicitly the cognitive elements of work (Militello & Hutton, 1998). CTA is considered as an extension of traditional task analysis that allows identifying, describing, and assessing the cognitive processes that are not observable, for example, selection, information processing, and decision-making.

Although there are several methods to develop CTA, few methods assign a value/score to each task being assessed. Cognitive Task Load Model (CTLM) was developed by Neerincx (2003) to assign a cognitive effect on the tasks analyzed. In addition to the classical measure percentage of time occupied, CTLM considers two load factors that affect cognitive task performance and mental effort: 1) the level of information processing and, 2) the number of task-set switches. These three aspects are contrasted against the duration of the task considered at three levels, *short*, *medium*, and *long*. The five cognitive effects are *no problem, under-load, vigilance, cognitive lock-up*, and the extreme case the *overload*. Table 5 shows the way information is organized in the method.

Task Load Analysis model has been applied mainly in the design and evaluation of software interfaces (Grootjen, Neerincx, Stolk et al., 2007; Grootjen, Bierman, & Neerincx, 2006; Streefkerk, Van Esch-Bussemakers et al., 2006; Toet, 2005) and workload measurement (Hossain & Yeasin, 2015; Siegel & Schraagen, 2014; Siegel & Schraagen, 2014).

PROPOSED METHOD

Identification and Assessment of Mental Tasks (IAMT) method considers three main steps to identify and characterize the mental tasks performed by a worker. An additional step is to assign a complexity level or a cognitive effect to each task. In the first step, a semi-structured interview is conducted among the participants. In

Table 5. Overview of four negative effects of cognitive task demands for a certain period (Neerincx, 2003)

<table>
<tr><th rowspan="2">Task Characteristics</th><th colspan="3">Task Performed Period</th></tr>
<tr><th>Short (<5 min)</th><th>Medium (5-0 min)</th><th>Long (>20 min)</th></tr>
<tr><td>Time occupied: low</td><td rowspan="3">No problem</td><td rowspan="3" colspan="2">Under-load</td></tr>
<tr><td>Info processing: low</td></tr>
<tr><td>Task switches: low</td></tr>
<tr><td>Time occupied: high</td><td rowspan="3" colspan="2">No problem</td><td rowspan="3">Vigilance</td></tr>
<tr><td>Info processing: low</td></tr>
<tr><td>Task switches: low</td></tr>
<tr><td>Time occupied: high</td><td rowspan="3" colspan="3">Cognitive lock-up</td></tr>
<tr><td>Info processing: all</td></tr>
<tr><td>Task switches: high</td></tr>
<tr><td>Time occupied: high</td><td rowspan="3" colspan="3">Overload</td></tr>
<tr><td>Info processing: high</td></tr>
<tr><td>Task switches: high</td></tr>
</table>

the second step, the task flow chart is developed. In the third step, the mental tasks involved in a Decision Making Process (DMP) are selected. An additional step is used to assign a complexity level to the identified tasks. A full description of the four steps just enunciated is given below.

Step 1: Semi-structured interview

- **Participant's Selection Criteria:** Prior to starting the interviews, it is necessary to identify between 5 and 10 expert workers/participants. The selection should be based on the participants´ seniority in the company, and the experience in the current position (at least six months). Only workers who meet these criteria should be invited to contribute to the study.
- **Interview:** It is conducted looking for activities or tasks the participants consider generate mental and physical efforts during their daily work. The interview exercise must be conducted in conditions that ensure there will be no interruptions. Wherever possible, in a space away from the work area. Participants must be informed about the general and specific objectives of the study; then they are asked to sign a consent form. The researcher must state unequivocally that the information gathered will be treaded confidentially. Once the participants are ready, they are invited to answer four questions,

probing on those activities/tasks the participants consider as demanding both mental and physical efforts during their daily work. It is recommendable to use an audio recorder during the interview.

The question posed to the participants are:

- Which tasks/activities demand only physical efforts in your daily work? State their frequency.
- Which tasks/activities demand only mental efforts in your daily? State their frequency.
- Which tasks/activities demand both physical and mental efforts simultaneously in your daily work? State their frequency.
- Please mention other issues that you consider may add mental and/or physical efforts in your daily work.
- Collect the information in a frequency table

Table 6 is an example of the frequency table constructed to collect the data obtained in the interview.

Step 2: Flow chart development

Making a decision is an indicator of mental effort (Wickens, 2014). Thus, the most important part of the flow chart is the identification of those tasks that involve a Decision Making Process (DMP). Figure 1 shows a common DMP where, after completing task 1, the worker must make a decision whether to continue with task 2 or task 3. In this context, Dharwada, Sadasivan, Nickles, & Gramopadhye (2006) used task flowcharts to describe an aircraft inspection task. Using this approach, the IAMT method uses the flowchart symbols to develop a task flowchart of the activities developed by a worker.

Special attention must be put on the DMP´s. The flow chart must include all the decisions taken by the operators during the tasks analyzed. It is important to use

Table 6. Frequency table

Task	Frequency	Type of Effort		
		Only Physical	Only Mental	Physical and Mental
Name of the task	Number of participants mention that mention this issue?	Mark only one option		
Write other issues that add mental or physical effort during the task				

Figure 1. Example of Making Decision Process (MDP)

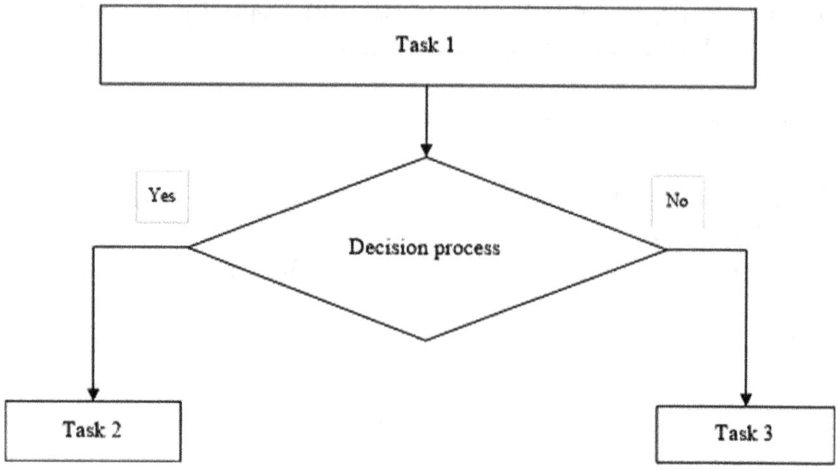

correctly the flowchart symbols (arrows, rhombus, boxes, and circles). Figure 2 shows a task flowchart with two MDP.

Step 3: List of mental tasks

In this step, the mental and combined tasks mentioned by the workers and the MDP identified in the tasks flowchart should be listed and described. Table 7 shows an example of the format used to complete this step.

Step 4: Assessment of cognitive tasks

In the last step, the IAMT method suggests applying the Cognitive Task Load Model (CTLM) (Neerincx, 2003) to assign the complexity level or cognitive effect of each cognitive task identified. Table 8 shows an example of the format used to complete this step.

COMMON EXAMPLE

This theoretical example is related to turn on the TV and to find a specific TV channel using the remote control.

Step 1: Semi-structured interview

- Select participant's criteria.

Figure 2. Example of a task flowchart

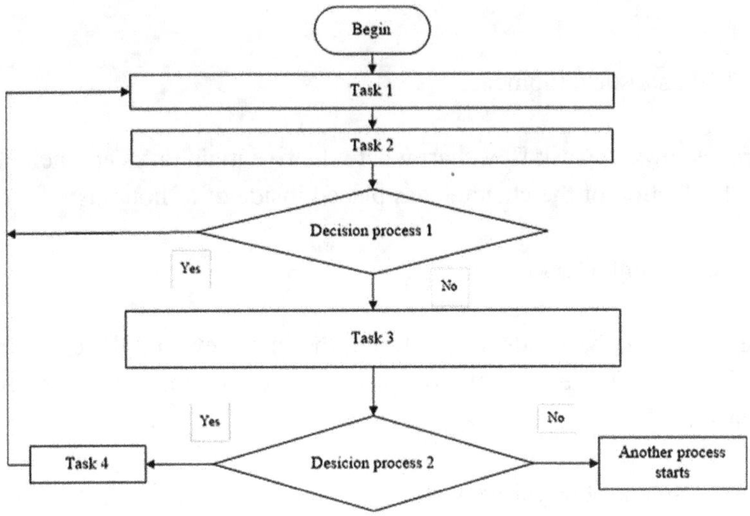

Table 7. Description of mental tasks

Task	Description	Task Duration
Name of the task	Description of the task	

Table 8. Cognitive task analysis

Task	Subtask	Cognitive Effect	Performance Time	Frequency
Name of the task	Name of the subtask	Result		

  - Five daily TV viewers were recruited. They were explained about the overall objective of this example.
- Ask for activities users consider demand mental and physical efforts. Four basic question are next:
  - Using the questions proposed by this method, the participants were questioned about the physical, mental, and combined tasks performed during two phases: 1) before, during, and after they turn on the TV, and 2) finding a TV channel using the remote control.
- Collect the information in a frequency table.

Five main tasks were mentioned by the users. Table 9 shows the information.

Step 2: Flow chart development

Figure 3 shows the task flowchart where the five main tasks are included. Only the task of selection of the channel was placed inside of a rhombus.

Step 3: List of mental tasks

Three main tasks were identified during the interview and the development of the task flowchart. Table 10 shows the tasks, the description, and the performance time of each task.

Step 4: Assessment of cognitive tasks

The Cognitive Task Load Model was applied to the tasks identified. Vigilance was assigned to the subtask related to watching TV indefinitely, and no cognitive effect was assigned to the other tasks. Table 11 shows the cognitive task analysis.

STUDY CASE

A study case is presented to exemplify the IAMT method proposed in this chapter. The work performed by an operator of a Control Numerical Computerized (CNC)

Table 9. Frequency table

Tasks	Frequency	Type of Effort		
		Only Physical	Only Mental	Physical and Mental
Looking for the remote control	5			X
Take the remote control	4	X		
Push the turn on button	5	X		
Watch the TV	5		X	
Select a specific TV channel	4			X
Other issues that add mental or physical effort during the task • None were mentioned				

Figure 3. Turn on TV and selection of a TV channel

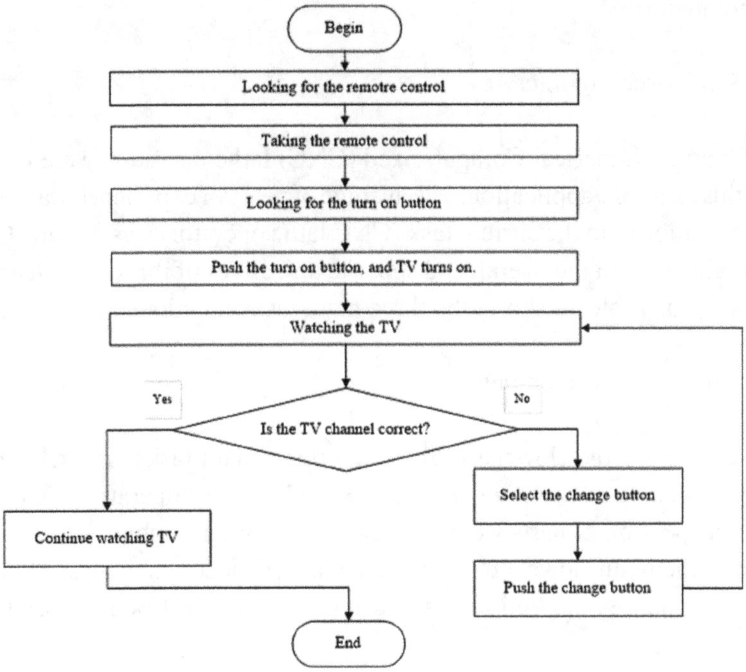

Table 10. Description of mental tasks

Task	Description	Task Duration
Looking for the remote control	The user looks for the remote control in a specific place	Less than 1 minute
Watch TV	Watch TV and decide if the channel is correct	1-5 seconds
Selection of a TV channel	The user select a specific TV channel to watch TV	10-15 seconds

Table 11. Cognitive task analysis

Task	Subtask	Cognitive Effect	Performance Time	Frequency
Looking for the remote control	NA	No effect	A few seconds	NA
Watching TV	Only for a few seconds	No effect	A few seconds	NA
	Indefinitely	Vigilance	Undefined	NA
Selection of a TV channel	Decide if the channel is correct	No effect	2-5 seconds	NA
	Select the correct button	No effect	2-5 seconds	NA

lathe is analyzed applying the proposed method. Three main tasks and five sub-tasks were identified.

Step 1: Semi-structure interview

Ten Control Numerical Computerized (CNC) lathe operators were recruited to develop this example/application. The average of years of experience was 5 while the average of seniority in the current task (CNC lathe operator) was 3 years. Operators were explained about the overall and specific objectives of this research and signed a consent form. Table 12 shows the three main tasks mentioned by the workers.

Step 2: Flow chart development

Figure 4 shows the flowchart where the three main tasks are included. Other sub-tasks were included to complete the task of CNC lathe operation. Only the tasks related to inspection of parts were included inside of a rhombus.

Because the main flowchart included a quality inspection process after the second MDP, the quality inspection was drawn in a separated flowchart (see Figure 5).

Step 3: List of mental tasks

Tasks of inspection and control panel operation are described in Table 13.

Step 4: Assessment of cognitive tasks

Using the Cognitive Task Load Model (CTLM), tasks of inspection of parts and control panel operation were evaluated. The inspection includes two different scenarios: 1) continuous inspection, and 2) identification of quality errors during the inspection. Table 14 shows the complete information.

Table 12. Frequency table

Tasks	Frequency	Type of effort		
		Only Physical	Only Mental	Physical and Mental
Load/unload parts	Every cycle	X		
Control panel operation	Once in a shift		X	
Inspection of parts	Every cycle			X

Figure 4. Flowchart of machining parts

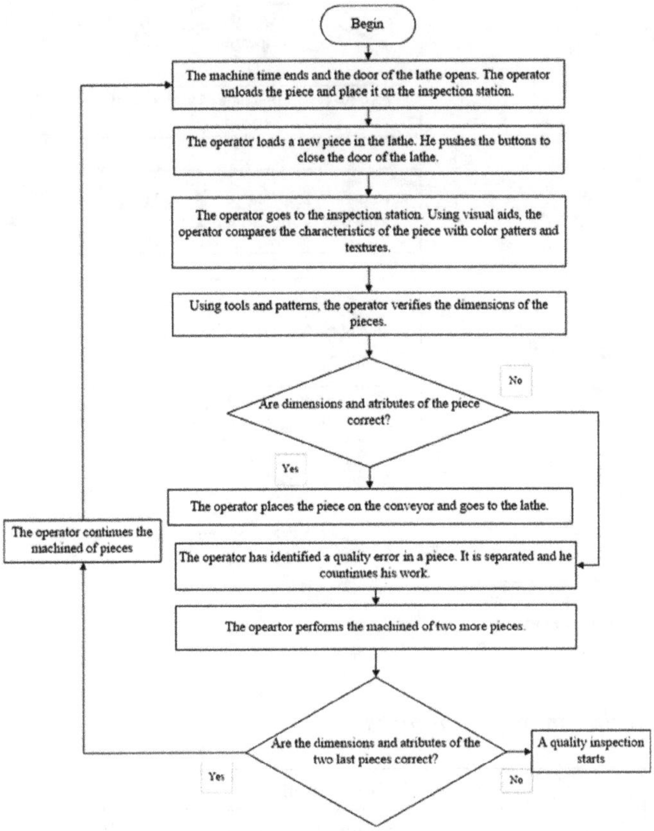

SOLUTIONS AND RECOMMENDATIONS

During the development of occupational activities, the physical tasks can be observed easily, but the mental tasks are difficult to identify. IAMT method, using a systematic procedure, helps to identify and assess the mental tasks developed by workers during occupational tasks. Although the proposed method suggests the use of Cognitive Task Load Model (CTLM), other methods could be applied to complete the cognitive assessment if required.

This method was developed to identify and assess mental task mainly during occupational tasks in industrial environments, and IAMT method has shown acceptable results when has been applied. However, the method needs to be applied in different contexts and work environments to validate its reliability.

Figure 5. Flowchart of quality inspection

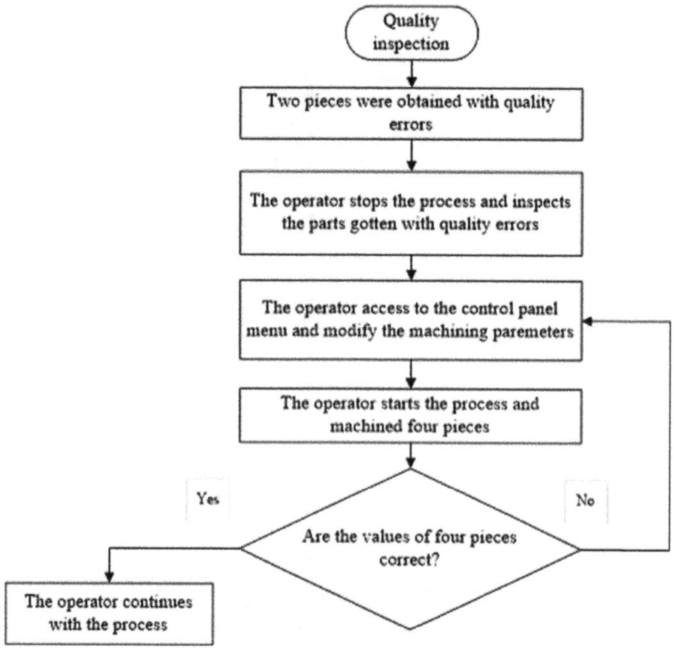

Table 13. Description of mental tasks

Task	Description	Task Duration
Inspection	When removing the part of the lathe, the operator revised specifications of dimensions and appearance. It is predominantly an operation against contrast parameters.	5 sec/piece
Control panel operation	The operator performs activities as access to the menu, parameters adjusting, or modify menu. All of them using the control panel of the CNC lathe.	Undefined

Table 14. Cognitive task analysis

Task	Subtask	Cognitive Effect	Performance Time	Frequency
Inspection	Part revision without errors	No problem	5 seconds/piece	Twice by minute
	Part revision with errors	Cognitive lock-up/ overload	5 seconds/piece	Undefined
Control panel operation	Access to the menu	No problem	5 seconds	Undefined
	Parameters setting	Cognitive lock-up/ overload	Undefined	Undefined
	Modify menu	Cognitive lock-up.	10 seconds	Undefined

FUTURE RESEARCH DIRECTIONS

IAMT method was designed to identify and assess mainly mental tasks. However, because the main objective of the Step 1 is to identify physical and mental tasks, IAMT method could be upgraded to develop a systematic task analysis and ergonomic evaluation considering both, physical and mental assessments applying the appropriate methods.

Similarly to the REBA (Hignett & McAtamney, 2000), RULA (Mcatamney & Corlett, 1993), OWAS (Karhu et al., 1977), JSI (Steven Moore & Garg, 1995) methods, among others, that offer as a final result an index of the physical ergonomic evaluation, IAMT method could be modified to offer a cognitive index of the tasks evaluated. Finally, the IAMT method could perform the mental task analysis not only of activities performed by a individual but also by a teams.

CONCLUSION

The Identification and Assessment of Mental Tasks (IAMT) method was applied in two cases. The first was a common case where the task "using the TV control" was analyzed. The second was a real study case where the human-machine interaction of an operator and a machine classified as Advance Manufacturing Technology (AMT) was analyzed. In both cases, the mental tasks were identified and assessed using the method proposed.

AIMT allowed identifying successfully the mental tasks developed by the worker, and consequently to assign a cognitive effect to each task. After the IAMT method is applied, results should be used by production planers and industrial engineers in the design of tasks and work schedules.

REFERENCES

Bligard, L.-O., & Osvalder, A. L. (2014). CCPE: Methodology for a Combined Evaluation and Physical Ergonomics in the Interaction between Human and Machine. *Human Factors and Ergonomics in Manufacturing*, *24*(6), 685–711. doi:10.1002/hfm.20512

Colombini, D., Occhipinti, E., Álvarez-Casado, E., Hernández-Soto, A., & Tello Sandoval, S. (2012). *El Método OCRA Checklist Revisado. Gestión y evaluación del riesgo por movimientos repetitivos de las extremidades superiores*. Editorial Human Factors Barcelona.

de la Torre-Caldera, V., Hernandez-Arellano, J. L., García-Alcaraz, J. L., & Ibarra-Mejia, G. (2014). Workload Assessment in Industrial Settings: A Proposal Applying the Analytic Hierarchy Process. Proceedings of the XXVI Annual occupational Ergonomics and Safety Conference, El Paso, TX, USA (pp. 32–37).

Dharwada, P., Sadasivan, S., Nickles, G., & Gramopadhye, A. (2006). Task Analytic Methodology for the Design of an Aircraft Inspection Training Program. In W. Karwowski (Ed.), International Encyclopedia of Ergonomics and Human factors (2nd ed., pp. 2366–2374). Taylor & Francis.

Embrey, D. E. (1986). SHERPA: A systematic human error reduction and prediction approach.*Proceedings of the international topical meeting on advances in human factors in nuclear power systems* (pp. 184–193).

Fanger, P. O. (1973). *Thermal Comfort*. New York, NY: McGraw Hill.

Gómez-Bull, K. G., Hernández-Arellano, J. L., & Ibarra-Mejía, G. (2015). A Proposed Methodology for Task Analysis in Ergonomic Evaluations. *Procedia Manufacturing*, *3*, 4756–4760. doi:10.1016/j.promfg.2015.07.573

Grootjen, M., Bierman, E.P.B., & Neerincx, M.A. (2006). Optimizing cognitive task load in naval ship control centers: Design of an adaptive interface. *Proceedings of the16th World Congress on Ergonomics*.

Grootjen, M., Neerincx, M.A., Stolk, K.D., van Weert, J.C.M., & Bierman, E.P.B. (2007). Design and user evaluation of an interface prototype that adapts to the operator's cognitive task load. In HFES/ACI Baltimore. Retrieved from http://www.researchgate.net/publication/228403104_Design_and_user_evaluation_of_an_interface_prototype_that_adapts_to_the_operator's_cognitive_task_load/file/9fcfd50e7648b88cf9.pdf

Guelaud, F., Beauchense, M. N., Gautrat, J., & Roustrang, G. (1977). *Pour une analyse des conditions du travail ouvrier dans l'entreprise* (Vol. 11). Paris: Espirit.

Hart, S. G., & Staveland, L. E. (1988). Development of NASA-TLX (Task Load Index): Results of empirical and theoretical research. *Advances in Psychology*, *52*, 139–183. doi:10.1016/S0166-4115(08)62386-9

Hernandez-Arellano, J. L., Ibarra-Mejía, G., Serratos-Pérez, J. N., Garcia-Alcaraz, J. L., & Brunette, M. J. (2012). Construction of a survey to assess workload and fatigue among AMT operators in Mexico. *Work (Reading, Mass.)*, *41*, 1790–1796. doi:10.3233/WOR-2012-0387-1790 PMID:22316973

Hignett, S., & McAtamney, L. (2000). Rapid Entire Body Assessment (REBA). *Applied Ergonomics*, *31*(2), 201–205. doi:10.1016/S0003-6870(99)00039-3 PMID:10711982

Hossain, G., & Yeasin, M. (2015). Effect of Ability-Demand Gap on Cognitive Dissonance and Overload. *IEEE Transactions on Autonomous Mental Development*, PP(99), 1. Doi:10.1109/TAMD.2015.2450681

Jung, H. S., & Jung, H.-S. (2001). Establishment of overall workload assessment technique for various tasks and workplaces. *International Journal of Industrial Ergonomics*, *28*(6), 341–353. doi:10.1016/S0169-8141(01)00040-3

Karhu, O., Kansi, P., & Kuorinka, I. (1977). Correcting working postures in industry: A practical method for analysis. *Applied Ergonomics*, *8*(4), 199–201. doi:10.1016/0003-6870(77)90164-8 PMID:15677243

Luximon, A., & Goonetilleke, R.S. (2001). Simplified subjective workload assessment technique. *Ergonomics*, *44*(3), 229–243. Doi:10.1080/00140130121511

Mcatamney, L., & Corlett, E. N. (1993). RULA: a survey method for the investigation of world-related upper limb disorders. Applied Ergonomics, *24*(2), 91–99. Doi:10.1016/0003-6870(93)90080-S

Militello, L. G., & Hutton, R. J. (1998). Applied Cognitive Task Analysis (ACTA): A practitioners toolkit for understanding cognitive task demands. *Ergonomics*, *41*(11), 1618–1641. doi:10.1080/001401398186108 PMID:9819578

Miyake, S. (2001). Multivariate workload evaluation combining physiological and subjective measures. *International Journal of Psychophysiology*, *40*(3), 233–238. doi:10.1016/S0167-8760(00)00191-4 PMID:11228350

Neerincx, M. A. (2003). Cognitive Task Load Analysis: allocation Tasks and Designing Support. In E. Hollnagel (Ed.), *Handbook of Cognitive Task Design* (pp. 283–305). Mahwah, NJ: Lawrence Erlbaum Associates; doi:10.1201/9781410607775.ch13

Papantonopoulos, S., & Salvendy, G. (2008). Analytic Cognitive Task Allocation: A decision model for cognitive task allocation. *Theoretical Issues in Ergonomics Science*, *9*(2), 155–185. doi:10.1080/14639220600765386

Rodgers, S. H. (2005). Muscle Fatigue Assessment: Functional Job Analysis Technique. In N. Stanton, A. Hedge, K. Brookhuis, E. Salas, & H. Hendrick (Eds.), *Handbook of Human Factors and Ergonomics Methods* (pp. 12–1–12–10). CRC Press.

Salmon, P., Stanton, N., Walker, G., & Green, D. (2006). Cognitive Task Analysis. In W. Karwowski (Ed.), *International Encyclopedia of Ergonomics and Human factors* (pp. 3044–3048). Taylor & Francis.

Siegel, A., & Schraagen, J. (2014). A Method to Reveal Workload Weak-Resilience-Signals at a Rail Control Post. In D. Harris (Ed.), *Engineering Psychology and Cognitive Ergonomics SE - 9* (Vol. 8532, pp. 82–93). Springer International Publishing; doi:10.1007/978-3-319-07515-0_9

Siegel, A. W., & Schraagen, J. M. C. (2014). Measuring Workload Weak Resilience Signals at a Rail Control Post. *IIE Transactions on Occupational Ergonomics and Human Factors*, *2*(3-4), 179–193. doi:10.1080/21577323.2014.958632

Snook, S. H., & Ciriello, V. M. (1991). The design of manual handling tasks: Revised tables of maximum acceptable weights and forces. *Ergonomics*, *34*(9), 1197–1213. doi:10.1080/00140139108964855 PMID:1743178

Sonne, M., Villalta, D. L., & Andrews, D. M. (2012). Development and evaluation of an office ergonomic risk checklist: ROSArapid office strain assessment. *Applied Ergonomics*, *43*(1), 98–108. doi:10.1016/j.apergo.2011.03.008 PMID:21529772

Stanton, N. (2006). Hierarchical task analysis: Developments, applications, and extensions. *Applied Ergonomics*, *37*(1), 55–79. Doi:10.1016/j.apergo.2005.06.003

Stanton, N. A., Ashleigh, M., & Cale, T. (2006). Design Issues: Action Research in Control Operations. In W. Karwowski (Ed.), International Encyclopedia of Ergonomics and Human factors (2nd ed., pp. 1403–1405). Taylor & Francis.

Steven Moore, J., & Garg, A. (1995). The strain index: A proposed method to analyze jobs for risk of distal upper extremity disorders. *American Industrial Hygiene Association*, *56*(5), 443–458. doi:10.1080/15428119591016863 PMID:7754975

Streefkerk, J. W., Van Esch-Bussemakers, M. P., & Neerincx, M. A. (2006). Designing personal attentive user interfaces in the mobile public safety domain. *Computers in Human Behavior*, *22*(4), 749–770. doi:10.1016/j.chb.2005.12.006

Toet, A. (2005). Integrated design of intelligent surveillance systems and their user interface. In *Proceedings of the 2005 International Conference on Artificial Intelligence IC-AI'05* (Vol. 1, pp. 17–23). Retrieved from http://h3b1jq.bay.livefilestore.com/y1pIgG86fKS56YPhVoAK_ROutWU5Co0j2wx5YfYCTcsyj_LYfXFJr_lCeidb6243F1e10elmFrgqL3Oj7fPF030Kw/Toet2005b.pdf?download\n:\Library\Toet\Toet2005b.pdf

University of Michigan. (2012). 3DSSPP. Retrieved from http://c4e.engin.umich.edu/tools-services/3dsspp-software/

Waters, T. R., Putz-Anderson, V., & Garg, A. (1994). *Applications manual for the revised NIOSH lifting equation*. Cincinnati, Ohio.

Wickens, C. D. (2014). Effort in Human Factors Performance and Decision Making. Human Factors. *The Journal of the Human Factors and Ergonomics Society*, *56*(8), 1329–1336. doi:10.1177/0018720814558419 PMID:25509817

KEY TERMS AND DEFINITIONS

Cognitive Task Analysis: Is the procedure developed to analyze the mental work performed by a worker in a specific environment.

Cognitive Task Load Model: Is a cognitive procedure applied to assign a cognitive effect on the tasks analyzed.

Combined Task: Is an activity developed by a person that demands physical and mental efforts.

Flowchart: A flowchart is a type of diagram that represents an algorithm, workflow or process, showing the steps as boxes of various kinds, and their order by connecting them with arrows.

Mental Task: Is an activity developed by a person that demands a mental effort.

Physical Task: Is an activity developed by a person that demands a physical effort.

Physical Task Analysis: Is the procedure developed to analyze the physical work performed by a worker in a specific environment.

Task Analysis: Is the procedure developed to analyze the work performed by a worker in a specific environment.

Chapter 2
Organizational Climate as a Predictor to Employees' Behavior

Shashi Singh
Sunbeam College For Women, India

ABSTRACT

There are many behavioral challenges lying in the front of employees, management and their organization due to globalization. The present investigation attempts to identify few of them like organizational role stress, job satisfaction and organizational climate. The study is also determining the effect of organizational climate on role stress and job satisfaction. The Stress has always been a part of human existence. Organizational climate is an individual's perception about the environment of the organization one is working with. Job satisfaction is the result of the individual perception of what is expected and what is receive from different facts of the work situation. Primary data is collected through standard psychometric devices. Prevailed climatic conditions are very important in the determination of stress levels and its consequences in an individual. The link between role stress and employees job satisfaction are of great relevance to organizational health. It will be useful for organizations in utilizing its human capital in a better and effective manner.

DOI: 10.4018/978-1-5225-1974-4.ch002

INTRODUCTION

Since the dawn of Human consciousness, mankind has been engaged in the pursuit of happiness, peace and stress free life. These are accountable too for the growth of an organization and its role incumbents on the one hand and society at large on the other hand. Very often the human element is reduced to a mere insignificant cog in the wheel of the total technological system. This tends to generate a feeling of powerlessness, meaninglessness, normlessness and consequent stress. The Indian Government has made various changes in its industrial, trade and fiscal policies after liberalization in the business environment. Through this modification Indian organization started facing the changes and competition with domestic as well as international business players. The organizations and its management were expected to be more efficient and productive against the multinational and other global players which were competing in the domestic market in the new liberalized scenario. The overall changing business structure had forced every organization to modify or alter their perspective on their on their function and role overnight. The companies having obsession to focus exclusively on bottom line i.e. customer, mission and organization's role, were forced to make changes in their organization to given emphasis primarily to productivity.

The Indian organizations, to survive in the present scenario, were forced to undergo massive changes. Thus the important factor with the most positive impact on the performance had been identified from the organizational environment. It had been found that human behavior issues have never been bothered in Indian organization. And the factors like stress, satisfaction of the individual employees regarding their jobs were found to have significant effect on the employee's behavior. Any organization is being established with a common goal and involvement of a group of individuals. To achieve the predetermined goal, it is very important to understand behavior related problems of employees for management. It has been observed that Indian organizations too have started bothering about behavioral issues now. The highlighted issues these days were, whether the employees are under organizational role stress, whether working climate is matching to their requirement or not, whether employees are satisfied with their jobs and if managerially they are successful or not. The level of these behavioural issues, Organiastional Role Stress and Job Satisfaction will vary from person to person, group to group and organisation to organisation. These psychological problems are not easy to ignore in Indian organisations also. Even the better facilities provided, the increasing level of stress among the employees can be seen. Particularly in a labour intensive organization, it will not be possible to sustain effectiveness unless the workforce is in a stress free and satisfied work environment.

Stress arises essentially from their way of responding to a particular situation. Stress is a part of everybody's life. Stressed employee may be unhappy and thus produce nominally. Stress can deteriorate family and social relationship. It can cause poor work performance and lower employee morale. These factors in turn, increase employee turnover rate and lessen quality of life. Therefore, organization needs to recognize stress as a problem and take necessary steps to act upon it. Stress is dependent on the individual appraisal of what is at stake and what resources are available for meeting the demands posed. The modern view of stress is that it arises from a lack of fit between a person and his/her environment when there is an inability to cope with the demands made. Survey of the literature on organisational role stress reveals that there are so many factors related to job which affect the behavior of the employees and which results to disturbance in a normal life. Different stressors in work can be categorized to be caused by job content, working conditions, employment conditions and social relations at work. In following table some general job-related stressors are presented.

Researches indicate that nearly one third of the working population report high to very high levels of stress in developed countries. Role conflicts, ergonomic deficiencies, time pressures, excessive demands job security and relationship with customers are specifically common stressors amongst employees in the financial services sector. Similarly, evidence for newly industrialized countries is also indicative of the prevalence of stress.

Table 1. Categories of Job Related Stressors

Category	Stressor
Job content	Monotonous work Too much responsibility Work over/under load Complex work Conflicting/ambiguous demands
Working conditions	Poor conditions Physically demanding work Work posture
Employment conditions	Poor career prospects Low pay Job insecurity Flexible labor contract
Social relations at work	Poor leadership Low participation in decision making Low social support Liberties Discrimination

Source: Information technology-related stress, Reetta Raitoharju

ORGANISATIONAL ROLE STRESS

An Organisational Role is defined by the expectations of its role senders, which includes the role occupant, the superior (or boss), the direct reports (or subordinates), the peers, and in some cases, customers, suppliers, partners, team members and process owners. On the contrary, an interaction is needed invariably to an organisational role with a set of connected roles within or outside the organisation. The role occupant is expected to perform and deliver on his/her role expectations in spite of impediments, such as the following: role occupant finds it difficult to interact with the related roles; role is unimportant and does not make an impact in the organisation (this is highly de motivating for the role occupant); role occupant is not clear about his/her role expectations; adequate resources have not been provided for performing in the role; role occupant does not have the competence required for performing in his/her role; role involves conflicting expectations; role occupant is compelled to do what he does not like; role does not offer opportunities for growth and development of the role occupant; role occupant cannot utilise his/her strengths in the assigned role; role involves excessive workload. In total, a role occupant encounters problems, constraints, deficiencies or conflicts in some form or the other during the course of his/her role performance.

Occupation of an organisational role is, therefore, a potential source of stress. Stress experienced in roles is referred to as Role Stress. High role stress is the result of poor person - environment fit or poor role design. Work stress jeopardizes the role performance and wellbeing of the role occupant. Any organization may be perceived as a system of roles. Such role stresses enacted in the context of organizations are called organisational role stress. These roles are different from positions or offices in the organization. Role stress refers to the tensions and conflict due to the roles being enacted by a person at any given point of time. Each individual is a member of social systems and the expectation as well as demand of one may put pressure on the other.

Effects of Stress

Stress can have various effects on the individual as well as on the organization. Clearly not only the individual suffers but the organization may also be affected by absenteeism, work related accidents, turnover and impaired decision – making. While stress is typically discussed in a negative context, it also has a positive value. The inverted U relationship between stress level and performance is illustrated by Figure. 1. From the organizations stand point, management may not be concerned when employee experience low to moderate level of stress which may lead to higher employee performance. But high level or even low levels of stress sustained over a long period of time, can lead to reduced level of performance and thus require action by management.

Organizational Climate

Organization differs not only in physical structure but also in attitudes and behaviors they elicit in people and these differences are related to differing individual perception. Individual personalities and job requirements interact to produce a climate that can be significant to both individual and to the organization. Some people like the place where they work and for the same reason others may express dislike.

Climate means all those characteristics that distinguish one organization from the other and in turn influence the behavior of the people in the organization. It not only affects the behavior of an individual but also how organizations interact within themselves. At an individual level, it can be stated that essentially, climate is an individual's description of the social setting (which comprises of physical structure, organizational policies and interpersonal relations developed within the group or the context of which the person is the part. The individual description are called "psychological climate" and aggregation of psychological climate has been used to represent the climate of larger units of analysis i.e. organizational Climate. It is relatively enduring quality of the internal environment of an organization that

Figure 1. Inverted U relationship between stress level and performance

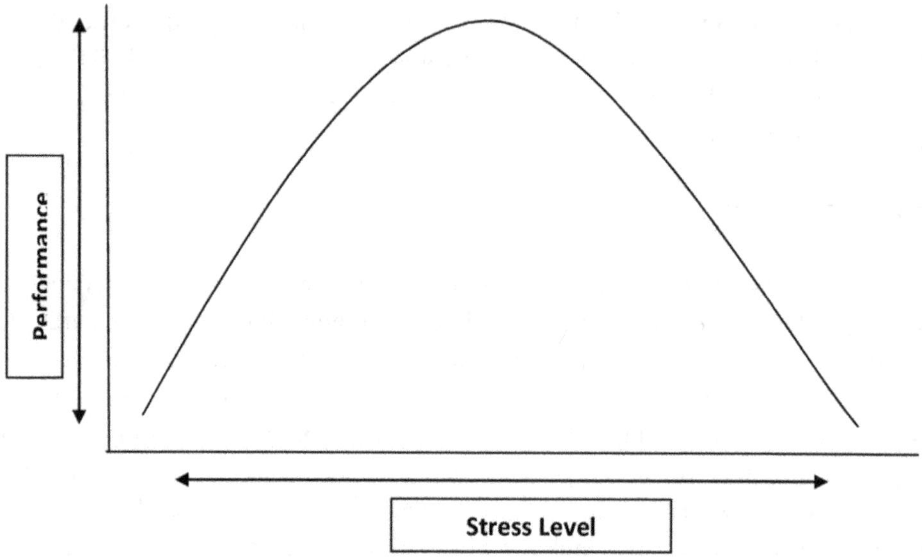

is experienced by its members. It influences their behavior and can be described in terms of the values of a set of characteristics or attributes of the organization.

Organizational climate is about the perception of the climate and about absolute measure. For organization, the climate may be regarded in absolute term and measured by instruments, but is felt differently by individuals. The absolute climate may suit one person and not another. Climate is worthwhile to understand and measure because there are organizational and human benefits of a good climate, and possible disadvantages of many kind of a bad climate.

Dimensions of Good Climate

The true keys to positive work climate are reflected through respect, support, entrepreneurialism, innovation, cooperation, performance, profitable management practices, knowledge management, organizational learning, employee readiness to change and Collective learning.

Dimensions of Bad Climate

The employees' behavior in terms of fear, crisis, anxiety, workplace aggression, employee burnout, employee turnover, politicking, decay, hopelessness and stagnation shows the bad climate.

Organizational climate is relatively and enduring quality of the internal environment of an organization that is experience by its members, influence their behavior and can be described in terms of the values of a particular set of characteristics or attributes of the organization. This shows that all organizations are based on differentiation of functions and the whole structure is a neat arrangement of the hierarchy of power. Besides this one more important dimension of the organization is its psychological atmosphere, i.e. climate. In this context, it is necessary to clarify the meaning of climate. By climate we mean those characteristics that distinguish the organization from other organizations and that influence the behavior of people in the organization. Each organization differs from the other not only in structure but also in the attitudes and behavior they elicit in people and these differences are associated with psychological structure. In fact, employee personalities and their requirement interact to influence the organizational climate. Organizational climate affects the behaviors of people in organizations.

Litwin and Stringer (1968) stated that organizational climate refers to a set of measurable properties of the work environment, perceived directly or indirectly by the people who live and work in this environment and assume to influence motivation and behavior of the employee. Their model of the concept of organizational climate was used as an intervening variable mediating between organizational factors and motivation tendencies. Organizational factors such as leadership, managerial practices and the decision processes are realities. According to their point of view the perceived organizational climate arouses motivation causing emergence of behavior which results in various consequences for the organization such as satisfaction, productivity or performance.

Organizational climate as a relatively enduring quality of the internal environment of an organization that

1. Is experienced by its members;
2. Influences their behavior;
3. Can be described in the terms of the value of a particular set of characteristics or attributes of the organization.

A lively controversy has been waged as to whether the organizational climate is the quality of the environment of perception of the various members of the total organization and the organizational unit. Thus, the organizational climate is the shared perception of the employees who work and live in the organization. It is the sum of individual perception regarding the organizational procedure, policies and practices. The organizational climate has been described as a molar concept reflecting the content and strength of prevalent value, norms, attitude and behavior of the member of social system. It represents the psychological environment of the organization consisting of the individual opinion formed upon micro events that happen to them as well as to the others around over period of time.

Job Satisfaction

Job satisfaction is another frequent associate of high role stress. Job Satisfaction in the field of organizational behaviour has been researched invariably thus depicting its importance in the organizations. It is positive emotional state resulting from the appraisal of one's job or job experience or pleasurable. Job satisfaction is a result of perception of employees about how well their job provides those important things that are expected. The following three important dimensions to job satisfaction can be positioned:

- Job satisfaction is often determined by how well outcome meet with exceed expectations.
- Job satisfaction is an emotional response to a situation at workplace. As such it cannot be seen, it can only be inferred.
- Several related attitudes are represented by Job satisfaction which is most important characteristics of a job about which people have effective response.

Understanding of job satisfaction can be work out with the responses of employees to the way the individual reacts to unpleasant situations, the facility with which he adjusts himself to other persons, his relative status in the social and economic group with which he identifies himself, the nature of the work in relation to his abilities, interest and preparation, security and loyalty.

The other category of definitions tried to focus attention on the factors whether intrinsic or extrinsic, which contribute directly or indirectly to job satisfaction like the job factors which were found by various investigators as underlying causes of satisfaction and dissatisfaction of workers. These are factor in the individual i.e. ability, health, age, desires and expectations, neurotic tendencies, unconscious conflicts, etc., factor in life away from work i.e. home condition, concern problems, labour union activities, socio-politico economic conditions, etc., and factors in employment relations i.e. wages or earning sturdiness of employment, transfer, layoff, and rehiring procedures, kind of work performed, supervision, training conditions of work opportunities, opportunity to use ability, social relationship on job, recognition and fair evaluation of work opportunities for advancement participation, free interchange of ideas, prompt and fair setting of grievances, understanding and respect by employer. The above classification suggests that worker satisfaction does not arise merely from factors on the job out runs the whole gamut of man's needs and aspiration.

Job Satisfaction is one part of life satisfaction. Since a job is an important part of life for many workers, it influences general life satisfaction, which results into spillover effect. So, attitude towards other parts of life should also be monitored by the manager.

Pestonjee (1967) is of the opinion that job satisfaction can be taken as summation of employee's feelings in four important areas. Two of these areas encompass factors directly connected with the job (intrinsic factors), and other two include factors not directly connected with the job but which are persuading to have a bearing on job satisfaction. These four areas have been defined as follows:

Table 2. Determinants of job satisfaction

ORGANISATIONAL DETERMINANTS	INDIVIDUAL DETERMINANTS
Pay	Age
Work itself	Gender
Quality of supervision	Status and seniority
Working conditions	Marital status

1. **Job:** Nature of work-dull, dangerous, interesting, hours of work, fellow workers, opportunities on the job for promotion and advancement (prospects), overtime regulations, interest in the work, physical environment, machine and tools, etc.
2. **Management:** Supervisory treatment, participation, rewards and punishment praises and blames, leave policy, favoritism, etc.
3. **Personal Adjustment:** Emotionality, health, home and living conditions, finances, relations with family members, etc.
4. **Social Relations:** Neighbours, friends and associates, attitudes towards people in community, participation in social activities, sociability, cast barriers, etc.

Sinha (1972) holds that job satisfaction covers both the satisfaction derived from being engaged in a piece of work, or in any pursuit of a higher order. It is essentially related to human needs and their fulfillment through work. In fact, job satisfaction is generated by individual's perception of how well his job on the whole is satisfying to his various needs.

A pair of researchers in 1972 examined nine definitions of job-satisfaction advanced during the previous several years and found that people different meanings to what is to be satisfied in another study, job-satisfaction was defined as the pleasurable emotional state resulting from the appraisal of one's job as achieving or facilitating the achievement of one's job values. In contrast, job satisfaction was defined as the unpleasurable, emotional state resulting from the appraisal of one's job as frustrating or blocking the attainment of one's job values or as entailing disvalues. Both satisfaction and dissatisfaction were seen as a function of the perceived relationship between what one wants from one's job and what one perceives it as offering or entailing. Other scholars have confined their definition of job satisfaction to persistent feelings toward discriminable aspects of the job situation (Discriminable aspects refer to such factors as the work itself, pay, promotional opportunities, the supervisor, co-workers, and the hours of work). Some definitions see moral and satisfaction as being synonymous. For example, one important psychologist believes that moral is the extent to which an individual's needs are satisfied and the extent to which the individual perceives that satisfaction as stemming from his total job situation.

We have gone through various definitions of job satisfaction in the previous chapter and also how its concept has evolved through various theories. Now, we move on to find out the various literature available relating satisfaction to other variables present in the environment of an organization Let's have a look at what have been going on recently regarding job satisfaction and its relationship to other relevant variables.

The above are the results that different scholars have found about the relationship of job satisfaction to many other variables relate to organization, individual and job.

Table 3. Some Important outcomes of job satisfaction

Variable Related with Job Satisfaction	Direction of Relationship
Life satisfaction	Positive
Job performance	Positive
Worker motivation	Positive
Job involvement	Positive
Organizational commitment	Positive
Organizational citizenship behavior	Positive
Worker health	Positive
Employee tardiness	Negative
Employee absenteeism	Negative
Withdrawal cognitions	Negative
Employee turnover	Negative
Perceived stress	Negative

Compiled from various sources

Generally, job satisfaction is the result of the individual perception of what is expected and what is receive from different facts of the work situation. The closer the expectation is to what is received, the greater the job satisfaction. Job satisfaction sometimes refers to an overall feeling of satisfaction or satisfaction with the situation as a whole (global satisfaction). At other times, job satisfaction refers to a person's feelings towards specific dimensions of the work environment refer to such things as pay, benefits, promotional opportunities, work conditions, supervision, the work itself, co-workers and the organizational structure. As everyone knows who has ever held a job; it is quite possible to be satisfied with some dimensions and dissatisfied with others. Global satisfaction, amounts to a feeling toward all of these various facts of the work environment. If person feels good about his or her job in a global sense, that individual probably does have job satisfaction. But when only a cumulative attitude such as this is known, it is difficult for people to influence and improve it. For practicing managers concerned with improving the work environment it is more helpful to obtain worker feelings about facet satisfactions than about global satisfaction. Managers can take more direct action in eliminating pockets of dissatisfaction when they know what facets are causing or contributing to low global dissatisfaction.

LITERATURE REVIEW

It has been universally acknowledged that no work can be meaningfully conceived and soundly accomplished without critically studying what already exists in relation to it. Review of literature is concerned with searching the relevant literature which compelled the researcher to go for the present study. It consists of going through as much possible available studies as possible which were done by the different scholars and are also relevant in one way or the other to the present study.

Azizi Yahaya et.al. (2009) found in his study that the causes of organisational role stress within the organization and the implication on job satisfaction and intention to leave and absenteeism. The finding showed that organisational role stress does not have direct effect on intention to leave and absenteeism but have direct negative effect on job satisfaction. Job satisfaction has negative effect on intention to leave and absenteeism. Some recommendation needed to be applied by management to reduce the number of turnover. First organization need to increase job satisfaction by reducing organisational role stress. By reducing stress companies can reduce the level of intentional to leave and absenteeism.

Anthonia Adenike (2011) aims in their study Organisational Climate as a Predictor of Employee Job Satisfaction: Evidence from Covenant University to explore organisational climate as a predictor of employees job Satisfaction of academic staff from a private Nigerian University. Three hypothesis were tested and the results of the finding showed a significant positive relationship between these two variable. Thus the relation between the variable are different in academics from those of south west Nigeria.

Monica J. Parzinger, Mary A. Lemons & Karen McDaniel (2012) in their research paper on The Impact of Organizational Climate on Turnover and Job Satisfaction: A Multi-Analysis Study of Bank Employees found that with the recent turmoil of the financial industry, banks have more challenges today than ever. Some of these challenges, such as government involvement and restriction, are out of the control of financial organizations. One problem that may be predicted and controlled by institutional leaders, however, involves the satisfaction and retention of their own employees.

Javed et.al. (2013) in their research paper titled The Impact of Role Conflict on Job Satisfaction: An Analysis of Gomal University Lecturers (Regular and Contract) and concluded in Gomal University, the level of participation of teachers (lecturers) in decision making was found high and they are satisfied, majority of the respondents were of the view that they have conflict in performing their roles on the job therefore, their level of satisfaction is suffering.

Kavita Jain, Preeti Jain (2013) in their research paper titled job satisfaction: a comparative study of private and public Sector reveals that that there is no significant difference between the mean score of public and private sector regarding employees-management relationship, in relation to the nature of job and in relation to the working conditions. Astonishingly researcher found that though there are several measures to improve the job satisfaction but the most important measures are good remuneration, promotional opportunities, and Job security.

Santosh Dev (2013) conducted a study on titled a study of Client Satisfaction and impact of Work Culture on Employee Satisfaction. In this study, an attempt has been made to gauge the satisfaction level of clients and employees and also to see the impact of work culture on the level of employee satisfaction and study the relationship of employee satisfaction and client satisfaction. The research has been carried out in a systematic and methodical manner.

Hunnur and Bagli (2014) have identified many of the stresses that are placed on police personnel, and various stressors and the relationship between the stress dimensions and the demographic variables like age, education qualification and work experience. Research indicated that there is no significant relation between the organisational role stress dimensions and the demographic variables i.e. age of respondents.

Yıldız and Özcan (2014) have studied the main purpose to find out the moderating role of organizational climate on the effect of transformational leadership on creativity. The survey was conducted on 178 employees in Istanbul, Turkey. As a result, it was noticed that pressure factor of the organizational climate has a significant negative moderating effect on this relationship. In addition there was a significant moderating effect of cohesion climate dimension on the relationship between transformational leadership and followers' creativity.

Gautam and Sharma (2014) investigated the effect of organizational climate on job stress and the findings were that teacher educators who are working in self-financed colleges have highly job stress in comparison to the teacher's educators working in aided B.Ed. College, aided B.Ed. institutions have better organizational climate in comparison to the self-financed B.Ed. institutions, a significant negative correlation existed between the job stress and organizational climate, job stress level of B.Ed. teachers was independent of their gender differences, the obtained results of the present study concluded that if organizational climate of B.Ed. institutions is rich, job stress of B.Ed. teachers will be less.

After going through the above literature, we can say that all the three variables have been studied by different scholars at different times and at different places. The findings have been mixed, from strongly related to moderately to weakly and sometimes unrelated were reported, but very few studies have been done on all the three variables together.

Need and Significance of the Study

One of the greatest challenges organization face today is how to manage turnover of workforce that may be caused by migration of a lots of industrial workers. Such turnover is related with the costs of recruitment, selection and training a replacement and also lost production until the newcomer becomes as skilled as the worker who quit. High rates of turnover may also harm an organisation's reputation as an employer or render it unable to exploit growth opportunities because of lack of satisfied staff which finally also will surely affect the performance of an organization. Therefore, it has become an important area of research that how to work on the climate in order to reduce stress, turnover and absenteeism and improve performance, satisfaction of employees in the organization.

Due to the rapid and striking changes in Indian industries like to technological changes, time pressure, role conflict, appointment of contract labour, the employees are experiencing a high level of stress. The problems due to high level of stress can be exhibited physically or behaviorally by the individual. Absenteeism, high turnover, less commitment to the job, poor performance, moodiness, fatigue, anxiety, frustration, and ultimately, reduced job satisfaction. etc. are caused by such stress. Stress can have serious consequences on an individual's physical as well as psychological health and their work performance. It can undermine their relationship at home and on the job. This evidence makes a strong case for understanding and examining organizational role stress. Researches show that conflicting demands at the workplace causes confusion among employees which leads to the stressful situations. Prolonged work hours and pressures may also form the cause for work related stress. When people go the workplace knowing that they are going to spend a large part of their day in a hostile environment, this will consequently put pressure on them.

Everybody is different and responding differently to the stressors. What causes one person to stress out can be a relaxation to another. Due to varying personality traits, different people react differently to any worse situation which can lead to stress. Even if the level of stress is high and climate is good or bad, the level of satisfaction can be low or high respectively. Again, if level of stress is low and climate is good or bad, the level of employee satisfaction can be high or low respectively. Prevailed climatic conditions are very important in the determination of stress levels and its consequences in an individual. The link between role stress and employees job satisfaction are of great relevance to organizational climate. According to management experts, the best method of stress management depends on both the organizational climate and the individual employee.

The present study focuses on impact of organizational role stress and climate on employee's job satisfaction. This study has been designed to gain a better understanding of the factors that contribute to organizational stress experienced by the employee in industrial sector.

Objectives of the Study

The present investigation is directed to explore and understand the dynamic relationship between the three variables i.e. role stress and climate on job satisfaction of the employees in industrial sector. It also aims at studying the organisational climate as a moderator variable affecting the relationship between stress and job satisfaction. An accurate diagnosis will provide the way to minimize stress and maximize job satisfaction. This study will also help you to evaluate the impact of organisational climate on job satisfaction of employees in the organization and to find the impact of employee's stress on organisational climate

In the light of available literature concerning the relationship among organisational role stress and job satisfaction, and the moderating effect of organisational climate, the following hypothesis have been formulated:

$H_0$1: There is no significant difference between mean job satisfaction score of the employees on good or bad climate group of employee in the organization.

$H_0$2: There is no significant difference between mean organizational climate scores of the employees belonging to high or low organizational role stress groups.

Design and Methodology

The research is usually designed to be a descriptive as well as exploratory one, as the research is supposed to be about finding the facts and drawing the conclusions based on that and exploring something new to some extent. As stated earlier, the present investigation has been aimed at studying intensively the levels of organizational role stress and job satisfaction among the employees of the industrial organisation, then the impact of organizational stress level on job satisfaction of employees and finally, the moderating effect for climate adopted by the employees to reduce their occupational stress level and increase level of satisfaction.

The cause and effect relationship in the study has been determined by the 2X2 factorial design and hence two levels – High and Low of the independent variable (organizational role stress) is taken. Such a design permits the investigator to test the influence of independent variable (organizational role stress) on dependent variable (job satisfaction) at the same time.

It may be the basic analytical framework of the study has involved few of the logical steps. Firstly the independent variable (organizational role stress) is split into two groups – High and Low – with reference to the median of the variable score in question. Secondly the dependent variable (job satisfaction) scores of employees corresponding to High and Low groups of the independent variable (organizational role stress) were noted and then these scores were taken as the bases for the computation of the entire statistic used in the study.

Research design being used is 2x2 factorial designs. Therefore, for application of valid statistics on all the four quadrants, at least sample size of 100 on each quadrant is required. Due to this, the selected sample size considered for the study is 400.

Data Collection and Measures

The data collected for the purpose of the study was primary and secondary both. Various psychometric tools were used in this study to investigate the various relationships existing among the three variables. Secondary data has been collected from books, management & HR Journals, research papers, research articles and websites, published Ph.D theses etc. The primary data used for the study was collected through three different questionnaires build by different experts.

Organizational Role Stress Scale (ORS) has been developed by Udai Pareek (1977). This scale assessed the extent of role stress in 10 different role dimensions i.e. Inter-role Distance, Role Stagnation, Role Expectation Conflict, Role Erosion, Role overload, Role Isolation, Personal Inadequacy, Self Role Distance, role Ambiguity and Resource Inadequacy. The scale comprised of 50 items, five for each dimension of role stress. The frequency of the role stress-situation was rated on the five-point-scale (i.e., Never or rarely/occasionally/sometimes/ frequently/always). The score on each item ranged from 0 to 4. The summation of the scores on each item makes the index of perceived role stress. The validity of the scale was well ascertained by internal consistency method. The score on each item was correlated with the total score on the scale for 500 respondents. All but two efficient were found to be significant at .001 level. The rest two were significant at .002 and .003 level, respectively. The results proved high internal consistency of the scale. The construct validity of the instrument was ascertained by factor analysis method and it was found to be acceptable by its statistical norms. The retest reliability for each type of stress was found to be .45 for self-role distance, .58 for inter-role distance .63 for role stagnation, .65 for role ambiguity, .53 for role overload, .37 for role erosion, and .58 for role inadequacy. The overall reliability of the scale was found to be .73.

The organizational climate questionnaire developed and standardized by Udai Pareek (1975) was employed in the investigation to assess the extent of perceived organizational orientation in various dimensions of psycho-social climate of the organizations. The questionnaire consists of 30 items covering five aspects of organizational climate. The items in each dimension assess the extent of general orientation of the organization, interpersonal relationship, and modes of managing conflicts, rewards, mutual trust and support. Each of five dimensions of organizational climate comprises six items to be rated on 4-point scale (namely, absolutely true, almost true, partially true and false) by the employees to indicate the extent of adequacy and congeniality of the social and psychological climate of their work organization. High score on the scale indicates high level climate i.e. good climate perceived by employee. The reliability of the five subscales of the organisational climate questionnaire was determined by half split method stands for 0.91 (N=400). The validity of the scale has been established against the measure of job performance, attitude and health.

The job satisfaction scale developed by Srivastava (1999) has been employed in the study to assess the extent of employee's job satisfaction, employee's attitudes and liking for various aspects of their job, such as job activities (task), work condition, social relations, job security and compensation system etc. The scale comprises of 15 item to be rated on four-point rating scale namely, absolutely true, almost true, partially true and false. High score on the scale indicates high level job satisfaction among employees. Split half reliability of the scale was found to be .79 (N=200). Validity of the scale has been established against the measures of job stress, job performance and psychological well-being. The employees scoring high on the job satisfaction scale scored significantly low on the measure of stress and high on the measure of job performance and psychological well-being.

Sample Size

The investigation was conducted at Diesel Locomotive Works, Varanasi, Uttar Pradesh, which is a government undertaking possessing both rural and urban characteristics. The investigation is related to 400 employees (approximate to rationale of sample size), consisting officers, supervisors, and clerical staff, workers, who were selected randomly from a total of 5941 total employees working in different departments of the unit, viz. administration, quality control, engineering, electrical, store, production, marketing, design etc.

Analysis and Discussions

The results of investigation obtained through a careful analysis of the response scores with the help on the SPSS software. The raw scores of the present study are the responses of workers on the three standardized measuring devises, namely, organisational role stress (ORS), organizational climate (OC) and job satisfaction (JS) scale. The appropriate statistic which has been used for data analysis in this study is mean, median, standard deviation, t-test and analysis of variance. These statistics are expected to test the various hypotheses of study and to explain in un-

Table 4. Mean JS scores and standard deviation pertaining to high & low levels of ORS

ORS High and Low	N	Mean	S.D.	t- Test for Equality of Means		
				T	DF	Sig. (2-Tailed)
Low	210	29.51	6.246	- 9.625	398	.000
High	190	23.18	6.907			

ambiguous terms how and to what extent the organisational climate and role stress level of employees can affect their job satisfaction.

The above table reproduces the results of the test of significance of the difference between the two mean scores of the dependent variable (job satisfaction) obtained on the basis of the high and low levels of the independent variable (organisational role stress). To test whether there is any significant difference between mean job satisfaction scores of employees in high and low organisational role stress groups; the independent samples t- test has been applied. The value of t-static calculated was found to be significant, it may, thus be conveniently interpreted that the job satisfaction scores of employees in the two groups of low and high organisational role stress are expected to be markedly different, enabling one to conclude on the basis of their mean job satisfaction scores that the employees having high organisational role stress usually are less stressed and employees having low organisational role stress are more satisfied with their job. It can be easily said that Organisational role stress is inversely related with job satisfaction.

Thus, our null hypothesis: There is no significant difference between mean job satisfaction scores of the employees belonging to high and low role stress groups of the organization; is rejected and, it can be said that as the level of organisational role stress increased, the job satisfaction of the employees goes down and vice-versa.

Table 5. reproduces the results of the test of significance of the difference between the two mean scores of the dependent variable (job satisfaction) obtained on the basis of the high and low levels of the independent variable (organisational climate). In the above table, the independent samples t- test has been applied to test whether there is any significant difference between mean job satisfaction scores of employees in good and bad perceived Climate groups. The value of t-static calculated was found to be significant, it may, thus be conveniently interpreted that the job satisfaction scores of employees in the two groups of good and bad organisational climate are expected to be markedly different, enabling one to conclude on the basis of their mean job satisfaction scores that the employees perceiving good climate are highly satisfied with their job in the organisation and employees perceiving bad organisational climate are less satisfied with their job. It means Organisational climate is directly related with the job satisfaction.

Table 5. Mean JS scores and standard deviation pertaining to Good and Bad OC

Organisational Climate	N	Mean	S.D.	t- Test for Equality of Means		
				T	df	Sig. (2-tailed)
Good	192	28.03	6.731	- 5.027	397.95	.000
Bad	208	24.49	7.374			

Thus, our null hypothesis: There is no significant difference between mean job satisfaction scores of the employees belonging to good and bad perceived climate groups of the organisation; is rejected and, it can be said that as the perception level of employees increases towards good organisational climate, the level of employee's job satisfaction also goes up and when it goes down along with bad organisational climate.

Table 6. reproduces the results of the test of significance of the difference between the two mean scores of the independent variable (organisational climate) obtained on the basis of the high and low levels of the independent variable (organisational role stress). The significance of the difference between the means has been tested with the help of independence samples t-test. The value of the t-static, its degree of freedom and its significance obtained has also been shown in the last three columns of the respective tables indicating clearly whether the differences between the two sets of mean scores is significant or insignificant.

The independent samples t- test has been applied to test whether there is any significant difference between mean climate scores of employees in high and low organisational role stress groups. The value of t-static calculated was found to be significant, it may, thus be conveniently interpreted that the organisational climate scores of employees in the two groups of high and low organisational role stress are expected to be markedly different. It enables to conclude on the basis of their mean organisational climate scores that the employees with more role stress perceives bad organisational climate and less stressed employee in their role perceives good

Table 6. Mean OC scores and standard deviation pertaining to high & low levels of ORS

ORS High and Low	N	Mean	S.D.	t- Test for Equality of Means		
				T	df	Sig. (2-tailed)
Low	210	59.83	12.42	- 6.110	398	.000
High	190	51.80	13.86			

organisational climate. It means organisational climate is inversely related with the organisational role stress.

CONCLUSION AND RECOMMENDATION

After the interpretations of the results obtained above and discussions regarding earlier relevant literature works following conclusions may be drawn:

The study revealed that 47.5% employees were having high role stressed, whereas 52.5% employees were having low role stress. The employees scored more on three stresses, namely, role stagnation, role erosion and role isolation. They found to be dominating stress indicating that there is a slow erosion of role and authority and a sense of isolation from the rest of organization. The study revealed that 42.2% employees were highly satisfied with their job whereas 57.8% employees were less satisfied with their job. The more satisfied employee is an asset of the organisation. The management should, therefore, pay due attention to this fact and should strive to ensure such working culture/environment and should design jobs (job enrichment) in such a way that it keeps the employees satisfied and hence committed. In case of Job satisfaction, the management must pay attention to certain factors like- proper promotion system, less favoritism, proper working conditions, proper utilization of ability and qualification, improving learning skills, high level of team spirit and cooperation etc.

It also revealed that reward and conflict management kind of practices in the organization gives a good perception of climate to employees. The result of the study concluded that if more focus is placed on rewards and recognition, it could have a resultant positive impact on motivation and thus result in higher levels of job performance & satisfaction. Again, it should be noted that conflict is a reality that crosses all organizational boundaries to affect individuals, groups and disciplines. It can initiate productive change and vitality or it can lead to the demise of an organization. Handled properly through an appropriate conflict management style, conflict can enhance administrator's efforts in reaching school goals. For administrators who realistically confront it, conflict can represent a dynamic force which facilitates organizational growth, change, adaptation and survival. In order to meet organizational obligations, its top management must develop a relationship between the organization and employees that will fulfill the continually changing needs of both parties.

In previous findings, there is a significant relationship has been found between organizational climate and job satisfaction. It means that employee's good perception of the climate gives satisfaction to the employees for their job whereas bad perception gives dissatisfaction for their job. In our industrial settings, the satisfaction level of employees has a great bearing on their levels of climate in their organization.

The organizational role stress has its impact on organizational climate. It has been revealed from the study that high stressed employees do not found their climate good but low stressed employees found their climate good.

The efficiency of employees depends, to a great extent, on the environment in which they work. Work environment consists of all the factors which act and react on the body and mind of an employee. The attitudes, feelings and emotions of employees towards organization play a vital role in determining their performance and behaviour. These in turn determine the success and growth of the organization. It is for this reason that organizations need to pay increasing attention on understanding Organizational Climate, enhancing the Job Satisfaction of their employees and reducing the role stress of employees.

REFERENCES

Adenike, A. (2011, January). Organisational Climate as a Predictor of Employee Job Satisfaction. *Business Intelligence Journal*, *4*(1), 151–165.

Dev, S. (2013). What makes employees stay?: Exploring the dimensions in context of urban-centric business process outsourcing industry in India, Strategic Outsourcing. *International Journal (Toronto, Ont.)*, *6*(3), 258–276.

Gautam, S., & Sharma, V.K. (2014). A study of job stress among b.ed. teachers in relation to organizational climate. *Indian Streams Research Journal*, *3*(12).

Hunnur, R.R., Bagli, M.M. (2014). A Study On Relationship Between Occupation Stress Index Dimensions And Demographic Variables Of Police Sub Inspectors And Asst. Sub Inspectors In Police Department. *International Journal of Business and Administration Research Review*, *1*(3), 161-175.

Jain, K., & Jain, P. (2013). Job Satisfaction: A Comparative Study of Public & Private Sector Banks. *International Journal of Organizational Behaviour and Management Perspectives*, *2*(1).

Parzinger, M. J., Lemons, M. A., & McDaniel, K. (2012, Spring). The Impact Of Organizational Context On Turnover And Job Satisfaction: A Multi-Analysis Study Of Bank Employees. *International Journal of the Academic Business World*, *6*(1), 39–50.

Pestonjee, D. M. (1973). *Organization Structure and Job Attitudes*. Calcutta: The Minnerva Association.

Pestonjee, D. M. (1987). Executive Stress: Should it always be avoided? *Vikalpa*, *12*(1), 23–30.

Pestonjee (1999). *Stress and Coping the Indian Experience*; Sage Publications, New Delhi.

Postonjee, D.M., & Singh, G.P. (1987). *Organizational behaviour issues for managers and systems analysis*. Indian institute of Managements, Ahmadabad.

Yahaya, A., Yahaya, N., Arshad, K., Ismail, J., Jaalam, S., & Zakariya, Z. (2009). Occupational Stress and its Effects towards the Organization Management. *Journal of Social Sciences*, *5*(4), 390-397.

Yildiz, M. L., & Özcan, E. D. (2014). Organizational Climate as a moderator of the Relationship between Transformational Leadership and Creativity. *International Journal of Business and Management*, *2*(1), 76–87.

Chapter 3
Managing Organized Crime

Roberto Musotto
University of Messina, Italy

Giacomo Morabito
University of Messina, Italy

Davide Di Fatta
University of Messina, Italy

Vittorio D'Aleo
University of Messina, Italy

Walter Vesperi
University of Messina, Italy

Salvatore Lo Bue
University of Messina, Italy

ABSTRACT

This chapter describes the way in which organised crime networks are structured and operate. Every general manager, no matter which kind of business he/she deals with, has to transform the daily chaos of events and decisions into an orderly way of sizing up the firm's position in its environment. At first, this chapter focuses on organised crime networks: how they are shaped and how they differ from others business. Secondly, how such a structure protects itself from exterior threats and how it moves and operates in a market among other legal and illegal firms and networks.

DOI: 10.4018/978-1-5225-1974-4.ch003

INTRODUCTION

This paper describes the way in which organised crime networks are structured and operate. In particular, the analysis will be held from strategic management point of view, using an industrial organisation approach (Porter, 1980, 1981; Bain, 1968; Mason, 1939) applied to network management structure (Tikkanen and Halinen, 2003).

The idea is that every general manager, no matter which kind of business he/she is dealing with, "has to transform the daily chaos of events and decisions into an orderly way of sizing up the firm's position in its environment" (Porter, 1981, p. 610). Whether managers will have to coordinate drug production and racket market or organise biotechnology drugs distribution, in the end of the day, both will have set strategies, pointed out choices and decisions that will affect the future of the firm.

This paper aims to focus on organised crime networks considering at first how they are shaped and how they differ from others business and, secondly, how such structure protects itself from exterior threats and how it moves and operates in a market among other legal and illegal firms and networks.

Prior to further analysis, it must be assumed that organised crime can be considered and, thus studied, as any other firm. This idea is not new nor original as it appeared at first on the Task Force Report on Organized Crime of the 1967 President's Commission on Law Enforcement and Administration Of Justice where it stated: "the core of organised crime activity is the supplying of illegal good and services - gambling, loansharking, narcotics and other forms of vice - to countless numbers of citizen customers". This definition clearly establishes a direct link between the core activities of organised crime and the management of illegal markets (Fiorentini and Peltzman, 1995). At first glance literature (among all: Schelling, 1971) was focused on activities held just as businesses and "although it is not denied that the criminal organisation can use violence in order to achieve economic results in its legal activities, this is typically not so when it is involved in its activities in illegal markets" (Fiorentini and Peltzman, 1995, p. 3).

Kerner (1973), at first, and Kerner and Mack (1975) gave the idea that criminal organisations work like a firm, where its business is to produce illegal goods and services for a broad variety of consumers. Eventually, also prosecutor's thesis in Maxiprocesso against the heads of Sicilian mafia was based on the evidences about a cupola acting as the core of a centralized decision-maker for their more important economic activities and risks management.

Considering criminal organizations like any other firm, it brings the idea that they have similar issues concerning paths to take, set out strategies against rivals and bring towards strategic choices that can maximize their objective functions. In specific, each organization might decide to structure itself as a network for the advantages that will be discussed (Fatta, D. D., Caputo, F., Evangelista, F., & Dominici, G. (2016b).

ORGANISED CRIME NETWORKS

What is a Network?

In many industries traditional markets and hierarchical organizations are partly being replaced by networks of interorganizational relationships (Ring and Van de Ven, 1992). The reason of this shift is explained by the fact that their existence helps knowledge, information and resources to flow on a more efficient way. This approach is slightly different from the traditional one (Porter, 1980) as it keeps the framework of industrial organisation paradigm structure, where firm's performance depends on the structure of the industry on the market where it competes but not all the actors manage to compete in an impersonal market place (Gulati, Nohria and Zaheer, 2000). Organisations might decide to cooperate to overcome the limit of internal resources (Tikkanen & Halinen, 2003) or to adapt themselves into new environments (Venkatraman & Subramaniam, 2002; Di Fatta et al., 2016a)

What is a network? Broadly speaking, a network is a series of connected 2 nodes, employed in strategic management to solve problems and improve performance. A node is an individual, a car or every other possible asset. Each node has a linkage to other nodes, creating connections and thus a network (Xu and Chen, 2004). Those links might be formal if they bound each node by contract: that is the case of joint ventures or cartels; or informal when the connection goes through the ruled relation and bounds on a different efficient way (Krackhardts & Hanson, 1993)[1]. Formal and informal networks usually coexist and they shape interactions over the devised structure. Managers can leverage these networks to solve organisational problems, restructuring their formal organisations to complement the informal, to make them work with company goals, maximising efficiency.

They might differ for size, shape, membership, cohesion and purpose[2] and the concept of network might fit multiple fields as it was just formulated. Network is critical to the effective functioning of the market (Williams, 1998) because it provides essential links between suppliers and customers. It might be considered superior to hierarchies in terms of electiveness especially for innovation and teamwork as networks have two main characteristics:

1. They resist to disruption better that a hierarchical organization
2. They have a higher degree of resilience than a regular firm

Every network has a core and a periphery; this latter can have subgroups.

Although every network has common features, it will be pointed out how organised crime networks differ from other business ones and this organizational architecture it is set to implement legal and illegal activities.

ORGANISED CRIME NETWORKS FEATURES

Considering Organised Crime Networks Xu and Chen (2005) pointed out how it is different to analyse such structures than phone market network for example, as those groups usually operate in secret and every information that can be spilled out is most of the times incomplete, incorrect and inconsistent. Nevertheless, data can be interpreted trough a social structure of competition (Burt, 1992) though the pattern might not always be evident (Xu & Chen, 2004; Williams, 1998).

Network analysis applied to organised crime networks helps to organise data that need to be transformed and reveals patterns in the nature and extent of relationships between data points to give a better understanding of the phenomenon for implementing criminal intelligence.

As already spotted, before analysing organised crime networks, a criminal organisation has to be assumed as a firm and thus to be able, as any other legal firm, to take investment decisions[3] or to set a competitive behaviour with respect to the rivals in the market. According to Polo (1995) and Gambetta and Reuter (1995) the necessary condition for criminal organisations to carry out their activities is the control over the turf [4].

When such control is gained, it still remains an incentive to invest in appropriate activities to dissuade further attempts to contest such control from other criminal groups and also from government. Such an investment could take place in military technology or corruption and it could be considered the equivalent to investment in research and development or in advertising in legal firms (Fiorentini & Peltzman,

Figure 1. Network structure

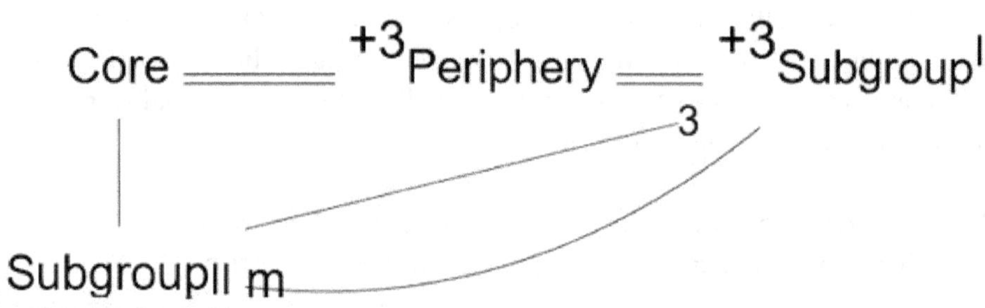

1995), because it is not directly aimed at the production of goods and services but instead at increasing their profitability by deterring (or limit as much as possible) the entry of rival firms[5].

Criminal organisations can decide to be part of a network at first to overcome their control and coercion problems and secondly this kind of structure is functional to a larger scale of operations (among all money laundering and international production of drugs) where it is useless to have a complete monopoly and it is more effective to cooperate to reach greater outcomes.

In next subsections, organised crime networks will be examined concerning density, cohesion, membership and shape under the light of a revised industrial organization point of view.

Density

One first important instrument to "measure" criminal networks is density[6], which is also a feature that allows to differ criminal groups from their networks. In effect, it is shown (McAndrews, 1999) that organised crime networks have not a stable and hierarchical structure just as other legal firms: most of the times they have a horizontal, straggling and spread structure like, for example, terrorist groups[7]. The reason of such a difference can be explained considering that it is a group under constant multiple attacks and threats from law enforcement and competitive rivals: when a subgroup or a unit is busted, it will be easier to replace it with another one. In such a context, all the subgroups gain centrality as they will be the most visible part insuring core concealment (Baker and Faulkner, 1993). However, as much as the core might be impalpable, there will be a node of the chain where there will be: A high degree of trust[8]; High level of cohesion[9].

Cohesion

Among all the features, cohesion is the most important element in organised crime networks, for the reasons that are going to be explained. Concerning this element, literature argued about the fact that it must be found something that unifies every individual at the core. This might be family (Aoki, 1990), religion or ethnicity; while at periphery all those connections are weaker. If it is true that those elements create cohesion, concerning periphery the first binding element is coercion. Skaperdas and Syropoulos (1995) argue about the fact that "the mafioso rise to power is inextricably linked to his willingness and ability to use force successfully" (p. 72). This is another difference from legal firms because physical punishments or minor threats are used as an instrument of control of members and workers are protected by institutions against those subordination methods. According to Skaperdas and

Syropoulos (1995) Mafia organisation try to act primitive states and since those kind of organisations do not benefit of protection from state law.[10]

Nevertheless, organised crime networks can experience cohesion problems (Polo, 1995) and although the punishment threat could be present the function variables of monitoring, intelligence and violence decline in effectiveness when the periphery operates far from the core so with large networks it will be more complex to keep control[11], but at same time expansion allows criminal organisation to reach new markets and gain more strength. In this sense cohesion is increasing in the dimension of the network and decreasing in the spatial and time distance between core and periphery. According to Polo (1995) this effectiveness reduction problem can be solved by contract agreements as "criminal managers" will have to minimize betrayal incentives paying more all the agents that are part of periphery and are less linked to the core or simply they are not bounded with religious or family reasons.

Cohesion is important even for interactions between more networks as it is the element that keeps cartels and agreements stationary. In such a situation, each member of the network is under a double obligation, hence more stringent from the original network and the new one crafted after the agreement. There are some examples of such agreements between Camorra and Cosa Nostra and Colombian Narcos for drug import and agents protection[12], where nodes mix up to serve both organisations.

From a strategic point of view this peripheral weakness is somehow the result of "the strength of weak ties" (Granovetter, 1973) that, on one hand, allows the periphery to be easily attacked or infiltrated, but on the other it allows to overcome technological and geopolitical barriers that might be a problem for the expansion and diversification of the same network.

Cohesion gives also the idea that it could be useful to consider an Industrial Organization approach (Scherer, 1980 & Porter, 1980) and its principal paradigm of structure-conduct-performance to examine the effect in a market system of organised crime behaviour. The reason of such approach stands in the fact that empirically there might be industry structures that facilitate collusion, corruption and illegal activities, that are a specific kind of conduct and thus influence economic performance for every part in the market.

Dynamism

In organised crime networks nodes are considered to be dynamic (Xu and Chen, 2005). This means that each node might come off without affecting all the structure and sideways: the inclusion of new nodes does not change the general structure. The logic behind this stands on the fact that periphery nodes aim naturally to expand themselves (Barzilai & Nahon, 2008). Dynamic networks also help the inclusion of individuals that formally are not part of the structure but they can profit and get benefits from illicit activities and at same time help the network with other tasks[13].

Dynamic networks could explain the success and failure of diamond or drug cartels (Levenstein & Suslo, 2006; Gupta, Polonsky, Woodside et al., 2010) because the impact of external forces on business networks may alter network structures over time (Eccles & Crane, 1987). Sinaloa cartel for example changed structure multiple times over decades:

Every node of the cartel had different functions or provided a specific service. For example, Mara Salvatrucha organization (MS-13) was an El Salvador native criminal group that became affiliated to Sinaloa Cartel providing security services and military functions; while Latin Kings are basically distributors and retail traders in U.S.A. of drugs produced and smuggled through the borders by other members of the group.

This same cartel changed and reduced its structure after arrests and rivalry with other criminal groups and become few years before its disappearing like in the following picture. This reduced network has not to get misleading conclusions about its effectiveness as it used to have the same functionality as the previous one but cohesion was kept higher than the previous structure.

One explanation of such dynamism can be traced back to the same definition of network from earlier, since the structure supplies links between different nodes that are put in communication, It must be considered that the same structure is neutral to its purpose as they are an instrument to reach multiple goals (Williams, 1998).

Knowledge

It was stated how networks might be more efficient and effective rather than traditional hierarchies and competition structures. In specific, networks help knowledge, information and resources to flow from each node to the other. Considering organised crime networks, it can be shown that information is procured on a more effective way, but at the same time it can be efficiently protected from other threats.

According to Williams (1998), this is possible thanks to a compartmental sharing of knowledge. Each node in periphery will have a very limited disposal of information restricted to duties that each unit has to carry out.

In such a system, a peripheral unit can lead just to a superior unit or to a close one, but none can lead or relate itself to the main unit. This protection system allows also to explain how hard it is to trace back such network structure and identify the core[14]. The most famous and brilliant example of such ex post reconstruction was the one that led to the arrest of Bernardo Provenzano following all the long transitions of a laundry bucket (Oliva & Palazzolo, 2006).

However, there are multiple factors that can help to protect organised crime networks (Skaperdas, 2001). Geography, society, inefficient institutions (Musotto, 2012) and even ethnic communities. Varese (2011) points out that ethnicity is at same time an element that favours protection[15] and expansion with reallocation of members and resources. The principle of guanxi (reciprocal obligation) is a case that shows how one tie can span generations and continents and thus spread over space and time, providing a basis for trust and cooperation (Williams, 1998). That is the case about how Chinese organised crime managed to spread into new continents (Paoli, 2002).

Compartmental information has the virtue to get virtually invisible the association because:

- A node could not consider itself part of the network;
- Each node can complete tasks without even knowing to do it for a certain network.[16]

This strategy allows the organised crime network to better adapt itself to complex processes (Miles, Snow, Meyer & Coleman, 1978) lowering risks which might expose all the network. Adaptation is possible also thanks to the high resiliency already spotted. Basically, organised crime networks have loose coupling that facilitate the entrance and ease every structural modification without the need to reveal themselves (Barzilai & Nahon, 2008). Eventually, they can get so loose that they become redundant. Now if this is usually considered one of the first sources of inefficiencies[17] concerning regular businesses, it is effective on organised crime networks and what a criminal manager would look for his/her structure. The ratio is that redundant nodes might be recovered easily once they are impaired. Every node of the network, if set free to act, tends per se to expand itself towards new nodes and creating new links (Krackhardt & Hanson, 2000). This means that there will not be gaps or holes inside the structure because at the same moment one unit stop existing one other will take charge, thus helping in its perpetuation even in most inhospitable environments.

Shape

As stated before in this same section, connections and links shape networks (Xu & Chen, 2004). Considering the high degree of resilience, a network might be cohesive or diffusive. The first case shapes union between all its nodes; while the latter spreads them out. This gives the idea that more shapes could exist since a network could group more individuals but also it could be surrounded by more organizations, like the Cartel of Sinaloa was. According to Williams (1998) the reason why criminal network shapes could be so different lies on the fact that usually there might be different products or services to offer (also Rumelt, 1974).

Considering organised crime networks, there are multiple activities that each network might deal with[18]. Although supply chain might not be so complex as biotech industries, it looks like these networks are highly structured into multiple levels and interactions.

For example, in case of trafficking, there will be a manager who will have to choose how to set production, as he might prefer to outsource it to avoid risks or to internalize it to get a bigger revenue. Then, once the product is ready to hit the market, it needs to arrive to final consumer with the help of other nodes or even other networks. Such revenues then need to be dematerialised not to trace them back to illicit activities.

According to Castells (2011) more networks can also organise themselves together to deal with some specific business. Networks here do not lack an organizational identity, but at the same time they are not overly preoccupied with organizational form. Depending on the kind of agreement, they can be with reciprocal benefits or subjected one to the other. Collaboration or subordination, work exactly as in the licit businesses, as their main objective is to facilitate cooperation.

CONCLUSION ABOUT ORGANISED CRIME FEATURES

In this subsection all the network features analysed in the section are going to be summed up to simplify reading and support conclusions.

Organised crime networks help cooperation between criminal groups. This structure favours the intake of external resources on a less costly way and, at same time, it reaches markets on a more effective and coordinated way.

Those networks are concealed to protect themselves and although the core is characterised by trust and cohesion, those two elements are more disperse on go-

Figure 2. Illicit flowchart

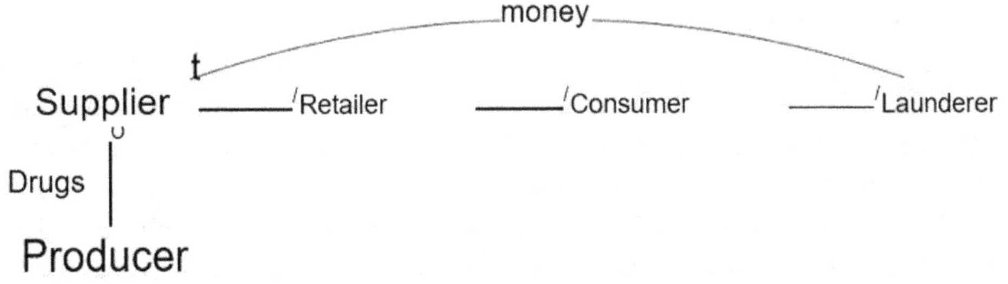

ing further from the centre. The most important point of this research is that it is possible to picture the existence of Mafia with sparse and decentralised networks, although they might keep a highly hierarchical structure between core and periphery (Mastrobuoni & Patacchini, 2012).

The concept of network in organised crime studies explains also the commitment and involvement of non-members on criminal activities that are kept off from traditional definitions: since membership is usually exclusive the aim of every organisation is to perpetuate itself is eased by external forces (Musotto, 2012).

Network analysis applied to organised crime explains also that information processes work on a compartmental block to hide evanescent connections set to preserve more vital nodes, while the other "expendables" ones can be quickly recovered on account of their redundancy.

NETWORK COMPETITION IN LEGITIMATE INDUSTRIES

This section considers the role of organised crime networks among le-gitimate industries. Considering the kind of services that organised crime might provide, how organised crime decides to enter a market and which are its strategic decision about work organisation.

This paper will not consider further the role of organised crime networks in illegitimate industries. Since such networks tend to operate on a monopoly-based market, with a strict control of the turf, there will not be competition, but only cooperation among all the possible criminal groups in the area[19].

In next subsection, it will be analysed the role of such networks from theoretical arguments and secondly from empirical evidences.

Protection

In legitimate industries criminal networks "supply" protection (Schelling, 1971) . This kind of protection is offered from racketeers and it might work as intimidation to false competition market or also as an extortion (Reuter, 1987). Those are a group of activities that facilitate the market of coerced industries and enforce agreements through violence (Musotto, 2012).

In a monopoly market the main function would be to put a barrier to entry intimidating other industries to enter and operate. According to Gambetta and Reuter (1995), protectors on a monopoly have also an incentive to let firms enter the market. The reason of such incentive is that having more "clients" on a specific market avoids every risk linked to the legitimate firm business life. In a nutshell, depending on just one participant is not convenient for the criminal enterprise because "the larger the number of firms the higher is the mafia's autonomy from and bargaining power over any single of them" (Gambetta, 1993 page 22).

In a competitive market, organised crime works creating a collusive agreement between all the participants or a part of them. This agreement gets an anti-competitive outcome that is stable and effective. Since every participant will be sure that other parties will undertake the agreement, the option to exit the cartel as every party in the cartel will get benefits (Fiorentini, 1999). Protection is also considered as a structure that allows market sharing (Gambetta, 1993), where Mafia plays a regulation role[20] that organises agreements and keeps the enforcement of cartels because it might effectively execute violent threats against its violations.

The idea is that mafia provides a service where the state is unable or unwilling to meet the demands of entrepreneurs for profit-enhancing and risk reducing regulation (Stigler, 1971). This kind of network is able to produce less volatile profits because they are relied to markets where the risk of cartel and network exposure is lower than on illicit ones and at same time the total risk is shifted from exchange transactions into policy agreement (Campiglio, 1995; Musotto, 2012).

Funeral Homes and Other Agreements

According to Gambetta and Reuter (1995) mafia controlled cartels manage to grow on very specific markets, where racketeers provide regulation and can be able to share tasks and jobs between all the firms in the market equally. The benefit in this case is double: firms do not have to worry about job orders and they work as a barrier to entry for other firms. The service is not free, but the racketed price[21] might change according to the size of the firm, sector and incomes[22]

In Palermo, funeral homes shared hospitals[23] using a geographical sharing of territory where firm A got hospital X; firm B hospital Y and firm C hospital Z. In such a situation Mafia worked as barrier to entry for other enterprises not affiliated to the main network and as regulator of that kind of market[24].

One other form of agreement takes places when costumers are fixed in location and the service or good is delivered to them (Reuter, 1987, page 7). One example of such cartel is street food and beverages selling in Borgo Vecchio neighbourhood and precisely in its main place. Here, although there are several retailers of beverages and food, each costumer is directed to the "rival" that has permission to sell during that period of time. The other vendors will act the same at their turn. Violations on such a small place can be easily detected and that is how cartels keep being stable for long time. Service might also concern public goods such as water and electricity supplies in Z.E.N. neighbourhood (Musotto, 2014) provided from Mafia in exchange of a fixed monthly payment to specific retailers.

Eventually, one last strategy to share market is creating queues. This is more effective than the others when there is a large number of buyers and sellers and turns dictate each contract agreement. The most clear example concerns taxi drivers market where queued clients A, B, C, will only receive services from respectively sellers X, Y, Z, though other sellers are still available (Musotto, 2012).

CONCLUSION ABOUT ORGANISED CRIME NETWORKS

The aim of this paper was to show resiliency that criminal networks can get once fully operative. Although a criminal manager might have to deal with different matters such as concealment and military technology, he puts out a development strategy to improve efficiency and effectiveness from everyday deals.

How to defeat and dismantle such criminal networks then? According to Arquilla and Ronfeldt (1997) it takes a network to defeat another one. A good network where resources, technology and knowledge are put together with specific objective function of understanding the phenomenon and hit were it might manifest (Castells, 2011).

Another end of such networks could be trough a different institutional framework (Musotto, 2012) that would set under specific conditions[25] market agreements and get useless the use of uomini d'onore for market regulations. At same time law enforcement should be implemented seizing resources and technology, diminishing the threat power that such networks are able to express.

REFERENCES

Aoki, M. (1990). Toward an economic model of the Japanese firm. *Journal of Economic Literature*.

Arquilla, J., & Ronfeldt, D. (1997). In Athena's Camp: Preparing for Conflict in the Information Age. California, USA: RAND.

Bain, J. S. (1968). *Industrial organization*. New York: Wiley.

Baker, W. E., & Faulkner, R. R. (1993). The social organization of conspiracy: Illegal networks in the heavy electrical equipment industry. *American Sociological Review*, *58*(6), 837–860. doi:10.2307/2095954

Barzilai-Nahon, K. (2008). Toward a theory of network gatekeeping: A frame work for exploring information control. *Journal of the American Society for Information Science and Technology*, *59*(9), 1493–1512. doi:10.1002/asi.20857

Burt, R. S. (1992). *Structural Holes: The Social Structure of Competition*. Cambridge, MA: Harvard University Press.

Campiglio, L. (1995). Discussion about "Conspiracy among the many: the mafia in Legitimate industries". In G. Fiorentini & S. Peltzman (Eds.), *The economics of Organised Crime*. New York: Cambridge University Press.

Castells, M. (2011). A Network Theory of Power. *International Journal of Communication*, 5.

Di Fatta, D., Musotto, R., D'Aleo, V., Vesperi, W., Morabito, G., & Bue, S. L. (2016b). Weak Ties and Value of a Network in the New Internet Economy. Social Media Data Extraction and Content Analysis, 66.

Eccles, R. G., & Crane, D. B. (1987). Managing through networks in investment banking. *California Management Review*, *30*(1), 176–195. doi:10.2307/41165273

Fatta, D. D., Caputo, F., Evangelista, F., & Dominici, G. (2016a). Small world theory and the World Wide Web: Linking small world properties and website centrality. *International Journal of Markets and Business Systems*, *2*(2), 126–140.

Faust, K., and Wasserman, S. (1992). Blockmodels: Interpretation and evaluation. *Social networks*, *14*(1), 5-61. 15

Fiorentini, G. (1999). Cartels Run by Criminal Organizations and Market Contestability. Proceedings of the IEA Conference Series (*Vol. 124*). doi:10.1007/978-1-349-14540-9_3

Fiorentini, G., & Peltzman, S. (Eds.), *The economics of Organised Crime*. New York: Cambridge University Press. doi:10.1017/CBO9780511751882

Gambetta, D. (1993). *The Sicilian Mafia: The Business of Private Protection*. Cambridge, MA: Harvard University Press.

Gambetta, D., & Reuter, P. (1995). Conspiracy among the many: the mafia in Legitimate industries. In G. Fiorentini & S. Peltzman (Eds.), *The economics of Organised Crime*. New York: Cambridge University Press. doi:10.1007/978-1-349-62853-7_5

Granovetter, M. S. (1973). The strength of weak ties. *American Journal of Sociology*, *78*(6), 1360–1380. doi:10.1086/225469

Gulati, R., Nohria, N., & Zaheer, A. (2000). Strategic Networks. *Strategic Management Journal*, *21*(3), 203–215. doi:10.1002/(SICI)1097-0266(200003)21:3<203::AID-SMJ102>3.0.CO;2-K

Gupta, S., Polonsky, M., Woodside, A., & Webster, C. M. (2010). The impact of external forces on cartel network dynamics: Direct research in the diamond industry. *Industrial Marketing Management, 39*(2), 202–210. doi:10.1016/j.indmarman.2008.11.009

Hammer, M. (1990). Reengineering work: Don't automate, obliterate. *Harvard Business Review, 68*(4), 104–112.

Kerner, H. J. (1973). *Professionelles und organisiertes vercrechen. Versuch einer Bestandsaufnabme und Bericht unber neuere Entwicklunggstendenzen in der Bundesrepublik Deutschland und in des Niederlanden.* Wiesbaden: BKA.

Kerner, H. J., & Mack, J. A. (1975). *The crime industry.* Lexington Lexington Books.

Krackhardt, D., & Hanson, J. R. (1993). Mapping employees relationships can help managers harness the real power in their organizations. *Harvard Business Review*, 16.

Krebs, V. E. (2001). Mapping Networks of Terrorist Cells. *Connections, 24*, 43–52.

Lavezzi, A. M. (2008). Struttura economica e vulnerabilitá del crimine organizzato in Sicilia. La A. Spina (Eds.), I costi della illegalitá. Mafia ed estorsioni in Sicilia. Bologna, Italy: il Mulino.

Levenstein, M. C., & Suslow, V. Y. (2006). What determines cartel success. *Journal of Economic Literature, 44*(1), 43–95. doi:10.1257/002205106776162681

Mason, E.S. (1939). Price and production policies of large-scale enterprises. *American Economic Review, 29*, 61-74.

Mastrobuoni, G., & Patacchini, E. (2012). Organized crime networks: An application of network analysis techniques to the American mafia. *Review of Network Economics, 11*(3).

McAndrew, D. (1999). The structural analysis of criminal networks. In D. Canter & L. Alison (Eds.), *The Social Psychology of Crime: Groups* (Vol. 3). Aldershot, Dartmouth: Teams, and Networks, Offender Profiling Series.

Miles, R.E., Snow, C.C., Meyer, A.D., & Coleman, H.J. (1978). Organizational strategy, structure, and process. *Academy of Management Review, 3*(3), 546–562. PMID:10238389

Musotto, R. (2012). *Inefficient Institutions and Organised Crime.* Universitá degli Studi di Palermo.

Musotto, R. (2014). Criminalidad Organizada, Estado y Servicios Públicos: un Análisis Socioeconómico. In J.J. Martínez Bolaños (Ed.), *Criminalidad Organizada*. Spain: Estudios Internacionales. Criminologia y Justicia Editorial.

Oliva, E., & Palazzolo, S. (2006). *Bernardo Provenzano: il ragioniere di Cosa nostra*. Rubbettino Editore.

Paoli, L. (2002). The paradoxes of organized crime. *Crime, law and social change*, *37*(1), 51-97. 17

Polo, M. (1995). Internal cohesion and competition among criminal organizations. In G. Fiorentini & S. Peltzman (Eds.), *The economics of Organised Crime*. New York: Cambridge University Press.

Porter, M.E. (1980). *Competitive Strategy: Techniques for Analysing Industries and Competitors*. NY: The Free Press.

Porter, M.E. (1981). The contributions of industrial organization to strategic management. *Academy of Management Review*, *6*(4), 609–620.

Reuter, P. (1987). *Racketeering in Legitimate Industries: A Study in the Economics of Intimidation*. California: RAND.

Ring, P.S., & Van de Ven, A.H. (1992). Structuring Cooperative Relationships between Organizations. *Strategic Management Journal*, *13*(10).

Rumelt, R.P. (1974). *Strategy, structure and economic performance*. Boston: Harvard University Press.

Schelling, T.C. (1971). What is the business of organized crime? *The American Scholar*, 40(4), 643–652.

Scherer, F.M. (1980). *Industrial Market Structure and Economic Performance*. Chicago: Rand McNally.

Skaperdas, S. (2001). The political economy of organized crime: Providing protection when the state does not. *Economics of Governance*, *2*(3), 173–202. doi:10.1007/PL00011026

Skaperdas, S., & Syropoulos, C. (1995). Gangs as primitive states. In G. Fiorentini & S. Peltzman (Eds.), *The economics of Organised Crime*. New York: Cambridge University Press.

Stigler, G. J. (1971). The Theory of Economic Regulation. *The Bell Journal of Economics and Management Science*, 2(1), 3-21.

Tikkanen, J., & Halinen, A. (2003). Network approach to strategic management: Exploration to the emerging perspective. *Proceedings of the 19th IMP International Conference*, Lugano, Switzerland.

Varese, F. (2011). *Mafias on the move: How organized crime conquers new territories*. Princeton University Press. doi:10.1515/9781400836727

Venkatraman, N., & Subramaniam, M. (2002). Theorizing the Future of Strategy: Questions for Shaping Strategy Research in the Knowledge Economy. In A. Pettigrew, H. Thomas, & R. Whittington (Eds.), *Handbook of Strategy and Management*. London: Sage Publications.

Williams, P. (1998). The nature of drug-trafficking networks. *Current History (New York, N.Y.)*, *97*, 154–159.

Wilson, I. (2010). The Biggest Cock: Territoriality, Invulnerability and Honour amongst Jakarta's Gangsters. *Indonesian Studies Working Papers*, *13*, 1–19.

Xu, J., & Chen, H. (2005). Criminal network analysis and visualization. *Communications of the ACM*, *48*(6), 100–107. doi:10.1145/1064830.1064834

Xu, J. J., & Chen, H. (2004). Fighting organized crimes: Using shortest-path algorithms to identify associations in criminal networks. *Decision Support Systems*, *38*(3), 473–487. doi:10.1016/S0167-9236(03)00117-9

ENDNOTES

1 Those two authors define formal networks as the skeleton of the company while the informal one as "the central nervous system driving the collective thought processes, actions and reactions of its business units".

2 All those elements will be further analysed

3 One of those choices could be joining or creating a network.

4 This control could be merely geographical, meaning that only one criminal group is allowed to work on a specific and bounded territory; or functional this could be the case of Mexican cartels, where one specific group controls completely a certain activity: for example, Commando negro of Los Zetas cartel that deals basically on tracking phones, cars and people (Musotto, 2012).

5 Concerning criminal organisations, there are major limits to their expansion which are internal cohesion and government attacks.

6 In Network literature density usually refers to the proportion of all possible ties that are present. Hypothesized relations among actors occupying structur-

ally equivalent positions (blocks) in networks are studied trough blockmodel theory (Wasserman and Faust (1994) and in criminal network analysis it can reveal patterns of group interactions and associations. According to Xu and Chen (2005) the link density between two subgroups i and j can be calculated by: $d_{ij} = \frac{m_{ij}}{n_i n_i}$ where mij is the actual number of links between subgroups i and j; n_i and n_j represent the number of nodes within subgroups i and j, respectively

7 One very interesting application of such theory was exactly concerning Al Quaeda network, because density studying helped literature to quantify and qualify connections between individuals and groups (Krebs, 2001).

8 That is prodromal to cohesion in such kind of groups (Lavezzi, 2008).

9 Wise (2014?) is opposed to such statement as he considers that nodes and teams with an high level of cohesion can affect negatively performance. In specific, he uses same arguments of Baker and Faulkner (1993) to show that there is an inverse curvilinear (U-shaped) relationship between social network structures and team performance.

10 Although an interesting exception can be found on Indonesian Preman gangs that were institutionalised by State and they even pay taxes from their racket revenues (Wilson, 2010)

11 That is a necessary element for organised crime networks to operate.

12 http://ricerca.repubblica.it/repubblica/archivio/repubblica/2010/07/20/mafia-camorra-in-affari-con-narcos.html

13 The clearest example of illicit activity in dynamic criminal networks in Italy might be the external participation in mafia groups concorso esterno in associazione di stampo mafioso expressed by the joint interpretation of artciles 416-bis and 110 of Italian Penal Code and decision from Cassazione Penale Sezioni Unite nÂř 22327/2003.

14 Xu and Chen (2005) observe that when data networks have to be analysed the best approach is to relate to manual speculation, while graphic and structural analysis help to expedite data processing.

15 Because organised crime members will establish on a compact society.

16That is the case of cargo ships transporting drugs into containers.

16 That is the case of cargo ships transporting drugs into containers.

17 Studying business process reengineering theories one of basic questions is: “why do we need to keep more people doing the same task if just one can do it?” Hammer (1990)

18 Exempli gratia: human, weapon and drug trafficking, money laundering, racket, corruption, collusion just to name a few.

19 Although it is possible to imagine competition and also war between more networks considering for example the enrolment of competitor's nodes and units: e.g. Cartel Wars in Mexico

20 Or it moves Adam Smith's invisible hand.

21 According to Gambetta and Reuters (1995) it is a tax, because Mafia behaves as a governmental institution.

22 E.G. Boss managers might decide to lower racketing price, just to get a wider class of businesses; see La Repubblica Palermo section on 24th of June 2014.

23 http://sosracketusurablog.wordpress.com/2012/01/30/scoperto-il-racket-delle-pompe-funebri-negli-ospedali-di-trapani-salemi-castelvetrano-mazara-del-vallo-palermo-partinico

24 http://reggiopress.wordpress.com/2014/06/27/mafia-a-palermo-pompe-funebri-nel-mirino-le-autorizzazioni-tutte-per-aprire-le-dettava-la-mafia

25 Among all possible conditions, customers care and product quality could be some of them.

Chapter 4
The Fundamentals of Human Capital

Kijpokin Kasemsap
Suan Sunandha Rajabhat University, Thailand

ABSTRACT

This chapter explains the overview of human capital; human capital and economic growth; human capital, innovation, and knowledge management; human capital and research and development (R&D); human capital, political regime, and foreign direct investment (FDI); human capital, employment, and labor markets; the measure of human capital; and the challenges and implications of human capital in the digital age. Human capital refers to knowledge, skills, and abilities acquired by an individual, traditionally through education and work experience. Human capital has a positive relationship with entrepreneurial success, business growth, and economic development. Creating an organization that relies on human capital for competitive advantage involves designing every organizational system with an essential approach to attracting, developing, retaining, and motivating the highly qualified people. The chapter argues that developing human capital has the potential to enhance organizational performance and gain sustainable competitive advantage in the digital age.

DOI: 10.4018/978-1-5225-1974-4.ch004

INTRODUCTION

Many organizations are increasingly recognizing the value of their human capital toward increasing organizational performance (Lajili, 2015). Human capital refers to the knowledge, skills, and abilities to generate a given set of outcomes (Hitt, Bierman, Shimizu, & Kochhar, 2001). Human capital in firms in terms of education, experience, and cognitive skills and the firm's overall access to human capital has a positive impact on firm productivity (Backman, 2014). The human capital of a firm as manifested by employee knowledge and experience represents an important resource of a firm's capabilities (Schulz, Chowdhury, & van de Voort, 2013).

Human capital provides a competitive advantage for firms in terms of skills, expertise, and their willingness to work (Hewitt-Dundas, 2006). Human capital investment is the most important input for the advancement of science and knowledge (Gallié & Legros, 2012). Human capital investment decisions are linked to the success of a business and ultimately to the probability of survival (Wyatt & Frick, 2010). The slow investment in human capital affects the sustainable development of the countries (Pelinescu, 2015). The compatibility between person and organization is encompassed in a research aimed to analyze the elements of human capital in an organization, such as training, competences, expertise, experience, creativity, and innovation (Zlate & Enache, 2015).

In any period, there are two types of capital (i.e., physical and human capital). Physical capital is accumulated during life through investment, while the human capital stock increases by allocating time to education (Alessandrini, Kosempel, & Stengos, 2015). The major elements of shared human capital are values, tacit knowledge, and social support (Suhonen & Paasivaara, 2011). Human capital and brand equity constitute a firm's most valuable resources (Vomberg, Homburg, & Bornemann, 2015). Firms and policymakers are faced with many constraints in light of the continued economic downturn and reduced budgets, indicating a need to take advantage of existing resources, human capital being one such resource (McGuirk, Lenihan, & Hart, 2015).

This chapter aims to bridge the gap in the literature on the thorough literature consolidation of human capital. The extensive literature of human capital provides a contribution to practitioners and researchers by describing the theory and applications of human capital in order to maximize the impact of human capital in the digital age.

Background

In the 1990s, strategic management interest in human capital became more widespread because it appeared that human capital could be a firm-level resource capable of enhancing competitive advantage (Fagan & Ployhart, 2015). Human capital is related to resource-based theory (RBT) (Barney & Wright, 1998). RBT holds that firms are heterogeneous in their endowment of resources, and these resource endowments contribute to variability in organizational performance and competitive advantage. Human capital is not something that can be owned by the organization (Coff, 1997), and thus firms must deploy human resource policies and practices that can accumulate through employee selection and develop through training it. The processes of accumulation and development are socially complex, causally ambiguous, and path dependent, thus making human capital difficult to imitate.

The economic human capital theory (Becker, 1993) is primarily focused on the individual level, while RBT is primarily focused on the firm level. The economics approach emphasized the study of education and experience to examine how these characteristics helped explain wage differentials over time (Becker, 2011). Human capital theory focused on two types of individual characteristics that were important for the purposes of the theory: generic human capital that could be applied to any firm and context, and specific human capital which was only applicable to a particular firm. This distinction was important for explaining wage differentials within the perspective of human capital theory, but strategy scholars took this distinction and applied it to competitive advantage (Fagan & Ployhart, 2015).

Generic human capital resources could not be a source of competitive advantage because the value that they produce corresponds to the costs of acquiring them. Specific human capital resources could be a major source of competitive advantage because there is no corresponding labor market where they can be acquired (Barney, 1986). Generic human capital (e.g., intelligence, personality, and values) have been shown to be related to the most important occupational and personal outcomes (Schmidt & Hunter, 2004). Specific human capital is the contextually-bound topic, such as the patterns of knowledge and skill (Fagan & Ployhart, 2015).

PERSPECTIVES OF HUMAN CAPITAL IN THE DIGITAL AGE

This section emphasizes the overview of human capital; human capital and economic growth; human capital, innovation, and knowledge management; human capital and R&D; human capital, political regime, and FDI; human capital, employment, and labor markets; the measure of human capital; and the challenges and implications of human capital in the digital age.

Overview of Human Capital

On the corporate level, human capital is the necessary production input and creator of the market value of the company (Kucharcíková, Tokarcíková, & Blašková, 2015).

Human capital development is one of the emerging areas of study concerning social science theory, practice, and research (Kaufman & Geroy, 2007). Human capital analysis has implications beyond the field of human resource management (Royal & O'Donnell, 2005). Organizations that embed the practices of human capital and competency across a range of human resource management activities effectively create and develop a boundary spanning culture connecting with various organizational disciplines in the global knowledge economy (Kasemsap, 2016a).

The field of strategic human resource management has rediscovered human capital with increasing research recognizing human capital as a mediator in the relationship between human resource practices and performance (Wright & McMahan, 2011). Human capital stock and method of leveraging human capital positively affect organizational performance (Carmeli & Schaubroeck, 2005). The internally developed human capital strategically fits better with high levels of expert human-capital leveraging (Kor & Leblebici, 2005). Human resource development and utilization are most effective when the human capital of employees is high (Rauch, Frese, & Utsch, 2005). Team-level human capital diversity is one of the potential antecedents of social capital for team creativity (Han, Han, & Brass, 2014).

Human capital management is a strategic and planned approach to managing organizational workforce (Kucharcíková et al., 2015). Both human capital management and human resource management can be recognized as the vital components in the process of people management and both perspectives establish the foundation for achieving human capital advantage through a resource-based strategy (Baron & Armstrong, 2007). Human capital management includes investment made by the organization on its employees to improve the performance and profitability of an organization by way of providing effective internal recruitment practices, improving career management programs, giving flexible working arrangements, focusing on both education and compensation issues of employees (Kucharcíková et al., 2015). Firm-specific human capital as a primary determinant of compensation (Slaughter, Ang, & Boh, 2007).

The positive impacts of employee and career development interventions on organizational process and customer competencies are fully mediated by the improved organizational human capital (Kim, 2015). Individuals' human capital assessed in the first stage of the career path is positively related to individuals' performance in the second stage of the career path and the value placed on individuals in the third stage of the career path (Harris, Pattie, & McMahan, 2015). Career commitment, job involvement, and learning motivation beneficially lead to the transfer of learning (Kasemsap, 2013a). Career adaptability and participation in decision making have a positive relationship with affective commitment in modern organizations (Kasemsap, 2013b). Cognitive ability and conscientiousness help explain the process through which human capital gets translated into performance effectiveness and tangible career attainments (Ng & Feldman, 2010).

Human Capital and Economic Growth

Human capital plays an important role in the theory of economic growth (Jones & Schneider, 2006). An economy can have different growth paths depending on the initial structure of human capital and the uncertainty about the nature of new technologies (Kim & Lee, 2011). Existing research on human capital in regional science has emphasized on the connection between human capital use and regional economic growth (Batabyal & Beladi, 2013). The economic growth is a numerical value to be able to measure the rate of real gross domestic product (GDP), while the economic development is a social criterion measuring the social levels of the human being, such as health, education, and human living standard (Atalay, 2015). Rapid economic growth encourages the increases in the return on education investment and the demand for education and thus achieve the virtuous circle of sustainable growth by providing more public educational resources and increasing the demand for high-skilled labor (Shao & Yang, 2014).

Human capital investments are good for economic development (Friebel, Leinyuy, & Seabright, 2015). Human capital composition is important in determining the probability of innovation and the economy's growth rate (Scicchitano, 2010). Human capital accumulation depends on both deliberate and non-deliberate learning (Blackburn & Varvarigos, 2008). Economic growth depends positively on the rate of human capital accumulation and positively or negatively on population growth (Strulik, 2005). The relevance of human capital accumulation to the process of economic development stems from its beneficial impact on macroeconomic productivity and on the long-run distribution of incomes (Ahmed & Krishnasamy, 2013). Productivity growth is primarily driven by physical capital and human capital accumulation (Henderson & Russell, 2005). The financial intermediation activities of banks and related institutions can encourage human capital accumulation (Abubakar, Kassim, & Yusoff, 2015).

Human capital is essential for the long-term growth of the economy (Choi & Shin, 2015). Human capital contributes to the economic growth, due to the capital accumulation and the improvement of labor productivity (Li, Wang, Westlund, & Liu, 2015). Economic misery increases human capital outflow (Ali, Mujahid, Rashid, & Shahbaz, 2015). There is a positive impact of human capital on the process of economic growth regarding traditional inputs, such as capital and labor (Mamuneas, Savvides, & Stengos, 2006). For example, Japan's growth rate has declined due to slowing growth in human capital, the stabilization of the rate of investment in physical capital concerning a shrinking labor force, a decline in weekly hours worked, higher oil prices, and convergence toward the steady state (Breton, 2015).

Generic human capital and specific human capital lead to economic growth and failure in different ways (Rauch & Rijsdijk, 2013). Human capital at the macro level is the source of extensive economic growth (Storper & Scott, 2009). Because the estimated impact that human capital has on economic growth is sensitive to the measures of human capital, accurate human capital measures are needed (Le, Gibson, & Oxley, 2006). An increase in the desire to pursue human capital will raise the long-run economic growth rate, but an increase in the desire to pursue physical capital will lower it (Chen, 2012).

Human Capital, Innovation, and Knowledge Management

In recent years, competition among companies has been intensified by globalization, innovation, and information technology (Iwamoto & Takahashi, 2015). Human capital is one of the most important organizational resources (Möller, Gamerschlag, & Guenther, 2011). Human capital is recognized as a main source of knowledge and skills in the innovation process (Koroglu & Eceral, 2015). Human capital is positively related to organizational innovation (e.g., OECD, 2011; Schneider, Günther, & Brandenburg, 2010). Human capital is the embodiment of knowledge, in better educated and productive people (Santos-Rodrigues, Dorrego, & Jardon, 2010). Bornay-Barrachina et al. (2012) indicated that human capital mediates the relationship between a mutual investment employment relationship and innovation, characterized by the high levels of incentives and expectations.

Quality of human capital predicts knowledge creation (Kwan & Chiu, 2015). Human capital affects the ability to build up knowledge capital as a by-product of learning-by-doing perspective (Greiner, 2012). Organizational innovation and knowledge management become a main source of competitive advantage in the digital age (Kasemsap, 2016b). Organizations aiming to increase organizational innovation and achieve business goals should focus on developing organizational learning, knowledge management, and knowledge-sharing behavior (Kasemsap, 2016c). Effective knowledge management is the key driver of new knowledge and ideas to the innovation process, innovative products, services, and solutions (Kasemsap, 2016d).

Business growth is positively related to the quality of human capital and the firm's investment in it (Gossling & Rutten, 2007). Human capital is an important element in innovation (Leiponen, 2005) and as most firm-level innovations are incremental, human capital relates to the generation, adaption, and diffusion of technical and organizational change (Toner, 2011). Research has identified middle management's establishment of an innovative climate and openness to technological innovation as the influences on innovation (Hosseini, Hamid, Azar, & Rostamy, 2003). Investment in financial assets is positively associated with returns to human capital investment (Brown & Taylor, 2005). Industrial innovation is recognized as a major approach to achieving long-term economic growth, especially for emerging nations (Merritt, 2015).

Firm-specific human capital is considered as a significant element of knowledge-based resources that have the potential for superior firm performance (Wang & Wong, 2012). There are various literatures examining more tacit characteristics including managers' capabilities (Fitjar, Gielsvik, & Rodriguez-Pose, 2013), the individual's creativity in innovation (Storper & Scott, 2009), founders' human capital (Gimmon & Levie, 2010), and leadership's essential role in developing innovation throughout the organization, especially in small and medium-sized enterprise (SME) innovation (McAdam, Moffett, Hazlett, & Shavlin, 2010). The level of human capital and the presence of foreign shareholders in the SMEs positively affect internationalization (Cerrato & Piva, 2012). The access of international newcomers in the entrepreneurial provision of internationalization strengthens local economies and make them more globally competitive (Kasemsap, 2016e).

Human Capital and Research and Development

Certain types of human capital can boost research and development (R&D) investment, which results in the increased innovation outcomes (Kato, Okamuro, & Honjo, 2015). Aspects of directors' human and relational capital (e.g., education, entrepreneurial finance experience, technical experience, and interlocks) significantly affect R&D spending regarding innovation (Dalziel, Gentry, & Bowerman, 2011). Specific human capital for innovation (e.g., prior innovation experience) is directly associated with innovation outcomes, whereas generic human capital (e.g., educational background) indirectly affects innovation outcomes through R&D investment (Kato et al., 2015).

Human capital and R&D significantly affect the regional total factor productivity growth in the manufacturing sector (Vogel, 2015). Firms that introduce practices related to continuous learning and the development of an innovative culture that encourages R&D projects improve the skills of their human capital (Palacios-Marques, Gil-Pechuán, & Lim, 2011). The higher levels of founders' human capital, especially their education levels, increase both actual and required investment in R&D (Honjo, Kato, & Okamuro, 2014).

Human Capital, Political Regime, and Foreign Direct Investment

Human capital defines the association between foreign direct investment (FDI) and income inequality (Lin, Kim, & Wu, 2013). Higher income inequality generally reduces economic growth (Chambers & Krause, 2010). The types of human capital determine the type of FDI inflow (Soltanpanah & Karimi, 2011). There is a mass of literature on the factors that determine the inflow of FDI into countries, depending on their levels of economic, social, and political development (Vindelyn & Omar, 2005). Governance has a positive relationship with advanced human capital, while government instability has a negative link with advanced human capital (Klomp & de Haan, 2013).

FDI is the cross-border investment by a resident entity in one economy with the objective of obtaining a lasting interest in an enterprise resident in another economy. FDI encourages the transfer of technology and know-how between countries, and allows the host economy to promote its products more widely in international markets. FDI involves not only financial capital, but also encompasses technological, organizational, and intellectual capital (Thangavelu & Narjoko, 2014). FDI and multinational enterprises (MNEs) grew substantially since after the Second World War (Cleeve, Debrah, & Yiheyis, 2015). FDI brings money, modern technology, and managerial capabilities in corporate functioning (Kar, 2013).

FDI only improves technical efficiency change in state-owned and state-controlled enterprises but reduces technical change in state-owned and state-controlled enterprises and joint ventures (Zhao & Zhang, 2010). Domestic human capital is a major determinant of FDI inflows for the developing world (Dutta & Osei-Yeboah, 2013). The relationships among FDI, human capital, and institutions play an important role in explaining FDI inflows to developing countries (Dutta & Osei-Yeboah, 2013). A foreign subsidiary sharing a parent firm's technology will invest more if it has more foreign-educated labor, since it can utilize this labor more productively because of the country-specific human capital (Kim & Park, 2013).

Human Capital, Employment, and Labor Markets

Attracting human capital is the important perspective to the participation of rural areas in national and global economic growth, especially in a knowledge economy (Olfert, Jelinski, Zikos, & Campbell, 2012). Moving from a centrally-planned economy to a market economy requires substantial restructuring of the labor market (Perna, Orosz, & Jumakulov, 2015). The labor market analysis and the determinants of human capital investment can determine the necessity to incorporate both internal and external labor markets and its mutual interaction (Giziene & Simanaviciene,

2015). Labor markets in most highly developed countries are marked by rising levels of segregation by skill and increasing inequality in skill-specific employment prospects (Schlitte, 2012). In labor markets which are not perfect, the distribution of education matters for per capita income, because a more unequal distribution of human capital lowers the probability that workers of similar skills can be matched together (Gille, 2015).

Human capital is considered as a key factor in the determination of individual wages and their growth over time (Psacharopoulos & Patrinos, 2004). In the long term, firms with greater variability in labor costs will achieve better performance (Bhattacharya, Doty, & Garavan, 2014). Taxation affects utilization rates of human capital through labor supply responses (Jacobs, 2005). If the government adequately chooses tax rates, human capital grows faster and welfare levels become higher under the public education regime than under the private education (Futagami & Yanagihara, 2008). If human capital is observable and correlated with income, then a signaling equilibrium in which poor individuals tend to spend a large fraction of their income on obvious consumption can emerge (Moav & Neeman, 2012).

It is important for the company to choose the specific individuals with appropriate skills, knowledge, and abilities, aiming to succeed in the job market (Giziene & Simanaviciene, 2015). Human capital-related skill levels are viewed as occupational groups (Stark, Hyll, & Wang, 2012). Each occupation practically values all human capital types but to a different degree (Silos & Smith, 2015). Occupations are greatly related to income (Levenson & Zoghi, 2010). Employment, learning effort, and output growth significantly increase with more effective learning, enhanced labor-market matching, and less costly vacancy creation (Chen, Chen, & Wang, 2011).

The velocity with which human capital depreciates depends on the duration and repetition of unemployment period (Mooi-Reci & Ganzeboom, 2015). For instance, a single occurrence of unemployment leaves a significant scar on re-employment wages (Jacobson, LaLonde, & Sullivan, 1993), which becomes larger with more frequent (Stevens, 1997) and longer unemployment period (Gangl, 2004). Afonso (2010) stated that wage inequality is encouraged by relative changes in supply and demand of both human capital types (i.e., generic human capital and specific human capital).

Measure of Human Capital

The difference between human capital as a physical capital and human capital as an intangible asset is at the root of the difficulty of its measurement (Soboleva, 2010). The increases in human capital significantly can raise the per-worker physical capital stock, and the increases in the physical capital significantly can enhance primary education levels (Grier, 2005). Becker (1993) distinguished between generic human capital and specific human capital: generic human capital relates to knowledge and skills that are easily transferable, whereas specific human capital relates to knowledge and skills that are less transferable and have a narrower scope of applicability.

In a study of human capital of firms' founders, Ganotakis (2012) found that specific human capital (regarding specific education and experience including managerial, commercial, and technical experience) provides positive contributions to firms' performance and survival. Other human capital measures include industry experience and learning (Santarelli & Tran, 2013), generic human capital, and specific human capital, measured by age, gender, parental background, and education (Robson, Akuetteh, Westhead, & Wright, 2012). Earnings are conceptualized as a function of human capital (Mane & Waldorf, 2013). Employment, earning potential, and prospects of training are higher in all perspectives for employees of higher skills than for those of lower skills (Hofheinz, 2009).

While global education inequality has been declining over the past four decades, global human capital inequality remains largely steady, as the decrease in between-country human capital inequality is largely balanced by the increase in the within-country human capital inequality (Lim & Tang, 2008). The possibility of a low-skilled guest-worker employment in a higher wage foreign country lowers the relative attractiveness of the skilled employment in the home country (Azarnert, 2012). Measuring the flows of human capital is a meaningful way to observe how migration affects the potential of regional distribution of development (Fan, 2009).

Generic human capital is assessed using experience depth and formal education (Marvel, 2013). Specific human capital is measured using prior start-up experience (Marvel, 2013). While recognizing the challenge of the task of measuring human capital, Teixeira and Tavares-Lehmann (2014) emphasized the intensity of human capital by measuring specific human capital as referring to top-skilled workers and generic human capital as relating to top-educated workers. Where a firm is foreign-owned, this factor has the impacts on its generic human capital (education) and its specific human capital (skills) (Teixeira & Tavares-Lehmann, 2014). Investment in human capital is believed to improve the performance of employees (Bosma, van Praag, Thurik, & de Wit, 2004).

Human capital is captured by individual-level professional education, start-up experience, and learning (Santarelli & Tran, 2013). There is a strong relationship between higher levels of education and technical training and an increased demand for the supply of technical and organizational innovation (Toner, 2011). Educational attainment, an indicator of the human capital accumulated by a population, is a primary determinant of a nation's prosperity and global economic competitiveness (Acemoglu & Robinson, 2012). Hofheinz (2009) stated that educational attainment is an effective method of evaluating the levels of skills in a workforce, where higher skills indicate tertiary attainment and medium skills indicate the attainment of secondary or equivalent education. Growth theory predicts that greater educational attainment will increase the real income per person (Yamarik, 2011).

Education has the long-run impacts on social preferences, norms, and institutions beyond the human capital directly produced (Jakiela, Miguel, & te Velde, 2015). Human capital-related technical skills are the important approach to profitable innovations (Leiponen, 2005). Education can indicate greater productivity (Ucbasaran, Westhead, & Wright, 2008). Business owners' human capital (measured by education) promotes firm survival (Saridakis, Mole, & Storey, 2008). Organizations utilize entrepreneurship education and knowledge management as the major assets and organizational resources for producing high-technology products and services in order to obtain sustainable competitive advantage in modern organizations (Kasemsap, 2016f).

Challenges and Implications of Human Capital in the Digital Age

Human capital growth expands future possibilities (Gorostiaga, Hromcová, & López-García, 2013). High human capital relaxes financial constraints, due to greater productivity of human capital in wage work than in self-employment (Åstbro & Bernhardt, 2005). Human capital and social capital affect the level of entrepreneurial export (Evald, Klyver, & Christensen, 2011). Entrepreneurial earnings crucially depend on the level of job-related human capital (Ohyama, 2015). When the return on human capital internationally differs, the growth rates of consumption and gross national product (GNP) vary across countries even when there is the free capital mobility (Perera-Tallo, 2005). In the culinary tourism, human capital factors include general business training, specific training in food and drink hospitality, and previous experience as a business owner (Rey-Martí, Ribeiro-Soriano, & Palacios-Marqués, 2016).

Human capital drivers of value practically vary across industry groups (O'Donnell, Kramar, & Dyball, 2009). Certain industries (e.g., manufacturing, agriculture, and information technology industries) strongly require specific knowledge and skills to conduct the core businesses (Ooi, Hooy, & Som, 2015). Entrepreneurial human capital, measured as educational background, is important in reducing the probability of bankruptcy in the high-tech sectors (Kato & Honjo, 2015). Appropriate human capital and age of the entrepreneurs are critical in the case of new business creation (Fourati & Affes, 2011). The human capital of the board of directors in these industries is important to the important decision making (Ooi et al., 2015). Greater diversity of human capital can provide a wider range of alternatives to cope with the complicated problems faced by the firms (Pitcher & Smith, 2001).

Firms appoint chief executive officers (CEOs) with different types of human capital in order to manage organizational resource dependencies (Peng, Sun, & Markóczy, 2015). Human capital, as represented by the board's CEO experience and industry experience, and social capital, as represented by directors' experience on the board and external directorship ties to other corporate boards, will affect the stock market reactions to the appointment of new CEO (Tian, Haleblian, & Rajagopalan, 2011). The accumulation of specific human capital for CEO's task is achieved through general leadership experience (Ahrens, Landmann, & Woywode, 2015). There is positive relationship between diversity in expertise of the board of directors and firm innovation performance (Wincent, Thorgren, & Anokhin, 2014).

Qualified human capital is an essential factor needed by advanced and emerging economies (Giordano & Pagano, 2013). Through enhancement of human capital-related competencies, qualifications, and skills, organizations can increase their absorptive capacity and acquire an ability to recognize the potential and value of cooperation for their own advancement and economic benefit (Pinto, Cruz, & Combe, 2015). The distribution of education matters if there are externalities of education, through learning spillovers (Gille, 2015). Learning spillovers are assumed to organize from the highly educated workers to the lowly educated workers (Moretti, 2004), in which case a less equally distributed human capital should have a positive impact on per capita income.

Inequality affects per capita income when individuals decide to invest in education taking into account their life expectancy, which depends on the human capital of their parents (Castelló-Climent & Doménech, 2008). The strong correlation between the formation of human capital and life expectancy is attributed not only to a higher marginal benefit arising from a longer payback period, but also to a lower marginal cost arising from a prolonged intergenerational overlap (Stark & Wang, 2005).

FUTURE RESEARCH DIRECTIONS

The classification of the extensive literature in the domains of human capital will provide the potential opportunities for future research. Establishing social capital dimensions (e.g., social networks, social norms, social trust, and institutional trust) should be executed in order to minimize the obstacle of lack of knowledge and to improve the knowledge sharing (Kasemsap, 2014a). Talent management introduces new strategic goals to streamline hiring and leadership succession processes (Kasemsap, 2016g). Productivity is a measure of the efficiency of a person, machine, factory, and system in converting inputs into useful outputs (Kasemsap, 2014b). Labor productivity is a key indicator of a successful business and economy. Labor productivity measures the amount of products and services produced by one hour of labor. The relationship between human capital, social capital, talent management, and labor productivity in the labor markets will be the beneficial topics for future research directions.

CONCLUSION

This chapter highlighted the overview of human capital; human capital and economic growth; human capital, innovation, and knowledge management; human capital and R&D; human capital, political regime, and FDI; human capital, employment, and labor markets; the measure of human capital; and the challenges and implications of human capital in the digital age. Human capital refers to knowledge, skills, and abilities acquired by an individual, traditionally through training, education, and work experience. Human capital has a positive relationship with entrepreneurial success, business growth, and economic development. Human capital increases employees' capabilities of discovering and exploiting business opportunities and helps employees obtain other useful resources, such as physical capital and financial asset in modern organizations.

Human capital results the success of business only if it is effectively utilized and transferred to the specific tasks in the organizations that need to be performed. Making human capital a source of competitive advantage requires attracting and retaining the right people as well as organizing and managing them effectively. Attracting the right people and retaining them require the right managerial behaviors as well as the right design of most of an organization's major operating systems in order to create a human capital-centric organization.

Knowledge about human capital management, human resource management, and organizational effectiveness is an obvious foundation that executives need in order to make the high-quality human capital management decisions. Effective human capital management requires a great deal of expertise in organizational systems and a great deal of understanding of motivation, competencies, traits, and organizational behavior. Human capital must be effectively organized, trained, and developed in ways that lead to the important development of the right core competencies and organizational capabilities toward creating business value.

Investing in human capital perspectives (e.g., training and education) is extremely important in order for a business to thrive in today's global marketplace, and also for economic improvement. Creating an organization that relies on human capital for competitive advantage involves designing every organizational system with an essential approach to attracting, developing, retaining, and motivating the highly-qualified people. Developing human capital has the potential to enhance organizational performance and gain sustainable competitive advantage in the digital age.

REFERENCES

Abubakar, A., Kassim, S. H. J., & Yusoff, M. B. (2015). Financial development, human capital accumulation and economic growth: Empirical evidence from the Economic Community of West African States (ECOWAS). *Procedia: Social and Behavioral Sciences*, *172*, 96–103. doi:10.1016/j.sbspro.2015.01.341

Acemoglu, D., & Robinson, J. A. (2012). *Why nations fail: The origins of power, prosperity, and poverty*. New York, NY: The Crown Publishing Group.

Afonso, O. (2010). Growth and wage inequality in a scale-independent model with R&D and human-capital accumulation. *The Manchester School*, *78*(2), 149–182. doi:10.1111/j.1467-9957.2009.02135.x

Ahme, E. M., & Krishnasamy, G. (2013). Human capital investment to achieve knowledge-based economy in ASEAN5: DEA applications. *Journal of the Knowledge Economy*, *4*(4), 331–342. doi:10.1007/s13132-011-0059-2

Ahrens, J. P., Landmann, A., & Woywode, M. (2015). Gender preferences in the CEO successions of family firms: Family characteristics and human capital of the successor. *Journal of Family Business Strategy*, *6*(2), 86–103. doi:10.1016/j.jfbs.2015.02.002

Alessandrini, D., Kosempel, S., & Stengos, T. (2015). The business cycle human capital accumulation nexus and its effect on hours worked volatility. *Journal of Economic Dynamics & Control*, *51*, 356–377. doi:10.1016/j.jedc.2014.11.004

Ali, A., Mujahid, N., Rashid, Y., & Shahbaz, M. (2015). Human capital outflow and economic misery: Fresh evidence for Pakistan. *Social Indicators Research*, *124*(3), 747–764. doi:10.1007/s11205-014-0821-5

Åstbro, T., & Bernhardt, I. (2005). The winner's curse of human capital. *Small Business Economics*, *24*(1), 63–78. doi:10.1007/s11187-005-3097-y

Atalay, R. (2015). The education and the human capital to get rid of the middle-income trap and to provide the economic development. *Procedia: Social and Behavioral Sciences*, *174*, 969–976. doi:10.1016/j.sbspro.2015.01.720

Azarnert, L. V. (2012). Guest-worker migration, human capital and fertility. *Review of Development Economics*, *16*(2), 318–330. doi:10.1111/j.1467-9361.2012.00664.x

Backman, M. (2014). Human capital in firms and regions: Impact on firm productivity. *Papers in Regional Science*, *93*(3), 557–575. doi:10.1111/pirs.12005

Barney, J. B. (1986). Strategic factor markets: Expectations, luck, and business strategy. *Management Science*, *32*(10), 1231–1241. doi:10.1287/mnsc.32.10.1231

Barney, J. B., & Wright, P. M. (1998). On becoming a strategic partner: The role of human resources in gaining competitive advantage. *Human Resource Management*, *37*(1), 31–46. doi:10.1002/(SICI)1099-050X(199821)37:1<31::AID-HRM4>3.0.CO;2-W

Baron, A., & Armstrong, M. (2007). *Human capital management: Achieving added value through people*. London, UK: Kogan Page.

Batabyal, A. A., & Beladi, H. (2013). Human capital, knowledge spillovers, and one kind of semi-endogenous regional economic growth. *Letters in Spatial and Resource Sciences*, *6*(3), 121–135. doi:10.1007/s12076-013-0092-9

Becker, G. S. (1993). *Human capital: A theoretical and empirical analysis, with special reference to education*. Chicago, IL: University of Chicago Press. doi:10.7208/chicago/9780226041223.001.0001

Becker, G. S. (2011). Forward. In A. Burton-Jones & J. Spender (Eds.), *The Oxford handbook of human capital* (pp. xiii–xvi). Oxford, UK: Oxford University Press.

Bhattacharya, M., Doty, D. H., & Garavan, T. (2014). The organizational context and performance implications of human capital investment variability. *Human Resource Development Quarterly*, *25*(1), 87–113. doi:10.1002/hrdq.21182

Blackburn, K., & Varvarigos, D. (2008). Human capital accumulation and output growth in a stochastic environment. *Economic Theory*, *36*(3), 435–452. doi:10.1007/s00199-007-0280-1

Bornay-Barrachina, M., de la Rosa-Navarro, D., López-Cabrales, A., & Valle-Cabrera, R. (2012). Employment relationships and firm innovation: The double role of human capital. *British Journal of Management*, *23*(2), 223–240. doi:10.1111/j.1467-8551.2010.00735.x

Bosma, N., van Praag, M., Thurik, R., & de Wit, G. (2004). The value of human and social capital investment for the business performance of start-ups. *Small Business Economics*, *23*(3), 227–236. doi:10.1023/B:SBEJ.0000032032.21192.72

Breton, T. R. (2015). Human capital and growth in Japan: Converging to the steady state in a 1% world. *Journal of the Japanese and International Economies*, *36*, 73–89. doi:10.1016/j.jjie.2015.03.001

Brown, S., & Taylor, K. (2005). Wage growth, human capital and financial investment. *The Manchester School*, *73*(6), 686–708. doi:10.1111/j.1467-9957.2005.00472.x

Carmeli, A., & Schaubroeck, J. (2005). How leveraging human resource capital with its competitive distinctiveness enhances the performance of commercial and public organizations. *Human Resource Management*, *44*(4), 391–412. doi:10.1002/hrm.20081

Castelló-Climent, A., & Doménech, R. (2008). Human capital inequality, life expectancy and economic growth. *The Economic Journal*, *118*(528), 653–677. doi:10.1111/j.1468-0297.2008.02136.x

Cerrato, D., & Piva, M. (2012). The internationalization of small and medium-sized enterprises: The effect of family management, human capital and foreign ownership. *Journal of Management and Governance*, *16*(4), 617–644. doi:10.1007/s10997-010-9166-x

Chambers, D., & Krause, A. (2010). Is the relationship between inequality and growth affected by physical and human capital accumulation? *The Journal of Economic Inequality*, *8*(2), 153–172. doi:10.1007/s10888-009-9111-x

Chen, B. L., Chen, H. J., & Wang, P. (2011). Labor-market frictions, human capital accumulation, and long-run growth: Positive analysis and policy evaluation. *International Economic Review*, *52*(1), 131–160. doi:10.1111/j.1468-2354.2010.00622.x

Chen, H. J. (2012). Social status, human capital formation and the long-run effects of money. *Journal of Economics*, *105*(3), 225–246. doi:10.1007/s00712-011-0227-7

Choi, K. H., & Shin, S. (2015). Population aging, economic growth, and the social transmission of human capital: An analysis with an overlapping generations model. *Economic Modelling*, *50*, 138–147. doi:10.1016/j.econmod.2015.05.015

Cleeve, E. A., Debrah, Y., & Yiheyis, Z. (2015). Human capital and FDI inflow: An assessment of the African case. *World Development*, *74*, 1–14. doi:10.1016/j.worlddev.2015.04.003

Coff, R. W. (1997). Human assets and management dilemmas: Coping with hazards on the road to resource-based theory. *Academy of Management Review*, *22*(2), 374–402.

Dalziel, T., Gentry, R. J., & Bowerman, M. (2011). An integrated agency-resource dependence view of the influence of director's human and relational capital on firms' R&D spending. *Journal of Management Studies*, *48*(6), 1217–1242. doi:10.1111/j.1467-6486.2010.01003.x

Dutta, N., & Osei-Yeboah, K. (2013). A new dimension to the relationship between foreign direct investment and human capital: The role of political and civil rights. *Journal of International Development*, *25*(2), 160–179. doi:10.1002/jid.1739

Evald, M. R., Klyver, K., & Christensen, P. R. (2011). The effect of human capital, social capital, and perceptual values on nascent entrepreneur's export intentions. *Journal of International Entrepreneurship*, *9*(1), 1–19. doi:10.1007/s10843-010-0069-3

Fagan, J., & Ployhart, R. E. (2015). The information processing foundations of human capital resources: Leveraging insights from information processing approaches to intelligence. *Human Resource Management Review*, *25*(1), 4–11. doi:10.1016/j.hrmr.2014.09.003

Fan, L. (2009). Measuring interprovincial flows of human capital in China: 1995–2000. *Population Research and Policy Review*, *28*(3), 367–387. doi:10.1007/s11113-008-9103-8

Fitjar, R., Gielsvik, M., & Rodriguez-Pose, A. (2013). The combined impact of managerial and relational capabilities on innovation in firms. *Entrepreneurship & Regional Development: An International Journal*, *25*(5/6), 500–520. doi:10.1080/08985626.2013.798353

Fourati, H., & Affes, H. (2011). Financial constraints, human and social capital, and risk-taking attitude in the foundation of new firms. *Strategic Change*, *20*(5/6), 219–232. doi:10.1002/jsc.897

Friebel, G., Leinyuy, J., & Seabright, P. (2015). The Schubert effect: When flourishing businesses crowd out human capital. *World Development*, *68*, 124–135. doi:10.1016/j.worlddev.2014.11.022

Futagami, K., & Yanagihara, M. (2008). Private and public education: Human capital accumulation under parental teaching. *The Japanese Economic Review*, *59*(3), 275–291. doi:10.1111/j.1468-5876.2008.00417.x

Gallié, E. P., & Legros, D. (2012). Firm's human capital, R&D and innovation: A study on French firms. *Empirical Economics*, *43*(2), 581–596. doi:10.1007/s00181-011-0506-8

Gangl, M. (2004). Welfare states and the scar effects of unemployment: A comparative analysis of the United States and West Germany. *American Journal of Sociology*, *109*(6), 1319–1364. doi:10.1086/381902

Ganotakis, P. (2012). Founder's human capital and the performance of UK new technology based firms. *Small Business Economics*, *39*(2), 495–515. doi:10.1007/s11187-010-9309-0

Gille, V. (2015). Distribution of human capital and income: An empirical study on Indian States. *Journal of Macroeconomics*, *43*, 239–256. doi:10.1016/j.jmacro.2014.11.003

Gimmon, E., & Levie, J. (2010). Founder's human capital, external investment, and the survival of new high-technology ventures. *Research Policy*, *39*(9), 1214–1226. doi:10.1016/j.respol.2010.05.017

Giordano, A., & Pagano, A. (2013). Brazil in the transition towards knowledge economy: Between qualification and internationalization of human capital. *Transition Studies Review*, *20*(1), 19–31. doi:10.1007/s11300-013-0267-5

Giziene, V., & Simanaviciene, Z. (2015). The impact of human capital on labour market: Lithuanian case. *Procedia: Social and Behavioral Sciences*, *191*, 2437–2442. doi:10.1016/j.sbspro.2015.04.331

Gorostiaga, A., Hromcová, J., & López-García, M. (2013). Optimal taxation in the Uzawa–Lucas model with externality in human capital. *Journal of Economics*, *108*(2), 111–129. doi:10.1007/s00712-012-0285-5

Gossling, T., & Rutten, R. (2007). Innovation in regions. *European Planning Studies*, *15*(2), 253–270. doi:10.1080/09654310601078788

Greiner, A. (2012). Human capital formation, learning by doing and the government in the process of economic growth. *Scottish Journal of Political Economy*, *59*(1), 71–89. doi:10.1111/j.1467-9485.2011.0569.x

Grier, R. (2005). The interaction of human and physical capital accumulation: Evidence from Sub-Saharan Africa. *Kyklos*, *58*(2), 195–211. doi:10.1111/j.0023-5962.2005.285_1.x

Han, J., Han, J., & Brass, D. J. (2014). Human capital diversity in the creation of social capital for team creativity. *Journal of Organizational Behavior*, *35*(1), 54–71. doi:10.1002/job.1853

Harris, C. M., Pattie, M. W., & McMahan, G. C. (2015). Advancement along a career path: The influence of human capital and performance. *Human Resource Management Journal*, *25*(1), 102–115. doi:10.1111/1748-8583.12047

Henderson, D. J., & Russell, R. R. (2005). Human capital and convergence: A production-frontier approach. *International Economic Review*, *46*(4), 1167–1205. doi:10.1111/j.1468-2354.2005.00364.x

Hewitt-Dundas, N. (2006). Resource and capability constraints to innovation in small and large plants. *Small Business Economics*, *26*(3), 257–277. doi:10.1007/s11187-005-2140-3

Hitt, M. A., Bierman, L., Shimizu, K., & Kochhar, R. (2001). Direct and moderating effects of human capital on strategy and performance in professional service firms: A resource-based perspective. *Academy of Management Journal*, *44*(1), 13–28. doi:10.2307/3069334

Hofheinz, P. (2009). EU 2020: Why skills are key for Europe's future. *Policy Brief*, *IV*(1), 1–23.

Honjo, Y., Kato, M., & Okamuro, H. (2014). R&D investment of start-up firms: Does founder's human capital matter? *Small Business Economics*, *42*(2), 207–220. doi:10.1007/s11187-013-9476-x

Hosseini, H., Hamid, K., Azar, A., & Rostamy, A. (2003). The intervening role of innovative climate: A study of middle managers in manufacturing organisations in Iran. *Public Organization Review*, *3*(2), 151–170. doi:10.1023/A:1024288830211

Iwamoto, H., & Takahashi, M. (2015). A quantitative approach to human capital management. *Procedia: Social and Behavioral Sciences*, *172*, 112–119. doi:10.1016/j.sbspro.2015.01.343

Jacobs, B. (2005). Optimal income taxation with endogenous human capital. *Journal of Public Economic Theory*, *7*(2), 295–315. doi:10.1111/j.1467-9779.2005.00205.x

Jacobson, L. S., LaLonde, R. J., & Sullivan, D. G. (1993). Earnings losses of displaced workers. *The American Economic Review*, *83*(4), 685–709.

Jakiela, P., Miguel, E., & te Velde, V. L. (2015). You've earned it: Estimating the impact of human capital on social preferences. *Experimental Economics*, *18*(3), 385–407. doi:10.1007/s10683-014-9409-9

Jones, G., & Schneider, W. J. (2006). Intelligence, human capital, and economic growth: A Bayesian Averaging of Classical Estimates (BACE) approach. *Journal of Economic Growth*, *11*(1), 71–93. doi:10.1007/s10887-006-7407-2

Kar, S. (2013). Exploring the causal link between FDI and human capital development in India. *DECISION*, *40*(1), 3–13. doi:10.1007/s40622-013-0001-5

Kasemsap, K. (2013a). Practical framework: Creation of causal model of job involvement, career commitment, learning motivation, and learning transfer. *International Journal of the Computer, the Internet and Management*, *21*(1), 29–35.

Kasemsap, K. (2013b). Innovative business management: A practical framework and causal model of participation in decision making, career adaptability, affective commitment, and turnover intention. Paper presented at the 2nd International Conference on Economics, Business Innovation (ICEBI 2013), Copenhagen, Denmark.

Kasemsap, K. (2014a). The role of social capital in higher education institutions. In N. Baporikar (Ed.), *Handbook of research on higher education in the MENA region: Policy and practice* (pp. 119–147). Hershey, PA, USA: IGI Global. doi:10.4018/978-1-4666-6198-1.ch007

Kasemsap, K. (2014b). Unifying a framework of organizational culture, organizational climate, knowledge management, and job performance. In R. Perez-Castillo & M. Piattini (Eds.), *Uncovering essential software artifacts through business process archeology* (pp. 336–362). Hershey, PA, USA: IGI Global. doi:10.4018/978-1-4666-4667-4.ch013

Kasemsap, K. (2016a). Analyzing the roles of human capital and competency in global business. In S. Sen, A. Bhattacharya, & R. Sen (Eds.), *International perspectives on socio-economic development in the era of globalization* (pp. 1–29). Hershey, PA, USA: IGI Global. doi:10.4018/978-1-4666-9908-3.ch001

Kasemsap, K. (2016b). The roles of knowledge management and organizational innovation in global business. In G. Jamil, J. Poças-Rascão, F. Ribeiro, & A. Malheiro da Silva (Eds.), *Handbook of research on information architecture and management in modern organizations* (pp. 130–153). Hershey, PA, USA: IGI Global. doi:10.4018/978-1-4666-8637-3.ch006

Kasemsap, K. (2016c). The role of knowledge sharing on organisational innovation: An integrated framework. In *Business intelligence: Concepts, methodologies, tools, and applications* (pp. 406–429). Hershey, PA, USA: IGI Global. doi:10.4018/978-1-4666-9562-7.ch022

Kasemsap, K. (2016d). Creating product innovation strategies through knowledge management in global business. In A. Goel & P. Singhal (Eds.), *Product innovation through knowledge management and social media strategies* (pp. 330–357). Hershey, PA, USA: IGI Global. doi:10.4018/978-1-4666-9607-5.ch015

Kasemsap, K. (2016e). Exploring the roles of entrepreneurship and internationalization in global business. In L. Carvalho (Ed.), *Handbook of research on entrepreneurial success and its impact on regional development* (pp. 481–512). Hershey, PA, USA: IGI Global. doi:10.4018/978-1-4666-9567-2.ch021

Kasemsap, K. (2016f). Advocating entrepreneurship education and knowledge management in global business. In N. Baporikar (Ed.), *Handbook of research on entrepreneurship in the contemporary knowledge-based global economy* (pp. 313–339). Hershey, PA, USA: IGI Global. doi:10.4018/978-1-4666-8798-1.ch014

Kasemsap, K. (2016g). Promoting leadership development and talent management in modern organizations. In U. Aung & P. Ordoñez de Pablos (Eds.), *Managerial strategies and practice in the Asian business sector* (pp. 238–266). Hershey, PA, USA: IGI Global. doi:10.4018/978-1-4666-9758-4.ch013

Kato, M., & Honjo, Y. (2015). Entrepreneurial human capital and the survival of new firms in high- and low-tech sectors. *Journal of Evolutionary Economics*, *25*(5), 925–957. doi:10.1007/s00191-015-0427-3

Kato, M., Okamuro, H., & Honjo, Y. (2015). Does founder's human capital matter for innovation? Evidence from Japanese start-ups. *Journal of Small Business Management*, *53*(1), 114–128. doi:10.1111/jsbm.12094

Kaufman, N. A., & Geroy, G. D. (2007). An energy model for viewing embodied human capital theory. *Performance Improvement Quarterly*, *20*(1), 37–47. doi:10.1111/j.1937-8327.2007.tb00430.x

Kim, J., & Park, J. (2013). Foreign direct investment and country-specific human capital. *Economic Inquiry*, *51*(1), 198–210. doi:10.1111/j.1465-7295.2012.00478.x

Kim, T. (2015). Impacts of learning interventions on organizational human capital and performance. *Performance Improvement Quarterly*, *27*(4), 7–28. doi:10.1002/piq.21180

Kim, Y. J., & Lee, J. W. (2011). Technological change, human capital structure, and multiple growth paths. *The Japanese Economic Review*, *62*(3), 305–330. doi:10.1111/j.1468-5876.2009.00507.x

Klomp, J., & de Haan, K. (2013). Political regime and human capital: A cross-country analysis. *Social Indicators Research*, *111*(1), 45–73. doi:10.1007/s11205-011-9983-6 PMID:23378681

Kor, Y. Y., & Leblebici, H. (2005). How do interdependencies among human-capital deployment, development, and diversification strategies affect firm's financial performance? *Strategic Management Journal*, *26*(10), 967–985. doi:10.1002/smj.485

Koroglu, B. A., & Eceral, T. O. (2015). Human capital and innovation capacity of firms in defense and aviation industry in Ankara. *Procedia: Social and Behavioral Sciences*, *195*, 1583–1592. doi:10.1016/j.sbspro.2015.06.196

Kucharcíková, A., Tokarcíková, E., & Blašková, M. (2015). Human capital management: Aspect of the human capital efficiency in university education. *Procedia: Social and Behavioral Sciences*, *177*, 48–60. doi:10.1016/j.sbspro.2015.02.332

Kwan, L. Y. Y., & Chiu, C. Y. (2015). Country variations in different innovation outputs: The interactive effect of institutional support and human capital. *Journal of Organizational Behavior*, *36*(7), 1050–1070. doi:10.1002/job.2017

Lajili, K. (2015). Embedding human capital into governance design: A conceptual framework. *Journal of Management and Governance*, *19*(4), 741–762. doi:10.1007/s10997-014-9295-8

Le, T., Gibson, J., & Oxley, L. (2006). A forward-looking measure of the stock of human capital in New Zealand. *The Manchester School*, *74*(5), 593–609. doi:10.1111/j.1467-9957.2006.00511.x

Leiponen, A. (2005). Skills and innovation. *International Journal of Industrial Organization*, *23*(5/6), 303–323. doi:10.1016/j.ijindorg.2005.03.005

Levenson, A., & Zoghi, C. (2010). Occupations, human capital and skills. *Journal of Labor Research*, *31*(4), 365–386. doi:10.1007/s12122-010-9098-x

Li, Y., Wang, X., Westlund, H., & Liu, Y. (2015). Physical capital, human capital, and social capital: The changing roles in China's economic growth. *Growth and Change*, *46*(1), 133–149. doi:10.1111/grow.12084

Lim, A. S. K., & Tang, K. K. (2008). Human capital inequality and the Kuznets curve. *The Developing Economies*, *46*(1), 26–51. doi:10.1111/j.1746-1049.2007.00054.x

Lin, S. C., Kim, D. H., & Wu, Y. C. (2013). Foreign direct investment and income inequality: Human capital matters. *Journal of Regional Science*, *53*(5), 874–896. doi:10.1111/jors.12077

Mamuneas, T. P., Savvides, A., & Stengos, T. (2006). Economic development and the return to human capital: A smooth coefficient semiparametric approach. *Journal of Applied Econometrics*, *21*(1), 111–132. doi:10.1002/jae.813

Mane, K. M., & Waldorf, B. S. (2013). Human capital and wages: A comparison of Albanian and Italian immigrants. *The Annals of Regional Science*, *51*(1), 53–72. doi:10.1007/s00168-012-0532-2

Marvel, M. R. (2013). Human capital and search-based discovery: A study of high-tech entrepreneurship. *Entrepreneurship Theory and Practice*, *37*(2), 403–419. doi:10.1111/j.1540-6520.2011.00465.x

McAdam, R., Moffett, S., Hazlett, S. A., & Shavlin, M. (2010). Developing a model of innovation implementation for UK SMEs: A path analysis and explanatory case analysis. *International Small Business Journal*, *28*(3), 195–214. doi:10.1177/0266242609360610

McGuirk, H., Lenihan, H., & Hart, M. (2015). Measuring the impact of innovative human capital on small firm's propensity to innovate. *Research Policy*, *44*(4), 965–976. doi:10.1016/j.respol.2014.11.008

Merritt, H. (2015). The role of human capital in university-business cooperation: The case of Mexico. *Journal of the Knowledge Economy*, *6*(3), 568–588. doi:10.1007/s13132-015-0258-3

Moav, O., & Neeman, Z. (2012). Saving rates and poverty: The role of conspicuous consumption and human capital. *The Economic Journal*, *122*(563), 933–956. doi:10.1111/j.1468-0297.2012.02516.x

Möller, K., Gamerschlag, R., & Guenther, F. (2011). Determinants and effects of human capital reporting and controlling. *Journal of Management Control*, *22*(3), 311–333. doi:10.1007/s00187-011-0138-3

Mooi-Reci, I., & Ganzeboom, H. B. (2015). Unemployment scarring by gender: Human capital depreciation or stigmatization? Longitudinal evidence from the Netherlands, 1980–2000. *Social Science Research*, *52*, 642–658. doi:10.1016/j.ssresearch.2014.10.005 PMID:26004486

Moretti, E. (2004). Human capital externalities in cities. In J. Henderson & J. Thisse (Eds.), *Handbook of regional and urban economics* (pp. 2243–2291). Amsterdam, The Netherlands: Elsevier.

Ng, T. W. H., & Feldman, D. C. (2010). Human capital and objective indicators of career success: The mediating effects of cognitive ability and conscientiousness. *Journal of Occupational and Organizational Psychology*, *83*(1), 207–235. doi:10.1348/096317909X414584

O'Donnell, L., Kramar, R., & Dyball, M. C. (2009). Human capital reporting: Should it be industry specific? *Asia Pacific Journal of Human Resources*, *47*(3), 358–373. doi:10.1177/1038411108099293

OECD. (2011). *Skills for innovation and research.* Paris, France: OECD Publishing.

Ohyama, A. (2015). Entrepreneurship and job-relatedness of human capital. *Economica*, *82*(328), 740–768. doi:10.1111/ecca.12144

Olfert, M. R., Jelinski, M., Zikos, D., & Campbell, J. (2012). Human capital drift up the urban hierarchy: Veterinarians in Western Canada. *The Annals of Regional Science*, *49*(2), 551–570. doi:10.1007/s00168-011-0448-2

Ooi, C. A., Hooy, C. W., & Som, A. P. M. (2015). Diversity in human and social capital: Empirical evidence from Asian tourism firms in corporate board composition. *Tourism Management*, *48*, 139–153. doi:10.1016/j.tourman.2014.11.002

Palacios-Marques, D., Gil-Pechuán, I., & Lim, S. (2011). Improving human capital through knowledge management practices in knowledge-intensive business services. *Service Business*, *5*(2), 99–112. doi:10.1007/s11628-011-0104-z

Pelinescu, E. (2015). The impact of human capital on economic growth. *Procedia Economics and Finance*, *22*, 184–190. doi:10.1016/S2212-5671(15)00258-0

Peng, M. W., Sun, S. L., & Markóczy, L. (2015). Human capital and CEO compensation during institutional transitions. *Journal of Management Studies*, *52*(1), 117–147. doi:10.1111/joms.12106

Perera-Tallo, F. (2005). Missing markets for human capital and differences in growth. *Economica*, *72*(286), 241–265. doi:10.1111/j.0013-0427.2005.00413.x

Perna, L. W., Orosz, K., & Jumakulov, Z. (2015). Understanding the human capital benefits of a government-funded international scholarship program: An exploration of Kazakhstan's Bolashak program. *International Journal of Educational Development*, *40*, 85–97. doi:10.1016/j.ijedudev.2014.12.003

Pinto, H., Cruz, A. R., & Combe, C. (2015). Cooperation and the emergence of maritime clusters in the Atlantic: Analysis and implications of innovation and human capital for blue growth. *Marine Policy*, *57*, 167–177. doi:10.1016/j.marpol.2015.03.029

Pitcher, P., & Smith, A. D. (2001). Top management team heterogeneity: Personality, power, and proxies. *Organization Science*, *12*(1), 1–18. doi:10.1287/orsc.12.1.1.10120

Psacharopoulos, G., & Patrinos, H. A. (2004). Returns to investment in education: A further update. *Education Economics*, *12*(2), 111–134. doi:10.1080/0964529042000239140

Rauch, A., Frese, M., & Utsch, A. (2005). Effects of human capital and long-term human resources development and utilization on employment growth of small-scale businesses: A causal analysis. *Entrepreneurship Theory and Practice*, *29*(6), 681–698.

Rauch, A., & Rijsdijk, S. A. (2013). The effects of general and specific human capital on long-term growth and failure of newly founded businesses. *Entrepreneurship Theory and Practice*, *37*(4), 923–941. doi:10.1111/j.1540-6520.2011.00487.x

Rey-Martí, A., Ribeiro-Soriano, D., & Palacios-Marqués, D. (2016). Entrepreneurial attributes of human capital and contingency factors in the culinary tourism. *The International Entrepreneurship and Management Journal*, *12*(1), 67–85. doi:10.1007/s11365-015-0375-2

Robson, P. J. A., Akuetteh, C. K., Westhead, P., & Wright, M. (2012). Innovative opportunity pursuit, human capital and business ownership experience in an emerging region: Evidence from Ghana. *Small Business Economics*, *39*(3), 603–625. doi:10.1007/s11187-011-9333-8

Royal, C., & O'Donnell, L. (2005). Embedding human capital analysis in the investment process: A human resources challenge. *Asia Pacific Journal of Human Resources*, *43*(1), 117–136. doi:10.1177/1038411105050308

Santarelli, E., & Tran, H. T. (2013). The interplay of human and social capital in shaping entrepreneurial performance: The case of Vietnam. *Small Business Economics*, *40*(2), 435–458. doi:10.1007/s11187-012-9427-y

Santos-Rodrigues, H., Dorrego, P. F., & Jardon, C. F. (2010). The influence of human capital on the innovativeness of firms. *International Business and Economics Research Journal*, *9*(9), 53–63.

Saridakis, G., Mole, K., & Storey, D. J. (2008). New small firm survival in England. *Empirica*, *35*(1), 25–39. doi:10.1007/s10663-007-9049-9

Schlitte, F. (2012). Local human capital, segregation by skill, and skill-specific employment growth. *Papers in Regional Science*, *91*(1), 85–106. doi:10.1111/j.1435-5957.2011.00373.x

Schmidt, F. L., & Hunter, J. (2004). General mental ability in the world of work: Occupational attainment and job performance. *Journal of Personality and Social Psychology*, *86*(1), 162–173. doi:10.1037/0022-3514.86.1.162 PMID:14717634

Schneider, L., Günther, J., & Brandenburg, B. (2010). Innovation and skills from a sectoral perspective: A linked employer-employee analysis. *Economics of Innovation and New Technology*, *19*(2), 185–202. doi:10.1080/10438590902872887

Schulz, E., Chowdhury, S., & van de Voort, D. (2013). Firm productivity moderated link between human capital and compensation: The significance of task-specific human capital. *Human Resource Management*, *52*(3), 423–439. doi:10.1002/hrm.21537

Scicchitano, S. (2010). Complementarity between heterogeneous human capital and R&D: Can job-training avoid low development traps? *Empirica*, *37*(4), 361–380. doi:10.1007/s10663-009-9113-8

Seghers, A., Manigart, S., & Vanacker, T. (2012). The impact of human and social capital on entrepreneur's knowledge of finance alternatives. *Journal of Small Business Management*, *50*(1), 63–86. doi:10.1111/j.1540-627X.2011.00344.x

Shao, S., & Yang, L. (2014). Natural resource dependence, human capital accumulation, and economic growth: A combined explanation for the resource curse and the resource blessing. *Energy Policy*, *74*, 632–642. doi:10.1016/j.enpol.2014.07.007

Silos, P., & Smith, E. (2015). Human capital portfolios. *Review of Economic Dynamics*, *18*(3), 635–652. doi:10.1016/j.red.2014.09.001

Slaughter, S. A., Ang, S., & Boh, W. F. (2007). Firm-specific human capital and compensation organizational tenure profiles: An archival analysis of salary data for it. *Human Resource Management*, *46*(3), 373–394. doi:10.1002/hrm.20169

Soboleva, I. (2010). Paradoxes of the measurement of human capital. *Problems of Economic Transition*, *52*(11), 43–70. doi:10.2753/PET1061-1991521103

Soltanpanah, H., & Karimi, M. (2011). Accumulation of human capital and FDI inflows in ASEAN-3 countries (Malaysia, Thailand, Indonesia). *African Journal of Business Management*, *7*(17), 1599–1605. doi:10.5897/AJBM11.1681

Stark, O., Hyll, W., & Wang, Y. (2012). Endogenous selection of comparison groups, human capital formation, and tax policy. *Economica*, *79*(313), 62–75. doi:10.1111/j.1468-0335.2010.00876.x

Stark, O., & Wang, Y. (2005). The intergenerational overlap and human capital formation. *Review of International Economics*, *13*(1), 45–58. doi:10.1111/j.1467-9396.2005.00491.x

Stevens, A. H. (1997). Persistent effects of job displacement: The importance of multiple job losses. *Journal of Labor Economics*, *15*(1), 165–188. doi:10.1086/209851

Storper, M., & Scott, A. J. (2009). Rethinking human capital, creativity and urban growth. *Journal of Economic Geography*, *9*(2), 147–167. doi:10.1093/jeg/lbn052

Strulik, H. (2005). The role of human capital and population growth in R&D-based models of economic growth. *Review of International Economics*, *13*(1), 129–145. doi:10.1111/j.1467-9396.2005.00495.x

Suhonen, M., & Paasivaara, L. (2011). Shared human capital in project management: A systematic review of the literature. *Project Management Journal*, *42*(2), 4–16. doi:10.1002/pmj.20211

Teixeira, A. A. C., & Tavares-Lehmann, A. T. (2014). Human capital intensity in technology-based firms located in Portugal: Does foreign ownership matter? *Research Policy*, *43*(4), 737–748. doi:10.1016/j.respol.2014.01.001

Thangavelu, S. M., & Narjoko, D. (2014). Human capital, FTAs and foreign direct investment flows into ASEAN. *Journal of Asian Economics*, *35*, 65–76. doi:10.1016/j.asieco.2014.11.002

Tian, J., Haleblian, J., & Rajagopalan, N. (2011). The effects of board human and social capital on investor reactions to new CEO selection. *Strategic Management Journal*, *32*(7), 731–747. doi:10.1002/smj.909

Toner, P. (2011). Workforce skills and innovation: An overview of major themes in the literature. Paris, France: OECD Directorate for Science, Technology and Industry (STI), Centre for Educational Research and Innovation (CERI).

Ucbasaran, D., Westhead, P., & Wright, M. (2008). Opportunity identification and pursuit: Does an entrepreneur's human capital matter? *Small Business Economics*, *30*(2), 153–173. doi:10.1007/s11187-006-9020-3

Vindelyn, A. S., & Omar, M. (2005). FDI, international business and regulation: The behavior of UK multinational corporations. *European Business Review*, *17*(1), 69–82. doi:10.1108/09555340510576276

Vogel, J. (2015). The two faces of R&D and human capital: Evidence from Western European regions. *Papers in Regional Science*, *94*(3), 525–551. doi:10.1111/pirs.12084

Vomberg, A., Homburg, C., & Bornemann, T. (2015). Talented people and strong brands: The contribution of human capital and brand equity to firm value. *Strategic Management Journal*, *36*(13), 2122–2131. doi:10.1002/smj.2328

Wang, H., & Wong, K. F. E. (2012). The effect of managerial bias on employee's specific human capital investments. *Journal of Management Studies*, *49*(8), 1435–1458. doi:10.1111/j.1467-6486.2012.01053.x

Wincent, J., Thorgren, S., & Anokhin, S. (2014). Entrepreneurial orientation and network board diversity in network organizations. *Journal of Business Venturing*, *29*(2), 327–344. doi:10.1016/j.jbusvent.2013.04.002

Wright, P. M., & McMahan, G. C. (2011). Exploring human capital: Putting "human" back into strategic human resource management. *Human Resource Management Journal*, *21*(2), 93–104. doi:10.1111/j.1748-8583.2010.00165.x

Wyatt, A., & Frick, H. (2010). Accounting for investments in human capital: A review. *Australian Accounting Review*, *20*(3), 199–220. doi:10.1111/j.1835-2561.2010.00104.x

Yamarik, S. (2011). Human capital and state-level economic growth: What is the contribution of schooling? *The Annals of Regional Science*, *47*(1), 195–211. doi:10.1007/s00168-010-0365-9

Zhao, G., & Zhang, Z. (2010). Uncovering the relationship between FDI, human capital and technological progress in Chinese high-technology industries. *China & World Economy*, *18*(1), 82–98. doi:10.1111/j.1749-124X.2010.01182.x

Zlate, S., & Enache, C. (2015). The interdependence between human capital and organizational performance in higher education. *Procedia: Social and Behavioral Sciences*, *180*, 136–143. doi:10.1016/j.sbspro.2015.02.096

ADDITIONAL READING

Aloi, M., & Tournemaine, F. (2013). Inequality, growth, and environmental quality trade-offs in a model with human capital accumulation. *The Canadian Journal of Economics. Revue Canadienne dEconomique*, *46*(3), 1123–1155. doi:10.1111/caje.12046

Arauzo-Carod, J. M. (2013). Location determinants of new firms: Does skill level of human capital really matter? *Growth and Change*, *44*(1), 118–148. doi:10.1111/grow.12004

Baye, F. M., & Epo, B. N. (2015). Impact of human capital endowments on inequality of outcomes in Cameroon. *Review of Income and Wealth*, *61*(1), 93–118. doi:10.1111/roiw.12077

Bedasso, B. E. (2015). Educated bandits: Endogenous property rights and intra-elite distribution of human capital. *Economics and Politics*, *27*(3), 404–432. doi:10.1111/ecpo.12063

Cañibano, C., & Woolley, R. (2015). Towards a socio-economics of the brain drain and distributed human capital. *International Migration (Geneva, Switzerland)*, *53*(1), 115–130. doi:10.1111/imig.12020

Coen-Pirani, D. (2015). Human capital accumulation in a federation. *European Economic Review*, *76*, 104–124. doi:10.1016/j.euroecorev.2015.02.002

Dias, J. (2015). Human capital demand in Brazil: The effects of adjustment cost, economic growth, exports and imports. *Economia*, *16*(1), 76–92. doi:10.1016/j.econ.2015.03.002

Gao, Q., Zhai, F., Yang, S., & Li, S. (2014). Does welfare enable family expenditures on human capital? Evidence from China. *World Development*, *64*, 219–231. doi:10.1016/j.worlddev.2014.06.003

Ghosh, S., & Mastromarco, C. (2013). Cross-border economic activities, human capital and efficiency: A stochastic frontier analysis for OECD countries. *World Economy*, *36*(6), 761–785. doi:10.1111/twec.12010

Grichnik, D., Brinckmann, J., Singh, L., & Manigart, S. (2014). Beyond environmental scarcity: Human and social capital as driving forces of bootstrapping activities. *Journal of Business Venturing*, *29*(2), 310–326. doi:10.1016/j.jbusvent.2013.02.006

Johnson, B. J., & Pierce, J. C. (2014). Is county level of social, creative, and human capital associated with winning humanities grants in Kansas? *Nonprofit Management & Leadership*, *24*(4), 503–520. doi:10.1002/nml.21103

Jones, G., & Potrafke, N. (2014). Human capital and national institutional quality: Are TIMSS, PISA, and national average IQ robust predictors? *Intelligence*, *46*, 148–155. doi:10.1016/j.intell.2014.05.011

Kobayashi, J., Kagawa, M., & Sato, Y. (2015). How to get a longer job? Roles of human and social capital in the Japanese labor market. *International Journal of Japanese Sociology*, *24*(1), 20–29. doi:10.1111/ijjs.12037

Lara, J. (2015). International migration and human capital in Mexico: Networks or parental absence? *International Journal of Educational Development*, *41*, 131–142. doi:10.1016/j.ijedudev.2015.02.006

Leitch, C. M., McMullan, C., & Harrison, R. T. (2013). The development of entrepreneurial leadership: The role of human, social and institutional capital. *British Journal of Management*, *24*(3), 347–366. doi:10.1111/j.1467-8551.2011.00808.x

McGowan, P., Cooper, S., Durkin, M., & O'Kane, C. (2015). The influence of social and human capital in developing young women as entrepreneurial business leaders. *Journal of Small Business Management*, *53*(3), 645–661. doi:10.1111/jsbm.12176

Mendolicchio, C., Paolini, D., & Pietra, T. (2014). Income taxes, subsidies to education, and investments in human capital. *Journal of Public Economic Theory*, *16*(1), 24–47. doi:10.1111/jpet.12051

Miller, D., Xu, X., & Mehrotra, V. (2015). When is human capital a valuable resource? The performance effects of Ivy League selection among celebrated CEOs. *Strategic Management Journal*, *36*(6), 930–944. doi:10.1002/smj.2251

Ngoma, A. L., & Ismail, N. W. (2013). The impact of brain drain on human capital in developing countries. *The South African Journal of Economics*, *81*(2), 211–224. doi:10.1111/saje.12014

Nyberg, A. J., Moliterno, T. P., Hale, D., & Lepak, D. P. (2014). Resource-based perspectives on unit-level human capital: A review and integration. *Journal of Management*, *40*(1), 316–346. doi:10.1177/0149206312458703

Pablo-Romero, M. D. P., & Sánchez-Braza, A. (2015). Productive energy use and economic growth: Energy, physical and human capital relationships. *Energy Economics*, *49*, 420–429. doi:10.1016/j.eneco.2015.03.010

Perdreau, F., Le Nadant, A. L., & Cliquet, G. (2015). Human capital intangibles and performance of franchise networks: A complementary view between agency and critical resource perspectives. *Managerial and Decision Economics*, *36*(2), 121–138. doi:10.1002/mde.2656

Shaw, J. D., Park, T. Y., & Kim, E. (2013). A resource-based perspective on human capital losses, HRM investments, and organizational performance. *Strategic Management Journal*, *34*(5), 572–589. doi:10.1002/smj.2025

Shimada, A. (2013). Wage inequality and human capital formation under migration possibilities. *Australian Economic Papers*, *52*(3/4), 190–201. doi:10.1111/1467-8454.12016

Sundaramurthy, C., Pukthuanthong, K., & Kor, Y. (2014). Positive and negative synergies between the CEO's and the corporate board's human and social capital: A study of biotechnology firms. *Strategic Management Journal*, *35*(6), 845–868. doi:10.1002/smj.2137

Wietzke, F. B. (2015). Long-term consequences of colonial institutions and human capital investments: Sub-national evidence from Madagascar. *World Development*, *66*, 293–307. doi:10.1016/j.worlddev.2014.08.010

Winters, J. V. (2014). STEM graduates, human capital externalities, and wages in the U.S. *Regional Science and Urban Economics*, *48*(1), 190–198. doi:10.1016/j.regsciurbeco.2014.07.003

Yu, J., Shen, K., & Liu, D. (2015). Rural–urban migration, substitutability of human capital and city productivity: Evidence from China. *Review of Development Economics*, *19*(4), 877–891. doi:10.1111/rode.12178

Zivin, J. G., & Neidell, M. (2013). Environment, health, and human capital. *Journal of Economic Literature*, *51*(3), 689–730. doi:10.1257/jel.51.3.689

KEY TERMS AND DEFINITIONS

Education: The process of teaching or learning, especially in a school or college.

Human Capital: The collective skills, knowledge, or other intangible assets of individuals that can be used to create economic value for the individuals, their employers, or their community.

Human Resource Management: The process of hiring and developing employees so that they become more valuable to the organization.

Innovation: The process of translating an idea or invention into product or service that creates value.

Knowledge: The understanding of a circumstance, gained through experience.

Knowledge Management: The strategies and processes designed to identify, capture, structure, value, leverage, and share an organization's intellectual assets to enhance its performance and competitiveness.

Skill: The ability acquired through systematic effort to effectively execute the complex activities.

Training: The organized activity aimed at informing instructions to improve the recipient's performance.

Chapter 5
Analyzing and Studying the Selection Tests based on their Capabilities in Evaluation of Various Jobs Proficiencies and Abilities

Mohamamd Abdolshah
Azad University, Iran

Ali Mollaaghamirzaei
Semnan University, Iran

Nahid Farazmand
Semnan University, Iran

Fateme Eshragh
Semnan University, Iran

Khashayar Ghadiri Nezhad
Semnan University, Iran

ABSTRACT

Nowadays, finding qualified labor force among the job applicants is one of the main problems in organizations and companies, so employee selection is one of the main challenges in human resource management. In this case, the variety of methods and tests has been represented and used in order to evaluate the employees' abilities up to now. However, determining the best selection methods according to the job requirements is one of the basic challenges in organizations and companies. In this chapter, different selection methods and their capabilities have been studied in order to assess various job abilities. The results, of this research, showed that the methods such as Assessment centers have significantly assessed a persons' job abilities, however we should pay attention to some parameters such as time, cost, the method's validity, and moral and legal aspects for an appropriate selection method.

DOI: 10.4018/978-1-5225-1974-4.ch005

1.INTRODUCTION

Nowadays, organizations compete strongly in order to find the best human resources. The majority of them spend enormous expenses for employment advertisements and strategies to attract the best applicants; as today managers have found that one of the most important resources in organizations is the human resources (Pulakos, 2005). Nowadays, this fact has been accepted that each organization's success depends on the labor-force's abilities and characteristics who want to work there. Not surprisingly, the selection's subject has attracted many researchers and managers' attention (Breaugh, 2009).

Here, there are numerous evaluation methods (formal methods) that organizations can use for their employees' selection, however not all of them are appropriate to select a person for a certain position in the organisation. The first step for choosing the suitable evaluation method in a position or a special job status is the exact determination of what the person must do after standing in the mentioned position. This aim is acheived by job analysis (Gael, 1988; Brannick& Levine, 2002).

Job analysis is generally divided into two categories: 1) Job-oriented analysis, and 2) Worker-oriented analysis. The first category refers to the analysis that results in providing a complete list of the defined job responsibilities for the mentioned position. The second one indicates the analysis dealing with the recognition of the considered KSA[1]s for doing the job (Pulakos, 2005).

In general, the steps of job analysis are as follows:

Step 1: Specialists are interviewed and their performance is observed in order to determine the list of their tasks in the mentioned job position.

Step 2: Specialists are interviewed and their performance is perceived for representing the list of the essential knowledge, skill and abilities for doing the job effectively.

Step 3: studying and polling the supervisors and officers in order to emphasize the responsibilities and KSAs.

Step 4: Analyzing the results for giving the priority to crucial tasks and KSAs related to the job.

Step 5: Selecting the appropriate evaluation methods and their development to measure the most important responsibilities and KSAs (Pulakos, 2005).

After job analysis and determining the required abilities, skills and knowledge for the considered job, the selection process, finding the appropriate person among the applicants, begins. The main purpose in this chapter is studying and analyzing different selection methods and specifying the proper ones to evaluate the variety of job abilities of job applicants. Therefore, at first, the following figure has illustrated an employment process model, then in the second section articles about different and common selection tests that are often noticeable in employment process have been studied. In the third section, the variety of job applicants' capabilities has been studied. The next section has represented the effective parameters on selection methods' evaluation. Finally, in the last section, various job abilities have been compared by each selection test and the results have been represented at the end of the chapter.

Figure.1 suggests that, before making decisions concerning such issues as what recruitment methods to use, an organization should thoughtfully establish its recruitment objectives) (Breaugh et al, 2008).

2. INTRODUCTION TO DIFFERENT EMPLOYEES' SELECTION TESTS

Organizations' selection tests have been used for both choosing the applicants from outside of the organization and assessing its current employees (Pulakos, 2005). These tests can be divided into two groups, the first one is related to the evaluation of employees' selected abilities, skills and knowledge and they're called "KSA-

Figure 1. A model of recruitment process (Breaugh et al, 2008)

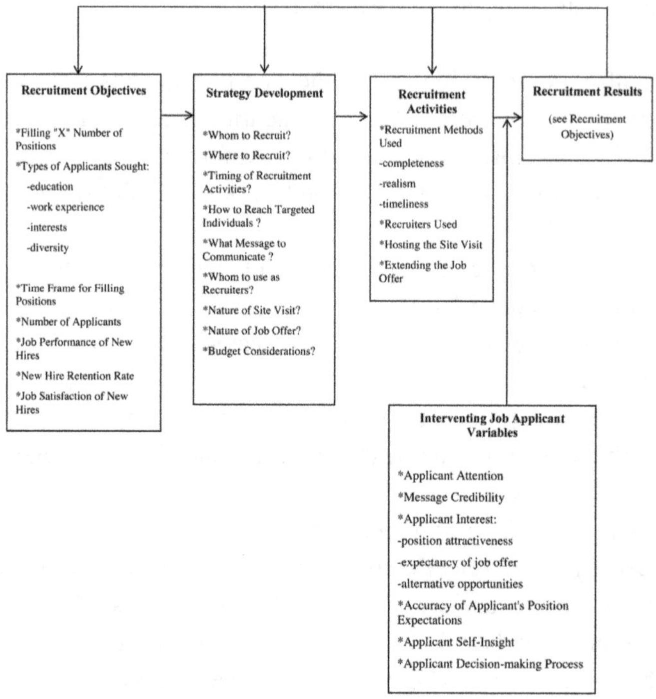

Oriented" tests. The other category, known as "Task-Oriented" tests, compare the employees' abilities for the special tasks that must be performed after standing on the specific job position. Figure 2 shows the most common ranking of the employees' selection tests that have been described in the rest of the chapter.

2.1. Cognitive Abilities Test

A variety of abilities, including the verbal, math, logic and comprehension abilities have been assessed by these. These tests have been proved very useful for the prediction of employees' performance, so they have been applied to select the workforce for different jobs (Ree et al., 1994, Hunter, 1986).

Some of these tests include the sections that evaluate different abilities, but finally, the person is given just one score indicating his mental capability. The score, related to every section, will indicate the person's certain mental ability if the scores of different parts are separately calculated (Pulakos, 2005). These tests are conducted in a specific written form.

Figure 2. Employees' selection tests (Pulakos, 2005)

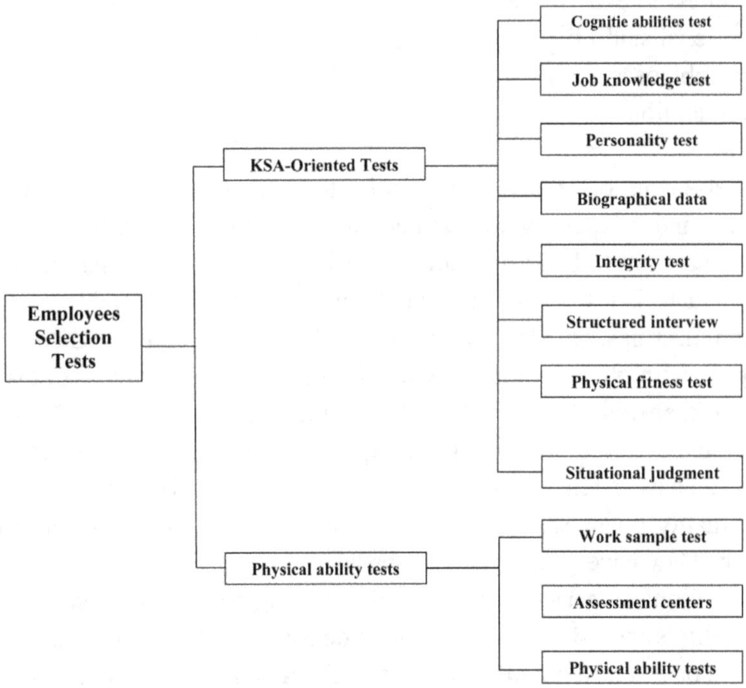

2.2. Job Knowledge Test

These tests have been used in order to evaluate the required knowledge domains resulted in the effective job performance (Hunter, 1986). The mentioned tests are applied where the applicant must have the desirable level of the considered knowledge before employment. In contrast, it's not necessary to carry out these tests when the employees will be trained after the employment (Pulakos, 2005). These tests are also conducted in a written form.

2.3. Personality Test

Personality doesn't have a simple and objective concept to be defined simply. It has a conceptual meaning, in fact, it is a complicated structure. Being so concepyual and stractured makes personality, difficult to define (Ross, 1992). Representing some theories such as "Cattell 16 personality factors " (Cattell, 1970), "Eysenck's three personality traits theory" and "Five-factor model" or "The Big Five" (Gerald et al., 1998) and their evolution have significantly developed the personality theories since the 1940s. The personality features that are assessed in personality tests include (Barrick& Mount, 1991; Costa & McCrae, 1992):

- Extraversion
- Openness to experiences
- Emotional stability
- Agreeableness
- Conscientious

Extraverts tend to verbal and physical activities and introverts are interested in dependence and privacy. A normal person selects the combination of social and introversive activities. Extraverts are the sociable people but sociability is just one of their characteristics. These people not only like others and tend to participate in parties and meetings, but also are practically determined, active, talkative and they like to speak with other people (McCrae & Costa, 1980). Openness to experiences as a main dimension of personality has been noticed much lesser than emotional instability and extraversion among the experts. A person, who has openness to experience, can have extensive interests and like new things. This parameter is related to intellectuality, openness to new ideas, cultural interests, educative approaches and innovation. They have active visions, aesthetic-sensitivity, great tendency towards internal emotional experiences and an absolute judgment (Costa & McCrae, 1985).

Personality's extensive dimensions include compatibility comparison, emotional stability, inconsistency, neuralgia and neurosis. A neurotic person is often worried, moody and depression prone (Howard, O.J & Howard, K.J.M., 1998). Just like extraversion, the agreement index emphasizes on interpersonal relationship tendency. A friendly person is basically altruist and sympathizes with others. They are interested in helping others and believe that other people have the same characteristic as well. The agreeableness factor is also determined by self-devotion. The agreeable people are friendly, humble and sympathetic (Costa & McCrae, 1992). The conscionable person has strong and pre-determined aims and. They are efficient, disciplined and responsible. They manage their affairs carefully and orderly, they are reliable and accomplish their tasks in the best way (Booth & Vickers, 1994).

Now, the personality tests which are used in order to evaluate the personality traits related to the job, have shown that the efficiency scales are referred to the employed person's future performance (Raymark et al., 1997; Lett et al., 1991). These tests are conducted in a written form and contain multiple-choice and true-false questions (Pulakos, 2005).

2.4. Biographical Data

This test includes the questions in which our main aim is gaining the information about the employees' past performance, their personality traits and interests. Moreover, these tests are based on the fact that each person's past performance will truly indicate his future performance (Pulakos, 2005). Thus the part of employees' past performance that is being evaluated in this test is the part which is related to the position they have applied for. These tests are conducted in two models: the first one consists of multiple-choice questions, but the other one has an oral form and it's called "accomplishment record". In the second model, the applicants are asked to note their own best and the most proper accomplishments about the skills and abilities related to the job. (for example, about planning and organizing, customer services and solving the conflicts (Hough, 1984)).

In these tests, the applicant must note another important person's name, such as their previous supervisor, that can confirm their statements (Pulakos, 2005). It has been proved through experience, the mentioned method is very effective on predicting the applicants' future performance (Hough et al., 1983).

2.5. Integrity Test

These tests evaluate the employee's attitudes and experiences that are related to his integrity, empathy and reliability (Ones et al., 1993; Sackett&Wanek, 1996; Camera &Scheider, 1994; Goldberg et al., 1991). This test aims at minimizing the probability of employing the employees with the negative job behaviors in industries, such as using narcotic substances or alcoholic beverages and causing controversy in the working environment, thievery from other employees, equipment's destruction and other unpleasant behaviors (Schmit& Hunter, 1998). This test is conducted as multiple-choice (I agree/ I disagree) questions and in a written form (Pulakos, 2005).

2.6. Structured Interview

The employment interviews can be structured or unstructured. Unstructured interviews don't have any specified structure and definite questions for responding. In fact, an interviewer usually asks applicants different questions (Schmit& Hunter, 1998). However, the structured interviews include the questions that are designed for comparing the required KSAs for profession (Eder & Ferris, 1989; Campion et al., 1988; Campion et al., 1998; Judge et al., 2000).

Another basic feature of structured interview that distinguishes it from unstructured interview is providing the standard scoring criteria for interviewer, so that the quality and effectiveness of interviewee's answers can be judged (Pulakos, 2005). The structured interview's questions can be designed in a way that they evaluate all of the KSAs related to the job, but this test has often been used in order to assess the person's social skills and personality traits, such as relationship skills, leadership, planning, organizing and compatibility with others (Pulakos, 2005).

The major finding in the performed researches about using interviews for selecting employees is that interviewer's judgment in a structured interview is more reliable for predicting the interviewee's future performance rather than an unstructured interview (Therese, 2009). In other words, qualitative and quantitative studies regarding this finding show that adding a structure to the interview process increases the interviewer reliability and his evaluative credibility (Conway et al., 1995; Huffcutt& Arthur, 1994; Huffcutt&Woehr, 1999; Posthuma et al., 2002). As a result, a structured interview has a high degree of reliability, although its organizing and application needs more expense rather than an unstructured interview (Schmit& Hunter, 1998).

2.7. Physical Fitness Test

Physical fitness tests are practical tests, (like running a definite distance) in which the person's strength, power and physical ability is being evaluated. In other words, these tests evaluate the employees' general health (Pulakos, 2005).

2.8. Situational Judgment Test (SJT)

These tests are multiple-choice in a written form, and they consist of the questions in which the special situation confronting an employee is posed. In addition, each choice is described indicating a kind of performance in a certain situation (Motowidlo et al., 1990; Chan & Schmitt, 1997; Weichmann et al., 2001). As a matter of fact, these tests have been applied in order to assess the applicants' judgment related to the position that they may encounter in working environment (Deborah et al., 2009).

THE mentioned tests are suitable not only for training the labor-force and developing their abilities, but also for appointing the competent persons for international occupations (Ployhart, 2006).

2.9. Work Sample Test

The work sample tests include the tasks or activities that a person must carry out after standing on the selected job position (Asher &Sciarrino, 1974; Hunter & Hunter, 1984; Howard, 1983). These tests can be used in order to compare all of the tasks related to occupations, however, they are also applied for evaluating the technical activities, such as using a special machine, its repair and fault detection and for the jobs associated with organizing and planning. As mentioned about job knowledge test, the work sample tests are also applied when the person must have the required abilities for the considered profession before employment and they are not appropriate when the employees are to be trained after being employed. (Pulakos, 2005).

2.10. Assessment Centers

There is an idea that states that psychologists can select the people for high classes jobs, however it hadn't been extensively noticed since world war II (Stagner, 1957).

It had been seen that the method that has been used to select German, Britain and American armies' officers can have a significant potential to be applied in industrial applied in industries after war (Brody & Powell, 1947; Taft, 1948). An assessment center is a kind of work sample test that has often been used to evaluate the employees' abilities and aptitudes in managerial and supervisory high class positions (Gaugler et al., 1987; Thornton&Byham, 1982; Thornton, 1992). The assessment centers usually include the programs that are followed for one or more days (Pulakos, 2005).The conducted tests in assessment centers are ranked in Figure 3, then each test has separately been described.

2.10.1. Role-Play Exercises

A scenario is predesigned in these tests in which a special situation is illustrated in organization, and the job applicant undertakes a role for this scenario. Moreover, his performance is assessed for implementing the mentioned role.

Figure 3. Assessment Centers

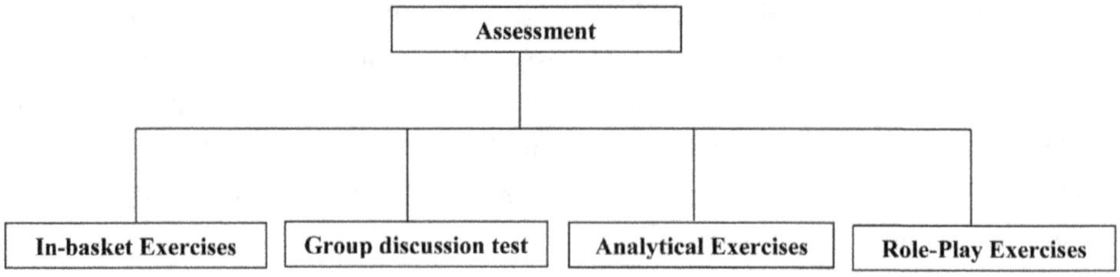

2.10.2. Analytical Exercises

A problem is presented in this test and the applicant is asked to analyze it and solve it in an appropriate way.

2.10.3. Group Discussion

This test looks like the analytic test, however there's a minor difference in which one must analyze the problem and represent the solution for it in a group discussion and by consultation.

2.10.4. In-basket Exercises

During this test, the applicant deals with the certain tasks, such as considering the letters, phone calls, etc. in the special period of time. In other words, he/she can bring out the tasks from the in-basket exercises orderly, and finally his managerial performance and fulfilling the mentioned responsibilities will be evaluated.

In addition, some of the assessment centers consist of the cognitive abilities tests, job knowledge test and personality tests (Pulakos, 2005). The assessment centers not only select the applicants outside the organization, but also have been used in order to evaluate the present employees for enhancing their position, etc (Thornton & Gibbons, 2009).

2.11. Physical Ability Tests

These tests have been usually applied to select employees for the professions in which the employed persons need the certain physical abilities, like police officers and firefighters (Hogan, 1991; Campion, 1983; BlakleyQuinones,Crawford, &Jago, 1994). As noted in the work sample test, the applicants are asked to perform the activities that they encounter then when they are carrying out the tasks, so their physical ability has been assessed for doing the mentioned job. It should be noted that the applicants usually need to perform the mentioned tasks in a defined period of time, therefore the rate of their performance will be compared in doing the tasks (Pulakos, 2005).

3. JOB-RELATED SKILLS AND ABILITIES

As mentioned before, organizations compete strongly with each other to attract the most proper employees. This statement is true about the job applicants, and at the present century, to be a successful person in finding an appropriate job regarding the changes in working area one needs to have abilities and skills agreeable with this area. Among the conditions for the present business area that require the special capabilities, we can mention the examples such as globalization (Wagschal, 1994), the relationship between organizations with universal scale, such as providing the resources and creating the institutional networks (Lee &Sirch, 1994), information burst, especially digital information (Wagschal, 1994), developing software like information systems under web (Resnick, 1994) and increasing focus on efficiency (Marchionini, 1991), which makes it difficult to find jobs in 21century. Zalaquett and Turner (1997) have introduced the set of required abilities and skills for getting a proper job in an article called "succeeding in the 21st Century", showed in Table 1.

4. EVALUATING THE EMPLOYEES' SELECTION METHODS

The test's theoretical parameters, especially neutrality, reliability and validity have been studied in order to evaluate the employee's selection methods. In addition to these statements, the selection tools must be assessed based on the structural efficiency, social validity and moral and legal aspects.

4.1. Validity

Among the psychometric qualitative criteria, the validity is the most important factor, and as the aim is usually the job achievement's prediction in future, so the predictive assaying of the validity plays a vital role among the other variables or strategies. Regarding this subject, it has been represented that the following tests have good or sufficient validity (Salgado 1999; Schmidt & Hunter 1998). Some of the tests, such as "General intelligence test", "Work sample test", "Job-related structured interviews", "biographical data" and some of the certain personality tests (such as integrity, conscience, success motivation) and multimodal procedures (such as, as-

Table 1. Job-related abilities and skills (Zalaquett&Turner, 1997)

Definition	Skills and abilities
Exchanging the thoughts and beliefs verbally or in the written form	Communications
The ability to understand others and working with them	Multicultural awareness
The ability to communicate with other languages	Multilingual
The ability to lead and organize people in order to use different policies and inventions and solving the disagreements among them	Managerial skills
Assisting efforts in a group for getting the appropriate target	Group working/ Cooperation
Training the artistic and imaginative abilities and the ability to find the new solutions for problems	Creativity
The ability to be changed and accommodated with a new situation	Adaptability
The ability to understand others' beliefs and affections	Sympathy
Controlling the stressful factors encountered the person and controlling the clues resulting from the stress	Stress management
The set of defined good and bad things for the person that they can make his/her fair performance	Work ethics
Controlling the behavior for improving the personal performance and the ability to control the fleeting desires for getting the permanent aims	Self-discipline
Tendency to accept responsibility	Responsibility
The ability to distinguish the real data from unreal ones	Pure thinking
Proper using the grammar rules in order to state thoughts and beliefs in a correct way	Grammar skills
The ability to use defined bases in logic and applying the abstract thinking in order to achieve the perception and dominance	Analytical logic
Using the dominant rules on business and economical relationships	Business/ Economics
The ability to use the basicmathematic theories and primary perception of the math and its applications	Mathematics skills
The ability to use computer effectively, such as widespread text, page processing softwareand internet	Computer skills
The ability to work with remote communicational tools	Remote communications

sessment centers and potential analysis), job knowledge tests and job performance evaluation are also included in the similar range. It must be noted that some of the conditions have to get adjust in some special cases (for example, biographical data test has a low validity for young people).

4.2. Organizational Efficiency

The organizational efficiency is used by its practical aspects. The most important aspects consist of the selection process cost, the required competency for application and availability of the considered test. Above all the instances, the procedure's economical interests are mostly considered which are the basic element of the organizational efficiency. The expected interests will be measured by implementing the economical indices.

4.3. Applicants' Reaction

The acceptance of selection process by the applicants and their reaction towards the employees' selection methods is considered as an independent qualitative criterion. The procedures that are more acceptable in this basis are distinct from other features such as job requirements, clarity, reaction and the ability to control the situation. These features are more available in interactional tests (e.g, interviews) rather than written tests or biographical documentation such as educational scores.

4.4. Moral and Legal Aspects

The moral, professional and legal aspects of employee's selection have been increasingly emphasized, and some examples about the drastic moral problems on this basis consist of using inappropriate and illegitimate diagnostic methods, ignoring job requirements, generating the intentional anxiety in selection procedure, improper invasion of personal sanctum, not respecting the confidentiality of personal information, conflict of interests between the customers and employees' relationship. On this basis, the efforts have significantly increased in order to organize the employees' selection methods that are possibly righteous and accepted by the society (Schuler et al., 1993).

5.ANALYSIS AND CONCLUSION

In this section, the capabilities of each of the selection methods have been studied for evaluating the job skills regarding the available literatures about the different ways of selection and the various occupational skills and abilities. Therefore, an expert polling is applied and the experts ideas have converged by using the "Delphi"[2] method. Thus, at first, the research literature is described for three expert persons and then they are asked to specify the competence and incompetence of evaluating each of the abilities with every test. To reach convergence of opinion, their collection has been sent for people during two turns. Consequently, the ultimate agreement in a personal meeting has been acquired to get the final result. Table 2 shows the obtained results.

Table 2. The competence of defined abilities and skills by each employee's selection test

Assessment centers	Work sample test	Situation judgment test	Structured interview	Integrity test	Biographical test	Personality test	Job knowledge test	Cognitive abilities test	Tests/ skills & abilities
*			*			*		*	Communications
*		*	*		*				Multicultural awareness
*	*		*		*		*		Multilingual
*		*			*		*		Managerial skills
*		*			*	*			Group working/ Cooperation
*	*	*			*			*	Creativity
*		*	*		*	*			Adaptability
*		*	*	*		*			Sympathy
*	*	*	*		*	*			Stress management
*		*	*	*	*	*			Working ethics
*		*	*		*	*			Self-discipline
*		*	*		*	*			Responsibility
*	*	*	*					*	Pure thinking
*							*	*	Grammar skills
*	*	*						*	Analytic logic
*	*	*					*		Economy/ Business
*							*	*	Mathematics skills
*	*	*					*		Computer skills
*	*								Remote communications

As you can see in Table 2, some of the selection tests have the ability to evaluate more than one job skills in a person. Meanwhile, it can be noted that the assessment centers method has evaluated the employees' professional skills more comprehensively than the other methods, whereas the integrity test compares just two cases of the skills and abilities. As the mentioned skills are basically introduced about the educated job applicants, it's evident that physical health tests and physical abilities don't have the competence to evaluate the above-mentioned proficiencies. So, they have been omitted from the table.

It must be mentioned that this table doesn't aim to show the better and weaker methods for evaluating the job applicant, instead a test must be selected after determining the job characteristics and the required skills regarding the time and cost remarks. Moreover, this test has to have the most compatibility for those abilities and skills' evaluation.

For example, it's not appropriate to ask the younger applicants "biographical questions" or it is not necessary to perform the "integrity test" for sensitive occupations. A test like "structured interview" has more basic and disciplined structure rather than the "unstructured interview" but it's more expensive.

Although a test like assessment centers test demands more time and cost and it can't be used in every situation, it is a suitable test in which the high-class job applicants such as managers and supervisors can be assessed and a variety of dimensions of employee's abilities can be studied.

In-basket exercises test can be applied for the assessment of job applicants' who should doa bulk of works orderly, for example applicants for a secretary position. Physical abilities test is also used for comparing the particular job applicants that need preparation and high physical health, e.g, fire-fighting and lifesaving applicants.

In this chapter evaluating applicants' skills and abilities through different tests, is considered to have absolute results which can lead to a more precise selection process if the weight factors for the elements are chosen properly. On this basis it can be concluded that the employee selection tests are becoming more efficient so that the results will include reduced test time and cost and an attitude towards loyal employees.

Suggested fields for future research include, studying the selection tests regarding cost and time, how they're affected by organizational culture, environmental customs and changes that can be made to the tests according to this culture.

REFERENCES

Asher, J. J., & Sciarrino, J. A. (1974). Realistic work sample tests: A review. *Personnel Psychology, 27*(4), 519–533. doi:10.1111/j.1744-6570.1974.tb01173.x

Barrick, M. R., & Mount, M. K. (1991). The big five personality dimensions and job performance: A meta-analysis. *Personnel Psychology, 91*(1), 1–26. doi:10.1111/j.1744-6570.1991.tb00688.x

Blakley, B. R., Quinones, M. S., Crawford, M. S., & Jago, I. A. (1994). The validity of isometric strength tests. *Personnel Psychology, 47*(2), 247–274. doi:10.1111/j.1744-6570.1994.tb01724.x

Booth-Kewley, S., & Vickers, R.R., Jr. (1994). Associations between major domains of personality and health behavior. *Journal of personality, 62*(3), 281-298.

Brannick, M. T., & Levine, E. L. (2002). *Job analysis*. Thousand Oaks, CA: Sage.

Breaugh, J. A. (2009). Employee selection at the beginning of the 21st century[Editorial]. *Human Resource Management Review, 19*(3), 167–168. doi:10.1016/j.hrmr.2009.03.009

Breaugh, J. A. (2009). The use of biodata for employee selection: Past research and future directions. *Human Resource Management Review, 19*(3), 219–231. doi:10.1016/j.hrmr.2009.02.003

Breaugh, J. A., Macan, T. H., & Grambow, D. M. (2008). Employee Recruitment. *Current Knowledge and Directions for Future Research, International Review of Industrial and Organizational Psychology, 23*, 45–82.

Brody, W., & Powell, N. J. (1947). A new approach to oral testing. *Educational and Psychological Measurement, 7*(2), 289–298. doi:10.1177/001316444700700206 PMID:20256563

Camara, W. J., & Schneider, D. L. (1994). Integrity tests: Facts and unresolved issues. *The American Psychologist, 49*(2), 112–119. doi:10.1037/0003-066X.49.2.112

Campion, M. A. (1983). Personnel selection for physically demanding jobs: Review and recommendations. *Personnel Psychology, 36*(3), 527–550. doi:10.1111/j.1744-6570.1983.tb02234.x

Campion, M. A., Palmer, D. K., & Campion, J. E. (1997). A review of structure in the selection interview. *Personnel Psychology*, *50*(3), 655–702. doi:10.1111/j.1744-6570.1997.tb00709.x

Campion, M. A., Pursell, E. D., & Brown, B. K. (1988). Structured interviewing: Raising the psychometric properties of the employmentinterview. *Personnel Psychology*, *48*, 289–308.

Casta, P. T., & McCrae, R. R. (1992). NEO PI-R professional manual. Odessa, FL: Psychological Assessment Resources.

Cattell, R. B., Eber, H. W., & Tatsuoka, M. M. (1970). *The handbook for the Sixteen Personality Factor Questionnaire*. Champaign, IL: Institute for Personality and Ability Testing.

Chan, D., & Schmitt, N. (1997). Video-based versus chapter and pencil method of assessment in situational judgment tests: Subgroup differences in test performance and face validity perceptions. *The Journal of Applied Psychology*, *82*(1), 143–159. doi:10.1037/0021-9010.82.1.143 PMID:9119795

Conway, J. M., Jako, R. A., & Goodman, D. F. (1995). A meta-analysis of interrater and internal consistency reliability of selection interviews. *The Journal of Applied Psychology*, *80*(5), 565–579. doi:10.1037/0021-9010.80.5.565

Costa, P.T. &McCrae, R.R. (1985). Comparison of EPI and psychoticism scales with measures of the five-factor model of personality. *Personality and Individual Differences*, 6(5), 587- 597.

Costa, P. T. Jr, & McCrae, R. R. (1992). Four ways five factors are basic. *Personality and Individual Differences*, *13*(6), 653–665. doi:10.1016/0191-8869(92)90236-I

Eder, R. W., & Ferris, G. R. (Eds.). (1989). *The employment interview: Theory, research, and practice*. Newbury Park, CA: Sage Publishing.

Gael, S. (Ed.). (1988). *The job analysis handbook for business, industry, and government* (Vol. 1 & 2). New York: Wiley.

Gatewood, R. D., Feild, H. S., & Barrick, M. (2008). *Human resource selection*. Mason, Ohio: Thompson South-Western.

Gaugler, B. B., Rosenthal, D. B., Thornton, G. C. III, & Bentson, C. (1987). Meta-analyses of assessment center validity. *The Journal of Applied Psychology*, *72*(3), 493–511. doi:10.1037/0021-9010.72.3.493

Gerald, M., Deary, I. J., & Whiteman, M. C. (1998). *Personality traits* (2nd ed.). Cambridge: Cambridge University Press.

Goldberg, L. R., Grenier, R. M., Guion, L. B., Sechrest, L. B., & Wing, H. (1991). *Questions used in the prediction of trustworthiness in pre-employment selection decisions: An APA Task Force Report.* Washington, D.C.: American Psychological Association.

Gottredson, L. S. (Ed.). (1982). The g factor in employment. *Journal of Vocational Behavior, 29*(3).

Hogan, J. (1991). Physical abilities. In M.D. Dunnette& L.M. Hough (Eds.), Handbook of industrial and organizational psychology (Vol. 2, pp. 753-831). Palo Alto, CA: Consulting Psychologists Press.

Hough, L. M. (1984). Development and evaluation of the accomplishment record methods of selecting and promoting professionals. *The Journal of Applied Psychology, 69*(1), 135–146. doi:10.1037/0021-9010.69.1.135

Hough, L. M., Keyes, M. A., & Dunnette, M. D. (1983). An evaluation of three alternative selection measures. *Personnel Psychology, 36*(2), 261–276. doi:10.1111/j.1744-6570.1983.tb01436.x

Howard, A. (1983). Work samples and simulations in competency evaluation. *Professional Psychology, Research and Practice, 14*(6), 780–796. doi:10.1037/0735-7028.14.6.780

Howard, O.J., & Howard, K.J.M. (1998). An introduction to five- factor model for personality for Human resource professionals.

Huffcutt, A. I., & Arthur, W. Jr. (1994). Hunter and Hunter (1984) revisited: Interview validity for entry-level jobs. *The Journal of Applied Psychology, 79*(2), 184–190. doi:10.1037/0021-9010.79.2.184

Huffcutt, A. I., & Woehr, D. J. (1999). Further analysis of employment interview validity: A quantitative evaluation of interviewer-related structuring methods. *Journal of Organizational Behavior, 20*(4), 549–560. doi:10.1002/(SICI)1099-1379(199907)20:4<549::AID-JOB921>3.0.CO;2-Q

Hunter, J. (1986). Cognitive ability, cognitive aptitudes, job knowledge, and job performance. *Journal of Vocational Behavior, 29*(3), 340–362. doi:10.1016/0001-8791(86)90013-8

Hunter, J., & Hunter, R. F. (1984). Validity and utility of alternative predictors of job performance. *Psychological Bulletin, 96*(1), 72–98. doi:10.1037/0033-2909.96.1.72

Judge, T. A., Higgins, C. A., & Cable, D. M. (2000). The employment interview: A review of recent research and recommendations for future research. *Human Resource Management Review*, *10*(4), 383–406. doi:10.1016/S1053-4822(00)00033-4

Lee, C. C., & Sirch, M. L. (1994). Counseling in an enlightened society: Values for a new millennium. *Counseling and Values*, *38*(2), 90–97. doi:10.1002/j.2161-007X.1994.tb00826.x

Macan, T. (2009). The employment interview: A review of current studies and directions for future research. *Human Resource Management Review*, *19*(3), 203–218. doi:10.1016/j.hrmr.2009.03.006

Marchionini, G. (1991). Technological trends and implications: Toward the new millennium. *School Library Media Annual*, *9*, 182–187.

McCrae, R. R., & Costa, P. T. J. R. (1980). Openness to experience and ego level in Loevingers sentence completion test: Dispositional contribution to developmental models of personality. *Journal of Personality and Social Psychology*, *39*(6), 1179–1190. doi:10.1037/h0077727

Motowidlo, S. J., Dunnette, M. D., & Carter, G. (1990). An alternative selection procedure: A low fidelity simulation. *The Journal of Applied Psychology*, *75*(6), 640–647. doi:10.1037/0021-9010.75.6.640

Ones, D. S., Viswesvaran, C., & Schmidt, F. L. (1993). Comprehensive meta-analysis of integrity test validities: Findings and implications for personnel selection and theories of job performance.[monograph]. *The Journal of Applied Psychology*, *78*(4), 531–537. doi:10.1037/0021-9010.78.4.679

Ployhart, R. E. (2006). Staffing in the 21st Century: New Challengesand Strategic Opportunities. *Journal of Management*, *32*(6), 868–897. doi:10.1177/0149206306293625

Ployhart, R. E., Schneider, B., & Schmitt, N. (2006). *Staffing organizations: Contemporary practice and theory* (3rd ed.). Mahwah, NJ: Lawrence Erlbaum.

Posthuma, R. A., Morgeson, F. P., & Campion, M. A. (2002). Beyond employment interview validity: A comprehensive narrative review of recent research and trends over time. *Personnel Psychology*, *55*(1), 1–81. doi:10.1111/j.1744-6570.2002.tb00103.x

Pulakos, E. D. (2005). *Selection Assessment Methods: a guide to implementing formal assessments to build high-quality workforce*. SHRM Foundation.

Raymark, M. J., Schmit, M. J., & Guion, R. M. (1997). Identifying potentially useful personality constructs for employee selection. *Personnel Psychology*, *50*(3), 723–736. doi:10.1111/j.1744-6570.1997.tb00712.x

Ree, M. J., Earles, J. A., & Teachout, M. S. (1994). Predicting job performance: Not much more than g. *The Journal of Applied Psychology*, *79*(4), 518–524. doi:10.1037/0021-9010.79.4.518

Resnick, H. (1994). Future of electronic technology in human service practice and education. Special topic: Electronic tools for social work practice and education: II. *Computers in Human Services*, *11*, 379–384.

Ross, A. (1992). Personality psychology (theories and processes) (trans. Siavash-jamalfar). Besat publication institute.

Sackett, P. R., & Wanek, J. E. (1996). New developments in the use of measures of honesty, integrity, conscientiousness, dependability, trustworthiness, and reliability for personnel selection. *Personnel Psychology*, *49*(4), 787–829. doi:10.1111/j.1744-6570.1996.tb02450.x

Salgado, J. F. (1999). Personnel selection methods. In C. L. Cooper & I. Robertson (Eds.), *International Review of Industrial and Organizational Psychology* (pp. 1–54). London, UK: Wiley.

Schuler, H. (2001). *International Encyclopedia of the Social & Behavioral Sciences*. Oxford: Pergamon Press.

Schuler, H., Farr, J. L., & Smith, M. (Eds.). (1993). *Personnel Selection and Assessment: Individual and Organizational Perspectives*. Hillsdale, NJ: Erlbaum.

Stagner, R. (1957). Some problems in contemporary industrial psychology. *Bulletin of the Menninger Clinic*, *21*, 238–247. PMID:13472270

Stokes, G. S. (1999). Introduction to special issue: The next one hundred years of biodata. *Human Resource Management Review*, *9*(2), 111–116. doi:10.1016/S1053-4822(99)00014-5

Taft, R. (1948). Use of the group situation observation method in the selection of trainee executives. *The Journal of Applied Psychology*, *32*(6), 587–594. doi:10.1037/h0061967

Tett, R. P., Jackson, D. N., & Rothstein, M. (1991). Personality measures as predictors of job performance: A meta-analytic review. *Personnel Psychology*, *44*(4), 703–742. doi:10.1111/j.1744-6570.1991.tb00696.x

Thornton, G. C. III. (1992). *Assessment centers in human resources management*. Addison-Wesley.

Thornton, G. C. III, & Byham, W. C. (1982). *Assessment centers and managerial performance*. New York: Academic Press.

Thornton, G. C. III, & Gibbons, A. M. (2009). Validity of assessment centers for personnel selection. *Human Resource Management Review*, *19*(3), 169–187. doi:10.1016/j.hrmr.2009.02.002

Wagschal, P. H. (1994). Hey Bucky, can you spare a paradigm? reflections on synergistic education. *NASSP Bulletin*, *78*(560), 51–61. doi:10.1177/019263659407856008

Weichmann, D., Schmitt, N., & Harvey, V. S. (2001). Incremental validity of situational judgment tests. *The Journal of Applied Psychology*, *86*(3), 410–417. doi:10.1037/0021-9010.86.3.410 PMID:11419801

Whetzel, D. L., & McDaniel, M. A. (2009). Situational judgment tests: An overview of current research. *Human Resource Management Review*, *19*(3), 188–202. doi:10.1016/j.hrmr.2009.03.007

Zalaquett, C. P., Michael T. Turner (1997), Succeeding in the 21st Century: A qualitative analysis. *TCA Journal*, *25*(1), 331 – 340.

ENDNOTES

1 Knowledge, Skill, Ability (KSA)

2 A structured communication technique, originally developed as a systematic, interactive forecasting method which relies on a panel of experts (Linstone & Turoff, 1975)

Chapter 6
Impact of Macroergonomic Organizational Elements on the Performance of Manufacturing Systems

Arturo Realyvásquez
Technological Institute of Tijuana, Mexico

Jorge Luis García-Alcaraz
Autonomous University of Ciudad Juarez, Mexico

Aidé Aracely Maldonado-Macías
Autonomous University of Ciudad Juarez, Mexico

Julio Blanco-Fernández
University of La Rioja, Spain

Jorge Limon-Romero
Autonomous University of Baja California, Mexico

ABSTRACT

This chapter analyzes the effects of macroergonomic compatibility of organizational elements on the performance of manufacturing systems in terms of Clients, Manufacturing Process, and Organizational Performance. As methods, a macroergonomic compatibility questionnaire is developed, statistically validated, and administered to middle and senior managers of manufacturing companies. Also, a hypothetical causal model is proposed and tested to find relationships among the constructs by using a Structural Equation Modeling. Direct, indirect, and total

DOI: 10.4018/978-1-5225-1974-4.ch006

effects are determined, and results show that macroergonomic organizational elements have significant direct effects among themselves. Likewise, it is found that Organizational Culture and Organizational Communication have significant direct effects over Clients and significant indirect effects over Manufacturing Process and Organizational Performance. Finally, the Manufacturing Process has significant direct effects over Clients and Organizational Performance, while Clients have a significant direct effect over the Organizational Performance.

INTRODUCTION

In today's highly competitive markets, effectiveness of manufacturing systems should be partly guided by an analysis of the macroergonomic factors that include human resources, the company's organization, technology implemented, tasks performed, and the physical environment in which employees perform their tasks. The model called Systems Engineering Initiative for Patient Safety (SEIPS) (Carayon et al., 2006, 2014) offers this macroergonomic approach to analyze manufacturing systems. It is a human factors systems approach successfully applied to healthcare research and practice (Carayon et al., 2014). Moreover, although it was initially developed for health work systems, it can be adapted and applied to various manufacturing systems thanks to its flexibility (Carayon et al., 2014; Chui, Mott, & Maxwell, 2012). Therefore, SEIPS serves as a useful framework to study work changes and the design of these work systems. Likewise, it provides a holistic view of a work system, instead of focusing on a single factor.

In this chapter the SEIPS model provides the macroergonomic organization factor and its elements of *Organizational Culture*, *Organizational Communication*, and *Teamwork* for the design of work systems. It also includes the dependent variables of *Clients*, *Manufacturing Process*, and *Organizational Performance*, which can be impacted by the macroergonomic organizational elements.

On the one hand, Macroergonomics is the study of work systems, on the other, macroergonomic compatibility exists when a work system supports an appropriate interaction between the personnel and the technological subsystems, including the relationship of the work system with external environment characteristics (Lange-Morales, Röbig, & Bruder, 2011). This compatibility of interaction should be considered at all levels, including the physical, perceptual, cognitive, emotional, social, organizational and environmental levels (Karwowski, 2000). Therefore, several authors have addressed ergonomic compatibility either at a micro- or macro-level (Haro & Kleiner, 2008; Karwowski, 2000, 2001; Lange-Morales et al., 2011; Maldonado, García, Alvarado, & Balderrama, 2013). However, it seems that so far no work has yet developed a method to measure macroergonomic compatibility.

Macroergonomic compatibility can provide benefits for manufacturing systems, such as *Manufacturing Process* optimization, reduction of occupational risks, and improvement of life quality at work (Beevis & Slade, 2003; García-Acosta & Lange-Morales, 2008; Hendrick, 1998, 2003; MacLeod, 2003). These benefits can be achieved by applying macroergonomic practices to the factors of a work system (García-Acosta & Lange-Morales, 2008; Haro & Kleiner, 2008). For this reason, the present chapter analyzes the impact of the organization factor in manufacturing systems from a macroergonomic perspective. In the SEIPS model the organization factor includes all the organizational elements under which tasks are performed in a company (Carayon et al., 2006, 2014; Chui et al., 2012).

This study proposes a structural equation model (SEM) and tests nine hypotheses concerning the effects of organizational elements on manufacturing systems. Elements with the highest positive impact over the benefits of manufacturing systems, or over themselves, will be considered the macroergonomic elements with the major impact on macroergonomic compatibility of manufacturing systems. It is hoped that results will be useful as a basis for manufacturing systems to develop strategies to increase their competitiveness.

The remainder of this chapter is hence organized as follows: section 2 introduces the literature review that deals with the effects of macroergonomic organizational elements over benefits obtained by companies. Section 3 shows the methodology proposed to test the hypotheses and presents the proposed hypothetical model. Similarly, section 4 discusses the final results, while section 5 provides conclusion and recommendations for future research. Finally, in section 6 authors acknowledge the participants and institutions involved in this project.

LITERATURE REVIEW

Macroergonomic Organizational Elements in Literature

A literature review is carried out to explore the presence of macroergonomic factors and organizational elements from the SEIPS model in the context of ergonomically compatible work system designs. Figure 1 shows how often macroergonomic factors are addressed in the literature review. For instance, it can be observed that organizational elements of the SEIPS model are the most frequently mentioned by literature. More specifically, *Teamwork*, and *Coordination, collaboration, and communication* appear as the most studied. Figure 2 depicts the frequency at which organizational elements from the SEIPS model are addressed in the literature review.

Impact of Macroergonomic Organizational Elements

Figure 1. Frequency of macroergonomic factors in literature

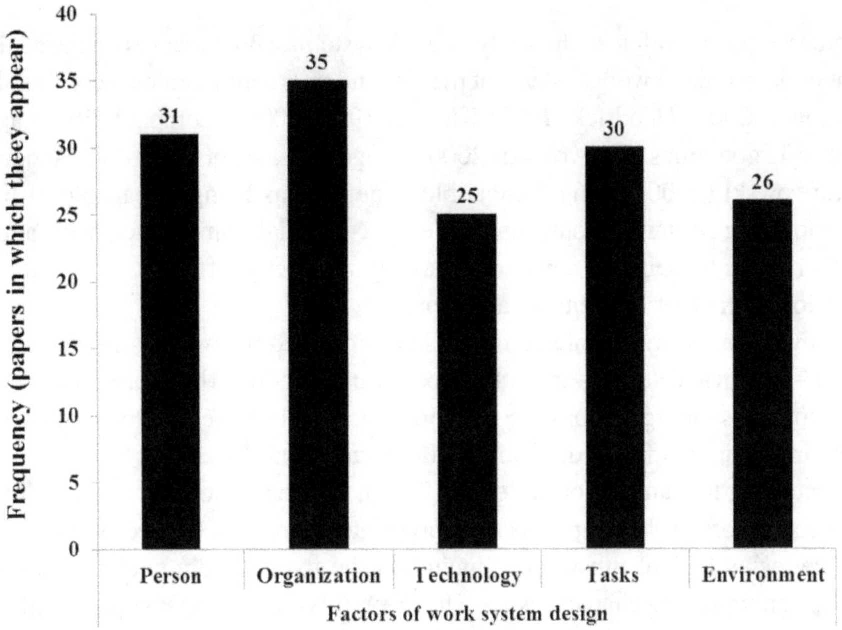

Figure 2. Frequency of organizational elements in literature

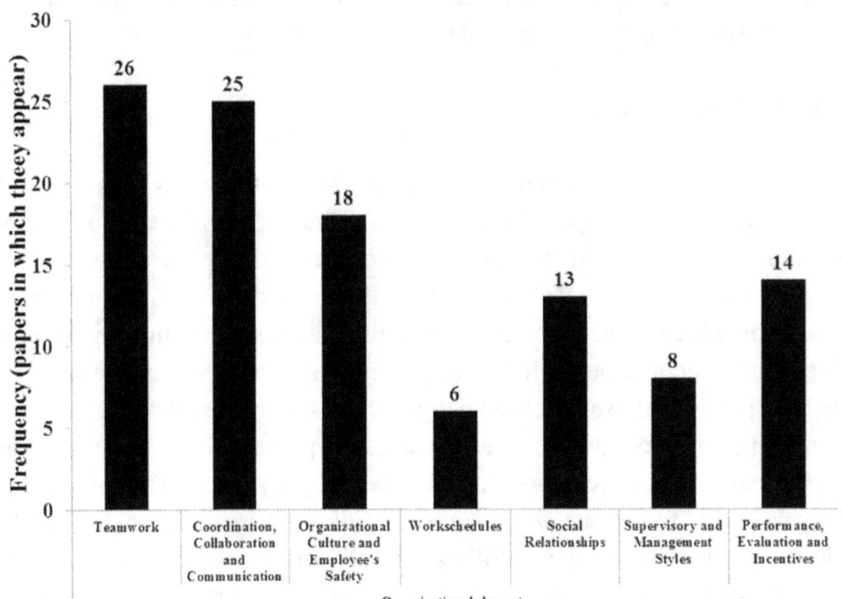

Macroergonomic Compatibility

Macroergonomics refers to the study of work systems, and it focuses on the achievement of harmonized work systems at macro- and microergonomic levels (Hendrick & Kleiner, 2000; Hendrick, 1987; Kleiner, 1998, 2006). Compatibility is a keyword in Ergonomics (Karwowski, 2000; Lange-Morales et al., 2011). According to Karwowski (2000), being compatible is defined as being 1) capable of living or performing in harmonious, agreeable, or congenial combination with another or others, and as being 2) capable of having an orderly, efficient integration and operation with other elements in a system.

In this chapter ergonomic compatibility is defined by evoking the concepts of human–system and human–artifact compatibility introduced by (Karwowski, 2001). Such concepts emerged from the need for a comprehensive treatment of compatibility in the human factor discipline (Maldonado et al., 2013).

According to Lange-Morales et al. (2011), macroergonomic compatibility exists when a work system supports an appropriate interaction between the personnel and the technological subsystems, including the work system´s relationship with external environment characteristics. However, this concept is still open to different personal interpretations in most of the Ergonomics literature. Therefore, in order to overcome the uncertainty and blurriness of this notion, Karwowski (2000) proposed the symvatology, a corroborative science to Ergonomics, in order to develop a universal measure of compatibility for designing, testing, and evaluating ergonomic systems (Karwowski, 2000; Lange-Morales et al., 2011).

Organizational Culture

Organizational Culture is defined as ‘‘the tacit, unwritten rules for getting along in the organization; the ropes that a newcomer must learn in order to become an accepted member" (Schein, 2006). Also, Schein (2010) proposed a three-level framework of *Organizational Culture.* The author provided a qualitative description of this factor, which ranged from visible public manifestations that people can see and feel to the unconscious beliefs and perceptions. The intermediate level of the framework included those espoused beliefs, values, norms, and rules.

Some other authors have proposed and tested hypotheses regarding the impact of *Organizational Culture* over other aspects of the company. For instance, Aktaş, Çiçek, and Kıyak (2011) found that *Organizational Culture* was related to organizational efficiency, and Nes, Solberg, and Silkoset, (2007) discovered that cultural distance between exporting and importing nations affected the communication between the exporter and its local foreign middleman. Likewise, Webber (2011) found that managers who felt identified with their own organization had significantly more loyal

Clients in comparison with those who did not feel identified. Similarly, MacIntosh and Doherty (2007) examined the external perception of *Organizational Culture* in one fitness company in Canada. Their results showed that the perception of *Clients* concerning the *Organizational Culture* of the company was significantly associated to their satisfaction and desire to continue exercising in that place.

Organizational Communication

Organizational Communication refers to the way businesses, companies, enterprises, firms, institutions, or groups communicate in their internal environment with their own members or employees and how organizations as a whole communicate with people (*Clients*, vendors, suppliers, stakeholders, media, general public, etc.) from outside their environment (Borca & Baesu, 2014). However, although this definition mostly addresses the exchange of knowledge and opinions in the workplace, *Organizational Communication* can also be credited for creating a positive atmosphere for employees (Borca & Baesu, 2014). Consequently, it has an interdisciplinary function, which integrates elements of human resources management, communication, and marketing (Verčič, Verčič, & Sriramesh, 2012).

Borca & Baesu (2014) offered an overview of *Organizational Communication* based on definitions, and they concluded that effective *Organizational Communication* had an impact on *Organizational Performance* and competitiveness, and it improved the corporation's image. Moreover, *Organizational Communication*, along with *Organizational Culture*, has been subject of study due to its impact on other aspects of companies. For instance, le Roux (2014) found that effective communication skills improved *Organizational Performance*. Similarly, Mitrofan and Bulborea (2013) carried out a study in a bank as a means to highlight the influence of communication exerts on structuring interpersonal relationships. Authors concluded that an efficient communication at the workplace was important for the success or failure of organizations, and that tight relationships of interpersonal communication between subordinates and managers could improve the activity within the organization at a long term.

In addition, it has been pointed out that *Organizational Communication* either encourages or hinders horizontal, upward, or downward communication among employees (Nordin, Sivapalan, Bhattacharyya, Ahmad, & Abdullah, 2014). For instance, in companies with defensive atmospheres, employees tend to avoid communicating their needs and may be low motivated. Similarly, Jaradat and Sy (2012) stated that since companies, business, or agencies that provided a product or service had to interact and operate with other people through communication, this influenced every aspect of the business. Hence, it has been demonstrated that communication plays a critical role in the decision-making process, and that businesses need it for their success. Moreover, companies with excellent communication patterns tend to motivate their employees to work cooperatively and more efficiently (Luthans, 2005).

Teamwork

Today, *Teamwork* is an essential component for companies to achieve high reliability (Baker, Day, & Salas, 2006). There are several definitions of *Teamwork* in literature; for instance, Beaubien and Baker (2014) defined *Teamwork* as the behaviors that facilitate team member interaction such as leadership, orientation, mutual performance monitoring, back up behaviors, and adaptability. However, another notion arose from the definition of team. A team consists of two or more individuals who have specific roles, perform interdependent tasks, are adaptable, and share a common goal (Baker et al., 2006). Therefore, in order to effectively perform together, team members must have specific knowledge, skills and attitudes, such as monitoring other´s performance, monitoring their teammate's tasks and responsibilities, and having a positive disposition towards working as a team. Such interrelated knowledge, skills, and attitudes comprise a *Teamwork* and facilitate a coordinated and adaptive performance (Baker et al., 2006; Baker, Gustafson, Beaubien, Salas, & Barach, 2003). Finally, Salas, Cooke and Rosen (2008) defined *Teamwork* as the interdependent components of the performance required to effectively coordinate the performance of multiple individuals.

Several studies have found a relationship between *Teamwork* and the *Organizational Performance* and success of companies. Baker et al. (2006) found that *Teamwork* played a critical role in the processes of gaining reliability. Also, Hoegl and Gemuenden (2001) stated that it was crucial to the success of innovative projects. Similarly, other authors, such as Tohidi and Tarokh (2006) proposed a model to determine the *Teamwork*'s performance based on the size of the team. They concluded that a certain size could yield the most cost efficient solution to increase team performance. Finally, Davidson and Tay (2003) argued that *Teamwork* influenced the competitiveness of companies, while Tabassi, Ramli and Bakar (2012), and Yang, Huang and Wu (2011) found that companies that improved their *Teamwork* activities also improved their *Organizational Performance* and faced fewer problems with their projects.

Manufacturing Process

According to Scheer and Nüttgens (2000), the term "business process" is universally defined, and it is described as a relevant procedure to add value to a company. Hence, every business process consists of a number of events. First of all, there are the initial requirements of the *Clients*, which lead to an order acceptance by the manufacturer's sales department. Then, the sales department relays information to the purchasing department in order to supply bought-in parts. Finally, the production department plans and executes the work order. Thus, the first event of the process are customer requirements, and the last event is the completion of the product in the manufacturing department.

Manufacturing Processes have an important impact on both the internal and external aspects of manufacturing systems. According to Lagacé and Bourgault (2003), a reliable and continuously improving *Manufacturing Process* is a key condition to ensure long-term sustainability. Similarly, Colledani et al. (2004) stated that manufacturing systems operated their processes in order to meet the required rates of high quality products and increase loyalty of *Clients*, while minimizing the use of resources.

Clients

The Lobbying Disclosure Act (LDA) defines a client as "any person or entity that employs or retains another person for financial or another compensation to conduct lobbying activities on behalf of that person or entity." (Luneburg & Susman, 2005). Today, *Clients* are the core of the *Manufacturing Process* of all industries; their needs must be met by developing correct product designs, solutions, and final high-quality products. This in turn enhances employees' performance (Oyedele & Tham, 2007). Therefore, it can be said that *Clients* play an important role in the general improvement of companies.

In fact, they are the most significant driver for competitiveness. For instance, Maister (2012) and Oyedele and Tham (2007) pointed out that the better the understanding of *Clients*, the greater the competitive advantage of a company. Similarly, Oyedele and Tham (2007) carried out a study where *Clients* assessed the performance of architects in a construction company in Nigeria. They found that by means of these assessments, architects could improve their skills and responsibilities as well as the process of construction. Similarly, Ahmad, Jaapar, Adnan, Bari and Rashid (2012) argued that when construction *Clients* lacked of knowledge and experience, the projects might fail to produce quality buildings. Finally, Etgar (2007) pointed out that the involvement of *Clients* could help improve the *Manufacturing Process* at different stages (assembly, packing, distribution and logistics, etc.) in manufacturing systems.

Organizational Performance

Performance has been a difficult concept to both define and measure (Dess & Robinson, 1984; Lee & Choi, 2003). However, most definitions of *Organizational*

Performance focus on the extent to which a company achieves its objectives (Lee & Choi, 2003). Therefore, *Organizational Performance* can be measured by four categories: 1) financial measure, 2) intellectual capital, 3) balanced scorecard, and 4) tangible and intangible benefits (Lee & Choi, 2003). In addition, some of the other indicators used to measure it are client satisfaction (Sharma & Fisher, 1997; Tracey, Vonderembse, & Lim, 1999), market share (Li, 2000; Sharma & Fisher, 1997), market share growth (Tracey et al., 1999), overall competitiveness (Lau, 2002), sales volume (Li, 2000), sales growth (Lau, 2002; Sharma & Fisher, 1997), overall plant success (Gordon & Sohal, 2001), and productivity (Ross, 2002; Sharma & Fisher, 1997).

Organizational Performance has also been related to other organizational aspects. For instance, Sirikrai and Tang (2006) affirmed that it could be considered a competitiveness indicator for manufacturing systems, while Adhikari and Regmī (2001) argued that excellence in *Organizational Performance* was caused by competition among enterprises. Also, Dess and Robinson (1984) found that there was a positive correlation between global *Organizational Performance* and the growth in sales and return on assets in manufacturing systems (Carayon & Smith, 2000).

METHODOLOGY

The methodology followed in this research comprises the following stages: 1) questionnaire development, 2) administration of the questionnaire, and 3) statistical analysis of information. These stages are explained in the following subsections.

Macroergonomic Compatibility Questionnaire (MCQ) Development

A questionnaire is developed in order to measure macroergonomic compatibility of manufacturing systems. The survey contains four sections: 1) demographic data, 2) employees' perception regarding the application of specific macroergonomic practices in their workplaces, 3) frequency at which companies apply such macroergonomic practices, and 4) the extent to which specific benefits are gained from the application of these macroergonomic practices.

On the one hand, the first section demands general information about every company as well as their manufacturing systems. On the other hand, the second section includes 92 items addressing ergonomic practices on five factors (humans, organization, tools and technology applied, tasks performed, and environment) of work systems. Also, the third section is composed of 22 items assessing the frequency at which companies apply macroergonomic practices. Finally, the fourth section comprises 18 questions addressing the benefits enjoyed by such companies.

Table 1 shows the items for every construct analyzed, as well as the references consulted for them. That is, an extensive literature review was conducted in order to determine both the macroergonomic organizational elements (independent latent variables) that impact on the compatibility of manufacturing systems and the benefits obtained from these elements (dependent latent variables). For instance, according to Dul and Neuman (2009), several benefits can be obtained when Macroergonomics is applied to the strategies of companies, including product design and innovation, *Manufacturing Process* innovation, marketing, and communication. Also, Ismail (2007) stated the principles and benefits of lean manufacturing implementation in manufacturing industries. These principles and benefits were considered to establish dependent latent variables in the model of this research, since they mainly emphasize on defects, productivity, and variety of products.

Table 1. References for MCQ items

Item	References
Teamwork	
Employees perform teamwork tasks.	(Humphrey, Nahrgang, & Morgeson, 2007; Morgeson & Humphrey, 2003, 2006; Nakata et al., 2004)
An employee receives support by the coworkers when he/she has questions or difficulties in performing a task.	(Humphrey et al., 2007; Morgeson & Humphrey, 2003; Nakata et al., 2004; Preziosi, 1980)
Employees give ideas, opinions, and suggestions that are respected.	(Axtell et al., 2000; Detert & Burris, 2007)
Employees receive feedback on their performance from coworkers and managers.	(Humphrey et al., 2007; Morgeson & Humphrey, 2003, 2006; Nakata et al., 2004; Preziosi, 1980)
Organizational Communication	
Employees strive to maintain coordination, collaboration and communication.	(Nakata et al., 2004)
Any employee can communicate with another one regardless of their hierarchical levels.	(Nakata et al., 2004)
Employees receive feedback in order to keep an effective organizational communication.	(Nakata et al., 2004; Preziosi, 1980)
The company uses different forms of communication (visual, oral, auditory, written).	(Nakata et al., 2004; Preziosi, 1980)
Organizational Culture	
The company's principles and values are clearly transmitted to employees from the beginning.	(Preziosi, 1980)

Item	References
Employees know the objectives of the company.	(Preziosi, 1980)
Employees strive to keep the company's principles and values.	(Preziosi, 1980)
This company is in favor of change.	(Preziosi, 1980)
Work division helps achieve the company's goals.	(Giunta, Nifo, & Scalera, 2012)
A safety culture is promoted among the employees.	(Choudhry, Fang, & Mohamed, 2007)
Safety inspections are performed regularly.	(Preziosi, 1980)
Work Schedules	
Work schedules are comfortable and stable.	(Anderson, Binder, & Krause, 2003; Lipscomb, Trinkoff, Geiger-Brown, & Brady, 2002; Trinkoff, Le, Geiger-Brown, & Lipscomb, 2007)
Employees are early informed about the tasks/ activities that would demand extra time.	(Åkerstedt, Fredlund, Gillberg, & Jansson, 2002; Beckers et al., 2004)
Employees decide how to program their tasks.	(Morgeson & Humphrey, 2003, 2006)
Social Relationships	
Employees can keep respectful social relationships inside the company.	(Morgeson & Humphrey, 2003, 2006; Nakata et al., 2004; Preziosi, 1980)
Employees interact with people from outside the organization (clients, providers, etc.).	(Humphrey et al., 2007; Morgeson & Humphrey, 2003, 2006)
Employees keep cordial professional relationships among them.	(Humphrey et al., 2007; Preziosi, 1980)
Employees share information among them.	(Humphrey et al., 2007; Preziosi, 1980)
Employees can gather to talk about any topic.	(Humphrey et al., 2007; Morgeson & Humphrey, 2003, 2006; Preziosi, 1980)
Supervisors are concerned about the welfare of all employees.	(Morgeson & Humphrey, 2003, 2006; Nakata et al., 2004; Preziosi, 1980)
Supervisory and Management Styles	
Tasks are supervised and monitored in order to improve the performance of employees.	(Morgeson & Humphrey, 2003, 2006; Nakata et al., 2004)
Managers provide continuous attention and support to employees.	(Morgeson & Humphrey, 2003, 2006; Nakata et al., 2004)
Clients	
Needs and expectations from clients are considered.	(Wilson & Carayon, 2014)
Clients are satisfied with the products they receive.	(Webber, 2011)
Clients are faithful to the company.	(Piegorsch et al., 2006; Webber, 2011)
The number of clients has increased with time.	(Piegorsch et al., 2006)
Manufacturing Process	
The number of complaints from clients is very low.	(Chen, Shie, & Yu, 2012)
The number of defects is very low.	(Ismail, 2007)
Inventory levels are low.	(Ismail, 2007)

Item	References
Productivity has increased with time.	(Ismail, 2007)
Organizational Performance	
Productivity has improved.	(Ismail, 2007)
The number of employees has increased.	(Ramlall, 2003)
The variety of products has increased.	(Ismail, 2007)
The business has improved.	(Caroly, Coutarel, Landry, & Mary-Cheray, 2010)

All organizational elements included in the SEIPS model are considered to develop the questionnaire. That is, questions about these elements from the literature and form the constructs are formed. Then, the items obtained are adapted to a macroergonomic approach. For the dependent variables, items are formulated based on the principles and benefits of lean manufacturing for *Clients*, *Manufacturing Process,* and *Organizational Performance* of the manufacturing systems. The search is conducted in databases such as Science Direct, Google Scholar, PubMed/MEDLINE, Taylor & Francis, Wiley Online Library, and SAGE. Once the questionnaire is drafted, judges proceed to validate it. They also make suggestions that help improve readability and comprehension of concepts and questions. Then, the questionnaire must be answered through a Likert scale including values from 1 to 5 with the following statements:

1. Totally disagree,
2. Disagree,
3. Neutral,
4. Agree,
5. Totally agree.

This scale is adopted since it has been effectively employed in other recent and similar studies by (García, Maldonado, Alvarado, & Rivera, 2014; Glover, Farris, Van Aken, & Doolen, 2011; Likert, 1932). Finally, an observations section is included so that participants add their comments regarding any specific macroergonomic situation from their manufacturing systems.

As previously stated, this chapter analyzes the effects of organizational elements over manufacturing systems. Therefore, benefits obtained for manufacturing systems include *Clients*' needs, their loyalty, and satisfaction. Similarly, the *Manufacturing Process* is analyzed by means of its productivity, inventory, and the number of defects and *Clients*' complaints. Finally, *Organizational Performance* is assessed by considering the number of employees, the variety of products offered, and the trend in the number of *Clients*.

Administration of the MCQ

The questionnaire is administered to manufacturing systems in Ciudad Juárez, Chihuahua, Mexico. Surveyed people are middle and senior managers, since they usually have a more complete perspective when offering opinions on macroergonomic organizational aspects, their deficiencies, and the opportunities for improvement. The questionnaire is thus administered by following these two steps:

Step 1. Contact the Management Department of the Company: The National Institute of Statistics, Geography and Informatics (INEGI) and the Maquiladoras Association, A. C. (AMAC) Index facilitate the registration list that includes those large industrial companies that are settled in the region. Large organizations are selected, since they cater for the main employment source in Chihuahua, Mexico. Then, one manager from every company is contacted by e-mail or telephone and he/she is introduced to the project, its objectives, and the benefits that it might bring to the company. At this stage managers are already familiar with the questionnaire.

Step 2. Establish an Appointment for Questionnaire Application: Managers from industrial companies contact their colleagues and inform them about the project. A meeting is then scheduled, specifying time and place to administer the questionnaire.

Statistical Analysis of Data

Statistical analysis of data comprises the questionnaire statistical validation and the analysis of relationships among the constructs. This analysis is carried out to test hypotheses regarding the impact of organizational elements on *Clients*, *Manufacturing Process*, and *Organizational Performance* of manufacturing systems.

MCQ Statistical Validation

Input data is made using SPSS® software (Coakes & Steed, 2009). A proper data screening is performed by substituting outliers and missing values by the median, since data are presented in an ordinal scale (Likert scale) (García et al., 2014; Hair, Black, Babin, & Anderson, 2010; Hair, Black, Babin, Anderson, & Tatham, 2006). Afterwards, the questionnaire is statistically validated. That is, the Cronbach's alpha index is determined for every dimension, considering a minimum cutoff value of 0.7 (Cronbach, 1951; García et al., 2014). During the validation process, all variables having a corrected item-total correlation lower than 0.3 are removed only if the Cronbach's alpha index remains higher than 0.7. Similarly, the average variance extracted (AVE) and cross-factor loadings are used as indicators of discriminant validity and convergent validity, respectively. For the latter, a minimum value of 0.5 is recommended for every item, not to mention that the *p* value must be significant (García et al., 2014; Ned, 2015). Also, the index of variance inflation factors (VIFs) is considered to detect collinearity between latent variables. The VIF value ought to be lower than 3.3 in every dimension or latent variable (Cenfetelli & Bassellier, 2009; García et al., 2014; Petter, Straub, & Rai, 2007). Moreover, the coefficient of Q-squared is used as a nonparametric measure of predictive validity, since data are presented in an ordinal scale. Validity is achieved when the Q-squared value is higher than zero (García et al., 2014; Ned, 2015).

Development of the Hypothetical Causal Model

Once the final variables are determined and based on the literature review, the following hypotheses are proposed:

H_1: Macroergonomic compatibility of *Organizational Culture* in manufacturing systems has a direct and positive effect on macroergonomic compatibility of *Organizational Communication.*

H_2: Macroergonomic compatibility of *Organizational Culture* in manufacturing systems has a direct and positive effect on *Clients*' loyalty.

H_3: Macroergonomic Compatibility of *Organizational Communication* in manufacturing systems has a direct and positive effect on the macroergonomic compatibility of *Teamwork.*

H_4: Macroergonomic compatibility of *Organizational Communication* in manufacturing systems has a direct and positive effect on *Clients*' loyalty.

H_5: Macroergonomic compatibility of *Organizational Communication* in manufacturing systems has a direct and positive effect on *Organizational Performance.*

H_6: Macroergonomic compatibility of *Teamwork* in manufacturing systems has a direct and positive effect on *Manufacturing Process.*

H_7: Macroergonomic compatibility of *Teamwork* in manufacturing systems has a direct and positive effect on *Organizational Performance.*

H_8: The *Manufacturing Process* of manufacturing systems has a direct and positive effect on *Clients*' loyalty.

H_9: The *Manufacturing Process* of manufacturing systems has a direct and positive effect on their *Organizational Performance.*

H_{10}: *Clients*' loyalty has a direct and positive effect on the *Organizational Performance* of manufacturing systems.

Figure 3 presents the hypothetical causal model including all the above mentioned hypotheses.

Analysis of The Structural Model

Structural equation modeling (SEM) is the best technique to perform an analysis when the model includes several independent and dependent variables (García et al., 2014). Therefore, once the final variables are defined for every construct, all relationships among the constructs are analyzed and tested. This analysis is performed with WarpPLS5® software. This piece of software does not use a conventional "linear" regression algorithm to analyze the data but a sophisticated series of algorithms based on partial least squares (PLS), which enables the use of non-linear models (Ned, 2015; Realyvásquez, Maldonado-Macías, García-Alcaraz, Cortés-Robles, & Blanco-Fernández, 2016). However, it must be mentioned that fit indexes of chi-square, the root mean squared error of approximation (RMSEA), and the goodness of fit index (GFI) are not provided, since they are irrelevant (Realyvásquez et al., 2016). Moreover, WarpPLS5® is widely recommended for small-sized samples (García et al., 2014; Ned, 2015), as it is the case of this research.

Fit indices employed to evaluate the model are: average path coefficient (APC), average R-squared (ARS), and average variance inflation factor (AVIF). The general criterion for APC and ARS to accept or reject a relationship is a p value lower than 0.05, since this inference analysis is carried out with a 95% of confidence level.

Figure 3. Proposed hypothetical model

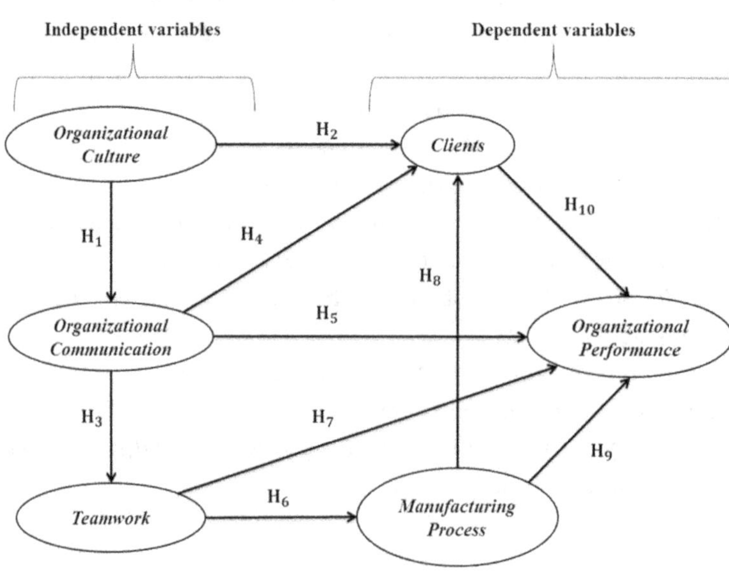

Thus, relationships with $p < 0.05$ are considered significant; otherwise, they are insignificant and removed. Once all significant relationships are determined, the loadings are analyzed. If a variable has a higher loading in a different dimension to the one where it belongs, it is then removed. Also, the null hypothesis to be tested is that APC and ARS equal zero, while the alternative hypothesis states that APC and ARS are different from zero. Finally, the maximum acceptable value for AVIF is set to 5 (García et al., 2014; Ned, 2015).

To validate hypotheses from Figure 3, direct effects between latent variables are considered. These effects indicate a direct relation between two given dimensions (García et al., 2014). However, indirect effects are also measured, and they concern effects between two latent variables but which are given through other dimensions or latent variables. They can be due to two or more segments from the model (García et al., 2014). Finally, the sum of direct and indirect effects between latent variables results in the total effects. Hypotheses H_a and H_b represented by equations (1) and (2), respectively, validate every kind of effect on each parameter:

$$H_a: \beta = 0 \qquad (1)$$

$$H_b: \beta \neq 0 \qquad (2)$$

RESULTS AND DISCUSSION

Statistical Analysis of Data

This section addresses the results from the statistical analyses, which include the statistical validation of the questionnaire and the structural model analysis. Table 2 shows values from the model fit and quality indices. Values significant at a 99.9% of confidence imply that although the analyses were performed at a confidence interval of 95%, they turned out to be more reliable, since their p values are less than 0.001 (Realyvásquez et al., 2016). This is the case of values from APC and ARS.

Moreover, the Tenenhaus goodness of fit (GoF) shows a value of 0.479, which means that the model as a whole has large and overall explanatory power and predictive quality (Ned, 2015). Similarly, values in the AVIF and the average full collinearity variance inflation factor (AFVIF) are both lower than the cutoff value – that is, 3.3. Likewise, the values from the Sympson's paradox ratio (SPR), the R-squared contribution ratio (RSCR), and the statistical suppression ratio (SSR) all equal 1. Therefore, all the paths in the model are in the correct direction, and the predic-

Table 2. Values of model fit and quality indices

Index	Value
APC	0.412*
ARS	0.380*
AVIF	1.527
AFVIF	1.911
GoF	0.479
SPR	1.000
RSCR	1.000
SSR	1.000
NLBCDR	1.000

*Significant at 99.9% of confidence level

tors have a positive contribution to R-squared. In addition, it can be concluded that the model is free from statistical suppression instances. Finally, since the value of nonlinear bivariate causality direction ratio (NLBCDR) equals 1, it is demonstrated that the hypothesized directions of causality are correct.

Table 3 introduces results from the validation processes for the latent variables analyzed (macroergonomic organizational elements and their benefits). According to the values obtained, it can be concluded that the survey has positive reliability. The value of the Cronbach's alpha index is higher than 0.7 in all analyzed dimensions. In addition, AVE values are greater than the minimum cutoff value (0.5) in all dimensions, which demonstrates that the survey has both discriminant and convergent validity.

Table 3. MCQ validation

Index	*Organizational Culture*	*Organizational Communication*	*Teamwork*	*Manufacturing Process*	*Clients*	*Organizational Performance*
R-squared		0.418	0.403	0.265	0.428	0.389
Composite reliability	0.864	0.825	0.858	0.855	0.883	0.873
Cronbach's alpha	0.810	0.713	0.779	0.770	0.822	0.782
AVE	0.514	0.545	0.601	0.600	0.654	0.697
Full VIF	1.825	2.171	2.062	1.672	2.133	1.601
Q-squared		0.422	0.406	0.270	0.433	0.392

Likewise, all R-squared values from dependent latent variables are acceptable, since they are higher than 0.02. As for the VIF index, even though there is a lack of consensus regarding its maximum value, if it is lower than 3.3, as in this case, it can be stated that there are no problems of collinearity between latent variables. Finally, Q-squared values for all dependent variables are higher than zero, and the nonparametric predictive validity is acceptable.

Effects Among Variables

This research analyzes the direct effects between latent variables as well as their indirect effects. The sum of direct and indirect effects between these latent variables is called total effects, and they are also discussed in this section.

Direct Effects

Direct effects quantify an influence that is not mediated by other latent variables in the SEM. More accurately, they measure the sensitivity to changes from a dependent latent variable caused by an independent latent variable, while all other variables in the analysis remain fixed (Pearl, 2001). Figure 4 introduces the significant and insignificant direct effects. The values expressed in β are standardized dependence measurement values. Similarly, *p* values are significance values from the hypothesis

Figure 4. Significant and insignificant direct effects between latent variables

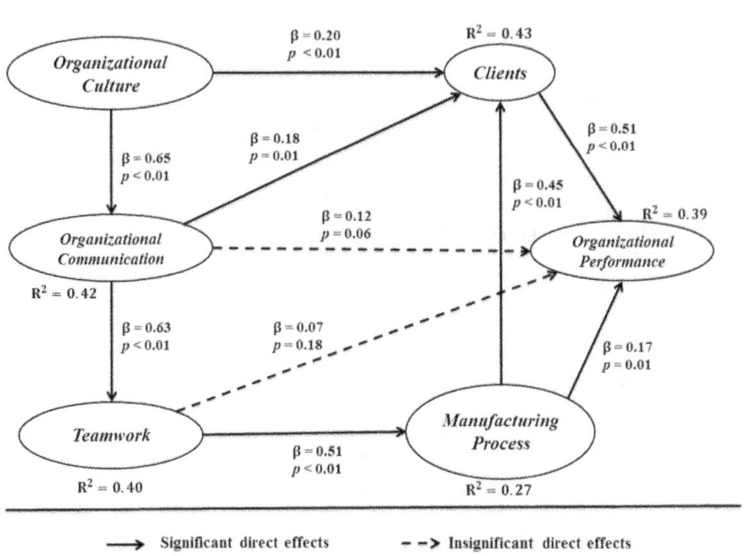

testing. Note that only two *p* values are higher than 0.05, which means that such relationships between latent variables are not significant.

Figure 4 also introduces the R-squared values, which stand for the contribution of independent (exogenous) variables to dependent (endogenous) variables. Such values also reflect the percentage of variance explained in every dependent latent variable (Ned, 2015). For instance, *Organizational Communication* has a R-squared value of 0.42. This implies that the variable is 42% explained by *Organizational Culture*. Likewise, *Teamwork* is 40% explained by *Organizational Communication,* while *Manufacturing Process* is 27% explained by *Teamwork*. However, note that certain latent variables may depend on two or many others. *Clients*, for example, is 43% explained by three latent variables in total. It is 8.4% explained through *Organizational Communication*, 8.9% through *Organizational Culture*, and 25.7% through *Manufacturing Process*. Also, *Organizational Performance* is 39% explained by *Clients* (31%) and *Manufacturing Process* (8%).

As for β values, which are dependency measures, similar interpretations can be provided for all the relationships in the model. For instance, it is observed that the relationship between *Clients* and *Organizational Performance* has $\beta = 0.51$. This implies that when the first dimension increases its standard deviation by one unit, the standard deviation of the second dimension also increases by 0.51 units. Note that the independent latent variable with the highest β value is *Organizational Culture*, while the dependent variable with the highest β value is *Clients*. This shows the indirect and direct effects that both variables can have on manufacturing systems. Therefore, based on values from Figure 4, relations (3-7) can be stated:

$$\textit{Organizational Communication} = 0.65 \times \textit{Organizational Culture} + \textit{Error} \tag{3}$$

$$\textit{Teamwork} = 0.63 \times \textit{Organizational Communication} + \textit{Error} \tag{4}$$

$$\textit{Manufacturing Process} = 0.51 \times \textit{Teamwork} + \textit{Error} \tag{5}$$

$$\textit{Clients} = 0.20 \times \textit{Organizational Culture} + 0.18 \times \textit{Organizational Communication} + 0.45 \times \textit{Manufacturing Process} + \textit{Error} \tag{6}$$

$$\textit{Organizational Performance} = 0.51 \times \textit{Clients} + 0.17 \times \textit{Manufacturing Process} + \textit{Error} \tag{7}$$

Indirect Effects

Indirect effects occur between two dimensions through other dimensions, and they can be represented by several segments in the structural model (García et al., 2014). Table 4 shows the sum of indirect effects between latent variables analyzed. All indirect effects are 99.9% significant based on the *p* values. For example, it can be observed that *Organizational Communication* has an indirect effect of 0.221 on *Organizational Performance*, which means that when the first dimension increases its standard deviation by one unit, the second goes up by 0.221 units, too. All indirect effects can be interpreted similarly. Also, note that all macroergonomic organizational elements in general have significant indirect effects over the other variables. This can be considered as a basis for the eventual design of ergonomic work systems.

Total Effects

As previously stated, total effects are the sum of direct and indirect effects (García et al., 2014). Table 5 shows the total effects between the dimensions analyzed. All of them are also 99.9% significant, which demonstrates that macroergonomic organizational elements truly and directly impact on all other subsequent dimensions. In addition, since *Organizational Performance* is the final dependent variable, all other variables have certain effect on it, either direct or indirect.

Total effects can be interpreted in the same form as indirect effects. For instance, the relationship between *Clients* and *Organizational Performance* has a total effect of 0.510, which means that when the first latent variable increases its standard deviation by one unit, the standard deviation of the second increases by 0.510 units. Finally, note that *Clients* shows the highest total effect over latent variable *Organizational Performance* of manufacturing systems. This highlights the importance of *Clients* for the competitiveness of businesses.

Table 4. Sum of indirect effects between latent variables

To	From			
	Organizational Culture	***Organizational Communication***	***Teamwork***	***Manufacturing Process***
Teamwork	0.410*			
Clients	0.210*	0.146*	0.231*	
Manufacturing Process	0.211*	0.327*		
Organizational Performance	0.242*	0.221*	0.206*	0.229*

*Significant at 99.9%

Table 5. Total effects between latent variables

To	From				
	Organizational Culture	**Organizational Communication**	**Teamwork**	**Manufacturing Process**	**Clients**
Organizational Communication	0.646*				
Teamwork	0.410*	0.634*			
Manufacturing Process	0.211*	0.327*	0.515*		
Clients	0.405*	0.324*	0.231*	0.448*	
Organizational Performance	0.242*	0.221*	0.206*	0.399*	0.510*

*Significant at 99.9%

CONCLUSION AND RECOMMENDATIONS

Conclusions Concerning the Hypotheses

According to the results from Figure 4, Table 4, and Table 5, it can be stated that macroergonomic compatibility of organizational elements positively influences on the competitiveness of manufacturing systems. Macroergonomic compatibility of *Organizational Culture* and *Organizational Communication* has an effect – direct, indirect, or total – on all other variables. This information can be considered a foundation to design compatible manufacturing systems. Moreover, *Clients* as a dependent variable play a critical role for the *Organizational Performance* of manufacturing systems. Therefore, it can be concluded that:

- Macroergonomic compatibility of *Organizational Culture* is required for macroergonomic compatibility of *Organizational Communication* in manufacturing systems.
- Macroergonomic compatibility of *Organizational Communication* is required for macroergonomic compatibility of *Teamwork* in manufacturing systems.
- Macroergonomic compatibility of *Teamwork* is required for a reliable *Manufacturing Process.*
- Macroergonomic compatibility of *Organizational Culture*, *Organizational Communication,* and a reliable *Manufacturing Process* are required for satisfied *Clients* in manufacturing systems.
- Satisfied *Clients* and a reliable *Manufacturing Process* are required for the *Organizational Performance* of manufacturing systems.

Since it is concluded that macroergonomic organizational elements help measure and improve macroergonomic compatibility of manufacturing systems, the following conclusions can be derived from the hypotheses stated in section 3:

H_1: There is enough statistical evidence to state that *Organizational Culture* has a direct, positive impact on *Organizational Communication*, since when the first latent variable or dimension increases its standard deviation by one unit, the second one increases by 0.65 units, too.

H_2: There is enough statistical evidence to state that *Organizational Culture* has a direct and positive impact on *Clients*. When the first latent variable or dimension increases its standard deviation in one unit, the second one also increases by 0.20 units.

H_3: There is enough statistical evidence to state that *Organizational Communication* has a direct and positive impact on *Teamwork*, since when the first latent variable or dimension increases its standard deviation in one unit, the second one rises 0.63 units.

H_4: There is enough statistical evidence to state that *Organizational Communication* has a direct and positive impact on *Clients*, because once the first latent variable or dimension increases its standard deviation in one unit, the second one also increases 0.18 units.

H_5: There is not enough statistical evidence to declare that *Organizational Communication* has a direct and positive impact on *Organizational Performance*.

H_6: There is enough statistical evidence to assert that *Teamwork* has a direct and positive impact on *Manufacturing Process*, since when the first latent variable or dimension increases its standard deviation in one unit, the second one also increases 0.51 units.

H_7: There is not enough statistical evidence to state that *Teamwork* has a direct and positive impact on *Organizational Performance*.

H_8: There is enough statistical evidence to state that *Manufacturing Process* has a direct and positive impact on *Clients*, because when the former increases its standard deviation in one unit, the latter also increases 0.45 units.

H_9: There is enough statistical evidence to state that *Manufacturing Process* has a direct and positive impact on *Organizational Performance*, since when the first latent variable or dimension increases its standard deviation in one unit, the second one goes up 0.17 units.

H_{10}: There is enough statistical evidence to state that *Clients* have a direct and positive impact on *Organizational Performance*, because when the first latent variable or dimension increases its standard deviation in one unit, the second one grows 0.51 units.

It is observed that hypotheses H_5 and H_7 were statistically rejected. The reason for such unfavorable results may be due to the fact that most respondents reported little or no feedback given on their *Teamwork* abilities and *Organizational Communication* performance. In addition, they reported a poor communication between operators and senior managers, which in turn may have prevented direct effects from *Teamwork* and *Organizational Communication* on *Organizational Performance.*

Industrial Implications

Results support the argument that designing work systems for manufacturing centers and all kinds of other companies must consider macroergonomic factors, since they can bring several long-term benefits. Also, it is demonstrated that philosophies pursuing clients' satisfaction by involving them into the manufacturing processes and meeting their needs can provide competitive advantages for companies. Finally, authors also recommend businesses being open to changes and applying ergonomic practices at both micro- and macroergonomic levels.

FUTURE RESEARCH

Future studies could expand macroergonomic research and practices to other fields of knowledge, such as education, construction, or health, among others. It is also advised to continue searching for a universal matrix to measure ergonomic compatibility of systems and artifacts, since the development of an effective index to evaluate manufacturing systems from an ergonomic perspective may help companies make decisions to improve quality of life at work, organizational culture, and organizational communication. Moreover, they will succeed in meeting clients' needs, which is the most significant variable that affects the organizational performance of manufacturing systems.

ACKNOWLEDGMENT

Authors wish to acknowledge all the reviewers who helped improve this chapter through their valuable suggestions and comments. Authors also want to thank the employees of the four surveyed manufacturing systems for being part of this research, and La Rioja University and Autonomous University of Ciudad Juarez for their valuable contributions of knowledge.

REFERENCES

Adhikari, R., & Regmī, D. (2001). *Anti-competitive practices in Nepal.* Discussion Paper. Kathmandu: South Asia Watch on Trade, Economic & Environment (SAWTEE) and Consumer Unity & Trust Society-Centre for International Trade, Economics & Environment (CUTS-CITEE).

Ahmad, N., Jaapar, A., Adnan, H., Bari, N. A. A., & Rashid, R. A. (2012). Important Qualities of Design Teams in Managing Clients Brief and their Impact on Delivering Quality Buildings. *Procedia: Social and Behavioral Sciences*, *35*, 728–738. doi:10.1016/j.sbspro.2012.02.143

Åkerstedt, T., Fredlund, P., Gillberg, M., & Jansson, B. (2002). Work load and work hours in relation to disturbed sleep and fatigue in a large representative sample. *Journal of Psychosomatic Research*, *53*(1), 585–588. doi:10.1016/S0022-3999(02)00447-6 PMID:12127175

Aktaş, E., Çiçek, I., & Kıyak, M. (2011). The Effect Of Organizational Culture On Organizational Efficiency: The Moderating Role Of Organizational Environment and CEO Values. *Procedia: Social and Behavioral Sciences*, *24*, 1560–1573. doi:10.1016/j.sbspro.2011.09.092

Anderson, D., Binder, M., & Krause, K. (2003). The Motherhood Wage Penalty Revisited: Experience, Heterogeneity, Work Effort, and Work-Schedule Flexibility. *ILR Review*, *56*(2), 273–294. doi:10.1177/001979390305600204

Axtell, C. M., Holman, D. J., Unsworth, K. L., Wall, T. D., Waterson, P. E., & Harrington, E. (2000). Shopfloor innovation: Facilitating the suggestion and implementation of ideas. *Journal of Occupational and Organizational Psychology*, *73*(3), 265–285. doi:10.1348/096317900167029

Baker, D. P., Day, R., & Salas, E. (2006). Teamwork as an essential component of high-reliability organizations. *Health Services Research*, *41*(4 Pt 2), 1576–1598. doi:10.1111/j.1475-6773.2006.00566.x PMID:16898980

Baker, D. P., Gustafson, S., Beaubien, J., Salas, E., & Barach, P. (2003). Medical teamwork and patient safety: The evidence-based relation. Washington, DC: American Institutes for Research. Retrieved from http://citeseerx.ist.psu.edu/viewdoc/download?doi=10.1.1.136.9246&rep=rep1&type=pdf

Beaubien, J. M., & Baker, D. P. (2004). The use of simulation for training teamwork skills in health care: how low can you go? *Quality and Safety in Health Care*, *13*(suppl 1), i51–i56. http://doi.org/<ALIGNMENT.qj></ALIGNMENT>10.1136/qshc.2004.009845

Beckers, D. G. J., van der Linden, D., Smulders, P. G. W., Kompier, M. A. J., van Veldhoven, M., & van Yperen, N. (2004). Working Overtime Hours: Relations with Fatigue, Work Motivation, and the Quality of Work. *Journal of Occupational and Environmental Medicine*, *46*(12), 1282–1289. PMID:15591981

Beevis, D., & Slade, I. M. (2003). Ergonomicscosts and benefits. *Applied Ergonomics*, *34*(5), 413–418. doi:10.1016/S0003-6870(03)00061-9 PMID:12963327

Borca, C., & Baesu, V. (2014). A Possible Managerial Approach for Internal Organizational Communication Characterization. *Procedia: Social and Behavioral Sciences*, *124*, 496–503. doi:10.1016/j.sbspro.2014.02.512

Carayon, P., Hundt, A., Karsh, B. T., Gurses, A. P., Alvarado, C. J., Smith, M., & Flatley Brennan, P. (2006). Work system design for patient safety: the SEIPS model. *Quality & Safety in Health Care, 15*(suppl 1), i50–8. http://doi.org/<ALIGNMENT.qj></ALIGNMENT>10.1136/qshc.2005.015842

Carayon, P., & Smith, M. J. (2000). Work organization and ergonomics. *Applied Ergonomics*, *31*(6), 649–662. doi:10.1016/S0003-6870(00)00040-5 PMID:11132049

Carayon, P., Wetterneck, T. B., Rivera-Rodriguez, A. J., Hundt, A., Hoonakker, P., Holden, R., & Gurses, A. P. (2014). Human factors systems approach to healthcare quality and patient safety. *Applied Ergonomics*, *45*(1), 14–25. doi:10.1016/j.apergo.2013.04.023 PMID:23845724

Caroly, S., Coutarel, F., Landry, A., & Mary-Cheray, I. (2010). Sustainable MSD prevention: Management for continuous improvement between prevention and production. Ergonomic intervention in two assembly line companies. *Applied Ergonomics*, *41*(4), 591–599. doi:10.1016/j.apergo.2009.12.016 PMID:20097327

Cenfetelli, R. T., & Bassellier, G. (2009). Interpretation of Formative Measurement in Information Systems Research. *Management Information Systems Quarterly*, *33*(4), 689–707.

Chen, C.-K., Shie, A.-J., & Yu, C.-H. (2012). A customer-oriented organisational diagnostic model based on data mining of customer-complaint databases. *Expert Systems with Applications*, *39*(1), 786–792. doi:10.1016/j.eswa.2011.07.074

Choudhry, R. M., Fang, D., & Mohamed, S. (2007). The nature of safety culture: A survey of the state-of-the-art. *Safety Science*, *45*(10), 993–1012. doi:10.1016/j.ssci.2006.09.003

Chui, M. A., Mott, D. A., & Maxwell, L. (2012). A qualitative assessment of a community pharmacy cognitive pharmaceutical services program, using a work system approach. *Research in Social & Administrative Pharmacy : RSAP*, *8*(3), 206–216. doi:10.1016/j.sapharm.2011.06.001 PMID:21824822

Coakes, S. J., & Steed, L. (2009). SPSS: Analysis Without Anguish Using Spss Version 14.0 for Windows. New York: John Wiley & Sons, Inc. Retrieved from http://dl.acm.org/citation.cfm?id=1804538

Colledani, M., Tolio, T., Fischer, A., Iung, B., Lanza, G., Schmitt, R., & Váncza, J. (2014). Design and management of manufacturing systems for production quality. *CIRP Annals - Manufacturing Technology, 63*(2), 773–796. http://doi.org/<ALIGNMENT.qj></ALIGNMENT>10.1016/j.cirp.2014.05.002

Cronbach, L. J. (1951). Coefficient alpha and the internal structure of tests. *Psychometrika, 16*(3), 297–334. doi:10.1007/BF02310555

Davidson, E. J., & Tay, A. S. M. (2003). Studying teamwork in global IT support. In *36th Annual Hawaii International Conference on System Sciences, 2003. Proceedings of the* (p. 10 pp.). IEEE. http://doi.org/ doi:<ALIGNMENT.qj></ALIGNMENT>10.1109/HICSS.2003.1173663

Dess, G. G., & Robinson, R. B. (1984). Measuring organizational performance in the absence of objective measures: The case of the privately-held firm and conglomerate business unit. *Strategic Management Journal*, *5*(3), 265–273. doi:10.1002/smj.4250050306

Detert, J. R., & Burris, E. R. (2007). Leadership behavior and employee voice: Is the door really open? *Academy of Management Journal*, *50*(4), 869–884. doi:10.5465/AMJ.2007.26279183

Dul, J., & Neumann, W. P. (2009). Ergonomics contributions to company strategies. *Applied Ergonomics*, *40*(4), 745–752. doi:10.1016/j.apergo.2008.07.001 PMID:18775532

Etgar, M. (2007). A descriptive model of the consumer co-production process. *Journal of the Academy of Marketing Science*, *36*(1), 97–108. doi:10.1007/s11747-007-0061-1

García, J. L., Maldonado, A. A., Alvarado, A., & Rivera, D. G. (2014). Human critical success factors for kaizen and its impacts in industrial performance. *International Journal of Advanced Manufacturing Technology*, *70*(9-12), 2187–2198. doi:10.1007/s00170-013-5445-4

García-Acosta, G., & Lange-Morales, K. (2008). Macroergonomic study of food sector company distribution centres. *Applied Ergonomics*, *39*(4), 439–449. doi:10.1016/j.apergo.2008.02.004 PMID:18377868

Giunta, A., Nifo, A., & Scalera, D. (2012). Subcontracting in Italian Industry: Labour Division, Firm Growth and the North–South Divide. *Regional Studies*, *46*(8), 1067–1083. doi:10.1080/00343404.2011.552492

Glover, W. J., Farris, J. A., Van Aken, E. M., & Doolen, T. L. (2011). Critical success factors for the sustainability of Kaizen event human resource outcomes: An empirical study. *International Journal of Production Economics*, *132*(2), 197–213. doi:10.1016/j.ijpe.2011.04.005

Gordon, J., & Sohal, A. S. (2001). Assessing manufacturing plant competitiveness - An empirical field study. *International Journal of Operations & Production Management*, *21*(1/2), 233–253. doi:10.1108/01443570110358567

Hair, J. F., Black, W. C., Babin, B. J., & Anderson, R. (2010). *Multivariate Data Analysis: A Global Perspective* (7th ed.). Englewood Cliffs, NJ: Prentice Hall.

Hair, J. F., Black, W. C., Babin, B. J., Anderson, R., & Tatham, R. L. (2006). *Multivariate data analysis (6th ed.)*. Upper Saddle River, NJ: Pearson Prentice Hall.

Haro, E., & Kleiner, B. M. (2008). Macroergonomics as an organizing process for systems safety. *Applied Ergonomics*, *39*(4), 450–458. doi:10.1016/j.apergo.2008.02.018 PMID:18407244

Hendrick, H. W. (1987). Human Factors in Organizational Design and Management. In A. H. Peter (Ed.), *Advances in Psychology* (pp. 347–398). Amsterdam: North-Holland Publishing Co. doi:10.1016/S0166-4115(08)62313-4

Hendrick, H. W. (1998). Measuring the economic benefits of ergonomics. In P. A. Scott, R. S. Bridger, & J. Charteris (Eds.), *Global ergonomics*. Amsterdam: Elsevier. doi:10.1016/B978-008043334-9/50170-0

Hendrick, H. W. (2003). Determining the cost-benefits of ergonomics projects and factors that lead to their success. *Applied Ergonomics*, *34*(5), 419–427. doi:10.1016/S0003-6870(03)00062-0 PMID:12963328

Hendrick, H. W., & Kleiner, B. M. (2000). *Macroergonomics: An Introduction to Work System Design* (Vol. 2). Santa Monica, CA: Human Factors and Ergonomics Society.

Hoegl, M., & Gemuenden, H. G. (2001). Teamwork Quality and the Success of Innovative Projects: A Theoretical Concept and Empirical Evidence. *Organization Science*, *12*(4), 435–449. doi:10.1287/orsc.12.4.435.10635

Humphrey, S. E., Nahrgang, J. D., & Morgeson, F. P. (2007). Integrating motivational, social, and contextual work design features: A meta-analytic summary and theoretical extension of the work design literature. *The Journal of Applied Psychology*, *92*(5), 1332–1356. doi:10.1037/0021-9010.92.5.1332 PMID:17845089

Ismail, R. B. (2007). *Implementations Problems in Lean Manufacturing: A study in manufacturing industries*. Malaysia Technical University of Melaka.

Jaradat, Y. M., & Sy, M. V. U. (2012). Organizational Communication Practices of Toc Glycol Company Ltd., Thailand. *Procedia: Social and Behavioral Sciences*, *40*, 122–127. doi:10.1016/j.sbspro.2012.03.170

Karwowski, W. (2000). Symvatology: The science of an artifact-human compatibility. *Theoretical Issues in Ergonomics Science*, *1*(1), 76–91. doi:10.1080/146392200308480

Karwowski, W. (2001). International Encyclopedia of Ergonomics and Human Factors (W. Karwowski, Ed.; 3rd ed.). New York: Taylor & Francis. Retrieved from https://books.google.com/books?hl=es&lr=&id=KeoMi5Y8Q_gC&pgis=1

Kleiner, B. M. (1998). Macroergonomic analysis of formalization in a dynamic work system. *Applied Ergonomics*, *29*(4), 255–259. doi:10.1016/S0003-6870(97)00034-3 PMID:9701539

Kleiner, B. M. (2006). Macroergonomics: Analysis and design of work systems. *Applied Ergonomics*, *37*(1), 81–89. doi:10.1016/j.apergo.2005.07.006 PMID:16226212

Lagacé, D., & Bourgault, M. (2003). Linking manufacturing improvement programs to the competitive priorities of Canadian SMEs. *Technovation*, *23*(8), 705–715. doi:10.1016/S0166-4972(02)00026-3

Lange-Morales, K., Röbig, S., & Bruder, R. (2011). Compatibility in multiplicity: towards a complex understanding of medical devices use. In S. Albolino, S. Bagnara, T. Bellandi, J. Llaneza, G. Rosal, & R. Tartaglia (Eds.), *Healthcare systems ergonomics and patient safety* (1st ed.; pp. 334–337). Taylor & Francis Group.

Lau, R. S. M. (2002). Competitive factors and their relative importance in the US electronics and computer industries. *International Journal of Operations & Production Management*, *22*(1), 125–135. doi:10.1108/01443570210412105 le Roux, T. (2014). The description of South African corporate communication practitioners that contribute to organisational performance. *Public Relations Review*, *40*(2), 193–215. doi:10.1016/j.pubrev.2013.11.008

Lee, H., & Choi, B. (2003). Knowledge Management Enablers, Processes, and Organizational Performance: An Integrative View and Empirical Examination. *Journal of Management Information Systems*, *20*(1). Retrieved from http://www.tandfonline.com/doi/abs/10.1080/07421222.2003.11045756

Li, L. X. (2000). An analysis of sources of competitiveness and performance of Chinese manufacturers. *International Journal of Operations & Production Management*, *20*(3), 299–315. doi:10.1108/01443570010294307

Likert, R. (1932). A technique for the measurement of attitudes. *Archives de Psychologie*, 22.

Lipscomb, J. A., Trinkoff, A. M., Geiger-Brown, J., & Brady, B. (2002). Work-schedule characteristics and reported musculoskeletal disorders of registered nurses. *Scandinavian Journal of Work, Environment & Health*, *28*(6), 394–401. doi:10.5271/sjweh.691 PMID:12539799

Luneburg, W. V., & Susman, T. M. (2005). *The Lobbying Manual: A Complete Guide to Federal Law Governing Lawyers and Lobbyists* (W. V. Luneburg & T. M. Susman, Eds.; 3th ed.). Chicago, IL: ABA Publishing. Retrieved from https://books.google.com/books?hl=es&lr=&id=DhL_4k4X5lEC&pgis=1

Luthans, F. (2005). *Organizational Behavior* (10th ed.). Boston: McGraw-Hill.

MacIntosh, E., & Doherty, A. (2007). Extending the Scope of Organisational Culture: The External Perception of an Internal Phenomenon. *Sport Management Review*, *10*(1), 45–64. doi:10.1016/S1441-3523(07)70003-7

MacLeod, I. S. (2003). Real-world effectiveness of Ergonomic methods. *Applied Ergonomics*, *34*(5), 465–477. doi:10.1016/S0003-6870(03)00066-8 PMID:12963332

Maister, D. H. (2012). *Managing The Professional Service Firm*. New York: Simon & Schuster UK. Retrieved from https://books.google.com/books?hl=es&lr=&id=2VpMK-uoJVMC&pgis=1

Maldonado, A., García, J. L., Alvarado, A., & Balderrama, C. O. (2013). A hierarchical fuzzy axiomatic design methodology for ergonomic compatibility evaluation of advanced manufacturing technology. *International Journal of Advanced Manufacturing Technology*, *66*(1-4), 171–186. doi:10.1007/s00170-012-4316-8

Mitrofan, N., & Bulborea, A. (2013). The Role of Organizational Communication in Structuring Interpersonal Relationships. *Procedia: Social and Behavioral Sciences*, *76*, 511–515. doi:10.1016/j.sbspro.2013.04.155

Morgeson, F. P., & Humphrey, S. E. (2003). *Work Design Questionnaire (WDQ): Developing and validating a comprehensive measure of work design.* Paper presented at the 62nd Annual Meeting of the Academy of Management, Seattle, WA.

Morgeson, F. P., & Humphrey, S. E. (2006). The Work Design Questionnaire (WDQ): Developing and validating a comprehensive measure for assessing job design and the nature of work. *The Journal of Applied Psychology*, *91*(6), 1321–1339. doi:10.1037/0021-9010.91.6.1321 PMID:17100487

Nakata, A., Haratani, T., Takahashi, M., Kawakami, N., Arito, H., Kobayashi, F., & Araki, S. (2004). Job stress, social support, and prevalence of insomnia in a population of Japanese daytime workers. *Social Science & Medicine (1982)*, *59*(8), 1719–30. http://doi.org/<ALIGNMENT.qj></ALIGNMENT>10.1016/j.socscimed.2004.02.002

Ned, K. (2015). WarpPLS© 5.0 user manual. Laredo, TX: ScriptWarp SystemsTM.

Nes, E. B., Solberg, C. A., & Silkoset, R. (2007). The impact of national culture and communication on exporter–distributor relations and on export performance. *International Business Review*, *16*(4), 405–424. doi:10.1016/j.ibusrev.2007.01.008

Nordin, S. M., Sivapalan, S., Bhattacharyya, E., Ahmad, H. H. W. F. W., & Abdullah, A. (2014). Organizational Communication Climate and Conflict Management: Communications Management in an Oil and Gas Company. *Procedia: Social and Behavioral Sciences*, *109*(8), 1046–1058. doi:10.1016/j.sbspro.2013.12.587

Oyedele, L. O., & Tham, K. W. (2007). Clients assessment of architects performance in building delivery process: Evidence from Nigeria. *Building and Environment*, *42*(5), 2090–2099. doi:10.1016/j.buildenv.2005.06.030

Pearl, J. (2001). Direct and indirect effects. In Proceedings of the Seventeenth conference on Uncertainty in artificial intelligence (pp. 411–420). San Francisco, CA: Morgan Kaufmann Publishers Inc.; Retrieved from http://dl.acm.org/citation.cfm?id=2074022.2074073

Petter, S., Straub, D., & Rai, A. (2007). Specifying Formative Constructs in Information Systems Research. *Management Information Systems Quarterly*, *31*(4), 623–656. Retrieved from http://www.jstor.org/stable/25148814

Piegorsch, K. M., Watkins, K. W., Piegorsch, W. W., Reininger, B., Corwin, S. J., & Valois, R. F. (2006). Ergonomic decision-making: A conceptual framework for experienced practitioners from backgrounds in industrial engineering and physical therapy. *Applied Ergonomics, 37*(5), 587–598. doi:10.1016/j.apergo.2005.11.002 PMID:16386700

Preziosi, R. C. (1980). Organisational Diagnosis Questionnaire (ODQ). In University Associates (Ed.), The 1980 annual handbook for group facilitators (pp. 112–120). Academic Press.

Ramlall, S. (2003). Organizational Application Managing Employee Retention as a Strategy for Increasing Organizational Competitiveness. *Applied H.R.M. Research, 8*(2), 63–72.

Realyvásquez, A., Maldonado-Macías, A., García-Alcaraz, J., Cortés-Robles, G., & Blanco-Fernández, J. (2016). Structural Model for the Effects of Environmental Elements on the Psychological Characteristics and Performance of the Employees of Manufacturing Systems. *International Journal of Environmental Research and Public Health, 13*(1), 1–21. doi:10.3390/ijerph13010104 PMID:26742054

Ross, A. (2002). A multi-dimensional empirical exploration of technology investment, coordination and firm performance. *International Journal of Physical Distribution & Logistics Management, 32*(7), 591–609. doi:10.1108/09600030210442603

Salas, E., Cooke, N. J., & Rosen, M. A. (2008). On Teams, Teamwork, and Team Performance: Discoveries and Developments. *Human Factors: The Journal of the Human Factors and Ergonomics Society, 50*(3), 540–547. doi:10.1518/001872008X288457 PMID:18689065

Scheer, A.-W., & Nüttgens, M. (2000). ARIS Architecture and Reference Models for Business Process Management. In W. van der Aalst, J. Desel, & A. Oberweis (Eds.), *Business Process Management* (Vol. 1806, pp. 376–389). Berlin: Springer Berlin Heidelberg; doi:10.1007/3-540-45594-9_24

Schein, E. H. (2006). Organizational Culture and Leadership (3rd ed.). John Wiley & Sons, Inc. Retrieved from https://books.google.com/books?hl=es&lr=&id=xhmezDokfnYC&pgis=1

Schein, E. H. (2010). Organizational culture and leadership (4th ed.). San Francisco, CA: John Wiley & Sons, Inc. Retrieved from https://books.google.com.mx/books?id=DlGhlT34jCUC

Sharma, B., & Fisher, T. (1997). Functional strategies and competitiveness: An empirical analysis using data from Australian manufacturing. *Benchmarking for Quality Management & Technology*, *4*(4), 286–294. doi:10.1108/14635779710195122

Sirikrai, S. B., & Tang, J. C. S. (2006). Industrial competitiveness analysis: Using the analytic hierarchy process. *The Journal of High Technology Management Research*, *17*(1), 71–83. doi:10.1016/j.hitech.2006.05.005

Tabassi, A. A., Ramli, M., & Bakar, A. H. A. (2012). Effects of training and motivation practices on teamwork improvement and task efficiency: The case of construction firms. *International Journal of Project Management*, *30*(2), 213–224. doi:10.1016/j.ijproman.2011.05.009

Tohidi, H., & Tarokh, M. J. (2006). Productivity outcomes of teamwork as an effect of information technology and team size. *International Journal of Production Economics*, *103*(2), 610–615. doi:10.1016/j.ijpe.2005.12.002

Tracey, M., Vonderembse, M. A., & Lim, J.-S. (1999). Manufacturing technology and strategy formulation: Keys to enhancing competitiveness and improving performance. *Journal of Operations Management*, *17*(4), 411–428. doi:10.1016/S0272-6963(98)00045-X

Trinkoff, A. M., Le, R., Geiger-Brown, J., & Lipscomb, J. (2007). Work Schedule, Needle Use, and Needlestick Injuries Among Registered Nurses. *Infection Control and Hospital Epidemiology*, *28*(2), 156–164. doi:10.1086/510785 PMID:17265396

Verčič, A. T., Verčič, D., & Sriramesh, K. (2012). Internal communication: Definition, parameters, and the future. *Public Relations Review*, *38*(2), 223–230. doi:10.1016/j.pubrev.2011.12.019

Webber, S. S. (2011). Dual organizational identification impacting client satisfaction and word of mouth loyalty. *Journal of Business Research*, *64*(2), 119–125. doi:10.1016/j.jbusres.2010.02.005

Wilson, J. R., & Carayon, P. (2014). Systems ergonomics: Looking into the future – Editorial for special issue on systems ergonomics/human factors. *Applied Ergonomics*, *45*(1), 3–4. doi:10.1016/j.apergo.2013.08.007 PMID:23684119

Yang, L.-R., Huang, C.-F., & Wu, K.-S. (2011). The association among project managers leadership style, teamwork and project success. *International Journal of Project Management*, *29*(3), 258–267. doi:10.1016/j.ijproman.2010.03.006

KEY TERMS AND DEFINITIONS

Clients: People or companies that by means of financial resources acquire a product or service that other people or companies offer.

Direct Effects: Effects that with no intermediate variables, a latent variable (dimension) has on a dependent latent variable.

Indirect Effects: Effects that a latent variable has on other latent variable through other latent variable that works as intermediate.

Insignificant Direct Effects: Directs effects that do not have a significant influence on a dependent latent variable

Macroergonomics: Branch of ergonomics that study work systems and their design having as goal the harmonization them and their subsystems (person, organization, technology, environment, tasks) at macroergonomic and microergonomic level.

Manufacturing Process: Process that by means of technology, tools and workforce transform different materials on a specific products.

Manufacturing Systems: Work systems related to manufacturing companies which include their corresponding subsystems of person, organization, technology, environment and tasks.

Organizational Communication: Communication that occurs in a company with employees of all hierarchical levels, and also the communication that this company has with its clients.

Organizational Culture: Way of working of a company by means of which it pursues its objectives.

Organizational Performance: The performance of a company measured on the basis of the achievement of its objectives in the short and long term.

Significant Direct Effects: Directs effects that have a significant influence on a dependent latent variable.

Teamwork: Combined actions of a group of workers that share their knowledges, abilities and skills to perform specific tasks in an efficient way to achieve the goals of a company.

Chapter 7

Mann Deshi Foundation:
Model for Women Empowerment Through Human Capital Formation and Development

Minakshi Balkawade
St. Mira's College for Girls, Savitribal Phule Pune University, India

ABSTRACT

Women in India, especially in the rural areas remain a deprived lot from mainstream education, employment, and productive resources, causing their marginalisation, poverty and social exclusion. The Government of India initiated various policies and programmes for development of rural entrepreneurship, including women. Nevertheless many of these programmes bungled owing to lack of tailor-made solutions to suit a particular rural environment. Thus SHGs, were used as a conduit to identify the needs of the rural community. Further various NGOs, and other voluntary organisations forayed in through their respective rural developmental models. This chapter attempts to demonstrate efforts and underscores the progress made by one such organisation, amidst a host of challenges in creating micro-entrepreneurs - the Mann Deshi Foundation in the State of Maharashtra, launched with an intent of human capital formation and human resource development through its b-school - Udyogini, in conjunction with the Mann Deshi Mahila Sahakari Bank and the Mann Deshi Chamber of Commerce for Rural Women.

DOI: 10.4018/978-1-5225-1974-4.ch007

1. INTRODUCTION

The extent to which society gives equal protection to women is a measure of its progress
– Swami Vivekananda

A daunting task before the government is that of inequality and lack of opportunities for participation in economic activities, as India is plagued by dissection in the social set-up on the basis of class, creed, caste and above all gender. These omnipresent partitions have indeed adversely impacted the scope for promoting economic development and provision of social opportunities (Dreze and Sen, 2002). This demands a major shift from growth to development – a shift embraced by economists in the 1970s, realising the fact that 40% of the population, majorly women in developing countries had remained outside the purview of economic growth throughout the 1950s and 1960s.

Thus the need for re-defining economic development as eradication of unemployment, inequality and poverty i.e. a progressive transformation was contemplated to be the key, focus being on human resource development, especially rural people and women. Hence it was realised that if a substandard or ineffective human resource policy can entail an economic and social burden on the economy, on the other hand a scientific man-power strategy will definitely assure enhanced economic development. This led to the emergence of a new measure of economic development – Human Development Index (HDI) as a substitute to Gross National Product (GNP). Further according to (Mahbub ul Haq, 1997) "Unless societies realise that their real wealth is their people, an excessive obsession with creating material wealth can obscure the goal of enriching human life". Thus with effect from 1990 human development has been defined by the Human Development Report as "expanding and broadening choices available to the population in terms of economic, social, cultural or political, thereby enhancing their welfare" (UNDP, 1997). Thus the main theme of the "Capability Approach" as advocated by Amartya Sen and later by Nussbaum and others implies granting freedom to people to achieve their well-being in terms of their capabilities.

This freedom centred view of development is closely linked to the rousing speech of Jawaharlal Nehru on the eve of India's independence, wherein he called upon the people of India to consider "freedom as an opportunity to end poverty and ignorance and disease and inequality of opportunity" (Sarvepalli, 1983). He further states that consideration of 'inequality of opportunity' is significant as it helps the State in the initiation and implementation of welfare policies in terms of either re-allocation of assets or establishment of microfinance and microcredit services or skill development. For instance a greater understanding of the ills of gender inequity will enable changing people's attitude by leading them to inquire into the hereditary forbearance of such an issue (Dreze and Sen, 2002).

1.1. Challenges Ahead for the Indian Economy

Statistics published by the World Bank indicates that the Indian economy has achieved a sensational Gross Domestic Product (GDP) growth of $2 trillion in 2014, with its Gross National Income (GNI) per individual increasing from $1,560 in 2013 to $1,610 (approximately Rs. one lakh) per annum during 2014 and a growth rate, at 7.4 per cent in the same fiscal converting it into one of the rapidly growing economies of the world just next to China (Raghavan, 2015). However in this scenario the Indian policy makers will be faced with a challenge of making this growth realistically inclusive, which necessitates enhancing employment opportunities and intensifying the velocity of deceleration in the poverty rates (Chandrasekhar, 2011).

Thus re-distributive growth is the primary purpose of any economic policy, of which poverty alleviation and eradication is an important aim i.e. guaranteeing sharing the fruits of growth with all segments (with emphasis on gender) of the economy (Government of India Planning Commission, 2014). This is extremely important because as (Nachane, 2011) has rightly observed, if benefits of growth are concentrated towards a particular segment of the society, poverty eradication will be a distant dream, further discouraging the course of growth, leading to social pressures, thereby destabilising the political system.

1.2. Objectives of the Study

1. To realize the importance of human capital formation and development in an economy.
2. To realise the significance of social capital in the creation and development of rural women entrepreneurship.
3. To scrutinize the policies undertaken by the government towards human resource development in the economy.
4. To comprehend the significance of women empowerment through creation of micro-enterprises.
5. To appreciate steps taken by the Mann Deshi Foundation (MDF) in fostering rural micro-enterprises with an objective of women empowerment.

2. HUMAN CAPITAL

2.1. Meaning

The most valuable of all capital is that invested in human beings.
– Alfred Marshall in Principle of Economics.

A broader definition of human capital was offered by the OECD (2001) as, "the knowledge, skills and competencies embodied in individuals that facilitate the creation of personal, social and economic well-being". This definition refutes the censure that a human capital approach equates individuals to physical instruments. Thus it implies investments in people in the form of education, training and health, which in turn result in enhancing their productivity (Golding, 2014). However if left undeveloped or underdeveloped it entails economic and social costs to a nation.

Thus human capital refers to both inherited and acquired skills, the latter being the most important indicator of the stage of the development of an economy, and which can be advanced through formal and informal education, training, vocational experience and job mobility (Mincer, 1981).

The concept of human capital dates back to (Smith, 1776) in his work on *Wealth of Nations* wherein he defines it as, "The acquisition of ... talents during ... education, study, or apprenticeship, costs a real expense, which is capital in [a] person. Those talents [are] part of his fortune [and] likewise that of society".

Irving Fisher is considered probably to be one of the first to formally employ the concept of human capital to economics, (which as per him although is a non-tradable asset, but leads to an inflow of income) along with Adam Smith and H. von Thunen. This concept, although espoused by others, was disregarded. Even Malthusian theory disregarded the concept of human capital i.e. the quality of general population. The reasoning for this lies in the fact that customarily; land, labour and physical capital, were the only three basic factors of production considered by the economists. The term rose to popularity during the 1960s with increased attention being given to the value of labour in terms of its level of skills, competencies and other attributes, enhanced through education and training (UK Centre for the Measurement of Economic Activity, 2008).

Similarly Theodore Schultz in his paper on "Investment in Human Capital" has a contrary opinion to that of J.S. Mill regarding the meaning of human capital. Whereas Mill failed to consider human capital as wealth, as in his view the latter was meant for use by people, Schulz opinionated that investment in oneself enables individuals to enhance their welfare by enlarging the scope of economic choices available to them (Schultz, 1961). Thus this necessitates inclusion of human beings in the concept of capital as any investment in individuals gives rise to an increase in personal incomes and growth for the economy.

2.2. Human Capital: Importance

Proponents of the neo-classical growth model did neglect human capital, as they proposed that an incremental physical capital augments growth in terms of GDP (Solow, 1956).

However the importance of human capital was realised due to the awareness that long term growth is possible only when increase in physical capital is complemented by human capital.

Thus the latter became a major constituent of the socio-economic development of a nation, leading to the notion of human capital accumulation and development (Leeuwen, 2007).

Human capital has been a cornerstone of a number of studies relating to the economic performance of nations and in the context of growth models which are endogenous in nature. These models state that economic growth is a result of endogenous and not exogenous factors, like investments in human capital in terms of knowledge and training. Thus economies rich in terms of reserves of human capital are found to grow at a faster pace (Barro, 1991). For instance, the stupendous growth rates experienced lately by economies like Japan, Taiwan and other Asian countries bears witness to the fact that this was achievable owing to high investments in education and training imparted to their workforce. Further as stated by (Becker, 2009) vocational know-how is also predicted to enhance human capital. Thus to ensure sustainable economic development, it is imperative to concentrate simultaneously on expansion and dispersal of human capital (Mincer, 1981), owing to its fabulous Returns on Investments (ROI).

2.3. Human Capital Formation

An important ingredient of economic development is human resource whose importance and efficiency can be increased through investments. Human capital formation and accumulation thus necessitates an investment outlay in education, health, on-the-job training, and information dissemination, leading to enhancement of their knowledge, skills and expertise.

The seventh five year plan in India (1985-1990) states, “human resources development has necessarily to be assigned a key role in any development strategy, particularly in a country with a large population. Trained and educated on sound lines a large population can itself become an asset in accelerating economic growth and in ensuring social change in desired directions" (Amala, 2004). Further looking at the growth prospects of the Indian economy it seems that higher growth will be achieved by India due to its strong human capital formation base (Dahlman and Utz, 2005).

However nations have to bear in mind one important fact that the presence of enabling institutions is an important capacity building mechanism of a nation to promote the accumulation of human capital. For instance, the existence of a highly effective judicial system defining individual's property rights is one such institution. This is highly imperative for rural and women entrepreneurship development keeping in mind the twin problems of the Indian rural economy that of unemployment and poverty (Golding, 2014).

2.4. Strategies for Human Capital Formation and Development

Human Resources Development is the process of increasing the knowledge, skills, and capacities of all people in the society. In economic terms, it could be described as the accumulation and effective investment of human capital in the development of any economy (Ejere, 2011). However creation and development of human resource requires human capital formation. A study conducted by (Ogunade, 2011) has tried to address the issue regarding the strategies to be adopted by the governments of developing nations in fostering human capital development, by attempting to seek answers to three relevant questions – a) the type of human capital available in these countries; b) the kind of knowledge, skills and competencies the personnel hold and c) the types of skills required to promote economic growth and development. The last question is highly imperative, as it will enable in recognising the directions of training and development of the labour force in such economies.

The Planning Commission in India has resolved this issue by following a strategy of expanding infrastructure for imparting education and training for skill enhancement related to employment and self-employment opportunities in agro-based and rural non-farm sector, along with industries and service sector. However the Indian economy is no exception to the fact that usually the human capital development policies followed by the governments are State-driven i.e. from the perspective of what the supplier feels right, with a total neglect of the demand side factors i.e. what the workforce requires. This leads to a mis-match between what is being offered by the training institutes and the demands of the industry or a particular vocation or a local community (Tan and Batra, 1996).

The problem is further aggravated due to the fact that these skill development strategies are politically driven, with several organisations (i.e. ministries, departments and NGOs) in charge of skill development with overlapping authorities and their overlapping agendas. This leads to duplication of efforts by the State, due to lack of harmonization, leading to wasteful expenditures on training without any real return on investment (ROI), which in turn negates the skill transfer and development process. This calls for a strategy of synchronization in imparting training, keeping in mind the aims of the National Skill Development Policy (Palmer, 2008).

Thus developing nations should tune their policies in line with different stages of their development process, especially in India for the simple fact that the Indian economy comprises of diverse groups in the community whose training requirements differ. Secondly the Indian government cannot give a blind eye to the training needs of the underprivileged groups (women, individuals with disabilities, individuals in certain castes), keeping in mind the Millenium Development Goals (MDGs) of skill enhancement aimed at poverty reduction and gender equality through inclusive growth (ILO, 2008).

As the Indian economy is exposed to a major unrelenting problem of gender disparity affecting the welfare of this class, in terms of their rights and privileges, one of the anti-dotes is the establishment of organisations and other hand-holding agencies, through creation of social capital, as enhanced economic growth does not mechanically warrant a reduction in such deprivations. Thus human interventions are a must for resolving this issue, preferably by providing gainful employment opportunities, for improving the status of women in their family as well as society, thereby leading to their empowerment. In this context (Dreze and Sen, 2002) have given the most important ingredient for equality in participation of economic activities and thereby targeting poverty reduction in such economies through creation of 'social capital', in the form of enterprise building especially in rural areas.

3. SOCIAL CAPITAL

3.1. Meaning of Social Capital

The concept of social capital pioneered by James Coleman, has been defined by the World Bank as, "it refers to the institutions, relations and norms that shape the quality and quantity of a society's social interactions. Increasing evidence shows that social cohesion is critical for societies to prosper economically and development to be sustainable. Social capital is just not the sum of institutions which underpin a society – it is the glue that holds them together".

(OECD, 2001) in its report defined social capital as, "networks together with shared norms, values and understandings that facilitate co-operation within or among groups".

3.2. Importance of Social Capital

According to Picciotto (OECD, 2001), "Gender discrimination squanders trust, hinders family relations, restricts social networks, and depletes social capital, the valuable capacity of societies to work towards common goals". Thus social capital is an important ingredient to foster equality of participation in economic activities, thereby necessitating its formation. Social capital has an economic value and therefore can be labelled as an "economic asset" because it supports social interactions, thereby enhances faith and restricts the use of moral hazards in economic contractual relationships, thereby trimming down the transaction costs. The best examples are that of women empowerment through creation of self-employment opportunities and entrepreneurship development through Self Help Groups (SHGs)/ Joint Liability Groups (JLGs).

Families, schools, local communities, civil society, firms, public sector, gender, etc can be tapped as the means for developing social capital, of which civil society comprising of both formal and informal organisations which are autonomous in nature can play a crucial role in creation of rural and women entrepreneurship as per the World Bank. The best examples of these are Grameen Bank (Bangladesh), SEWA and Mann Deshi Foundation (India) etc. which paved the way for women empowerment through micro-credit and allied facilities.

3.3. Social Capital for Entrepreneurship Development

A large number of research studies have shown a vital correlation between rural development and the presence of dynamic networks and local organisations at the grassroots level, in addition to investment in physical assets, apposite technology and availability of market mechanisms (Putnam, 1993). Social capital is also essential for entrepreneurial development as it makes available systems that can further the exploration of opportunities and also aid the apperception, assimilation and apportionment of sparse resources (Uzzi, 1999). Rather social capital aids potential entrepreneurs in the conception stage by manifesting distinct, novel concepts, and aspects, thereby making available a vast body of knowledge which is essential for the guidance and sustenance of their unique and latent conceptions or enterprises (Davidsson and Honig, 2003). The existence of social capital in the form of affiliations with trade associations referred to as "weak ties" by Granovetter enables new entrepreneurs to gain insights into latest technological innovations and critical information about its utility (Granovetter, 1983). According to (Davidsson and Honig, 2003) these "weak ties" provides opportunities to develop and maintain relations with local agencies, business networks in the form of mentoring, associations with fellow entrepreneurs and availing facilitation services like business incubators, business and market-related consultancy and networking services.

4. LITERATURE REVIEW

4.1. Challenges of Women Entrepreneurship Development in Rural Areas

The statement of Pandit Jawaharlal Nehru, "You can tell the condition of a nation by looking at the status of women" emphasizes the basic philosophy of the Indian economy as a 'welfare state', whose progress will be possible and meaningful only when women participate dynamically in the nation's socio-economic activities (Saha and Banerjee, 2001). However a major challenge facing India is, its major rural population (the main component being women) lives below the poverty line. Thus referring to poverty as 'feminisation of poverty' would not be a misnomer, as it leads to their marginalisation from the mainstream further aggravating the predicament of gender inequity. However realizing the significant contribution women can make towards their family, community and economy at large, the Government of India has initiated various steps in this direction. The Preamble, Fundamental Rights, Fundamental Duties and Directive Principles of State Policy of the Indian Constitution shield the principle of gender equality. For instance Articles 14 and 15 of the Indian Constitution.

According to (Goswami and Bhattacharya, 2014), the Eleventh 5-Year Plan aiming at inclusive growth has emphasized on gender equality, which is possible by promoting women entrepreneurship in the rural non-farm sector.

A study conducted by (Shah and Saurabh, 2015), highlights the importance of development of women entrepreneurs, as it transforms the lives of their families and people associated with them. However there are several impediments in this process as, lack of entrepreneurial skills, resulting in low confidence on the part of women, lack of access to credit and thereby dependency on money lenders following usurious practices, especially in countries like India, Pakistan, Bangladesh, and Sri Lanka. This led to introduction of programmes for creation of self-employment opportunities, through training in skill development by Indian government.

A study by (Tripathi, 2014) highlights the problems faced by women in terms of access to resources like land, financial assistance, technology, education and by (Pharm and Sritharan, 2013) like – family responsibilities, educational deficiency, male subjugated social set-up, lack of credit facilities, high production costs, lack of knowledge of legal formalities, exploitation at the hands of middlemen.

However (Kolluju, 2015) emphasizes on women emancipation and empowerment, through development of rural women entrepreneurship via the SBLP model. This has led to various government initiatives in the form of national policies, development programmes and establishment of SHGs for empowering women (Mazumdar and Ahmed, 2015).

4.2. Environment Conducive to Women Entrepreneurship

The (UN Publication, 2007) has highlighted the impediments to development of women entrepreneurship, in the form of access to ownership rights to property which in turn deprives them of participation in socio-economic activities. No doubt the Asia-Pacific region has made greater strides in decelerating gender inequality, but these are abysmal, causing the region to lose to the extent of $42 to $47 billion a year, a huge opportunity cost. For instance it is estimated that if women participation in India comes to par with that of United States, its GDP would rise by 4.2% a year and its growth rate by 1.08% point. A pertinent reason for this problem is women's voicelessness as far as the decision making process is concerned, owing to dominance of traditional male-dominated values which enable men to inherit ancestral property since birth. No doubt many countries have amended their property rights in favour of females; however marriage leads to the deprivation of such claims. As a result women are handicap to start any enterprise without any title to property rights depriving them of access to credit in the absence of collateral security, which is a hard core policy requirement of the traditional banking sector. A study by (Deininger, 2003) validates that bestowing property rights on women, affirmatively impact productivity in agriculture and their access to finance and credit. Similar kind of results were found by (Panda et al., 2005) wherein women land ownership rights have shown to drastically reduce the menace of domestic violence, thereby affecting the process of economic development of a nation. According to (Sharma, 2011) gender remains a key element which is susceptible to poverty and hence it is justified that women's access to finance in terms of micro-credit and micro-loans can help promote micro-enterprises providing them with a source of living, thereby improving their negotiating power and skills and a better position in the society. Thus a favourable outcome of these disparities can be said to be the formation of micro-credit institutions like the Grameen Bank. As Kofi Annan, Former United Nations Secretary-General has rightly stated - "Sustainable access to micro-finance helps alleviate poverty by generating income, creating jobs, allowing children to go to school, enabling families to obtain health care, and empowering people to make the choices that best serve their needs".

Thus the process of development in an economy is furthered through the provision of micro-credit, as the banks and financial institutions in the formal financial sector follow a collateral-based lending policy, and the informal sources of finance like money lenders follow usurious lending practices, with absence of professional norms in the valuation of the collaterals of borrowers. In such a scenario micro-credit can come to the rescue of the underprivileged women beneficiaries (Quaraishi, 2007).

In his study (Shah et al., 2007) has raised an important question about the efficacy of the local community organisations in supporting and nurturing micro-enterprises, with special reference to the (SBLP) Self Help Group Bank Linkage Model, which like other government programmes have met with failure, due to reasons like - lack of ancillary facilities like market backing, provision of suitable technology and skill development, in addition to financial assistance, unlike successful organisations like Myrada (Karnataka), DHAN (Tamil Nadu), SEWA (Ahmedabad), who have demonstrated the strength of local communities in solving problems of grass roots, unattainable even for the market and government organisations. With these supplementary facilities credit will be better absorbed and give a good return.

Thus the development of rural women entrepreneurship needs a distinct approach i.e. the "top down" approach co-ordinating with the "bottom up" approach i.e. programmes and assistance tailor made to suit the needs of the local community. Secondly the ownership, control and management of these initiatives should be in the hands of the members of the local community who are well versed with the challenges of their area. In this context social entrepreneurs can play a significant role in the socio-economic development of the community, by enabling local people to harness the local resources for promoting local micro enterprises (Sherief, 1994).

4.3. SHGS (Self Help Groups) As a Conduit for Women Empowerment

According to (Mishra, 2010), SHGs have been instrumental to sever the appalling loop of poverty in India, enabling people to develop their entrepreneurial skills. The author has highlighted the facilities provided by the SHG under study in several stages comprising of - motivating people to start enterprises, provision of training in production areas like basket making, rope knitting, making incense sticks, etc., direct and indirect marketing, contacting middlemen, accompanying beneficiaries to banks to acquire financial assistance, helping them in assessing the amount of investment and technology required. However, the SHG under study faced several constraints like - lack of competent trainers, low literacy level of women trainees and their busy family schedules.

The study conducted by (Pangannavar, 2012), highlights the fact that women are major victims of unemployment and poverty. Thus the Indian government initiated various steps in this direction, which were ineffective, owing to an ivory tower approach followed by Indian policy makers sitting in urban elite areas making policies for development of rural poor, not tuned to the needs of these local areas and their prevailing conditions. Thus the 9th and 10th 5-year plan have focussed on women empowerment in the form of SHGs – a concept launched by the government as an anti-poverty measure. The SHGs apart from being a micro finance agency is also an agency for socio-economic development of the poor i.e. a model for gender justice, women empowerment and economic development. However the impediments faced by the beneficiaries of the SHGs are – lack of counselling in selection of business enterprises, reliance on indigenous technology owing to lack of education to adapt to latest technology, investment risk due to competition from the organised sector, inadequate infrastructural facilities i.e. lack of proper production and marketing facilities, thus cheated by middlemen, absence of proper social security measures from SHGs during a crisis and above all problems of bank dealings i.e. lack of financial literacy.

Study conducted by (Lavanya, 2010) has made a reference to India's obligation to the Millenium Development Goals (MDGs) in the context of overcoming the problem of discrimination against women and the Eleventh 5 Year Plan (2007-2012) which has emphasized on women empowerment, which according to the author is possible through women entrepreneurship development. Efforts taken by the Indian government in this direction include – establishment of National Institute of Small Industry Extension Training, Hyderabad; NIESBUD in New Delhi and the EDII in Ahmedabad which launched programmes for women entrepreneurship development; and IDBI introduced two programmes - Mahila Udhyam Nidhi for giving seed capital assistance to women entrepreneurs and Mahila Vikas Nidhi under which NGOs dealing with women entrepreneurs were given assistance; amendment and enactment of women related legislations, increased supply of credit, marketing facilities, technology and skill training for large number of women farmers, ensuring land rights for women and provision of home loans for women entrepreneurs as these homes are a place of production for them. Finally the author concludes by stating that successful women entrepreneurship programmes entail important steps like identification and selection of potential women entrepreneurs, guiding them in preparation of project reports and undertaking feasibility study of such projects and preparing reports accordingly, post-training and follow-up with women entrepreneurs.

(Raheem, 2011) in his study has emphasized the fact that although women empowerment is important for economic development, but their contribution is statistically absent in national income accounting, particularly in countries like India and other South Asian countries owing to traditional mindsets. Thus the author is of the view that certain strategies are essential for ensuring women empowerment, like – improvement in infrastructure, Information and communication Technology (ICT), gender sensitive agricultural policies, income generation schemes for women

– by strengthening SHGs, skill development, gender friendly and low-cost insurance schemes, education and training of Women.

The Mann Deshi Foundation through its sister concern the Mann Deshi Mahila Sahakari Bank is a best example of this transformation.

5. MANN DESHI FOUNDATION: A STEP TOWARDS WOMEN EMPOWERMENT

"We not only want the piece of the pie we also want to choose the flavour and to know how to make it ourselves" - Ela Bhatt, founder Self-Employed Women's Association, (SEWA).

This statement highlights the importance of women empowerment through entrepreneurship formation and development. The concept introduced primarily in the International Women's Conference held in Nairobi in 1985. The Global Conference on Women Empowerment held in 1988 defined women empowerment as "the surest way of making women, partners in development", enabling them overcome their subservient socio-economic conditions. In a broader sense it entails enhancing women autonomy, to make life's choices and enabling her to be a part of the decision making process by provision of information and knowledge.

Accordingly the first four 5 year plans in India followed a welfare- oriented policy for women's development. The 5th plan changed its focus from welfare to women's development, the 8th plan from development to women empowerment and the 11th plan aimed at promoting self-employment among rural women through SHGs programmes (Pangannavar, 2012). However as stated earlier these governmental efforts need to be supplemented by the initiatives for entrepreneurship development at the local community levels by developing social capital by social entrepreneurs, who are well-versed with the local conditions and can therefore introduce programmes tailor-made to suit the needs of these areas. Mention needs to be made of one such social entrepreneur in Mhaswad, Satara district, Maharashtra – Chetna Gala Sinha, the founder of the NGO – Mann Deshi Foundation. Although born and brought up in a metropolis like Mumbai, but had exposure to principles of Jayaprakash Narayan, having worked as a leader of the youth wing of the Janata Dal party and actively involved in the movement for the well-being of marginalised communities during emergency period and landless labour movement in Bodh Gaya. On coming to Mhaswad after getting married to Vijay Sinha, she recalls, "It opened my eyes to the plight of people at the grassroots level and the challenge of working for their benefit came with the idealism I had grown up with." This paved the way for Mann Deshi Foundation.

Affected by severe and perennial droughts and failing monsoons, with majority people thriving as farmers, shepherds and daily wage earners, the Mann Taluka in Satara district was prone to rampant unemployment. The female folk were the hardest hit by this problem, falling prey easily to hunger and death. Thus Mhaswad was subjected to abject poverty, leading to large scale migrations to urban areas. Thus there was an urgent need to rescue the people from this vicious circle of unemployment and poverty and thus was born the Mann Vikas Samajik Sanstha (renamed as Mann Deshi Foundation), an NGO.

The main aim of this chapter is to understand the strategies adopted by MDF towards achieving the objective of women empowerment through rural women entrepreneurship and in the process understand the uniqueness of the organisation in fostering its objective.

5.1. Mann Deshi Foundation: Genesis

Mann Deshi foundation, a registered NGO established in 1994 by a social entrepreneur Chetna Gala Sinha with an objective of fostering the development of rural women and their families susceptible to poverty and socio-economic pressures, by enhancing their access to finance, development of business skills, provision of management and leadership training, information relating to property rights, personality development and adaptation to latest technology. The main aim is upgrading the lives of rural women with a long term perspective of poverty alleviation. The organisation believes that when financial control is centred in the hands of the female of the family, it leads to a holistic upliftment of the family from all angles be it children's education, healthcare and other household issues, leading to financial empowerment of rural women.

The Mann Deshi Foundation works towards achieving these objectives in partnership with its financial arm - the Mann Deshi Mahila Sahakari Bank.

5.2. Mann Deshi Mahila Sahakari Bank (MDMSB): Banking Re-Invented

The government of India and RBI have taken laudable efforts to foster the goal of women empowerment through financial inclusion. However these efforts are in vain because even today a major women rural population is dependent on the money lenders, despite governmental measures to regulate the latter. Thus there is a dire necessity to free these areas from the control of the exploitative practices of the money lenders through the policy of financial inclusion. As a result in 2013 the Union finance Minister in his Union Budget pronounced the need and intention of setting up a women's bank. In this context what Usha Thorat, former Deputy

Governor of the Reserve Bank of India and advisor to the government on new bank for women, said is worth noting – "If you have to be a women's bank, it's best to be like Mann Deshi,".

"A bank for, by and of rural Indian women" – is the motto of Mann Deshi Mahila Sahakari Bank (MDMSB). What led Chetna Sinha into an idea of establishing a bank solely for women? It was the woes of the rural women who saved money, but lacked a safe haven, as banks in the formal financial sector, found it financially and operationally unviable to operate very small accounts of these women. Thus Sinha recognised the problem that although world over the formal financial sector has acknowledged rural women as credit worthy, but they still face many procedural hurdles in accessing credit through these formal channels. This led to filing an application to Reserve Bank of India (RBI) in 1994 for establishment of a rural co-operative bank, which was out rightly rejected, for the simple reason that all the member directors were illiterate. However resolved to establish a bank the women took up a vow to learn to read and write which paved the way for adult literacy classes. Two years later when an application was made for the second time, the women proved their mettle to the RBI officials and thus returned with a feather in their cap, a license to start the first women-led rural co-operative bank in India - the first micro-finance bank in rural Maharashtra, established in 1997 with the goal of financial empowerment of rural women, through the promotion of micro-enterprises (a micro-enterprise being defined by the World Bank, "as an enterprise with less than 10 employees and assets and annual sales amounting to less than 10,000 USD"). Women as share holders play a decisive role in the Bank's policy making at the annual general meetings.

5.2.1. Mann Deshi Mahila Sahakari Bank (MDMSB): Overcoming Obstacles

However the primary exhilaration after starting the Bank faded in an instant when it was realised that owing to time constraints (i.e. to avoid loss of working hours) the customers discontinued their visits to the bank, which would have seriously affected the Bank's financial viability. Thus a novel concept of door-step banking, through the appointment of field officers was introduced, who provide following services to their clients:

1. Collection of daily savings through pigmy collection agents - average monthly savings of the women are Rs. 75/-.
2. Provision of daily, weekly and fortnightly loans is done through Bank's staff who operate in the form of human ATMs making loans available at the door-step i.e. work place of the borrower and at the most appropriate time when needed. A criterion for obtaining loans is that the husbands have to declare

their wives as co-partners in ancestral property. Finance is provided only through the channel of women, although males can become account holders in the form of depositors of the bank.

Another note-worthy step taken by the MDF was in the direction of gaining ownership rights in ancestral property for women, as this would improve their borrowing capacity in the form of a collateral and also serve as a protection measure in case of a divorce. Accordingly the Maharashtra Revenue Department was persuaded by the Foundation to write women's names also on property papers in 2004. Further the Bank follows a practice of providing cheaper loans (i.e. a rebate of 1%) to those women who own and hold properties in their names.

A unique product has been launched by the Bank for its weekly market micro-enterprise clients – the "cash credit" after conducting a research study of Satara. The study revealed unhealthy practices followed by wholesalers in these markets i.e selling goods (sub-standard in quality) to the vendors on credit basis at a daily interest rate of 1.4% owing to their vulnerable financial and thereby bargaining position relative to those who bought on cash basis. Under the cash credit scheme the Bank had 213 clients with total loan outstanding of INR 2.6 million covering 17 markets as on July 2014.

3. Recovery of loans (repayment rate approx. 97%) – Usurious practices of money lenders have been weeded out by the Bank by providing loans at reasonable rates of interest.
4. Introduction of e-cards to clients – Maintenance of a large number of pass books of small clients was operationally impractical Secondly the women clients of the bank wanted to conceal their savings from their male counterparts with the fear of squandering these on alcohol and other vices. Thus the Bank came up with a unique idea of personal e-cards to record the details of the clients banking transactions, with access to account status to the beneficiaries with the help of this technology.

By end of 2014 the Bank had 185000 clients. Thus MDMSB has acquired the status of one of the largest microfinance agency in Maharashtra, with an ISO 9001-2000 certification.

5.3. Beyond Micro-Lending

Sustainable women empowerment requires a step beyond micro-credit in the form of ancillary services i.e. non-financial services as well. The MDF has introduced following unique schemes in this regard as follows:

5.3.1. Micro-Pension Scheme

The Foundation realised that by the time women reach their late 40s especially in rural areas, they start suffering from joint and muscular pain owing to laborious physical tasks. However in a country like India they lack any kind of social security or medical or insurance benefits, thus have to rely on their sons or families during old age or fend for themselves. Keeping this in mind, the Foundation has launched a pension scheme in collaboration with the UTI Mutual Fund, which would work like a contingency fund in their old age. Women in the age group of 18-55 years can join the scheme and pension becomes payable on reaching the vesting age of 58. The unique feature of the scheme is the woman contributor under the scheme can also re-assign the pension benefits to a chosen beneficiary in the event of her death.

5.3.2. Mann Deshi Udyogini: Business School for Rural Women

Forget China, India and the Internet: economic growth is driven by women.
– The Economist 2006.

In 2006, the MDF initiated a Business School for Rural Women (BSRW) – the Udyogini, in collaboration with the HSBC Bank. The B-school provides training in skill development – financial, business, management and ICT, which enables them to either start their own micro-enterprises or upgrade their existing micro-enterprises, in street vending, goat de-worming, bag making, weaving, screen printing, photo laminating, computer operating, etc. The school designs and follows tailor-made curriculum and courses, to suit the needs of the local community. For instance the goat herding course is taught on the fields. The institute targets school drop-outs and women (Subramaniam, 2012).

The unique feature of the school is there are no minimum educational qualifications or age limits as entry barriers, nor exorbitant fees nor formal admission procedures and time periods i.e. admissions are on "any-day basis". The time period of the course may range from a few weeks to a few months and fees from Rs. 25 to Rs. 1200. Thus it aims at providing vocational and professional training to rural women, along with confidence building through personality development. The school has branches in Mhaswad, Vaduj, Dahiwadi, Satara and Hubli.

The unique feature of the school is it uses financial literacy as a safety net along with microfinance to overcome the problem of Non Performing Assets (NPAs) among its beneficiaries. This course is mandatory for every client of the MDMSB. An Impact Assessment of the beneficiaries of this course was undertaken, which indicated that out of the 54 women who studied this programme (none of whom had ever saved before), 48 started saving monthly, 22 took out a bank loan and 24 invested in bank shares. The subject matter of this course includes lessons on significance of savings, in-time repayment of borrowings and procedure for consulting banks in emergencies. The school has devised unique ways of delivering the course contents in collaboration with the Commonwealth of Learning (CoL), through voicemails, which are then converted for broadcast through the Foundations's community radio system formed in 2008.Thus the school is in the fore-front in providing training in technical, marketing, management and financial literacy skills.

The females are also provided with a free counselling to understand their current skills and aptitudes in helping them choose the appropriate courses and ventures.

The Foundation has also initiated a Mobile Business School for Rural Women - "Business School on Wheels" fitted with computers and sewing machines, who have temporal and spatial constraints i.e. door-step training is provided to them through a mobile bus travelling from village to village.

The school has launched a 1000 Deshi MBA Program whose goal is to create 10,000 rural entrepreneurs by providing them with training in business management through mentoring. Training is provided in management of working capital, supply chain management, branding, advertising, packaging and marketing their products. It also arranges field visits to expose them to the working of big enterprises. Mentors are put in charge of these trainee entrepreneurs, who work with them for 12 months, and they are also taken out to observe and learn from successful local enterprises. They are reimbursed for their transportation, food and lodging costs. On experiencing their enterprises grow these women become more self-confident and more self-empowered and also set an example for other women entrepreneurs. More than 70,000 students graduated from the B-school in 2013. The syllabus of this course has been framed by Mumbai's SP Jain Management Institute and US based non-profit organisation Accion (Desai, 2013). Sinha wants to create woman entrepreneurs as brands in the process. Management interns of Yale and Harvard universities' visit the b-school entrepreneurs to understand the complexities of running an enterprise.

Naina Lal Kidwai, country head for HSBC India and director of HSBC Asia-Pacific, while speaking about the B-school says, "The B-school has helped the women to be creative, resourceful and business savvy, enabling the mainstreaming of a significant number of women into India's economy".

5.3.3. Mann Deshi Chamber of Commerce for Rural Women (MCCRW)

As it has been rightly said "necessity is the mother of all inventions", so is the case with the Mann Deshi Chamber of Commerce established in 2012 by MDMSB. The need for starting this institution arose out of an incident which took place in the life of Bainabai Kantilal Sagar, an entrepreneur and client of the MDMSB, who operated a tea vending shop. Less did this lady know that using domestic gas connection for a commercial purpose was illegal, till she was arrested and detained by the police, who was rescued by Sinha. This paved the way for establishment of the MCCRW, in joint co-ordination with 'President Clinton Foundations' initiative - Clinton Global Initiative (CGI) based in New York, USA, to help such women entrepreneurs through a toll-free hotline (a complementary service) assisting them to sort out legal issues and seek business licenses.

The main intention behind the establishment of the MCCRW is the formation and development of rural women entrepreneurs by providing them with mentorship services, market accessibility, and connectivity with a network of like-minded peers, enhanced financial aid, advocacy tools, knowledge support and provision of solar lights to street vendors. These services are provided through workshops conducted on a monthly basis, wherein individual special needs of each member specific to their business enterprises are also addressed.

The women entrepreneurs graduating from the B-school can avail services of the MCCRW.

5.3.4. Technology: ICT

More than at any other time in history, the world is poised to leverage innovation to improve the lives of poor women and empower them to realise their potential.
– International Centre for Research on Women 2006.

The MDMSB has initiated ICT into its working to enhance women rural entrepreneurship in following ways:

1. Loans for mobile phones

The MDMSB offers loans of Rs. 5000/- to its clients to purchase mobile phones, who can use them to access market information on prices of raw materials and place orders for the same, and also enhance their customer base. Semi-literate or illiterate women can make use of voice data transmission through mobile phones.

A unique mobile phone application, "nano ganesh" - a water pump with a remote mobile starter, a latest technology developed by Mr. Santosh Ostwal, CEO and Founder Director of an Indian agro-based company – Ossian Agro Automation, is promoted for use by MDMSB among its women entrepreneurs. For instance, Sunita, a beneficiary of the MDMSB who runs a micro-enterprise for silk worm breeding, not only uses her mobile phone to contact her traders to notify the delivery dates of silk cocoons, but also uses the same to remotely turn on her mobile-operated water pump with the help of "nano ganesh", to send water to her silk worm shed, from the place where she is located.

2. Community Radio Station

Launched in 2008 under the aegis of the MDF, but owned by the Mhaswad village community and nearby areas, attracts a daily average of 15,000 listeners, is a means to reach illiterate and semi-literate folks of the village for providing information on procedure for establishing farmer co-operatives; accessing micro-credit; acquisition of land ownership rights; rationale for women's rights to property; importance of health and safety issues.

3. Information kiosks

These provide internet access to the beneficiaries of MDMSB for seeking latest and dependable market information, making online payment of electricity bills, opening an account in the bank, filing a loan application, thereby reducing personal visits to the bank leading to saving time and cost of the beneficiaries.

4. E-Mentoring

"[My mobile phone] saves me time and allows me to be on the move. I can do various transactions on the mobile, while overseeing operations or domestic responsibilities. I can stay in touch with various people ... and could convert the recognition into better and bigger business opportunities" – Varsha, Mann Deshi Entrepreneur (Malhotra et al., 2012). Under the 1000 Deshi entrepreneurship programme, the Foundation provides free airtime vouchers on mobile phones to women entrepreneurs to enable them to connect with their mentors (who are successful women entrepreneurs from local communities) for seeking targeted business advice and support.

5.3.5. Mann Deshi Mahila Bachat GAT Federation

A non-profit association aimed at organising rural women entrepreneurs, comprising of more than 2400 SHGs, which are used to conduct village surveys for identification of local needs, enabling development of courses for the B-school which are most suitable and beneficial to the trainees, at the same time has real value for them as per the market demands.

5.3.6. CSR Initiatives by MDF

The Foundation organises cattle camps to aid the owners of livestock especially during the periods of droughts. 14,000 animals along with their owners and families in 52 villages were taken care of during the Mhaswad drought in 2012.

Interest-free loans are provided to the school going girls under its scheme, "Freedom ride", initiated in 2004, to enable the girl child to attend school regularly, save her time and thereby avoid extensive school drop-outs.

6. IMPACT ASSESSMENT: MAJOR STRIDES BY MDF

An impact assessment of the MDF brings to light the progress made by the organisation in terms of number of students of the B-school, which increased from 4,300 in 2010 to 45,471 in 2013. During the same period number of chambers of commerce increased to 3 and its beneficiaries to 16,200 (Mann Deshi Foundation, 2010-13).

The Foundation along with its pioneer Chetna Sinha has won various accolades for their commendable achievements, like – the Ashoka Changemakers Innovation Award (2005), Jankidevi Bajaj Award for Rural Development (2006), Godfrey Phillips Bravery Amodini Award (2009), Edelgive Social Innovation Honors (2010). Schwab Foundation Social Entrepreneur of the Year - India (2013), Best Innovation Award By National Rural Livelihood Mission (2013), Best Eco Tech Bank Award by Indian Bank Association (2014) – Mann Deshi – A Story of Knowledge, Courage and Capital – Personal interview with the CAO of MDF, Vanita Shinde.

A feather in the cap of MDF is Vanita Pise an entrepreneur and client of the MDMSB who was awarded the CII-Bharti Women exemplar Award from the Prime Minister of India as a social entrepreneur creating employment opportunities to other women in her vicinity.

7. CONCLUSION

Ajit Rangnekar, dean of the Hyderabad-based Indian School of Business has stated that India is diverse and so are its education needs from top professionals to a small rural vendor, requiring different growth and development models to suit the specific needs of the specific classes of the society. Therefore he says, "The real challenge in India is not about doing these experiments, but about codifying the learning from such initiatives, and scaling the successful ones rapidly so that the growth can be shared across the society."

However experience has shown that government efforts in this direction have met with failure and probably that is the reason why social entrepreneurs like Chetna Sinha have taken the lead to educate and empower rural women with a bottom-up approach, thereby arresting the problem of unemployment, migration and poverty. Thus in this context Abha Thorat-Shah, director at the British Asian Trust, a London-based social fund in South Asia, while referring to Mann Deshi says, "I love the fact that it's rural, training and skilling people in the state, and not promoting migration." Thus Chetna Sinha has created social capital to uplift the rural women, enabling them to acquire financial empowerment lives leading to social sustainability.

SHGs and micro-enterprises usually face a risk of viability, which was also applicable to MDF. However the Foundation has been able to grow and sustain positively owing to a comprehensive and holistic approach to micro-finance, thereby overcoming all kinds of business and systemic risks. Thus according to Sinha, "Financial inclusion is not just a low-interest bank account or a loan ... you need to design your product based on the cash flow and needs of the population you are trying to serve".

8. GUIDELINES FOR FUTURE RESEARCH

Although an Impact Assessment has been conducted by the Foundation, however as of date no research study has been conducted by the research community to find a statistical relationship between impacts of the efforts of MDF on empowerment of women. Thus future research can be conducted in this untouched area.

REFERENCES

Amala. (2004). *History of Education*. Discovery Publishing House. Retrieved from https://books.google.co.in/books?isbn=8171418600

Anju, M., Anjala, K., & Payal, P. (2012). *How Mobile Phones, Computers and the Internet can Catalyse Women's Entrepreneurship: India – A Case Study*. Cherie Blair Foundation. Retrieved from http://www.icrw.org/files/publications/Connectivity-how-mobile-phones-computers-and-the-internet-can-catalyze-womens-entrepreneurship.pdf

Anusha, S. (2012, October 28). Of Milk and Honey. *Business Today*. Retrieved November 18, 2015, from http://www.businesstoday.in/cover-story/bestb-schools-2012-mann-deshi-udyogini-curriculum/story/188847.html

Barro, . (1991). Economic Growth in a Cross section of Countries. *The Quarterly Journal of Economics, 106*(2), 407. Retrieved from http://www.econ.nyu.edu/user/debraj/Courses/Readings/BarroGrowth.pdf doi:10.2307/2937943

Becker. (2009). *Human Capital: A theoretical and Empirical Analysis, with Special reference to Education.* Retrieved from https://books.google.co.in/books?id=9t69iICmrZ0C&source=gbs_navlinks_s

Brian, U. (1999). Embeddedness in the Making of Financial Capital: How Social Relations and Networks Benefit Firms Seeking Financing. *American Sociological Review, 64*. Retrieved from http://www.kellogg.northwestern.edu/faculty/uzzi/ftp/lending.pdf

Chandrama, G., & Manisha, B. (2014). The Non-Farm Sector - Rural Non-Farm Employment in Assam: A Gender Based Analysis. *Space and Culture, 2*(1). Retrieved from http://spaceandculture.in/index.php/spaceandculture/article/view/38

Chandrasekhar, S. (2011). Macro-economic Overview. In D.M. Nachane (Ed.), *India Development Report* (pp. 26-38). New Delhi: Oxford University Press. Retrieved October 11, 2015, from http://www.igidr.ac.in/pdf/publication/IDR-2011.pdf

Claudia, G. (2014). *Human Capital.* Harvard University and NBER – Handbook of Cliometrics. Retrieved from http://scholar.harvard.edu/files/goldin/files/human_capital_handbook_of_cliometrics_0.pdf

Dahlman & Utz. (2005). *India and the Knowledge Economy – Leveraging Strengths and Opportunities.* World Bank Institute. Retrieved from http://info.worldbank.org/etools/docs/library/145261/India_KE_Overview.pdf

Davidsson & Honig. (2003). The Role of Social and Human Capital Among Nascent Entrepreneurs. *Journal of Business Venturing*. Retrieved from http://eprints.qut.edu.au/5832/1/5832.pdf

Dreze & Sen. (2002). *India Development and Participation*. Oxford University Press.

Ejere. (2011). Human Capital Formation as Catalyst for National Development: Nigeria in Perspective. *International Business and Management, 2*(2). Retrieved from http://www.cscanada.net/index.php/ibm/article/view/j.ibm.1923842820110202.011

Gopal, S. (Ed.). (1983). *Jawaharlal's Nehru's Speech at the Constituent Assembly, New Delhi, 14th August 1947 reprinted in, Jawaharlal Nehru: An Anthology*. New Delhi: Oxford University Press.

Government of India Planning Commission. (2014). *Preface to Report of the Expert Group to Review the Methodology for Measurement of Poverty*. Retrieved October 11, 2015, from http://planningcommission.nic.in/reports/genrep/pov_rep0707.pdf

Haq. (1997). *Reflections on Human Development.* Delhi: Oxford University Press.

ILO. (2008). *Conclusions on Skills for Improved Productivity, Employment Growth and Development.* International Labour Conference. Retrieved from http://www.ilo.org/wcmsp5/groups/public/---ed_emp/---ifp_skills/documents/publication/wcms_103457.pdf

Jacob, M. (1981). *Human Capital and Economic Growth*. Working Paper No. 803. National Bureau of Economic Research. Retrieved from http://www.nber.org/papers/w0803.pdf

Klaus, D. (2003). *Land Policies for Growth and Poverty Reduction. A World Bank Policy Research Report.* World Bank and Oxford University Press. Retrieved from http://info.worldbank.org/etools/docs/library/34919/landpoliciesexecsummary.pdf

Kumud, S. (2011, October). Small Loans, Big Dreams: Women and Microcredit in a Globalising Economy. *Economic and Political Weekly*, *46*(43). Retrieved from http://www.epw.in.iproxy.inflibnet.ac.in:2048/journal/2011/43/review-womens-studies-review-issues-specials/small-loans-big-dreams-women-and

Lavanya, T. (2010). *Women Empowerment through Entrepreneurship*. New Delhi: New Century Publications.

Leeuwen. (2007). *Human Capital and Economic Growth in India, Indonesia and Japan: A Quantitative Analysis*. Retrieved from https://books.google.co.in/books?id=JAxpCWzpDuQC&dq=18.%09Bas+Van+Leeuwen.+().+Human+Capital+and+Economic+Growth&source=gbs_navlinks_s

Mann Deshi Foundation - Impact Report. (2013). Retrieved November 18, 2015, from http://www.thefundingnetwork.org.uk/wp-content/uploads/2013/07/Mann-Deshi-3-year-Impact-Report-Final.pdf

Mark, G. (1983). The Strength of Weak Ties: A Network Theory Revisited. *Sociological Theory*, *1*. Retrieved from http://www.soc.ucsb.edu/faculty/friedkin/Syllabi/Soc148/Granovetter%201983.pdf

Mazumdar & Ahmed. (2015). Empowerment of Rural Women Through Entrepreneurship: An Overview. *International Research Journal of Interdisciplinary and Multidisciplinary Studies, 1*(1). Retrieved from http://www.researchinformation.org/files/Mrs.-Manashi-Mazumdar.pdf

Mihir, S., Rangu, R., & Shankar, V. P. S. (2007). Rural Credit in the 20th Century: An Overview of History and Perspectives. *Economic and Political Weekly*. Retrieved from https://www.researchgate.net/publication/239783568_Rural_Credit_in_20th_Century_India_An_Overview_of_History_and_Perspectives

Nachane, D. M. (2011). Two decades of structural reforms: A balance sheet. In D.M. Nachane (Ed.), *India Development Report* (pp. 1-21). New Delhi: Oxford University Press. Retrieved October 11, 2015, from http://www.igidr.ac.in/pdf/publication/IDR-2011.pdf

Naveen, K. (2015). Poverty Reduction through Women's Entrepreneurial Activities in Rural Andhra Pradesh (Vol. 34). Ritsumeikan Journal of Asia Pacific Studies. Retrieved from http://www.apu.ac.jp/rcaps/uploads/fckeditor/publications/journal/RJAPS34_6_Kolloju.pdf

OECD Centre for Educational Research and Development. (2001). *The Well Being of Nations – The Role of Human and Social Capital– Education and Skills.* Retrieved October 9, 2015, from http://www.oecd.org/site/worldforum/33703702.pdf

Ogunade Adeyemi, O. (2011). *Human Capital Investment in the Developing World: An Analysis of Praxis.* Schmidt Labor Research Centre Seminar Series. Retrieved from http://www.uri.edu/research/lrc/research/papers/Ogunade_Workforce_Development.pdf

Panda, P., & Bina, A. (2005). Marital Violence, Human Development and Womens Property Status in India. *World Development*, *33*(5), 823–850. doi:10.1016/j.worlddev.2005.01.009

Pangannavar Arjun Yallappa. (2012). *Self-help Groups and Women Empowerment in India.* New Delhi: New Century Publications.

Pharm, A., & Sritharan, R. (2013). Challenges for Rural Women Entrepreneurs: Problems Being faced by Women Entrepreneurs in Rural Areas. *International Journal of Engineering Science*, *2*(3). Retrieved from http://www.theijes.com/papers/v2-i3/I023052055.pdf

UN Publication. (2007). *Economic and Social Survey of Asia and the Pacific 2007: Surging ahead in Uncertain Times.* UN.

Raheem, . (2011). *Women Empowerment through Self-help Groups (SHGs).* New Delhi: New Century Publications.

Robert, P. (1993). *The Prosperous Community: Social Capital and Public Life – The American Prospect*. Retrieved from http://prospect.org/article/prosperous-community-social-capital-and-public-life

Robert, P. (2008). *Skills and Productivity in the Informal Sector. International labour Office, Skills and employability Dept*. ILO Geneva. Employment Working Paper No. 5. Retrieved from http://www.ilo.org/wcmsp5/groups/public/---ed_emp/---ifp_skills/documents/publication/wcms_103983.pdf

Sabrina, Q. (2007). *How Empowering is Microcredit: A Look at Grameen Bank*. Sixth Congress of the U.S. Basic Income Guarantee Network. Retrieved from www.usbig.net/papers/173-Quaraishi-GrameenBank.doc

Saha & Banerjee. (2001) Women partners in development.Employment News, 25(49).

Shah & Saurabh. (2015). Women Entrepreneurs in Developing Nations: Growth and Replication Strategies and Their Impact on Poverty Alleviation. *Technology Innovation Management Review*. Retrieved from http://timreview.ca/sites/default/files/article_PDF/ShahSaurabh_TIMReview_August2015.pdf

Sharad, R. (2015, July 3). India is now a $2-trillion economy. *The Hindu*. Retrieved October 13, 2015, from http://www.thehindu.com/business/Economy/india-is-now-a-2trillion-economy-says-world-bank-data/article7380442.ece

Sherief. (1994). Entrepreneurship as an economic force in rural development. *Africa Economic Analysis*. Retrieved from http://www.africaeconomicanalysis.org/articles/gen/rural_entrepreneurship.html

Shivambhare, M. (2010). *Empowering Men and Women through self-Help Group (SHG)*. Jaipur: RBSA Publishers.

Shweta, D. (2013, May 17). MBAs for India's Rural Women. India Real Time. *The Wall Street Journal*. Retrieved from http://blogs.wsj.com/indiarealtime/2013/05/17/mbas-for-indias-rural-women/

Smith. (1776). *An Inquiry into the Nature and Causes of the Wealth of Nations*. Retrieved from http://www.ifaarchive.com/pdf/smith_-_an_inquiry_into_the_nature_and_causes_of_the_wealth_of_nations%5B1%5D.pdf

Solow, . (1956). A Contribution to the Theory of Economic Growth. *The Quarterly Journal of Economics*, *70*(1), 65. Retrieved from http://faculty.smu.edu/tosang/pdf/Solow_1956.pdf doi:10.2307/1884513

Tan, H. W., & Geeta, B. (1996). *Enterprise Training in Developing Countries: Overview of Incidence, Determinants and Productivity Outcomes*. The World Bank Private Sector Development Department. Occasional Paper 9. Retrieved from http://www.oecd.org/dev/2731650.pdf

Theodore, S. (1961). Investment in Human Capital. *The American Economic Review, 51*(1). Retrieved from http://www.ssc.wisc.edu/~walker/wp/wp-content/uploads/2012/04/schultz61.pdf

Tripathi. (2014). Women Entrepreneurship in Rural India and Sustainable Economic Development. *New Man International Journal of Multidisciplinary Studies, 1*(12). Retrieved from http://www.newmanpublication.com/admin/issue/br/Untitled4.pdf

UK Centre for the Measurement of Economic Activity. (2008). *Proposals for a Satellite Account on Human Capital Resource formation*. Retrieved October 10, 2015, from http://www.google.co.in/url?url=http://www.ons.gov.uk/ons/guide-method/ukcemga/ukcemga-publications/publications/archive/proposals-for-a-satellite-account-on-human-capital-resource-formation

UNDP. (1997). *Human Development Report*. New Delhi: Oxford University Press.

Chapter 8
Preparing Strategy for Emerging Bankers in Iran Banking Industries Using Blue Ocean Strategy:
A Case Study in Pasargad Bank of Iran

Mohamamd Abdolshah
Azad University, Iran

Venus Rahmati Govari
Azad University, Iran

Sahar Sharifi
Azad University, Iran

Hanieh Doust Mohammadi
Azad University, Iran

ABSTRACT

Banking industries in Iran is recently more competitive than last decade which may result of Private bankers' presence as well as modification performed in governmental bankers' plan. In fact the philosophy of these new strategies it is seeking for value creation in organization which obviously associate with innovation. The main aim of present research is to provide banker's emerging strategy using Blue ocean solution within Pasargad Bank of Iran. The current study is accomplished based on descriptive – analytical method and collection of required data has been implemented through designed questionnaire. Then, utilizing QSPM matrix, most attractive strategies prioritized (such as creation variety of services providing travelling banking services and enhance productivity, as well as to offer CCDM [CHECK/CASH DEPOSIT MODULE], increase in security and reduce misuse of related information, implement of updated software, establish a system to update expiration date of credit cards, and online payment of other currencies).

DOI: 10.4018/978-1-5225-1974-4.ch008

1. INTRODUCTION

From past decade up to now main focus of strategic thought has been concentrated to competitive strategies and matter of competition is located in core of consideration of model those are involved providing of strategies. There is no wonder if mentioned approach cause organization to learn competition method to each other tactically and construct their economic structure same as to what structure are currently in use. Today, we are living in a world that all people put their effort to increasing develop and compete each other in this way. With presence of private banking in Iran, banking industries have been looker of drastic variation which implemented aiming to qualitative and quantitative development of banking services considering social requirements to those services. Most of bankers are focused on proceeding with sales services and other factors, those are incorporated with improvement have not been paid high attention. So, the bankers to reach their objectives for improvement and hold more market share should apply particular strategies (Mohammad; 2013). Though, banking industry like every other industries is not lacking of competition. So, considering current competition space and presence of powerful competitors, our question is what solution the bankers and financial institutions should provide to resolve the problem they face in this respect? The Blue Ocean Strategy could develop proper solution this question. With implementing this strategy you are drawing one step than others (Shiri Ardeshir, 2014). The blue ocean strategy because of creation of unknown markets it made, recall the organization to exhaust from bloody ocean of competition to place where the term of competition is meaningless. A dominant concept of this strategy laying in creation of original markets through which they will involve with development of profit making opportunities. Within mentioned strategy, the new markets and industries in which demand is challenge substituted with demand and is not related to competition regulations. (Kim ; 2014, W.C.M. Kim R ; 2005). Prof. Hill for the first time proposed the concept of Blue Ocean in Michigan State University. He acclaimed that Porter concept is incomplete; since discrimination could interpreted as cost leadership and the company who provide his products in lower price than others, in fact implemented one aspect of discrimination strategy. He added that the companies to achieve sustainable competitive advantages, should employ a complex of both cost leadership and discrimination strategies in same time (WL Hill; 1988). Similarity of provided banking services and tight competition governing through, made situation more rigorous to them in view of marketing. Exclusiveness and limitation in banking services in Iran within long time interval and on the other hand, obligatory adopting of these services by client of what bankers serving, made a sever situation called vendor market. In this situation, normally the bankers dictated the services to customers and neglected many competitive tools and behaviors (MusaKhani;2012). Considering that present pattern imitation is dominant behavior in banking services and other bankers could easily make a copy of these actions, services or strategies, there is anxiousness about losing the customer. But adoption of Blue Ocean strategy consequences bankers to create new space in their business and attract new clients and as a result exhaust from competitive environment. Meanwhile, the bankers can take necessary action to maintain their clients and make loyalty in their new customers and simultaneously by inactivation of other bankers' imitation, move to achieve new Blue Oceans. Considering that today, there is strong competition between Iranian bankers and financial institution and successful in this market required to develop novel method in which while discrimination from other competitors, could response to current space of competition. So, we decided to drive their process to success introducing a new plan and method in banking industries. Within present research we plotted strategy situation as well as answered to the following questions:

1. What are the measures to removal in Blue Ocean strategy?
2. What are the indices to increase in Blue Ocean strategy?
3. What are the measures to decreasing in Blue Ocean strategy?
4. What are the indices to creation in Blue Ocean strategy?

2. REVIEW OF RESEARCH LITERATURE

Worldwide markets are governed by one of two following strategies: Blue Ocean and Red Ocean

2.1. Red Ocean

This term represent all presented industries in today markets and companies are now competing in. In fact, Red Ocean is included of recognized markets (W.C.M. Kim, R.: 2005). It mostly concentrate on new customer attraction and has no proper and right concept about making new markets or creational innovation. This strategy is focusing on costly products rather than reducing of costs. More competition space is crowded and there is a rush of competitor, less market share, profiting and growth would be. Most of products is graded as consumable material or cover only a particular part of market. This competition will probably result to wash many companies out and make this ocean bloody (W.C.M. Kim, R.: 2005). Within Red Ocean there is limitation for markets and all competitors knows others strategy. The main aim of this game is to obtain higher market share. In Red Ocean we could see low incoming of companies. Actually it suggested that there is no way through which companies could gain competition advantages. Knowing how production will reach to maturation, it could be describe the decrease in demand, reduction in profit, prevented improvement, and decrease in convincing of client attraction. (Georgopoulos;2011). Red Ocean is within competition – oriented strategies and companies are contending in this space. (WL. Hill; 1988, Porter; 1996, White; 1986). In this environment, competition, costs and price are most important elements accounting for survival of industries. Meanwhile there is huge different in costs within Red Ocean since companies are operated in best manner (Arthur; 1996).

2.2. Blue Ocean

Considering particular situation of business in today world and steady changes of environmental variables, there is no longer possible to freeze many information while long term planning for future. Hence, in recent years, all motion that has employed in strategic management have been placed in innovation and creativity in strategy and paradigmatic movement in strategic domain. One of the most important evolution in this arena which resulted in emerging a revolution in strategic area is Blue Ocean strategy. (http://www.blueoceanstrategy.com). In fact, blue ocean is as a metaphor for a natural, virgin and widespread market which its depth has not been explored yet. (W. C. M. Kim, R., 2005). Now, organization to achieve opportunities for growth and new profiting should create a Blue Ocean (Saini, 2006 September). What is diversifying between winners and losers in creation of Blue Ocean, is their approach to strategy. Creators of Blue Ocean tracking different strategy that call innovation in value. Blue Ocean strategy is a steady pattern derived from strategical thought prior to develop new markets and industries, where challenges substituted by expressed demand and competition regulations are irrelevant (W. C. & Mauborgne Kim, R., 2005a). Blue Ocean generation is not a permanent success but rather is a dynamic process for the company who developed competitive advantages and its superior practice will be revealed when imitators sooner or later will emerge in this present market. (W. C. M. Kim, R, 2005). Proper Blue Ocean strategy, is one that could not be easily imitated. Blue Ocean strategy illustrates decreasing expenses and increase value for customers simultaneously (http://www.blueoceanstrategy.com).

2.3. Innovation in Value

Innovation in value is the foundation of Blue Ocean strategy. The value innovation emphasizing on innovation and value similarly and considered as a novel thinking method to provide and execution of strategy which results to creation of Blue Ocean. Particularly, value innovation is one of the most ordinary and adopted principles to prevent competition. In today strategical literatures, usually it has believed that organization could either generate more value to their clients through higher expenses they spend or create an acceptable value with lower cost. In contrast to this concept, the organization who are seeking for creation of Blue Ocean, concern with both value strategy and lower costs simultaneously (W. C. & Mauborgne Kim, R., 2005) which is illustrated in Figure 1.

2.4. Four Steps Decision Making Framework of Blue Ocean Strategy

Kim and Mauborgne developed tools named Four Steps Decision Making model, due to renewal of value elements' structure to customers for development of new value diagram. Within this model, if there is value innovation, it should be observe within new and existed graphs. To challenge with strategical logic and presented model of business in industries, there is 4 key questions which would be answered (W. C. & Mauborgne Kim, R., 2005).

1. Which factors that industries assign them as warranty should be removed?
2. Which factors might reduce to the lower level than industries' standard?
3. Which factors shall be reduce to the higher level than industries' standard?

Figure 1. Value innovation, foot stone to Blue Ocean Strategy (W. C. M., R., 2005)

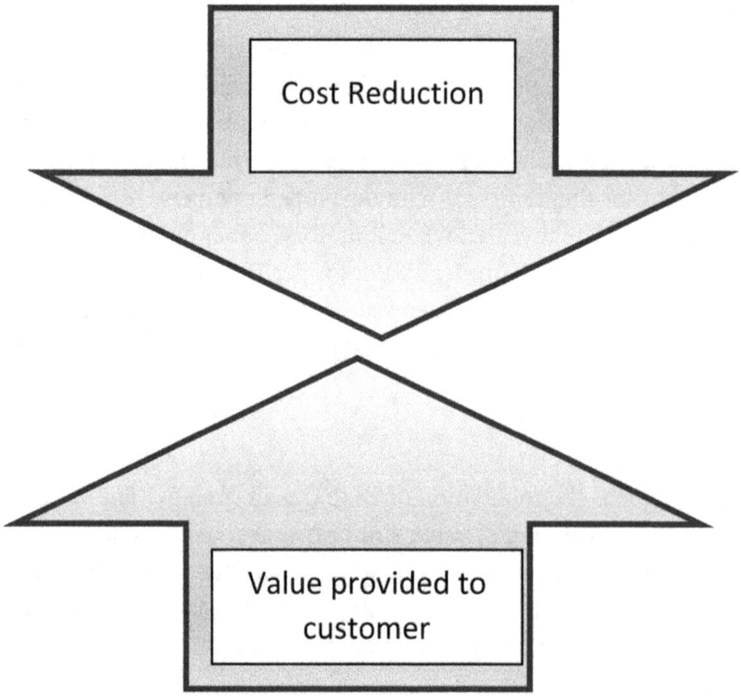

4. Which factors that never been provided in industries, shall be created?

The first questions suggested necessity of investigation of such factors that most of the bankers compete each other to achieve, but it could be removed.

The second question expressed necessity of investigation of such factors that are not cost effective and do not meet customer required value and might be reduced to the lower level than standard. The third one emphasizing on investigation necessarily required for elements that could not provide desired value while it is on high importance for customers. These factors shall enhance to the higher level than standards. The forth question provided that it deemed necessary to identify or create new factors for client upon which they can achieve more market share for their company.

2.5. Strategy Situation Map

Strategy Situation map is implied as a diagnostic and pragmatist frame work to generate Blue Ocean strategy which has two important applications: First the current situation within related industry and markets will be recognized and illustrated. In this way we will be aware that where other competitors have been invested. Second that which values will be obtained by customers from current competition? Here in below we figured out an example for strategy situation map:

Figure 2. An example to Blue Ocean strategy map considering existing parameters

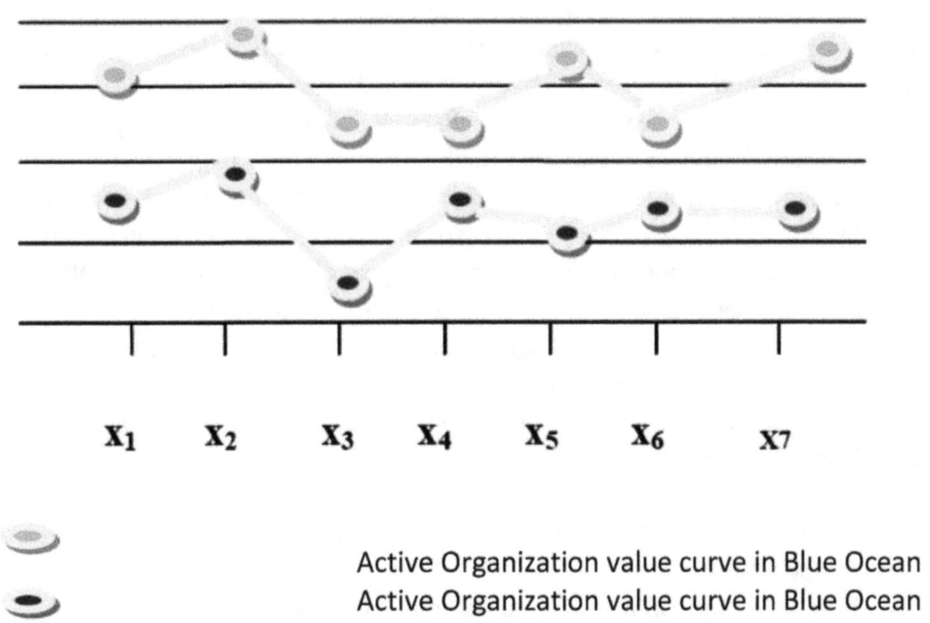

With plotting Blue Ocean Strategy situation map it could be possible to identify those factors that are in high importance for other competitors and using Four Steps Decision Making model as well as the strategies of removal, increase, reduction, creation, a value new diagram has been developed.

3. RESEARCH METHODOLOGY

The present research has been performed in term of Descriptive – Analytical and with practical concern. Thus, we needed an execution plan to create Blue Ocean, which developed through performed assessment and interviews which have been hold with related managers in this field. The relevant statistic population of present research is employees of Pasargad Bank of Iran which is consisting of 20 people. Analytical data have been collected through questionnaire. So, that some questions and total 25 questions introduced for each different part of Blue Ocean strategic Map. The scale for measuring the choices was derived from 5 scores of Likert spectra. So, after investigation has been finalized and considering 4 steps decision making model (removal, reduction, increase and creation), final output and its precedence have been obtained. It is deemed necessary to mentioned that, other methods for data collection which were included on interview with managers, librarian and study of other articles related to Blue Ocean strategy also have been utilized.

3.1. Research Implementation Environment: Pasargad Bank

The vision is defined as to provide a desired picture and an achievable ideal which serve social general management an overview and landscape in long term horizons and comprising some features as Socialism, Valuism, Realism and providence. Within vision document of Pasargad Bank it has mentioned that:

Pasargad Bank as a Bank for 3rd millennium intended that to attain at least 10 percent of market share in Card Banking over the country within related domains. (Maintain and increasing in market share up to year of 1404). As we are well aware mission of company is indicating its existence cause and philosophy. Mission manifest express nature and existence philosophy of the company in phrases and use as instruction to strategy compilation. Mission manifest describe cause of company existence and most general of organization objectives (Lorange, 2007). Pasargad Bank's mission manifest is as follow:

1. Issue of all type of banking card including of credit card, cash card, gift card, Coupon Card
2. Installation of POS terminals in trading and service centers.

3. Installation of PIN PAD terminals in Bank branches for the cash payment
4. Installation of CCDM (CHECK/CASH DEPOSIT MODULE) terminals in all Bank branches, Trading, Service and entertainment centers.
5. Adopting and issue of international Cards
6. Development of ADSL network all over the country (Pasargad Net)

Our Research flow chart is as follows:

Figure 3. Flow chart of implementation in Pasargad Bank

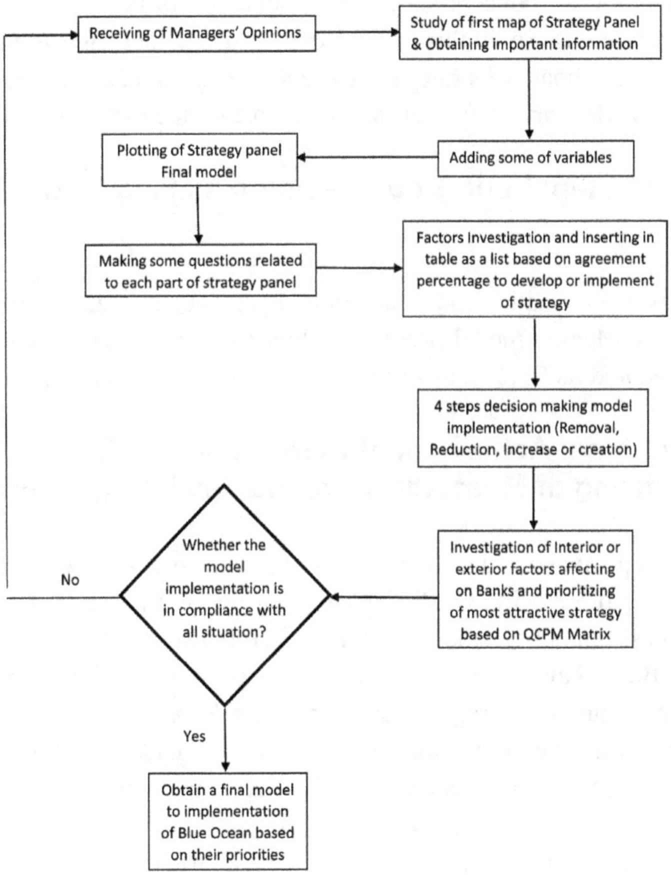

4. STRATEGY PREPARATION FOR EMERGING BANKERS IN IRAN BANKING INDUSTRIES USING BLUE OCEAN STRATEGY

To develop and provide an appropriate model to implement Blue Ocean strategy map within pasargad Bank, following steps applied:

4.1. First Step: Obtain Effective Indices in Banks

Within first step, we studied current strategy of Pasargad Bank. Then we held an interview with executive managers of Bank and some new items added up to relevant strategic map. Thereafter, we designed a questionnaire for each item separately to achieve employees' concept about implementation of present items in bank or creation of new items. So, in this way we explored weakness and strength point of the bank, and final board of strategy at the end of first step has plotted. Within following table, we described concisely about given data and its calculated percentage:

4.2. Second Step: Four Steps Decision Making Model for Indices

After strategy determination and calculation of percentage, some proposals for Four Steps Decision Making model (Removal, Reduction, Increase and Creation) have been provided and its final results illustrated at the end of Table 2.

3.4. Third Steps: Achievement of Internal and Exterior Factors and Prioritizing of Most Attractive Indices Using QSPM Matrix

During this step we decided to select the best and most attractive feasible strategy and prioritizing those using QSPM matrix. Considering the related questionnaire and employees' opinions gathering internal factors (Strength and weakness point of Pasargad Bank) have been listed. Meanwhile, paying attention to importance of working domain and receiving executive managers' opinion of Pasargad Bank exterior factors (Threatening and Opportunities) have been identified and determined.

The list of most important Strength and weak point of mentioned bank in view point of its employees is illustrated within Table 4.

A prepared list of most important of strength and weak points of Pasargad Bank considering importance of working domain and its executive managers' viewpoint has been Illustrated within Table 5.

Based on opinions collected from samples, the most attractive strategies are as follows:

Table 1. Percentage calculation for implementation or creation of new items in strategy board

Item no.	Indices	Description	Compliance (%)
1	Securities	Security implementation and safeguarding of information is accounting for first priorities of every organization. Information safekeeping is well implemented but it might be take necessary and beyond what is applying in this respect currently.	93
2	Variety in services	Implementation of variety and free charges services in Pasargad Bank	90
3	Phone and mobile banking services	Mobile and phone protocol in banking system of Pasargad Bank has been well established and implemented	87
4	Credit Services	Credit Cards cover variety of services but it would be take necessary action to create more variated services.	83
5	Traveling Bank	Creation of Traveler Bank would cause management of cash	80
6	Interest and profit fee	Profit and Interest fee has been adjusted with Islamic norms and contracts and with compliance with Central Bank of Islamic Republic of Iran regulations	73
7	Customer orientation	Customer orientation is well established and visible within Pasargad Bank	69
8	CCDM (CHECK/ CASH DEPOSIT MODULE) services	Development of CCDM (CHECK/CASH DEPOSIT MODULE) services could benefit of its exclusive advantages such as detection of fake monies, information regarding loan and etc.	60
9	Employees job satisfaction	Employees are key persons of every organization and their job satisfaction will bring profit to that organization.	56
10	Flexibility	Change against situation is within main objectives of Pasargad Bank which is well applicable.	53

- **Strategy no. 1:** Increasing in safeguarding and reduction of misuse of information through implementing updated software.
- **Strategy no. 2:** Implementation of a system purposing to automatic updating credit cards expiration date meanwhile currency online payment.
- **Strategy no. 3:** Creation of variety services providing Traveler Banking system and enhancement of productivity.
- **Strategy no. 4:** Creation of variety services providing CCDM systems and enhancement of productivity.

Figure 4. Pasargad Bank Strategy board. Legend: X1:interest fee, X2: Profit fee, X3: Security, X4: Variety in services X5: Customer orientation, X6: Flexibility, X7: Employees job Satisfaction, X8: Online payment of currencies, X9: telephone payment system, X10: CCDM (CHECK/CASH DEPOSIT MODULE), X11:Traveler Bank, Blue curves: Value curve of Bank in Blue Ocean. Red Curves: Value curve of Bank in Red Ocean

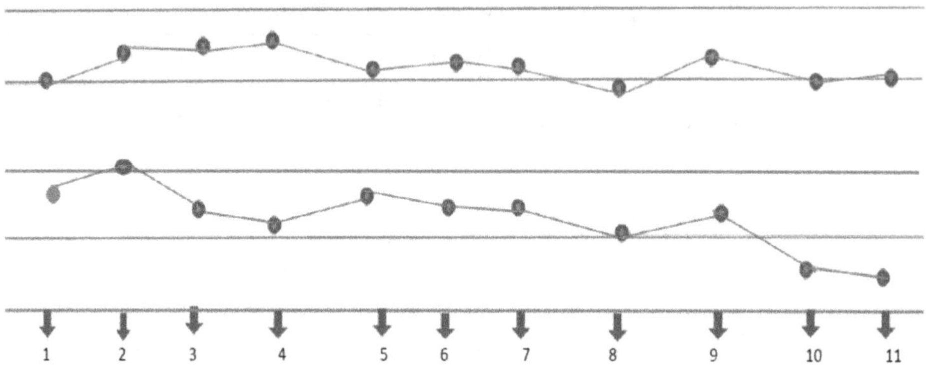

**For a more accurate representation of this figure, please see the electronic version.*

Table 2. Measures assessment and provide proposals

Item	Measures	Description
1	Safeguarding	Private information of people are thoroughly protecting safe in Pasargad Bank. Also, it could be possible to implement other control points which would cause decreasing in system vulnerability and misuse by destructive software so follow with enhancement in safeguarding.
2	Variety in services	Active bankers provide variety of services properly to their client, but they should move forward to present more variety in their services such as exchange services which inspire sense of confidence in their client.
3	Phone payment and mobile banking system	All active bankers comprising well covered services in this domain.
4	Credit Card Services	Dynamic bankers are able to submit full cover banking services. Meanwhile, creation of new electronic services like online payment of currencies with least wage and automatic updating of expiration date of related card needless to client request, it would be able to reduce charges and achieve client satisfaction
5	Traveler Banking	Pasargad bank is agreed to traveler banking services and believe that this would reduce of poverty and improve cash management.
6	Profit and Interest fee	Adopting with Islamic contact in interest and profit aspect within Pasargad Bank is indication of proper trend and is agreed by Central Bank of Islamic Republic of Iran, but reducing interest fee up to 10 percent, it could be able to achieve more client satisfaction

continued on next page

Table 2. Continued

Item	Measures	Description
7	Customer orientation	Operation of Pasargad Bank in this respect is evaluated as moderately but still there is some changes required. So, it has proposed that the bankers can create a grading system of customers (As Gold, Blue and silver grade). In this way, marginal costs will be reduced, delay in presenting of services will remove and provide services to loyal customers will be realized.
8	CCDM (CHECK/ CASH DEPOSIT MODULE)	The Bankers are in uncertainty to implement such these machine, since impose high charges to their system. But Blue Ocean believe that since the time is passing through, the provided value within today markets will be differed from the provided value in future markets. So, it shall be implemented within the Pasargad Bank base on an accurate plan.
9	Employee job Satisfaction	Improper operation of bank in this case resulted to dissatisfaction of personnel. The employees are accounting as key element of every organization. So, it could be possible to enhance personnel job satisfaction through following actions: Working facilitation, Increase of bonus, pay attention to their approach and opinion, reduction of stress and exhaustion, decrease of inefficient activities, creation of positive working space.
10	Flexibility against changes	In this case Pasargad Bank has operated so weak. To obtain inimitable market, most important factor is flexibility and accepting changes easily. We propose that, fear about failure and distrust should be leave away. So, based on an appropriate plan we pass over changes rather than avoided.

Table 3. Four Steps Decision Making Model

Increase:	Decrease:
5- Increase in safeguarding 6- Increase in facilitation working 7- Increase in bonus 8- Increase in payment coverage	4- Marginal charges 5- Reduction of ineffective activities 6- Reduction in interest fee
Creation: 7- Variety in services / Multiple services 8- Customer Grading 9- Creation of positive working space 10- Generation of developed systems to update information 11- Creation of Traveler Banking 12- Provide CCDM (Check/Cash deposit module)	Removal: 3- Delay in provided services 4- Fear of failure and distrust

As we could observe within table no. 10, significant coefficients or weight of each factors both interior or exterior to organization have been illustrated. Meanwhile, each strategy scored by its attractive points as follows:

1. Rarely attractive
2. mostly attractive
3. Rational attractive
4. High attractive

Table 4. Evaluation matrix of interior situation of Pasargad Bank

Interior Strategic Factors	Weight	Current Situation Score	Weighted Score	Description
Strength Point				
S1: Interest fee considering Islamic Contracts	0.156	3	0.47	After financial audit of operations, interest fee will be approved by Central Bank of Islamic Republic of Iran
S2:Variety in services	0.156	4	0.63	Variety in services is critical factor to success
S3: Safeguarding and keeping client's information in safe manner	0.156	4	0.63	Safekeeping imply a key norm to organization
S4: Payment Services well coverage	0.125	3	0.38	Variety in payment services are currently on going in mentioned Bank
Weak Points				
W1: Customer negligent	0.125	2	0.25	Customer services is implemented in low level
W2: Poor Job satisfaction	0.094	2	0.19	The active bankers ignore employees and their opinions
W3: Less Flexibility of employees	0.094	2	0.19	There is no innovating spirit in organization
Total:	1		2.74	

Table 5. Evaluation matrix for exterior conditions of Pasargad Bank

Exterior Strategic Factor	Weight	Current Situation Score	Weighted Score	Description
Opportunities				
O1: productivity level follow improvement trend	0.119	4	0.476	There is wide room to bankers to improve
O2: attitude regarding provide services to clients	0.07	3	0.21	Customer needs precedence
O3: Improving trend for technology to updating information	0.095	3	0.285	The bankers should update their information more.
O4: Government's support	0.119	4	0.476	The active bankers will benefit from government favorable services
O5: Promote authorization granted to Pasargad Bank to enhance knowledge level of its employees	0.119	3	0.357	Optimum utilization of opportunities

continued on next page

Table 5. Continued

Exterior Strategic Factor	Weight	Current Situation Score	Weighted Score	Description
Threats				
T1: Change in economic circumstances	0.119	2	0.238	The banker are not in proper situation in this view point
T2: Change in technology	0.095	3	0.285	This point will not cause, major problem
T3: Change in life style	0.095	2	0.19	There is poor attention paid to this case
T4: Increasing in interest fee and banking facilities and loan	0.07	2	0.14	The banker's operation due to this item is appeared too weak
T5: Losing market share due to incompliance with changes	0.095	2	0.19	There is no proper situation for this cases within Pasrgad Bank
Total	1		2.847	

Obvious difference between attraction scores within each set of strategy suggesting favorability of one strategy against other strategy. Then total score of attraction will be calculated i.e. sum of coefficient multiple to attraction scores. Grand total of attraction scores of each column of quantitative strategic planning shows that which strategy have higher attraction in each set of strategy.

5. CONCLUSION

It is clear that due to similarity of Banking Services, same methods of marketing would be imitated and this prove necessity of entering into new spaces within the market in which creation of new values and using recent marketing method, it could be possible to achieve significant share of market. Growth rate of competition considering limitation in investments and Banker's customers are increasing. Therefore, making to competent organizational structure we could move to change our main strategy and marketing in banking industries market and introducing new competitors make preparation to pass through old Blue Ocean and enter into new Blue Ocean. The result of research suggested that to be pioneer in Banking Industry, Blue Strategy have to implement in 4 steps as follows.

This study comparing with other research is featuring more option to make and enter into a Blue Ocean. Meanwhile, suggested proposals is more updated and selected in compliance with social daily requirements. Within all other available article there is made questions and collected data for 4 Steps Decision Making

Table 6. QSPM Matrix

Main factors to success	Significant Coefficient	Kind of practicable strategies							
		Strategy no. 1		Strategy no. 2		Strategy no. 3		Strategy no. 4	
Opportunities / Threats		Attraction score	Total score	Attraction score	Total score	Attraction score	Total score	Attraction score	Total score
O1: productivity level follow improvement trend	0.09	3	0.27	2	0.18	4	0.36	4	0.36
O2: attitude regarding provide services to clients	0.1	4	0.4	4	0.4	4	0.4	4	0.4
O3: Improving trend for technology to updating information	0.08	4	0.32	4	0.32	3	0.24	3	0.24
O4: Government's support	0.2	2	0.4	3	0.6	4	0.8	4	0.8
O5: Promote authorization granted to Pasargad Bank to enhance knowledge level of its employees	0.08	2	0.16	1	0.08	2	0.16	2	0.16
T1: Change in economic circumstances	0.1	1	0.32	2	0.2	3	0.3	3	0.4
T2: Change in technology	0.08	4	0.27	4	0.32	3	0.24	3	0.24
T3: Change in life style	0.09	3	0.16	4	0.36	3	0.27	1	0.27
T4: Increasing in interest fee and banking facilities and loan	0.08	2	0.3	1	0.08	2	0.16	3	0.08
T5: Losing market share due to incompliance with changes	0.1	3	0.3	3	0.3	3	0.3	3	0.3
Total Score of Exterior Factors	1		2.7		2.84		3.23		3.25

continued on next page

Table 6. Continued

Main factors to success	Significant Coefficient	Kind of practicable strategies							
		Strategy no. 1		Strategy no. 2		Strategy no. 3		Strategy no. 4	
Opportunities / Threats		Attraction score	Total score	Attraction score	Total score	Attraction score	Total score	Attraction score	Total score
Strength & Weakness Point									
S1: Interest fee considering Islamic Contracts	0.2	2	0.4	2	0.4	1	0.2	1	0.2
S2:Variety in services	0.12	3	0.36	4	0.48	4	0.48	4	0.48
S3: Safeguarding and keeping client's information in safe manner	0.2	4	0.8	3	0.6	3	0.6	3	0.6
S4: Payment Services well coverage	0.15	3	.45	4	0.6	3	0.45	3	0.45
W1: Customer negligent	0.15	2	0.3	3	0.45	3	0.45	3	0.45
W2: Poor Job satisfaction	0.09	1	0.09	2	0.18	2	0.18	2	0.18
W3: Less Flexibility of employees	0.09	2	0.18	3	0.27	2	0.18	1	0.09
Total Score of Interior Factors	1		2.58		2.29		2.54		2.45
Grand Total of Scores			5.27		5.13		5.77		5.7

Table 7. Prioritizing of practicable strategies

Item no.	Best Practicable Strategy	Final Score of Strategies Attraction	Priority of Each Strategy
1	Creation of variety services providing traveler banking services and enhance productivity	5.77	First
2	Creation of variety services providing CCDM systems and enhancement of productivity	5.7	Second
3	Increasing in safeguarding and reduction of misuse of information through implementing updated software.	5.27	Third
4	Implementation of a system purposing to automatic updating credit cards expiration date meanwhile currency online payment.	5.13	Fourth

Table 8. Final pattern for 4 steps decision making model in Pasargad Bank

Increasing:	Decreasing:
5. Increasing in safeguarding 6. Facilitation of work in progress 7. Increase in Bonus 8. Increasing of Payment Coverage	4. Marginal costs 5. Reduction in ineffective activities 6. Reduction in interest rate
Creation: 7. Multiple and variety services 8. Customer Grading 9. Creation of Positive working Space 10. Development of advanced systems to updating information 11. Creation of Traveler Banking 12. Provide CCDM (Check/Cash Deposit Module)	Removal: 3. Delay to provide services 4. Fear in failure and distrust

Model, but within present research first all options those are (or will be) effective, have been identified, then to increase, decrease, creation and removal some proposal have been made to users so, make this research more precise than other. In addition, in this study, all items, interior and exterior factors to mentioned bank have been scored and use QSPM to its prioritizing. It is necessary to draw the attention or reader of presented research to the point that this study has been performed within Pasargad Bank as private one, so its results could not be extended to governmental Bankers, since regulation and criterions as well as limitation governing in said banking system (governmental) are very different from those private bankers are currently apply.

REFERENCES

Arthur, W. (1996). Increasing returns and the new world of business. *Harvard Business Review*, 100–109. PMID:10158472

Blue Ocean Strategy. (n.d.). Retrieved from http://www.blueoceanstrategy.com

Georgopoulos, P. G. (2011). *Red ocean vs blue ocean strategy*. MBA-TQM, University of Piraeus.

Hill, W. (1988). Differentiation versus low cost or differentiation and low cost. *Academy of Management Review*, *13*(3), 401–412.

Karampour, A., Sharifi, K., & Safabakhsh, Sh. (2012). *A model-based approach for evaluating the effects of components on export performance based on cost leadership strategy in non-metallic mineral industry*. Business Management.

Kim, W. C. M. R (2004). Blue Ocean strategy: How to create uncontested market space and make competition irrelevant. Boston: Harvard Business School Press.

Kim, W. C. M. (2005a). Blue ocean strategy: From theory to practice. *California Management Review*.

Kim, W. C. M. (2005b). Blue ocean strategy. Cambridge, MA: Harvard Business School Press.

Kim, W. C. M. (2005c). Blue ocean strategy: How to create uncontested Market Space and Make the competition Irrelevant. Boston: Harvard Business School Press.

Kim, W. C. M. (2005d). Value Innovation: A leap the blue ocean. *The Journal of Business Strategy*, *26*(4), 22–28. doi:10.1108/02756660510608521

Lorange, P. (2007). *Scott Morton*. Strategic Control.

Musakhani, M., Haghighi, M., & Torkzadeh, S. (2012). A model for customer loyalty using customer knowledge management in the banking industry private banks. *Business Management*, *4*(12), 147–164.

Porter, M. E. (1996). What is strategy? *Harvard Business Review*, *74*, 61–78. PMID:10158474

Saini, D. S. (2006, September). *Book review: Blue ocean strategy: how to create uncontested market space and make competition irrelevant*. Academic Press.

White, R. E. (1986). Generic business strategies, organizational context and performance: An empirical investigation. *Strategic Management Journal*, *7*(3), 217–231. doi:10.1002/smj.4250070304

Chapter 9
Corporate Social Responsibility:
Theory and Applications

Kijpokin Kasemsap
Suan Sunandha Rajabhat University, Thailand

ABSTRACT

This chapter emphasizes the overview of corporate social responsibility (CSR); the practices and disclosure of CSR; CSR and human values; CSR in mining operations; CSR in sports tourism industry; CSR in emerging economies; and the perspectives of CSR in the digital age. A strategic approach to CSR is crucial to a company's success. CSR can bring various benefits in terms of risk management, cost savings, access to capital, customer relationships, human resource management, and innovation capacity. CSR encourages more social and environmental responsibility from the corporate sector at a time when the crisis has damaged consumer confidence and the levels of trust in business. Socially responsible companies can improve their brand reputation, attract more customers, and increase stakeholder engagement. The chapter argues that promoting CSR has the potential to enhance organizational performance and reach strategic goals in the digital age.

DOI: 10.4018/978-1-5225-1974-4.ch009

INTRODUCTION

Corporate social responsibility (CSR) has gained an increasing attention across the globe (Zhu & Zhang, 2015). CSR is a business strategy that enables organizations to act in a socially responsible manner based on their premises (Asif, Searcy, Zutshi, & Fisscher, 2013), and is recognized as an important instrument for driving sustainable development (Mutti, Yakovleva, Vazquez-Brust, & di Marco, 2012) and for maximizing long-term benefits for organizations (Mohr, Webb, & Harris, 2001). CSR is the volitional contribution by organizations to improve the environment, society, and economy based on either altruism value or competitive advantage enhancement (Huang, Ye, & Kao, 2015). CSR is the right thing to do because firms have responsibility to any person or entity that is affected by their CSR activities (Freeman, Wicks, & Parmar, 2004).

CSR positively relates to stakeholders' perceptions (Gonzalez-Rodriguez, Diaz-Fernandez, & Simonetti, 2015). The assessment of stakeholders' perceptions toward CSR considerably affect top management's decision to respond in an encouraging manner to CSR initiatives (Okpara & Wynn, 2012). The CSR perspectives (e.g., social activism, globalization, and transparency) have increased the requirements of companies beyond aspects of business, giving importance to economic, social, and environmental issues (Jamali, Safieddine, & Rabbath, 2008). Firms have adopted CSR practices to help increase both shareholder and social values by integrating stakeholder and shareholder interests into company's decision making (Detomasi, 2008).

Many business firms have started to assume social and political responsibilities that go beyond legal requirements and fill the regulatory vacuum in global governance (Scherer & Palazzo, 2011). Developed countries have initiated the national projects to promote CSR practices among companies (Cramer, 2005). CSR efforts in developed countries are demonstrated to bring performance improvement, such as productivity (Sun & Stuebs, 2013) and competitive success (Gallardo-Vazquez & Sanchez-Hernandez, 2014). CSR practices are usually voluntary for most companies in developed countries, such as Sweden, Denmark, and Germany (Oxfam Hong Kong, 2010). However, even in Organization for Economic Cooperation and Development (OECD) countries, governmental intervention is used to promote CSR practices (Gonzalez & Martinez, 2004).

This chapter aims to bridge the gap in the literature on the thorough literature consolidation of CSR. The extensive literature of CSR provides a contribution to practitioners and researchers by describing the theory and applications of CSR in order to maximize the business impact of CSR in the digital age.

Background

Since the 1990s, the discourse on CSR has been more prominent within companies, governments, and society (Anderson & Bieniaszewska, 2005). This has been achieved by bringing ethics closer to business (Swanson, 1995). Socially responsible tasks have frequently led firm's managerial practices to improve the general opinion of their brand image, making it appear as an essential element of their identity (Malsch, 2013). Organizations and companies previously considered only on the economic benefits (Anderson, 1989); however, recently companies have begun more focusing on the environment and social effects (Welford, Chan, & Man, 2008). CSR has evolved including the normative and philosophic issues regarding the company's role within society as a generator of benefits (Dahlsrud, 2008).

An enhanced level of interest in the topic of CSR has led to a significant increase in the volume of studies dealing with various dimensions (Fatemi, Fooladi, & Tehranian, 2015). While most of the earlier research was executed by practitioners and researchers in the fields of strategic management and business ethics (Orlitzky & Benjamin, 2001), scholars in the fields of economics and finance have recently joined the discussion in an endeavor to explore the relationship between social and financial performance (Servaes &Tamayo, 2013). Gonzalez-Rodriguez et al. (2015) indicated that the current economic situation has required the emergence and proliferation of good entrepreneurs as business founders and managers who are involved in firms and society.

The literature has increasingly emphasized the importance of implementing sustainable development principles in which the inclusion of stakeholders plays an important role (Matos & Silvestre, 2013). Ramasamy et al. (2010) defined stakeholders as individuals who should have to ensure that firms act in a socially responsible manner. Ruf et al. (2001) established the relationship between stakeholder theory and CSR and stated that CSR performance can be evaluated in terms of a company meeting the demands of its multiple stakeholder groups. Stakeholders can pressurize companies into taking responsibility for their industrial operations (Castka & Prajogo, 2013). The identification of stakeholders enables the organization to explore the business entities and leads to sustainable development (Sardinha, Craveiro, & Milheiras, 2013).

The concept of CSR is closely intertwined with the increased engagement with stakeholders and the integration of their concerns into core business processes (Skouloudis, Evangelinos, & Malesios, 2015). Firms are encouraged to manage their CSR and identity in accordance with the popular stakeholder theory (Heikkurinen & Ketola, 2012). Matten et al. (2003) stated that the stakeholder theory appears to be an essential process in the CSR perspectives. The notion of stakeholder personalizes CSR by specifying groups or persons to whom companies should be responsible (Branco & Rodrigues, 2007). The stakeholder theory is based on the idea that companies must recognize not only shareholders as a fundamental stakeholder category, and who are critical for the firm's survival and success, but also several agents who may be affected by business decisions (Freeman, 1984).

IMPLICATIONS OF CORPORATE SOCIAL RESPONSIBILITY

This section explains the overview of CSR; the practices and disclosure of CSR; CSR and human values; CSR in mining operations; CSR in sports tourism industry; CSR in emerging economies; and the perspectives of CSR in the digital age.

Overview of Corporate Social Responsibility

The perceived importance of environmental, social, and governance programs has arisen in recent years (Gao & Zhang, 2015). CSR is a key driver of corporate reputation given its potential to promote the hard-to-duplicate competitive advantage (Melo & Garrido-Morgado, 2012). The CSR literature has been faced from two perspectives: the domains of stakeholders and social issues (Mattingly & Berman, 2006). The CSR pattern established by the triple bottom line (TBL) is largely popular, current, and accepted. TBL classifies CSR into three dimensions: financial, environmental, and ethical perspectives (Elkington, 1997). TBL admits the relevance not only of the economic aspect, but also of the ethical and environmental components of a social initiative executed by the firm to measure its performance (Norman & MacDonald, 2004).

CSR is categorized according to its contribution to economic prosperity, environmental quality, and social capital (Gonzalez-Rodriguez et al., 2015). Social capital includes social networks, social norms, social trust, and institutional trust (Kasemsap, 2014a). García-Rodríguez et al. (2013) indicated that CSR is important for firms in the sectors, which are characterized by their close ties with their social and environmental context, especially multinational enterprises (MNEs) operating in resource-rich developing countries and, more specifically, in the oil sector. Regarding tourism industry, CSR and sustainable tourism development enhance the value-creating strategies in the competitive advantage of business organizations against potential competitors (Kasemsap, 2016a). Both better stakeholder engagement and transparency around CSR performance are important in reducing capital constraints (Cheng, Ioannou, & Serafeim, 2014).

As large companies integrate the principles of CSR into their business practices, company personnel are expected to show actions that are connected to communicated corporate values and related policies (Michailides & Lipsett, 2013). CSR activities enhance the value of the firm when they are accompanied by high public awareness (Servaes & Tamayo, 2013). Firms with environmental concerns face higher required returns by shareholders and end up paying higher rates on their bank loans (Chava, 2014). Environmental responsibility is found to have a positive and significant impact on institutional ownership only when financial performance is high (Wahba, 2008).

CSR continues to grow in importance among the press, political activists, managers, analysts, and investors (Carroll, Primo, & Richter, 2016). The improvements in CSR can enhance the value in organizations (Kruger, 2014). There is a positive relationship between a bank's performance and its CSR activities (Wu & Shen, 2013). The presence of an optimal level of CSR can maximize business profits (Benabou & Triole, 2010). Huppe (2011) found a positive relationship between CSR and investment performance. Concentrating on the environmental dimension of CSR, Chava (2014) provided evidence on both the cost of debt and cost of equity. CSR is influenced by various firm-specific factors, such as the organization's stage of development, strategy, and leadership (Mason & Simmons, 2011). Market orientation, learning orientation, and risk-taking attitudes are the major constructs that affect firms' CSR engagement (Nybakk & Panwar, 2015). CSR has a positive impact on product evaluation and this positive impact is greater for products with high brand familiarity than products with low brand familiarity (Perera & Chaminda, 2013).

Current trend of emphasis on CSR serves to divert the public's attention from the ethical issues facing business and society (Ludescher, Mahsud, & Prussia, 2012) as a marketing campaign (Viveros, 2016). Based on information collected from a survey of 280 Australian companies from the manufacturing and service sectors, Galbreath (2010) observed that CSR activities in economic, legal, ethical, and discretionary areas positively yield the traditional and financial outcomes in various areas, such as employee turnover, customer satisfaction, and corporate reputation. There is a positive relationship between financial resource availability and CSR (Julian & Ofori-dankwa, 2013).

Practices and Disclosure of Corporate Social Responsibility

The demand for information and transparency from corporations has increased over the last few years (Tagesson, Blank, Broberg, & Collin, 2009). Sierra-García et al. (2015) indicated that there is the increasing interest in the integrated reporting that includes the company's financial, governance, environmental, and social performance. There is the growing pressure on corporations for sustainability reporting (Asif, Searcy, Santos, & Kensah, 2013). Similar to environmental reporting (Mitchell & Quinn, 2005) or sustainability reporting (Samkin, 2012), it is an effective way to require companies to publicize their CSR reports. Firms practicing CSR behave differently from other firms in financial reporting and provide more value-relevant information (Gao & Zhang, 2015).

Positive CSR information about a firm significantly enhances consumers' intentions to purchase products from, potential employees' intentions to seek employment with, and potential investors' intentions to invest in the company (Alniacik, Alniacik, & Genc, 2011). When employees perceive that their organization invests in a CSR practice that is both intrinsic and extrinsic, they also tend to exert extra effort in their work (Story & Neves, 2015). MNEs that disclose information on a wider variety of social and environmental issues and frame CSR with a focus on internal issues are more inclined to integrate corporate governance into their CSR reporting (Kolk & Pinkse, 2010).

Better-performing firms are more likely than worse-performing ones to disclose CSR information and to produce higher quality CSR reports (Li, Luo, Wang, & Wu, 2013). CSR reporting is stronger in high-risk industries than in low-risk industries (Young & Marais, 2012). Lattemann et al. (2009) stated that the firm-level characteristics (e.g., size, duality of board chairperson, and percentage of external members on the board) have a significant influence on CSR communications. The importance of communicating CSR not only to socially responsible investors, but also to the mainstream of the financial community is gaining importance in a more competitive capital market environment (Fieseler, 2011).

In China, the government has encouraged CSR practices among all state-owned companies (SOCs) since 2008 (Bhatia, 2012). Chinese SOCs have made significant efforts to adopt CSR practices and develop their CSR reports (Bhatia, 2012). As early as 2000, developed countries (e.g., the Netherlands) developed national initiatives to promote CSR practices among companies (Cramer, 2005). Two key streams of CSR studies are developing measurements for CSR practices (de Villiers, 1999) and examining if and how much performance improvement can be achieved by CSR efforts (Wingard & Vorster, 2001). An empirical examination on the U.S. chemical companies showed that CSR practices can improve productivity (Sun & Stuebs, 2013).

Organizational core value has positive relationship with CSR practices (Duarte, 2010). For successful implementation, CSR should be embedded into corporate governance considering stakeholders' interests (Mason & Simmons, 2014). Business press plays an important role as an information intermediary and that media coverage affects a firm's information environment (Kim, Zhang, Li, & Tian, 2014). For CSR to affect a firm's wider media coverage, the media must have incentives to report more positively about good CSR firms (Cahan, Chen, Chen, & Nguyen, 2015). If firms that are good CSR performers receive more favorable media coverage, managers have incentives to actively manage their media image by being more socially responsible, as long as a positive media image is economically beneficial (El Ghoul, Guedhami, Kwok, & Mishra, 2011).

While the company-specific management systems vary in detail, the basic components of the systems often include formal policy documents (e.g., code of corporate conduct and policies addressing health, safety, environment, and community issues); designated health, safety, environment, and community units responsible for the implementation of CSR policies; a process for evaluating and monitoring environmental, social, and technical risks and impacts of business operations; and CSR reports (Kotilainen, Prokhorova, Sairinen, & Tiainen, 2015). Policymakers should promote the transparency of ownership information and enhance CSR performance (Dam & Scholtens, 2012). Firms that exhibit a higher CSR score behave in a responsible manner to constrain earnings management, thus delivering more transparent financial information to investors (Kim, Park, & Wier, 2012).

CSR often occupies a prominent position on corporate Internet sites (Meiseberg & Ehrmann, 2012). The disclosure of CSR-related sustainable information is the most frequently used way for companies to appear to be socially responsible to society, thus improving relationships with stakeholders (Deegan & Rankin, 1996). Because executives usually tend to take into account the demands of other stakeholders, not only shareholders (Ibrahim & Angelidis, 1995), it is expected that they tend to defend CSR disclosures that are useful for a wide range of interest groups. The disclosure of CSR information is useful for a wide range of interest groups, as it concerns social contributions, public safety, and environmental actions in modern organizations. CSR disclosure improves analyst forecast accuracy (Dhaliwal, Radhakrishnan, Tsang, & Yang, 2012). Firms with a better CSR score exhibit cheaper equity financing (El Ghoul et al., 2011).

Corporate Social Responsibility and Human Values

Human values have been largely studied in the academic literature as a proxy for both human attitudes and behaviors (Kirkman & Shapiro, 2001). Schwartz's theory (1992) specified ten universal values arranged into a circular structure where the side-by-side values are positively related to one another. The circular arrangement of human values represents a motivational continuum, both the compatibilities and conflicts among the ten value types being identified (Schwartz, 1992). The entrepreneurs' values and their managerial behaviors can determine the CSR managerial practices (Witt & Redding, 2011).

The structure of human values can be reorganized by four higher-order values with their own aims: self-enhancement versus self-transcendence and openness to change versus conservation (Schwartz, 1992). Basil and Weber (2006) indicated that consumers' prosocial behavior is motivated by altruism value and egotism value as well as by a combination of two values (i.e., altruism and egotism). Hemingway and Maclagan (2004) stated that individuals have an affinity with CSR due to altruistic values. Egocentric individuals can display the socially responsible behavior by being motivated by what other individuals might think about them (Clary, Snyder, Ridge, & Copel, 1998).

From a socio-psychological value perspective, the concept of human values is attached to the individuals who have them (Rokeach, 1973), human values have the main goals which can be summarized: the cognition about what the individual wishes to strive for (Rokeach, 1973); the activation of prime attitudes, biological and social individual needs and the guidance and selection of behaviors and events (Schwartz & Bilsky, 1987); and the individual adaptive response to the environment requires the joint, and not the separate, study of human values and their environment (Michod, 1993).

Corporate Social Responsibility in Mining Operations

With a shift from cheap and easy resources to expensive and more difficult, the global mining industry is expanding to new regions and facing the increasing challenges related to social and environmental constraints to the mining operations (Prior, Giurco, Mudd, Mason, & Behrisch, 2012). Regarding strategies within controversial industries (Du & Vieira, 2012), in order to overcome these social and environmental restraints, the mining industry has been adopting and developing CSR policies across regions and societies (Kotilainen et al., 2015).

Mining companies face the long-standing community expectations for the development of the infrastructure and improvement of social services, that were previously provided by the state through the state-owned mining companies (Bogdetsky & Novikov, 2012). Basu et al. (2015) indicated that the evaluations of costs and benefits to local communities affected by the mining activities must be undertaken on a case-by-case basis as circumstances across projects are not identical and although many issues may be common, outcomes can differ for a number of reasons. Advocacy for compensation to the mining communities for the negative result-related economic, social, and environmental impacts regarding mining activity has arisen (Esteves & Vanclay, 2009).

Mining operations are often conducted in the less-developed, remote, and relatively poor regions that serve as the major sources of raw materials for global markets while the benefits of mining operations are often acknowledged outside the mining areas (Gifford, Kestler, & Anand, 2010). Mining operations often run the risk of disturbing other sources of livelihoods and provide only small local benefits and compensations, thus causing the growing socioeconomic inequalities and land-use conflicts (Kotilainen et al., 2015). The mining industry has faced the growing demands from non-governmental organizations, local communities, and activists to improve its environmental and social performance (Warhurst, 2001).

The emergence of global CSR norms and intensified debates on sustainability in mining operations have promoted the adoption of CSR policies and practices among mining companies (Dashwood, 2007). Many transnational mining companies have started to forge global CSR strategies to be applied to all their operations (Kapelus, 2002). CSR strategies in mining operations aim at mitigating negative impacts of mining operations and maximizing their benefits for society, and include charitable giving, environmental management systems, tight safety regulations, and more systematic local economic mining development programs (Hamann, 2004). The significance of executing CSR procedures during the exploration stage of mining operations has recently been better acknowledged (Luning, 2012).

Corporate Social Responsibility in Sports Tourism Industry

Tourism-related industries (e.g., airlines, casinos, hotels, and restaurants) and the sports industry have engaged in various CSR activities (Inoue & Kent, 2012) including community involvement, customer connections, employee relations, green management (Holcomb, Upchurch, & Okumus, 2007), and environmental sustainability (Trendafilova, Babiak, & Heinze, 2013). Sports tourism (i.e., travel associated with physical activity and sports) has become one of the fastest growing aspects of tourism (Gibson, 1998), because it transcends the boundaries of culture, society, ethics, and religion.

There is an increase in CSR activities among sports-related organizations (Breitbarth & Harris, 2010). Tourism has become unified based on the power of sports attractions and has become a new participant in cross-cultural markets (Cappato & Pennazio, 2006). Cross-cultural understanding and cultural knowledge for global marketing approaches are the key issues to be recognized for a favorable integration into the cross-cultural organizations (Kasemsap, 2015a).

The strategic CSR approach significantly promotes an understanding of company's reputation, competitor differentiation, brand loyalty, competitive advantage, and economic performance (Walters & Tacon, 2010). Regarding CSR, as more people and businesses worldwide are becoming more concerned about sustainability and environmental initiatives, it is important that firms should focus on how sports marketing-related activities can add value to their strategic goals (Kasemsap, 2014b). Business corporations should seek the valuable sports sponsorship opportunities to realize their overall organizational objectives, sports marketing goals, and promotional strategies to enhance brand management in the global sports marketing (Kasemsap, 2015b).

Corporate Social Responsibility in Emerging Economies

CSR policies depend on issues, such as size of a company, its industrial profile, the country of its origin, and personal orientations of executives and managers (Jenkins & Yakovleva, 2006). CSR is adopted to increase the chance of bonding with the government (Lin, Tan, Zhao, & Karim, 2015). While recognized as voluntary activities that go beyond governmental regulation and core profit activities of businesses (Chapple & Moon, 2005), it has been suggested that business core activities and obedience to legislation can be viewed as the major CSR activities (Carroll, 1991). CSR practices have been found to vary between industrialized and developing countries, and comparative studies of CSR practices shedding light on the mechanisms behind such diversity have been called for (Lim & Tsutsui, 2012).

CSR has been studied within the context of developed industrialized economies, and it has been explained as emerging from civil activism and public demands for transparency, human rights, and ecological and social sustainability of businesses. For developing and emerging economies, CSR has been considered as a controversial practice (Kotilainen et al., 2015). There are major obstacles to achieving corporate responsibility in developing countries where the institutions, standards are relatively weak. CSR strategies have been argued not to address the actual problems in developing countries (Campbell, 2012).

Countries with a weak legal system and poor institutional and economic setting have been found to be the probable contexts for companies to underperform in CSR (Ringov & Zollo, 2007). CSR practices have a negative impact on emerging economies as there are fundamental problems concerning the capacity of private firms to deliver the practical development through local community development projects (Frynas, 2005). It is required to adjust CSR practices to the contexts of developing countries where the challenges faced by various societies and businesses differ from those in developed countries (Hilson, 2012).

Perspectives of Corporate Social Responsibility in the Digital Age

CSR implies that companies have collective responsibility beyond legal requirements (Weisenfeld, 2012). CSR is of immediate interest and relevance for scholars and practitioners (Dobers, 2009). CSR is being promoted as an instrument for global governance to address the regulatory vacuum surrounding transnational business activities and as a method for encouraging business to contribute to sustainable development at the national level (Gjølberg, 2010). CSR can be viewed as a process of institutional change in which norms are changed (de Bakker, 2012). CSR is becoming a strategic issue that has to be dealt with by top management (Setó-Pamies,

2015). Both CSR and Global Reporting Initiative (GRI) activities positively affect corporate environmental performance and financial performance (Lee & Maxfield, 2015). Cuadrado-Ballesteros et al. (2015) stated that corporate reputation is positively related to CSR.

The CSR-related economic, legal, ethical, social, and environmental aspects are usually involved in various decision-making processes of international businesses (Kolk & van Tulder, 2010). The main managerial decisions in a firm (e.g., growth, resources, performance, CSR commitments, and ethical goals) are strongly linked to the top management team (Carpenter, Geletkanycz, & Sanders, 2004). Top management team plays a crucial role in the implementation of the institutional corporate structures correlated with CSR in which firms are embedded (Gonzalez-Rodriguez et al., 2015). Corporate governance can positively moderate the association between corporate financial performance and CSR (Ntim & Soobaroyen, 2013).

When sustainability is part of the goal, the integration of the diverging needs of stakeholders is critical to encourage the socially responsible decision-making process (Gonzalez-Benito, Lannelongue, & Queiruga, 2011). The decision support methods have been suggested in the literature to take account of the stakeholders' needs and to promote sustainable development within an organization (de Brucker, Macharis, & Verbeke, 2013). The standard ISO 26000 aims to provide guidance on social responsibility and help all types of organizations contribute to sustainable development (Hahn, 2013). Using stakeholder analysis, the list of stakeholders is narrowed down to the most important issues in order to obviously understand their interests, objectives, and concerns, and to predict their CSR-related actions (Sperry & Jetter, 2012).

Formulating and translating CSR strategy into actual managerial practices and outcome values remain ongoing challenges for many organizations (Jamali, El Dirani, & Harwood, 2015). Various CSR-related stakeholder management approaches, utilizing multiple-criteria processes and incorporating stakeholders' circumstances into corporate decision-making processes, have been previously explored (Bendjenna, Charre, & Zarour, 2012). Defining a fair method for CSR-related stakeholder management is a significant goal as it can empower those who are most affected by the industry's operations (Poplawska, Labib, Reed, & Ishizaka, 2015). CSR-related stakeholder relationship management and strategic communication management can play in the development, implementation, and monitoring of corporate strategies in a sustainable manner (de Beer & Rensburg, 2011).

Fuzzy set theory and fuzzy logic have been applied for stakeholders' management, to capture the significant views of multiple stakeholders (Akter & Simonovic, 2005), to evaluate the company's commitment through its stakeholders, to evaluate the social and financial performance of an organization, and the relationship between them (Munoz, Rivera, & Moneva, 2008), to prioritize stakeholders' concerns in the environmental risk management (Paralikas & Lygeros, 2005), to evaluate stakeholders' influence to the important aspects, and to provide relevant information for the management of stakeholders' relationships (Susniene & Purvinis, 2013).

Fuzzy logic has been jointly applied with Decision Making Trial and Evaluation Laboratory (DEMATEL), for instance, to evaluate the drivers of CSR in the mining industry (Govindan, Kannan, & Shankar, 2014) and to explore the practices of green supply chain management (Lin, 2013). Stakeholder prioritization in the engineering process has been applied using fuzzy logic (Majumdar, Rahman, & Rahman, 2014). In order to take into account uncertainty and vagueness, the fuzzy logic algorithm has been employed to indicate the stakeholders' perspectives (Gil-Lafuente & de Paula, 2013).

FUTURE RESEARCH DIRECTIONS

The classification of the extensive literature in the domains of CSR will provide the potential opportunities for future research. CSR is the process of assessing an organization's impact on society and evaluating their responsibilities. Companies should have visible CSR campaigns is due to the importance and prevalence of social media. Companies that want to protect their brand understand that social media is an integral part of public perception. With the advent of Web 2.0 technologies, social media enables the creation of knowledge value chain to customize information and delivery for a technological business growth (Kasemsap, 2014c). Exploring the role of social media in encouraging CSR should be further studied. Social entrepreneurship becomes an important mechanism for reconciling the disparities in wealth, opportunity, educational access, and environmental issues in modern business (Kasemsap, 2016b). CSR and social entrepreneurship are certain to remain important issues for future research directions.

Sustainability is essential for businesses both as a long-term strategy to improve employee confidence, and as a short term response to government legislation. Sustainability regulation can assist competitiveness in business, as it forces industry to innovate and create new solutions, driving up profits for those companies that provide the high-quality products. Sustainable development can balance the economic, environmental, and social needs, allowing prosperity for now and future generations. Poor ethical climate and the lack of willingness of top executives in defining core values (e.g., accountability, control, deontology, independence, integrity, and responsibility) lead to organizational deviance (Kasemsap, 2015c). The relationship among CSR, sustainability, sustainable development, and ethical leadership will be the beneficial topics for future research directions.

CONCLUSION

This chapter highlighted the overview of CSR; the practices and disclosure of CSR; CSR and human values; CSR in mining operations; CSR in sports tourism industry; CSR in emerging economies; and the perspectives of CSR in the digital age. CSR requires the effective engagement with internal and external stakeholders so it enables business enterprises to take advantage of fast-changing expectations in the digital age. CSR has the significant effect on a company's stakeholders, its goals, and its performance. Companies that effectively engage in CSR significantly gain various benefits in terms of economic, social, and environmental perspectives. Socially responsible companies have the positive effect regarding staff retention, recruitment, job satisfaction, and organizational commitment in the modern workforce. Socially responsible companies can effectively detect and respond to risk, and can expect the needs of their stakeholders in a timely and effective manner.

Socially responsible companies can obtain customer satisfaction and customer loyalty when customers buy products and services based on corporate trust, corporate reputation, and brand. Socially responsible companies have an increased ability to develop new products toward customer satisfaction and to establish the business creativity of their stakeholders. Socially responsible companies can facilitate the development of new markets and create the attractive opportunities for entrepreneurial success, business growth, and economic development. Socially responsible companies can deliver business-related benefits through CSR activities and continuous engagement with their stakeholders. Socially responsible companies can gain operational efficiencies and earn the satisfaction, trust, and loyalty of their stakeholders, customers, and employees. Promoting CSR has the potential to enhance organizational performance and reach strategic goals in the digital age.

REFERENCES

Akter, T., & Simonovic, S. P. (2005). Aggregation of fuzzy views of a large number of stakeholders for multi-objective flood management decision-making. *Journal of Environmental Management*, *77*(2), 133–143. doi:10.1016/j.jenvman.2005.02.015 PMID:16046249

Alniacik, U., Alniacik, E., & Genc, N. (2011). How corporate social responsibility information influences stakeholders intentions. *Corporate Social Responsibility and Environmental Management*, *18*(4), 234–245. doi:10.1002/csr.245

Anderson, C. L., & Bieniaszewska, R. L. (2005). The role of corporate social responsibility in an oil companys expansion into new territories. *Corporate Social Responsibility and Environmental Management, 12*(1), 1–9. doi:10.1002/csr.71

Anderson, J. W. (1989). *Corporate social responsibility*. Westport, CT: Greenwood Press.

Asif, M., Searcy, C., Santos, P. D., & Kensah, D. (2013). A review of Dutch corporate sustainable development reports. *Corporate Social Responsibility and Environmental Management, 20*(6), 321–339. doi:10.1002/csr.1284

Asif, M., Searcy, C., Zutshi, A., & Fisscher, O. A. M. (2013). An integrated management systems approach to corporate social responsibility. *Journal of Cleaner Production, 56*(1), 7–17. doi:10.1016/j.jclepro.2011.10.034

Basil, D. Z., & Weber, D. (2006). Values motivation and concern for appearances: The effect of personality traits on responses to corporate social responsibility. *International Journal of Nonprofit and Voluntary Sector Marketing, 11*(1), 61–72. doi:10.1002/nvsm.38

Basu, P. K., Hicks, J., Krivokapic-Skoko, B., & Sherley, C. (2015). Mining operations and corporate social responsibility: A case study of a large gold mine in regional Australia. *The Extractive Industries and Society, 2*(3), 531–539.

Benabou, R., & Triole, J. (2010). Individual and corporate social responsibility. *Economica, 77*(305), 1–19. doi:10.1111/j.1468-0335.2009.00843.x

Bendjenna, H., Charre, P. J., & Zarour, N. E. (2012). Using multi-criteria analysis to prioritize stakeholders. *Journal of Systems and Information Technology, 14*(3), 264–280. doi:10.1108/13287261211255365

Bhatia, A. (2012). The corporate social responsibility report: The hybridization of a confused genre (20072011). *IEEE Transactions on Professional Communication, 55*(3), 221–238. doi:10.1109/TPC.2012.2205732

Bogdetsky, V., & Novikov, V. (2012). *Mining, development and environment in Central Asia: Case studies: A toolkit companion*. Joensuu, Finland: University of Eastern Finland.

Branco, M. C., & Rodrigues, L. L. (2007). Positioning stakeholder theory within the debate on corporate social responsibility. *Electronic Journal of Business Ethics and Organization Studies, 12*(1), 5–15.

Breitbarth, T., & Harris, P. (2008). The role of corporate social responsibility in the football business: Towards the development of a conceptual model. *European Sport Management Quarterly*, *8*(2), 179–206. doi:10.1080/16184740802024484

Cahan, S. F., Chen, C., Chen, L., & Nguyen, N. H. (2015). Corporate social responsibility and media coverage. *Journal of Banking & Finance*, *59*, 409–422. doi:10.1016/j.jbankfin.2015.07.004

Campbell, B. (2012). Corporate social responsibility and development in Africa: Redefining the roles and responsibilities of public and private actors in the mining sector. *Resources Policy*, *37*(2), 138–143. doi:10.1016/j.resourpol.2011.05.002

Cappato, A., & Pennazio, V. (2006). *Corporate social responsibility in sport: Torino 2006 Olympic Winter Games*. Turin, Italy: University of Turin.

Carpenter, M. A., Geletkanycz, M. A., & Sanders, W. G. (2004). Upper echelons research revisited: Antecedents, elements, and consequences of top management team composition. *Journal of Management*, *30*(6), 749–778. doi:10.1016/j.jm.2004.06.001

Carroll, A. B. (1991). The pyramid of corporate social responsibility: Towards the moral management of organizational stakeholders. *Business Horizons*, *34*(4), 39–48. doi:10.1016/0007-6813(91)90005-G

Carroll, R. J., Primo, D. M., & Richter, B. K. (2016). Using item response theory to improve measurement in strategic management research: An application to corporate social responsibility. *Strategic Management Journal*, *37*(1), 66–85. doi:10.1002/smj.2463

Castka, P., & Prajogo, D. (2013). The effect of pressure from secondary stakeholders on the internalization of ISO 14001. *Journal of Cleaner Production*, *47*, 245–252. doi:10.1016/j.jclepro.2012.12.034

Chapple, W., & Moon, J. (2005). Corporate social responsibility (CSR) in Asia: A seven-country study of CSR website reporting. *Business & Society*, *44*(4), 415–441. doi:10.1177/0007650305281658

Chava, S. (2014). Environmental externalities and cost of capital. *Management Science*, *60*(4), 2223–2247. doi:10.1287/mnsc.2013.1863

Cheng, B., Ioannou, I., & Serafeim, G. (2014). Corporate social responsibility and access to finance. *Strategic Management Journal*, *35*(1), 1–23. doi:10.1002/smj.2131

Clary, E. G., Snyder, M., Ridge, R. G., Copeland, J., Stukas, A. A., Haugen, J., & Miene, P. (1998). Understanding and assessing the motivation of volunteers: A functional approach. *Journal of Personality and Social Psychology*, *74*(6), 1516–1530. doi:10.1037/0022-3514.74.6.1516 PMID:9654757

Cramer, J. (2005). Experiences with structuring corporate social responsibility in Dutch industry. *Journal of Cleaner Production*, *13*(6), 583–592. doi:10.1016/j.jclepro.2003.12.008

Cuadrado-Ballesteros, B., Rodriguez-Ariza, L., & Garcia-Sanchez, I. M. (2015). The role of independent directors at family firms in relation to corporate social responsibility disclosures. *International Business Review*, *24*(5), 890–901. doi:10.1016/j.ibusrev.2015.04.002

Dahlsrud, A. (2008). How corporate social responsibility is defined: An analysis of 37 definitions. *Corporate Social Responsibility and Environmental Management*, *15*(1), 1–13. doi:10.1002/csr.132

Dam, L., & Scholtens, B. (2012). Does ownership type matter for corporate social responsibility? *Corporate Governance: An International Review*, *20*(3), 233–252. doi:10.1111/j.1467-8683.2011.00907.x

Dashwood, H. S. (2007). Towards sustainable mining: The corporate role in the construction of global standards. *Multinational Business Review*, *15*(1), 47–66. doi:10.1108/1525383X200700003

de Bakker, F. G. A. (2012). Exploring networks of activism on corporate social responsibility: Suggestions for a research agenda. *Creativity and Innovation Management*, *21*(2), 212–223. doi:10.1111/j.1467-8691.2012.00641.x

de Beer, E., & Rensburg, R. (2011). Towards a theoretical framework for the governing of stakeholder relationships: A perspective from South Africa. *Journal of Public Affairs*, *11*(4), 208–225. doi:10.1002/pa.414

de Brucker, K., Macharis, C., & Verbeke, A. (2013). Multi-criteria analysis and the resolution of sustainable development dilemmas: A stakeholder management approach. *European Journal of Operational Research*, *224*(1), 122–131. doi:10.1016/j.ejor.2012.02.021

de Villiers, C. (1999). Corporate social reporting in South Africa: Signs of a pygmy awakening? *Social and Environmental Accounting*, *19*(2), 5–7. doi:10.1080/0969160X.1999.9651613

Deegan, C., & Rankin, M. (1996). Do Australian companies report environmental news objectively? An analysis of environmental disclosures by firms prosecuted successfully by the environmental protection authority. *Accounting, Auditing & Accountability Journal*, *9*(2), 50–67. doi:10.1108/09513579610116358

Detomasi, D. A. (2008). The political roots of corporate social responsibility. *Journal of Business Ethics*, *82*(4), 807–819. doi:10.1007/s10551-007-9594-y

Dhaliwal, D. S., Radhakrishnan, S., Tsang, A., & Yang, Y. G. (2012). Nonfinancial disclosure and analyst forecast accuracy: International evidence on corporate social responsibility disclosure. *Accounting Review*, *87*(3), 723–759. doi:10.2308/accr-10218

Dobers, P. (2009). Corporate social responsibility: Management and methods. *Corporate Social Responsibility and Environmental Management*, *16*(4), 185–191. doi:10.1002/csr.201

Du, S., & Vieira, E. T. Jr. (2012). Striving for legitimacy through corporate social responsibility: Insights from oil companies. *Journal of Business Ethics*, *110*(4), 413–427. doi:10.1007/s10551-012-1490-4

Duarte, F. (2010). Working with corporate social responsibility in Brazilian companies: The role of managers values in the maintenance of CSR cultures. *Journal of Business Ethics*, *96*(3), 355–368. doi:10.1007/s10551-010-0470-9

El Ghoul, S., Guedhami, O., Kwok, C., & Mishra, D. (2011). Does corporate social responsibility affect the cost of capital? *Journal of Banking & Finance*, *35*(9), 2388–2406. doi:10.1016/j.jbankfin.2011.02.007

Elkington, J. (1997). *Cannibals with forks: The triple bottom line of 21st century business*. Gabriola Island, Canada: New Society Publishers.

Esteves, A. M., & Vanclay, F. (2009). Social development needs analysis as a tool for SIA to guide corporate-community investment: Applications in the minerals industry. *Environmental Impact Assessment Review*, *29*(2), 137–145. doi:10.1016/j.eiar.2008.08.004

Fatemi, A., Fooladi, I., & Tehranian, H. (2015). Valuation effects of corporate social responsibility. *Journal of Banking & Finance*, *59*, 182–192. doi:10.1016/j.jbankfin.2015.04.028

Fieseler, C. (2011). On the corporate social responsibility perceptions of equity analysts. *Business Ethics (Oxford, England)*, *20*(2), 131–147. doi:10.1111/j.1467-8608.2011.01616.x

Freeman, E. E. (1984). *Strategic management: A stakeholder approach.* Boston, MA: Pitman Publishing.

Freeman, R. E., Wicks, A. C., & Parmar, B. (2004). Stakeholder theory and the corporate objective revisited. *Organization Science, 15*(3), 364–369. doi:10.1287/orsc.1040.0066

Frynas, J. G. (2005). The false developmental promise of corporate social responsibility: Evidence from multinational oil companies. *International Affairs, 81*(3), 581–598. doi:10.1111/j.1468-2346.2005.00470.x

Galbreath, J. (2010). How does corporate social responsibility benefit firms? Evidence from Australia. *European Business Review, 22*(4), 411–431. doi:10.1108/09555341011056186

Gallardo-Vazquez, D., & Sanchez-Hernandez, M. I. (2014). Measuring corporate social responsibility for competitive success at a regional level. *Journal of Cleaner Production, 72*, 14–22. doi:10.1016/j.jclepro.2014.02.051

Gao, L., & Zhang, J. H. (2015). Firms earnings smoothing, corporate social responsibility, and valuation. *Journal of Corporate Finance, 32*, 108–127. doi:10.1016/j.jcorpfin.2015.03.004

García-Rodríguez, F. J., García-Rodríguez, J. L., Castilla-Gutiérrez, C., & Major, S. A. (2013). Corporate social responsibility of oil companies in developing countries: From altruism to business strategy. *Corporate Social Responsibility and Environmental Management, 20*(6), 371–384. doi:10.1002/csr.1320

Gibson, H. J. (1998). Sport tourism: A critical analysis of research. *Sport Management Review, 1*(1), 45–76. doi:10.1016/S1441-3523(98)70099-3

Gifford, B., Kestler, A., & Anand, S. (2010). Building local legitimacy into corporate social responsibility: Gold mining firms in developing nations. *Journal of World Business, 45*(3), 304–311. doi:10.1016/j.jwb.2009.09.007

Gil-Lafuente, A. M., & de Paula, L. B. (2013). Algorithm applied in the identification of stakeholders. *Kybernetes, 42*(5), 674–685. doi:10.1108/K-04-2013-0073

Gjølberg, M. (2010). Varieties of corporate social responsibility (CSR): CSR meets the Nordic Model. *Regulation & Governance, 4*(2), 203–229. doi:10.1111/j.1748-5991.2010.01080.x

Gonzalez, M. D., & Martinez, C. (2004). Fostering corporate social responsibility through public initiative: From the EU to the Spanish case. *Journal of Business Ethics, 55*(3), 275–293. doi:10.1007/s10551-004-0994-y

Gonzalez-Benito, J., Lannelongue, G., & Queiruga, D. (2011). Stakeholders and environmental management systems: A synergistic influence on environmental imbalance. *Journal of Cleaner Production, 19*(14), 1622–1630. doi:10.1016/j.jclepro.2011.05.013

Gonzalez-Rodriguez, M. R., Diaz-Fernandez, M. C., & Simonetti, B. (2015). The social, economic and environmental dimensions of corporate social responsibility: The role played by consumers and potential entrepreneurs. *International Business Review, 24*(5), 836–848. doi:10.1016/j.ibusrev.2015.03.002

Govindan, K., Kannan, D., & Shankar, K. M. (2014). Evaluating the drivers of corporate social responsibility in the mining industry with multi-criteria approach: A multi-stakeholder perspective. *Journal of Cleaner Production, 84*(1), 214–232. doi:10.1016/j.jclepro.2013.12.065

Hahn, R. (2013). ISO 26000 and the standardization of strategic management processes for sustainability and corporate social responsibility. *Business Strategy and the Environment, 22*(7), 442–455. doi:10.1002/bse.1751

Hamann, R. (2004). Corporate social responsibility, partnerships, and institutional change: The case of mining companies in South Africa. *Natural Resources Forum, 28*(4), 278–290. doi:10.1111/j.1477-8947.2004.00101.x

Heikkurinen, P., & Ketola, T. (2012). Corporate responsibility and identity: From a stakeholder to an awareness approach. *Business Strategy and the Environment, 21*(5), 326–337. doi:10.1002/bse.744

Hemingway, C. A., & Maclagan, P. W. (2004). Managers personal values as drivers of corporate social responsibility. *Journal of Business Ethics, 50*(1), 33–44. doi:10.1023/B:BUSI.0000020964.80208.c9

Hilson, G. (2012). Corporate social responsibility in the extractive industries: Experiences from developing countries. *Resources Policy, 37*(2), 131–137. doi:10.1016/j.resourpol.2012.01.002

Holcomb, J. L., Upchurch, R. S., & Okumus, F. (2007). Corporate social responsibility: What are top hotel companies reporting? *International Journal of Contemporary Hospitality Management, 19*(6), 461–475. doi:10.1108/09596110710775129

Huang, F. H., Ye, Y. J., & Kao, C. H. (2015). Developing a novel intuitionistic fuzzy importance–performance analysis for evaluating corporate social responsibility in sport tourism event. *Expert Systems with Applications: An International Journal, 42*(19), 6530–6538. doi:10.1016/j.eswa.2015.04.008

Huppe, G. A. (2011). *Alpha's tale: The economic value of CSR.* Paper presented at the 2011 PRI Academic Network Conference, Sigtuna, Sweden. doi:10.2139/ssrn.1969583

Ibrahim, N. A., & Angelidis, J. P. (1995). The corporate social responsiveness orientation of board members: Are there differences between inside and outside directors? *Journal of Business Ethics, 14*(5), 405–419. doi:10.1007/BF00872102

Inoue, Y., & Kent, A. (2012). Investigating the role of corporate credibility in corporate social marketing: A case study of environmental initiatives by professional sport organizations. *Sport Management Review, 15*(3), 330–344. doi:10.1016/j.smr.2011.12.002

Jamali, D., Safieddine, A. M., & Rabbath, M. (2008). Corporate governance and corporate social responsibility synergies and interrelationships. *Corporate Governance: An International Review, 16*(5), 443–459. doi:10.1111/j.1467-8683.2008.00702.x

Jamali, D. R., El Dirani, A. M., & Harwood, I. A. (2015). Exploring human resource management roles in corporate social responsibility: The CSR-HRM co-creation model. *Business Ethics (Oxford, England), 24*(2), 125–143. doi:10.1111/beer.12085

Jenkins, H., & Yakovleva, N. (2006). Corporate social responsibility in the mining industry: Exploring trends in social and environmental disclosure. *Journal of Cleaner Production, 14*(3/4), 271–284. doi:10.1016/j.jclepro.2004.10.004

Julian, S. D., & Ofori-dankwa, J. C. (2013). Financial resource availability and corporate social responsibility expenditures in a Sub-Saharan economy: The institutional difference hypothesis. *Strategic Management Journal, 34*(11), 1314–1330. doi:10.1002/smj.2070

Kapelus, P. (2002). Mining, corporate social responsibility and the community: The case of Rio Tinto, Richards Bay Minerals and the Mbonambi. *Journal of Business Ethics, 39*(3), 275–296. doi:10.1023/A:1016570929359

Kasemsap, K. (2014a). The role of social capital in higher education institutions. In N. Baporikar (Ed.), *Handbook of research on higher education in the MENA region: Policy and practice* (pp. 119–147). Hershey, PA: IGI Global. doi:10.4018/978-1-4666-6198-1.ch007

Kasemsap, K. (2014b). The role of sports marketing in the global marketplace. In M. Dos Santos (Ed.), *Strategies in sports marketing: Technologies and emerging trends* (pp. 279–298). Hershey, PA: IGI Global. doi:10.4018/978-1-4666-5994-0.ch017

Kasemsap, K. (2014c). The role of social media in the knowledge-based organizations. In I. Lee (Ed.), *Integrating social media into business practice, applications, management, and models* (pp. 254–275). Hershey, PA: IGI Global. doi:10.4018/978-1-4666-6182-0.ch013

Kasemsap, K. (2015a). The roles of cross-cultural perspectives in global marketing. In J. Alcántara-Pilar, S. del Barrio-García, E. Crespo-Almendros, & L. Porcu (Eds.), *Analyzing the cultural diversity of consumers in the global marketplace* (pp. 37–59). Hershey, PA: IGI Global. doi:10.4018/978-1-4666-8262-7.ch003

Kasemsap, K. (2015b). The roles of sports sponsorship and brand management in global sports marketing. In H. Leng & N. Hsu (Eds.), *Emerging trends and innovation in sports marketing and management in Asia* (pp. 1–21). Hershey, PA: IGI Global. doi:10.4018/978-1-4666-7527-8.ch001

Kasemsap, K. (2015c). The role of ethical leadership in ethical organizations: A literature review. In C. Anyansi-Archibong (Ed.), *Contemporary issues surrounding ethical research methods and practice* (pp. 135–168). Hershey, PA: IGI Global. doi:10.4018/978-1-4666-8562-8.ch006

Kasemsap, K. (2016a). Encouraging corporate social responsibility and sustainable tourism development in global tourism. In L. Guliani & S. Rizwan (Eds.), *Corporate social responsibility in the hospitality and tourism industry* (pp. 197–224). Hershey, PA: IGI Global. doi:10.4018/978-1-4666-9902-1.ch016

Kasemsap, K. (2016b). The role of social entrepreneurship in the global business environments. In Z. Fields (Ed.), *Incorporating business models and strategies into social entrepreneurship* (pp. 177–201). Hershey, PA: IGI Global. doi:10.4018/978-1-4666-8748-6.ch011

Kim, J. B., Zhang, H., Li, L., & Tian, G. (2014). Press freedom, externally-generated transparency, and stock price informativeness: International evidence. *Journal of Banking & Finance*, *46*, 299–310. doi:10.1016/j.jbankfin.2014.05.023

Kim, Y., Park, M. S., & Wier, B. (2012). Is earnings quality associated with corporate social responsibility? *Accounting Review*, *87*(3), 761–796. doi:10.2308/accr-10209

Kirkman, B. L., & Shapiro, D. L. (2001). The impact of team members cultural values on productivity, cooperation, and empowerment in self-managing working teams. *Journal of Cross-Cultural Psychology*, *32*(5), 597–617. doi:10.1177/0022022101032005005

Kolk, A., & Pinkse, J. (2010). The integration of corporate governance in corporate social responsibility disclosures. *Corporate Social Responsibility and Environmental Management*, *17*(1), 15–26.

Kolk, A., & van Tulder, R. (2010). International business, corporate social responsibility and sustainable development. *International Business Review*, *19*(1), 1119–1125.

Kotilainen, J., Prokhorova, E., Sairinen, R., & Tiainen, H. (2015). Corporate social responsibility of mining companies in Kyrgyzstan and Tajikistan. *Resources Policy*, *45*, 202–209. doi:10.1016/j.resourpol.2015.06.001

Kruger, P. (2014). Corporate goodness and shareholder wealth. *Journal of Financial Economics*, *115*(2), 304–329. doi:10.1016/j.jfineco.2014.09.008

Lattemann, C., Fetscherin, M., Alon, I., Li, S., & Schneider, A. M. (2009). CSR communication intensity in Chinese and Indian multinational companies. *Corporate Governance: An International Review*, *17*(4), 426–442. doi:10.1111/j.1467-8683.2009.00758.x

Lee, J., & Maxfield, S. (2015). Doing well by reporting good: Reporting corporate responsibility and corporate performance. *Business and Society Review*, *120*(4), 577–606. doi:10.1111/basr.12075

Li, Q., Luo, W., Wang, Y., & Wu, L. (2013). Firm performance, corporate ownership, and corporate social responsibility disclosure in China. *Business Ethics (Oxford, England)*, *22*(2), 159–173. doi:10.1111/beer.12013

Lim, A., & Tsutsui, K. (2012). Globalization and commitment in corporate social responsibility: Cross-national analyses of institutional and political-economy effects. *American Sociological Review*, *77*(1), 69–98. doi:10.1177/0003122411432701

Lin, K. J., Tan, J., Zhao, L., & Karim, K. (2015). In the name of charity: Political connections and strategic corporate social responsibility in a transition economy. *Journal of Corporate Finance*, *32*, 327–346. doi:10.1016/j.jcorpfin.2014.10.007

Lin, R. J. (2013). Using fuzzy DEMATEL to evaluate the green supply chain management practices. *Journal of Cleaner Production*, *40*, 32–39. doi:10.1016/j.jclepro.2011.06.010

Ludescher, J. C., Mahsud, R., & Prussia, G. E. (2012). We are the corporation: Dispersive CSR. *Business and Society Review*, *117*(1), 55–88. doi:10.1111/j.1467-8594.2011.00399.x

Luning, S. (2012). Corporate social responsibility (CSR) for exploration: Consultants, companies and communities in process of engagements. *Resources Policy*, *37*(2), 205–211. doi:10.1016/j.resourpol.2011.02.004

Majumdar, S. I., Rahman, M. S., & Rahman, M. M. (2014). Stakeholder prioritization in requirement engineering process: A case study on school management system. *Computing in Science & Engineering*, *4*(1), 17–27.

Malsch, B. (2013). Politicizing the expertise of the accounting industry in the realm of corporate social responsibility. *Accounting, Organizations and Society*, *38*(2), 149–168. doi:10.1016/j.aos.2012.09.003

Mason, C., & Simmons, J. (2011). Forward looking or looking unaffordable? Utilising academic perspectives on corporate social responsibility to assess the factors influencing its adoption by business. *Business Ethics (Oxford, England)*, *20*(2), 159–176. doi:10.1111/j.1467-8608.2011.01614.x

Mason, C., & Simmons, J. (2014). Embedding corporate social responsibility in corporate governance: A stakeholder systems approach. *Journal of Business Ethics*, *119*(1), 77–86. doi:10.1007/s10551-012-1615-9

Matos, S., & Silvestre, B. S. (2013). Managing stakeholder relations when developing sustainable business models: The case of the Brazilian energy sector. *Journal of Cleaner Production*, *45*, 61–73. doi:10.1016/j.jclepro.2012.04.023

Matten, D., Crane, A., & Chapple, W. (2003). Behind the mask: Revealing the true face of corporate citizenship. *Journal of Business Ethics*, *45*(1/2), 109–120. doi:10.1023/A:1024128730308

Mattingly, J. E., & Berman, S. L. (2006). Measurement of corporate social action: Discovering taxonomy in the Kinder Lydenburg Domini ratings data. *Business & Society*, *45*(1), 20–46. doi:10.1177/0007650305281939

Meiseberg, B., & Ehrmann, T. (2012). Lost in translation? The prevalence and performance impact of corporate social responsibility in franchising. *Journal of Small Business Management*, *50*(4), 566–595. doi:10.1111/j.1540-627X.2012.00367.x

Melo, T., & Garrido-Morgado, A. (2012). Corporate reputation: A combination of social responsibility and industry. *Corporate Social Responsibility and Environmental Management*, *19*(1), 11–31. doi:10.1002/csr.260

Michailides, T. P., & Lipsett, M. G. (2013). Surveying employee attitudes on corporate social responsibility at the frontline level of an energy transportation company. *Corporate Social Responsibility and Environmental Management*, *20*(5), 296–320. doi:10.1002/csr.1291

Michod, R. E. (1993). Biology and the origin of values. In M. Hechter, L. Nadel, & R. Michod (Eds.), *The origin of values* (pp. 261–271). New York, NY: Aldine de Gruyter.

Mitchell, C., & Quinn, N. (2005). Environmental reporting disclosure in South Africa: A comparative study of the expectations of selected groups of preparers and users. *Meditari Accountancy Research, 13*(2), 17–33. doi:10.1108/10222529200500010

Mohr, L. A., Webb, D. J., & Harris, K. E. (2001). Do consumers expect companies to be socially responsible? The impact of corporate social responsibility on buying behavior. *The Journal of Consumer Affairs, 35*(1), 45–72. doi:10.1111/j.1745-6606.2001.tb00102.x

Munoz, M. J., Rivera, J. M., & Moneva, J. M. (2008). Evaluating sustainability in organisations with a fuzzy logic approach. *Industrial Management & Data Systems, 108*(6), 829–841. doi:10.1108/02635570810884030

Mutti, D., Yakovleva, N., Vazquez-Brust, D., & di Marco, M. H. (2012). Corporate social responsibility in the mining industry: Perspectives from stakeholder groups in Argentina. *Resources Policy, 37*(2), 212–222. doi:10.1016/j.resourpol.2011.05.001

Norman, W., & MacDonald, C. (2004). Getting to the bottom of triple bottom line. *Business Ethics Quarterly, 14*(2), 243–262. doi:10.5840/beq200414211

Ntim, C. G., & Soobaroyen, T. (2013). Corporate governance and performance in socially responsible corporations: New empirical insights from a neo-institutional framework. *Corporate Governance: An International Review, 21*(5), 468–494. doi:10.1111/corg.12026

Nybakk, E., & Panwar, R. (2015). Understanding instrumental motivations for social responsibility engagement in a micro-firm context. *Business Ethics (Oxford, England), 24*(1), 18–33. doi:10.1111/beer.12064

Okpara, J. O., & Wynn, P. M. (2012). Stakeholders perceptions about corporate social responsibility: Implications for poverty alleviation. *Thunderbird International Business Review, 54*(1), 91–103. doi:10.1002/tie.21441

Orlitzky, M., & Benjamin, J. D. (2001). Corporate social performance and firm risk: A meta-analytic review. *Business & Society, 40*(4), 369–396. doi:10.1177/000765030104000402

Oxfam Hong Kong. (2010). *Corporate social responsibility survey of Hang Seng Index constituent companies 2009*. Hong Kong: Oxfam Hong Kong.

Paralikas, A., & Lygeros, A. (2005). A multi-criteria and fuzzy logic based methodology for the relative ranking of the fire hazard of chemical substances and installations. *Process Safety and Environmental Protection*, *83*(2), 122–134. doi:10.1205/psep.04236

Perera, L. C. R., & Chaminda, J. W. D. (2013). Corporate social responsibility and product evaluation: The moderating role of brand familiarity. *Corporate Social Responsibility and Environmental Management*, *20*(4), 245–256. doi:10.1002/csr.1297

Poplawska, J., Labib, A., Reed, D. M., & Ishizaka, A. (2015). Stakeholder profile definition and salience measurement with fuzzy logic and visual analytics applied to corporate social responsibility case study. *Journal of Cleaner Production*, *105*, 103–115. doi:10.1016/j.jclepro.2014.10.095

Prior, T., Giurco, D., Mudd, G., Mason, L., & Behrisch, J. (2012). Resource depletion, peak minerals and the implications for sustainable resource management. *Global Environmental Change*, *22*(3), 577–587. doi:10.1016/j.gloenvcha.2011.08.009

Ramasamy, B., Yeung, M. C. H., & Au, A. K. M. (2010). Consumer support for corporate social responsibility (CSR): The role of religion and values. *Journal of Business Ethics*, *91*(1), 61–72. doi:10.1007/s10551-010-0568-0

Ringov, D., & Zollo, M. (2007). Corporate responsibility from a socio-institutional perspective. The impact of national culture on corporate social performance. *Corporate Governance*, *7*(4), 476–485. doi:10.1108/14720700710820551

Rokeach, M. (1973). *The nature of human values*. New York, NY: The Free Press.

Ruf, B. M., Muralidhar, K., Janney, J. J., & Paul, K. (2001). An empirical investigation of the relationship between change in corporate social performance and financial performance: A stakeholder theory perspective. *Journal of Business Ethics*, *32*(2), 143–156. doi:10.1023/A:1010786912118

Samkin, G. (2012). Changes in sustainability reporting by an African defence contractor: A longitudinal analysis. *Meditari Accountancy Research*, *20*(2), 134–166. doi:10.1108/10222521211277834

Sardinha, I. D., Craveiro, D., & Milheiras, S. (2013). A sustainability framework for redevelopment of rural brownfields: Stakeholder participation at Sáo Domingos Mine, Portugal. *Journal of Cleaner Production*, *57*(1), 200–208. doi:10.1016/j.jclepro.2013.05.042

Scherer, A. G., & Palazzo, G. (2011). The new political role of business in a globalized world: A review of a new perspective on CSR and its implications for the firm, governance, and democracy. *Journal of Management Studies*, *48*(4), 899–931. doi:10.1111/j.1467-6486.2010.00950.x

Schwartz, S. H. (1992). In M. Zanna (Ed.), *Universal in the content and structure of values: Theoretical advances and empirical tests in 20 countries* (pp. 1–65). Advances in experimental social psychologyNew York, NY: Academic Press.

Schwartz, S. H., & Bilsky, W. (1987). Toward a universal psychological structure of human values. *Journal of Personality and Social Psychology*, *53*(3), 550–562. doi:10.1037/0022-3514.53.3.550

Servaes, H., & Tamayo, A. (2013). The impact of corporate social responsibility on firm value: The role of customer awareness. *Management Science*, *59*(5), 1045–1061. doi:10.1287/mnsc.1120.1630

Setó-Pamies, D. (2015). The relationship between women directors and corporate social responsibility. *Corporate Social Responsibility and Environmental Management*, *22*(6), 334–345. doi:10.1002/csr.1349

Sierra-García, L., Zorio-Grima, A., & García-Benau, M. A. (2015). Stakeholder engagement, corporate social responsibility and integrated reporting: An exploratory study. *Corporate Social Responsibility and Environmental Management*, *22*(5), 286–304. doi:10.1002/csr.1345

Skouloudis, A., Evangelinos, K., & Malesios, C. (2015). Priorities and perceptions for corporate social responsibility: An NGO perspective. *Corporate Social Responsibility and Environmental Management*, *22*(2), 95–112. doi:10.1002/csr.1332

Sperry, R., & Jetter, A. J. (2012). *Fuzzy cognitive maps to implement corporate social responsibility in product planning: A novel approach*. Paper presented at the 2012 Technology Management for Emerging Technologies (PICMET 2012), Vancouver, Canada.

Story, J., & Neves, P. (2015). When corporate social responsibility (CSR) increases performance: Exploring the role of intrinsic and extrinsic CSR attribution. *Business Ethics (Oxford, England)*, *24*(2), 111–124. doi:10.1111/beer.12084

Sun, L., & Stuebs, M. (2013). Corporate social responsibility and firm productivity: Evidence from the chemical industry in the United States. *Journal of Business Ethics*, *118*(2), 251–263. doi:10.1007/s10551-012-1579-9

Susniene, D., & Purvinis, O. (2013). Empirical insights on understanding stakeholder influence. *Journal of Business Economics and Management*, *16*(4), 1–15.

Swanson, D. L. (1995). Addressing a theoretical problem by reorienting the corporate social performance model. *Academy of Management Review*, *20*(1), 43–64.

Tagesson, T., Blank, V., Broberg, P., & Collin, S. O. (2009). What explains the extent and content of social and environmental disclosures on corporate websites: A study of social and environmental reporting in Swedish listed corporations. *Corporate Social Responsibility and Environmental Management*, *16*(6), 352–364. doi:10.1002/csr.194

Trendafilova, S., Babiak, K., & Heinze, K. (2013). Corporate social responsibility and environmental sustainability: Why professional sport is greening the playing field. *Sport Management Review*, *16*(3), 298–313. doi:10.1016/j.smr.2012.12.006

Viveros, H. (2016). Examining stakeholders perceptions of mining impacts and corporate social responsibility. *Corporate Social Responsibility and Environmental Management*, *23*(1), 50–64. doi:10.1002/csr.1363

Wahba, H. (2008). Exploring the moderating effect of financial performance on the relationship between corporate environmental responsibility and institutional investors: Some Egyptian evidence. *Corporate Social Responsibility and Environmental Management*, *15*(6), 361–371. doi:10.1002/csr.177

Walters, G., & Tacon, R. (2010). Corporate social responsibility in sport: Stakeholder management in the UK football industry. *Journal of Management & Organization*, *16*(4), 566–586. doi:10.1017/S1833367200001942

Warhurst, A. (2001). Corporate citizenship and corporate social investment: Drivers of tri-sector partnerships. *Journal of Corporate Citizenship*, *1*(1), 57–73. doi:10.9774/GLEAF.4700.2001.sp.00008

Weisenfeld, U. (2012). Corporate social responsibility in innovation: Insights from two cases of Syngentas activities in genetically modified organisms. *Creativity and Innovation Management*, *21*(2), 199–211. doi:10.1111/j.1467-8691.2012.00643.x

Welford, R., Chan, C., & Man, M. (2008). Priorities for corporate social responsibility: A survey of businesses and their stakeholders. *Corporate Social Responsibility and Environmental Management*, *15*(1), 52–62. doi:10.1002/csr.166

Wingard, H. C., & Vorster, Q. (2001). Financial performance of environmentally responsible South African listed companies. *Meditari Accountancy Research*, *9*(1), 313–332. doi:10.1108/10222529200100017

Witt, M. A., & Redding, G. (2011). The spirits of corporate social responsibility: Senior executive perceptions of the role of the firm in society in Germany, Hong Kong, Japan, South Korea and the USA. *Socio-economic Review*, *10*(1), 109–134. doi:10.1093/ser/mwr026

Wu, M., & Shen, C. (2013). Corporate social responsibility in the banking industry: Motives and financial performance. *Journal of Banking & Finance*, *37*(9), 3529–3547. doi:10.1016/j.jbankfin.2013.04.023

Young, S., & Marais, M. (2012). A multi-level perspective of CSR reporting: The implications of national institutions and industry risk characteristics. *Corporate Governance: An International Review*, *20*(5), 432–450. doi:10.1111/j.1467-8683.2012.00926.x

Zhu, Q., & Zhang, Q. (2015). Evaluating practices and drivers of corporate social responsibility: The Chinese context. *Journal of Cleaner Production*, *100*, 315–324. doi:10.1016/j.jclepro.2015.03.053

ADDITIONAL READING

Andreini, D., Pedeliento, G., & Signori, S. (2014). CSR and service quality in nonprofit organizations: The case of a performing arts association. *International Journal of Nonprofit and Voluntary Sector Marketing*, *19*(2), 127–142. doi:10.1002/nvsm.1488

Barthold, C. (2013). Corporate social responsibility, collaboration and depoliticisation. *Business Ethics (Oxford, England)*, *22*(4), 393–403. doi:10.1111/beer.12031

Beare, D., Buslovich, R., & Searcy, C. (2014). Linkages between corporate sustainability reporting and public policy. *Corporate Social Responsibility and Environmental Management*, *21*(6), 336–350. doi:10.1002/csr.1323

Becchetti, L., Ciciretti, R., & Giovannelli, A. (2013). Corporate social responsibility and earnings forecasting unbiasedness. *Journal of Banking & Finance*, *37*(9), 3654–3668. doi:10.1016/j.jbankfin.2013.05.026

Carbo, J., Langella, I. M., Dao, V. T., & Haase, S. J. (2014). Breaking the ties that bind: From corporate sustainability to socially sustainable systems. *Business and Society Review*, *119*(2), 175–206. doi:10.1111/basr.12029

Cheng, B., Ioannou, I., & Serafeim, G. (2013). Corporate social responsibility and access to finance. *Strategic Management Journal*, *35*(1), 1–23. doi:10.1002/smj.2131

Deng, X., Kang, J., & Low, B. (2013). Corporate social responsibility and stakeholder value maximization: Evidence from mergers. *Journal of Financial Economics, 110*(1), 87–109. doi:10.1016/j.jfineco.2013.04.014

Devinney, T. M., Schwalbach, J., & Williams, C. A. (2013). Corporate social responsibility and corporate governance: Comparative perspectives. *Corporate Governance: An International Review*, *21*(5), 413–419. doi:10.1111/corg.12041

Fabrizi, M., Mallin, C., & Michelon, G. (2014). The role of CEOs personal incentives in driving corporate social responsibility. *Journal of Business Ethics*, *124*(2), 311–326. doi:10.1007/s10551-013-1864-2

Fifka, M. S., & Pobizhan, M. (2014). An institutional approach to corporate social responsibility in Russia. *Journal of Cleaner Production*, *82*, 192–201. doi:10.1016/j.jclepro.2014.06.091

Fransen, L. (2013). The embeddedness of responsible business practice: Exploring the interaction between national-institutional environments and corporate social responsibility. *Journal of Business Ethics*, *115*(2), 213–227. doi:10.1007/s10551-012-1395-2

Graafland, J., & Smid, H. (2014). Does corporate social responsibility really make a difference? An explorative analysis for Chinese companies. *China & World Economy*, *22*(2), 102–124. doi:10.1111/j.1749-124X.2014.12064.x

Hah, K., & Freeman, S. (2014). Multinational enterprise subsidiaries and their CSR: A conceptual framework of the management of CSR in smaller emerging economies. *Journal of Business Ethics*, *122*(1), 125–136. doi:10.1007/s10551-013-1753-8

Heisler, K., & Markey, S. (2013). Scales of benefit: Political leverage in the negotiation of corporate social responsibility in mineral exploration and mining in rural British Columbia, Canada. *Society & Natural Resources: An International Journal*, *26*(4), 386–401. doi:10.1080/08941920.2012.695858

Herbohn, K., Walker, J., & Loo, H. Y. M. (2014). Corporate social responsibility: The link between sustainability disclosure and sustainability performance. *Abacus*, *50*(4), 422–459. doi:10.1111/abac.12036

Idemudia, U. (2014). Corporate social responsibility and development in Africa: Issues and possibilities. *Geography Compass*, *8*(7), 421–435. doi:10.1111/gec3.12143

Jo, H., & Harjoto, M. (2014). Analyst coverage, corporate social responsibility, and firm risk. *Business Ethics (Oxford, England)*, *23*(3), 272–292. doi:10.1111/beer.12051

Kim, D., & Choi, M. I. (2013). A comparison of young publics evaluations of corporate social responsibility practices of multinational corporations in the United States and South Korea. *Journal of Business Ethics, 113*(1), 105–118. doi:10.1007/s10551-012-1285-7

Memon, Z. A., Wei, Y. M., Robson, M. G., & Khattak, M. A. O. (2014). Keeping track of corporate social responsibility as a business and management discipline: Case of Pakistan. *Journal of Cleaner Production, 74*, 27–34. doi:10.1016/j.jclepro.2014.03.057

Noronha, C., Tou, S., Cynthia, M. I., & Guan, J. J. (2013). Corporate social responsibility reporting in China: An overview and comparison with major trends. *Corporate Social Responsibility and Environmental Management, 20*(1), 29–42. doi:10.1002/csr.1276

Pérez, A., & del Bosque, I. R. (2015). How customer support for corporate social responsibility influences the image of companies: Evidence from the banking industry. *Corporate Social Responsibility and Environmental Management, 22*(3), 155–168. doi:10.1002/csr.1331

Romolini, A., Fissi, S., & Gori, E. (2014). Scoring CSR reporting in listed companies: Evidence from Italian best practices. *Corporate Social Responsibility and Environmental Management, 21*(2), 65–81. doi:10.1002/csr.1299

Shah, K. U., & Arjoon, S. (2015). Through thick and thin? How self-determination drives the corporate sustainability initiatives of multinational subsidiaries. *Business Strategy and the Environment, 24*(6), 565–582. doi:10.1002/bse.1838

Walker, K., & Dyck, B. (2014). The primary importance of corporate social responsibility and ethicality in corporate reputation: An empirical study. *Business and Society Review, 119*(1), 147–174. doi:10.1111/basr.12028

Young, S., & Thyil, V. (2014). Corporate social responsibility and corporate governance: Role of context in international settings. *Journal of Business Ethics, 122*(1), 1–24. doi:10.1007/s10551-013-1745-8

Zhang, D. Y., Jiang, Q. J., Ma, X. M., & Li, B. J. (2014). Drivers for food risk management and corporate social responsibility: A case of Chinese food companies. *Journal of Cleaner Production, 66*, 520–527. doi:10.1016/j.jclepro.2013.11.075

Zheng, Q. Q., Luo, Y. D., & Wang, S. L. (2014). Moral degradation, business ethics, and corporate social responsibility in a transitional economy. *Journal of Business Ethics, 120*(3), 405–421. doi:10.1007/s10551-013-1668-4

KEY TERMS AND DEFINITIONS

Behavior: The response of an individual or group to an action, environment, person, or stimulus.

Community: The self-organized network of people with common agenda, cause, or interest.

who collaborate by sharing ideas: information, and other resources.

Corporate Social Responsibility: A company's sense of responsibility toward the community and environment in which it operates.

Shareholder: The individual, group, or organization that owns one or more shares in a company, and in whose name the share certificate is issued.

Stakeholder: A person, group or organization that has interest in an organization.

Sustainability: The continued development without significant deterioration of the environment and depletion of natural resources on which human well-being depends.

Sustainable Development: The economic development characterized by the low growth rate, the absence of pollution, and the diminished environment impact.

Triple Bottom Line: The financial, social, and environmental effects of a firm's policies and actions that determine its viability as a sustainable organization.

Chapter 10

A Descriptive Study About Burnout Syndrome and Obesity in Senior and Middle Managers:

A Case Study of the Maquiladora Industry in Ciudad Juarez, Mexico

Aide Aracely Maldonado-Macías
Autonomous University of Ciudad Juarez, Mexico

Jorge Luis García-Alcaraz
Autonomous University of Ciudad Juarez, Mexico

María del Rocío Camacho-Alamilla
Autonomous University of Ciudad Juarez, Mexico

Juan Luis Hernández-Arellano
Autonomous University of Ciudad Juarez, Mexico

ABSTRACT

Burnout syndrome (BS) and obesity have a high economic impact on different fields. This chapter presents a descriptive study of both conditions among middle and senior managers in the maquiladora industry of Ciudad Juarez. The Maslach Burnout Inventory General Survey- was administered to six companies. A sample of 361 participants informed their weight and height. Five levels of Burnout were obtained. Obesity was studied according to the World Health Organization criteria. Results found that 29.8% is exempt from BS, 10.5% has low level, 12.9% has a middle level, 28.2% a fairly level and 18.5% an extreme level of BS. In addition, 34% of the sample suffers from some degree of obesity. Work psychosocial aspects and their effects on human capital development in the industrial sector are not sufficiently studied in developing countries so that to develop strategies for the prevention and effective handling of both BS and obesity.

DOI: 10.4018/978-1-5225-1974-4.ch010

INTRODUCTION

According to Block, He, Zaslavsky, Ding, and Ayanian (2009) and Isasi et al. (2015), scientific research has lately emphasized on the fact that the increasing weight gain of workers is associated with greater levels of stress at work. Unfortunately, this problem has become a regular and costly issue in the Mexican industry, reaching 40% of the working population (Martínez, 2015) as the result of both physical and psychological exigencies demanded to remain competitive in this globalized world.

Work stress appears when demands in the work environment exceed individual resources. Prolonged exposure to stressors, therefore results in burnout syndrome (BS), which is an affective state presenting both emotional and physical exhaustion and mental fatigue, and it eventually reflects a gradual loss of energy (Shirom, 2003) and affects subjects in different aspects, especially their physical and psychological health. As a result, their performance is compromised, and so is the economy of companies.

Obesity may be considered one of the multiple adverse side effects of BS, and, from psycho-physiological and behaviorist perspectives, it is one of the major problems in public health worldwide due to its magnitude, rapid development, and the growing subsequent illnesses that it causes. The (World Health Organization [WHO], 2015) defines obesity as the abnormal or excessive accumulation of fat in the body. Mexico holds second place in the ranking of global prevalence of adult obesity, which is ten times greater than in countries like Japan or Korea (Dávila-Torres, González-Izquierdo, & Barrera-Cruz, 2015). Similarly, obesity is not an exclusive condition to work environment (Borak, 2011), but it is a risk factor for the development of chronic diseases. Moreover, according to the literature, it can be linked to BS (Ahola et al., 2012). Finally, studies on both obesity and BS agree on the fact that the work environment is a factor that favors their appearance. As a result, both conditions have become central subjects of research due to their economic and social impact on individuals, companies, and countries.

Mexico is a developing country, and great part of its industrial sector focuses on manufacturing. The manufacturing industry known as maquiladora is widely present in the country. For instance, it caters for 5,024 manufacturing establishments employing 2,280,504 workers and billing around 7,233.37 million US dollars. Particularly the state of Chihuahua, stands for 13.6% of the total income of the Mexican manufacturing transnational industry. In this region, the city of Juarez, occupies about 14.2% of the labor force in Mexico with 320 manufacturing companies approximately (National Institute of Statistics, Geography, and Informatics [INEGI], 2015). It offers the highest number of industrial job positions and production levels in exports.

In order to promote and achieve the human capital development of this region and increase its competitiveness, research on the psychosocial aspects of work must increase and be further encouraged. However, so far it is known too that middle and senior managers in the maquiladora industry are constantly emerged in stressful situations. They must work in a synergic way to achieve the different goals set by the company, clarify objectives, and spread their vision to their subordinates so they willingly adopt it. Similarly, they must be able to successfully face challenges and promote changes that guarantee an outstanding organizational behavior. Such positive behavior would be reflected on an organizational environment that will consequently favor a greater achievement of productivity, quality, team empowerment, enhanced integration, benefits, and goals.

Therefore, a descriptive study of both obesity and burnout syndrome in senior and middle managers can be beneficial for a better comprehension of their emergence in the industrial sector. Thus, this chapter aims to describe the prevalence of BS of the sample using five levels and the obesity will be described using sociodemographic and work variables where this disease prevails. The variable of obesity will be described and viewed as a single variable joining its three degrees (I, II, and III). By expanding knowledge of both conditions, this research seeks to raise awareness on the importance of early detection of BS and obesity and help companies to enhance preventive measures and pertinent interventions. Finally, this work also provides knowledge to collaborate in other fields of research, such as the maquiladora industry (Juárez-García, Idrovo, Camacho-Ávila, & Placencia-Reyes, 2014).

LITERATURE REVIEW

Burnout syndrome has recently become the popular description for work stress. The term "burnout" conveys the image of a flame consuming materials until they are reduced to ashes. According to C. Maslach (2009), the fire represents the enthusiasm, dedication, and commitment from a worker that "burns out" with the success, leaving behind smoking embers from exhaustion, cynicism, and inefficacy. However, the term became relevant when psychiatrist Herbert Freudenberguer (1974) explained what happened to volunteers of a drug clinic. He described how these people began working with extraordinary levels of enthusiasm and had high expectations regarding what they could achieve at the clinic, so they strived harder to accomplish their objectives. However, a year after their arrival, such enthusiasm and motivation started to decrease noticeable and caused negative stress, which reflected mentally and physically. This way, Freudenberguer (1974), defined burnout as "a feeling of failure and exhausted existence resulting from a work overload due to exigencies of energy, personal resources, or spiritual strength."

Nowadays, burnout syndrome is also widely used in casual conversations to describe fatigue and exhaustion. Authors McCormack and Cotter (2013) have pointed out that one of the most accepted definitions for the term in studies and academic research emerged from the work of Cristina Maslach, psychology professor, and Susan E. Jackson, human resources professor. They conceived BS as a "syndrome of emotional exhaustion, depersonalization, and reduced personal accomplishment that can occur in individuals who do 'people work' of some kind." (Juárez-García et al., 2014). However, the notion has changed as the etiologic theories and evaluations of BS have evolved. Hence, burnout syndrome is more general, and not exclusive to helping and assistance professions, now is defined as "a crisis in one's relationship with work and not necessarily a crisis in one's relationship with people at work" (Moreno-Jiménez, Rodríguez-Carvajal, & Escobar, 2001). The condition is composed of three dimensions described below.

- **Emotional Exhaustion (EE):** It is the basic individual stress component of BS. It concerns feelings of being over extended and depleted from physical resources to deal with situations. According to Maslach (2009), workers with EE tend to feel weakened and exhausted, and they lack from enough energy to start a new workday or deal with a problem. To the author, EE shows the expected positive correlation with work demands and results from the stress-health relationship.
- **Cynicism (CYN):** This is the essential characteristic of BS (Maslach, 2009). It represents the interpersonal context of the syndrome and refers to a negative, hostile, or excessively apathetic response to an excess of EE. First, it is self-protective (an emotional buffer of "detached concern"). Workers begin by working strenuously and performing several tasks, but they eventually withdraw and diminish their work. However, subjects eventually develop a negative reaction towards their works and the people. To Maslach (2009), as cynicism evolves, workers change their behavior, from doing their best effort to perform as little as possible. This affects consequently their performance.
- **Professional Efficacy (PE):** This dimension represents the self-evaluation component of burnout. It involves feelings of incompetence and inability to achieve goals and be productive at work. A decreased feeling of professional efficacy is due to a lack of resources to work, social support, and opportunities for professional development. People suffering from this dimension usually ask/tell themselves: "What am I doing?" "Why am I here?" "This may be the wrong job for me." Feelings of inefficacy also cause workers to think that they might chose the wrong profession, or they usually are unhappy with the type of people that they have become. They have a negative conception of themselves and the people around them (Maslach, 2009).

About the study of BS, researchers have developed various instruments to measure and quantify the population who suffers it. Respect to the instrument, the most prominent is the Maslach Burnout Inventory (MBI; Maslach y Jackson, 1986). In accordance with Juárez-García et al. (2014), the criterion commonly used to determinate the prevalence of the syndrome is the traditional categorization of grades low, medium and high of each dimension using cutoffs. Additionally, Guerrero and Vicente (2001), uses a method that allow a general perspective of the syndrome. This method consists of a general classification or levels obtained from the 27 combinations as results of using the 33.3 and 66.6 percentiles as cutoff points. In this way, the levels assigned a categorical variable as follows: none, low, middle, fairly and extreme.

In Mexico research on burnout has mainly targeted at helping and assistance professions, such as doctors, nurses, and professors (Juárez-García et al., 2014). Nevertheless, Camacho-Alamilla, Maldonado-Macias, García-Alcaraz, and Hernández-Arellano (2014) and Maldonado-Macías, Camacho-Alamilla, Torres, Alcaraz, and Limón (2015), have pointed out that BS is equally present in middle and senior managers in several companies of the maquiladora industry in Ciudad Juarez. Participants of these studies show that 25.8% is exempt from BS, 12.5% has low level, 15.5% has a medium level, 23.3% showed fair level and 23.0% a extreme level of BS.

Relationship Between Burnout Syndrome and Obesity

Negative effects of BS are noticeable in psychological and behavioral aspects, as well as in the individual's health and work environment (Guerrero & Vicente, 2001). According to authors O`Connor and Conner (2011), the relationship between BS and obesity enables to understand the origins of the latter, which is considered multifactorial. For instance, Ahola et al. (2012) have found that while PE is linked to obesity, EE and CYN are rather associated with little physical activity. Despite such efforts, insufficient literature has focused on studying this connection between BS and obesity. For Armon, Shirom, Berliner, Shapira, and Melamed (2008) and Foss and Dyrstad (2011), this fact may be due to a lack of consensus about the disjunctive of recognizing whether obesity is a cause or consequence of BS and their evolution is interrelated. Nevertheless, Foss and Dyrstad (2011) have also stated that studies pointing out stress as a cause of obesity are more accepted, while those who consider the opposite (stress as consequence of obesity) seem to be less common. However, the former conclusion concerns on the psycho physiological response of stress as a negative behavioral response to handle stressful situations particularly at work.

First, obesity (Body Max Index >= 30 kg/m^2) has become a major public health issue around the world due to its magnitude, increasing presence, and the negative effects that it causes on health. It is considered a systemic, chronic, and multifactorial disease that is not exclusive to developed countries, and the WHO (2015), defines it as an abnormal or excessive accumulation of fat in the body. From this perspective, Mexico ranks the second most obese country in the world with 30% of adults affected by this condition.. Moreover, obesity is the second cause of death in the world; it is responsible for about 3.4 millions of adult deaths due to several chronic, no transmissible diseases (NTDs) developed as result of excessive weight gain. Among them, in 2012, cardiovascular diseases (mainly cardiomyopathy and strokes) became the second cause of death, while diabetes, musculoskeletal disorders (e.g.: osteoarthritis, a debilitating disease), and certain types of cancer (endometrial, breast, and colon) have a strong negative impact.

Second, obesity usually begins during childhood or adolescence. It happens when an individual eats more calories than his/her body actually burns up, and many genetic and environmental factors may be an influence. As for the magnitude of the issue, the Organization for Economic Co-operation and Development (OECD) estimated that by 2020 more than two thirds of the world population would likely suffer from either overweight or obesity (Franco, 2012). Such scenario provides a better understanding of the problem in Mexico, since global experience has demonstrated that multi-sectorial strategies must be developed as a means to enhance preventive factors for health enhancement to modify individual, family, and community behaviors that have an impact on obesity development.

Psychophysiological Response Relationship

From a physiological perspective, stress is a state that threatens homeostasis of the body. In fact, a complex set of physical and behavioral responses react to the presence of a stressor (Kyrou & Tsigos, 2009). Authors such as Foss & Dyrstad (2011) point out that the stress system is composed of two major parts: the sympathetic nervous system (SNS) and the hypothalamic–pituitary–adrenal axis (HPA).

Figure 1 depicts the stress system. Firstly, the SNS innervates glands, viscera, and smooth muscle tissue of all organs from the body. Its main function is unconsciously maintaining homeostasis (internal stability and balance of the body). Moreover, activation of the SNS mainly releases adrenaline and noradrenaline hormones, and this provides ideal conditions for emergency responses, since the body becomes prepared to perform any strenuous activity. In addition, these two hormones are also responsible for increasing blood pressure, blood flow to working muscles, and muscle strength. Similarly, they are accountable for the rate of cellular metabolism, blood glucose, liver and muscle glycolysis, mental activity, and blood coagulation. In addition, they cause a state of alert, anxiety, and pupillary dilation, stimulate sweat and saliva secretion, and dilate bronchi and digestive tract motility (Serrano, Alacreu-Crespo, Costa, Abad, & González-Bono, 2015).

Secondly, if stress conditions are sustained and the individual perceives the situation as inevitable, the HPA is triggered (Guerrero y Vicente, 2001), mainly due to EE (Gómez-Alcaina, Montero-Marín, Demarzo, Pereira, & García-Campayo, 2013). This activation stimulates secretion of both the corticotropin releasing factor (CRF) and the adrenocorticotropic releasing factor (ACTH), which in turn increase glucocorticoid levels, especially cortisol (Serrano, Salvador, & Costa, 2015). Cortisol, plays a central role in the physiological responses of BS (Marchand, Juster, Durand, & Lupien, 2014). Additionally it is related with diseases such as metabolic syndrome and obesity, as it is argued by Epel, Lapidus, McEwen, and Brownell (2001), Foss and Dyrstad (2011), Gómez-Alcaina et al. (2013), Kyrou and Tsigos (2009), Marchand et al. (2014), Newman, O'Connor, and Conner (2007) and Torres and Nowson (2007).

Finally, when suffering from BS, both the SNS and HPA are activated. This causes diseases that affect the functions of organs involved in both systems since they are unable to fully recover. As a result, resources are depleted, and the individual suffers from several psychophysiological disorders, such as those introduced by Table 1 (Guerrero y Vicente, 2001).

Behavioral Response

Negative behaviors are another consequence of BS. That is, individuals are more prone to negatively react during critical moments (e.g.: dismissal from work). They may return to old smoking habits, drinking alcohol in excess, not exercising, or not sleeping and/or eating well. For instance, Dallman (2010) stated that around 80%

Figure 1. The Stress System

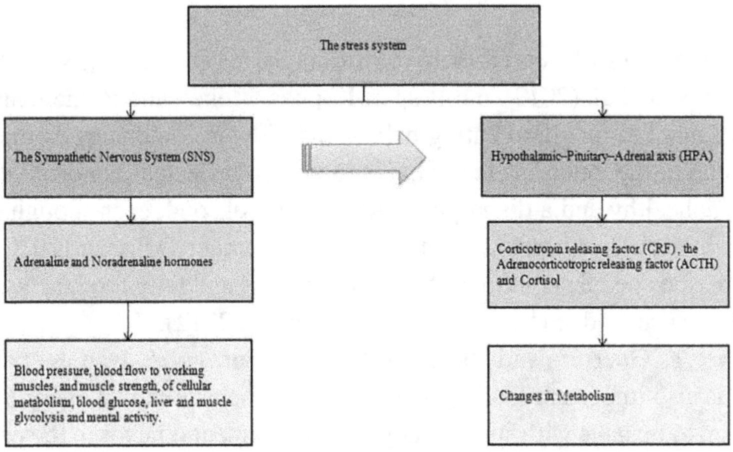

Table 1. Major Psychophysiological Disorders (Guerrero & Vicente, 2001)

Type of Disorder	Related Disease
Cardiovascular	• Essential hypertension • Coronary disease • Tachycardia • Cardiac arrhythmia • Raynaud disease • Migraine headaches
Respiratory	• Bronchial asthma • Hyperventilation syndrome • Allergies
Gastrointestinal	• Peptic ulcer • Functional dyspepsia • Irritable bowel syndrome • Ulcerative colitis
Muscular	• Tics • Tremors and cramps • Altered muscle reflexes • Lumbago • Tension headaches
Dermatologic	• Pruritus • Eczemas • Acne • Psoriasis
Sexual	• Sexual impotence • Premature ejaculation • Painful coitus • Vaginismus • Hypoactive sexual desire
Endocrine	• Hyperthyroidism • Hypothyroidism • Cushing syndrome
Immunological	• Deterioration of the immunological system

of people altered or decreased their caloric intake when they felt stressed. Similarly, Nevanpera et al. (2012) and Proper, Koppes, Meijer, and Bemelmans (2013) mentioned that EE modified eating habits. Individuals could start eating without measure due to the emotions felt. That is, a person reflected its negative feelings by eating unhealthy and a disproportioned amount of food, even though he/she is not really hungry. Furthermore, according to researcher Dallman (2010), during stressful periods people tend to prefer sweet, greasy, and fatty food, as well as soft and alcoholic drinks due to EE and PE (Ahola et al., 2012).

However, as Guerrero and Vicente (2001) and Serrano, Salvador, et al. (2015) affirm, it is also important to highlight the diverse behaviors that every individual can develop to manage with stress. They are a fundamental factor in the prevalence of any disease. That is, different people can experience a same negative situation in different ways. For instance, while some may eat more and gain weight during stressful moments, others may reduce their intake and therefore lose body mass (Barattucci, 2011). Finally, since both BS and stress can be originated in the work environment, they both imply economic consequences in employees' health and the productivity of companies. Thus, many efforts must be conducted toward their prevention by identifying those factors that favor them.

Burnout Syndrome in Companies

Although stressful situations at work are inevitable, research on BS focuses on the negative consequences of such chronic stressors (Guerrero & Vicente, 2001). Therefore, from an organizational perspective, etiology of BS principally centers on factors such as high work demand, lack of resources to cope with situations, and low adaptive organizational attitudes (Alarcon, 2011). For instance, Llaneza (2002) stated that consequences of working with employees that suffered from BS would be unfortunately reflected on the goals and results achieved by the company. Likewise, results from a survey administered by Regus Group (2009) mostly to managers of 11,000 companies worldwide indicated that competitiveness and wage rates were also relevant factors affecting BS. Most participants of the survey actually reported taking additional tasks and activities without being paid for them. In total, 79% of the Mexican sample reported such information, in comparison with 69% of Spanish respondents, 67% of Argentinean participants, and 54% of the British sample.

Among other BS affecting factors, Serrano and Salvador (2015) considered the physical work environment as one of them, while Llaneza (2002) emphasized on job dynamics, professional inadequacy, conflicts due to role ambiguity, stressors due to the use of new technology, the organizational structure and environment of the company, work challenges, work autonomy, commitment, and the relationships with co- workers. Also, a national survey administered by an insurance company in the United States found that 25% of the sample considered their work as the top life stressor, whilst seven out of ten respondents also reported it as a cause of frequent health problems and productivity loss (Hunter, 2009). Finally, Global Recruitment and Human Resources Consulting carried out a study and made two important discoveries. First, one of every seven managers surveyed had lost employees due to BS. Second, more than one third of the sample had witnessed productivity losses in other workers. Organizations experiencing such situations were management, technology, media and telecommunication, and financial service companies, while sectors affected concerned manufacturing, engineering, and marketing (Hudson, 2005).

Unfortunately, a lack of attention to stressors may lead to major levels of work absenteeism (Borritz et al., 2010), increased turnover (Van Bogaert, 2010; Zhang

& Feng, 2011), earlier departure from work, and high resignation rates (Leiter & Maslach, 2009). Additionally, employees' performance can decline, which would increase error making (Bosqued, 2008) and might bring quality issues, since individuals would pay less attention to details (Aranda Beltrán, López Gónzalez, & Barraza Salas, 2013). Also, as Ross (1993) and Rubio (2003) affirm, individuals suffering from BS may face problems in their relationships with colleagues and supervisors as a cause of CYN developed.

All these BS affecting factors consequently increase economic costs in companies. For example, the American Institute of Stress (AIS) in New York mentioned that occupational stress cost more than $300 billion dollars per year to the United States, let alone costs derived from healthcare compensation to stressed people, which is 46% higher than compensation given to unstressed employees (Schwartz, 2004). It is also important to highlight that the use of health services is higher and incapacity periods due to stress have become longer in comparison with other occupational injuries and diseases (Raffo, Ráez, & Cachay, 2013). Likewise, it was found that industrial employees over 45 years old had a 26% risk of death due to EE, 29% due to CYN, and 22% as a consequence of reduced PE (Ahola, Vaananen, Koskinen, Kouvonen, & Shirom, 2010).

In spite of this scenario, C. Maslach (2009), mentions that many companies still underestimate feelings of stress or BS symptoms from their employees They may believe that a bad day to such people is not relevant to the organization. Even little or no tolerance to general malaise from job demands has become desirable to detect and remove so called unskillful or weak employees. Yet this assumption completely lacks from research foundations. However, what studies have actually proved is that a more flexible work where employees do their jobs on a regular basis and part of their time at work can be done from their homes, does reduce occupational stress and improves productivity at 10% or 20%. This consequently diminishes costs for companies (Regus Group, 2009).

Obesity in Organizations

Actually, adverse characteristics of work tend to be considered as factors affecting obesity, since many people spend most of their time in their workplaces. Moreover, as Borak (2011) and Proper, Koppes, Van Zwieten, and Bemelmans (2012) mentions, that the fact that obesity is a considered a worldwide epidemic represents a challenge to both professionals in occupational health and companies. Therefore, according to Borak (2011), four elements are relevant when studying obesity in the workplace. First element is high economic costs as a result of – second element – health deterioration, deaths, and treatment of obesity-related diseases. For instance, a recent analysis on epidemiological transition in Mexico, found out that attention to illnesses caused by obesity and overweight had an annual cost of $42,246 million of Mexican pesos, about 2,283.6 million of American Dollars. Cancer, diabetes, and cardiovascular problems were some of the chronic diseases involved (Dávila-Torres et al., 2015). However, according to the Secretaría de Salud (2010), by 2017 this number may increase up to $77,919 million of Mexican pesos, about 4,211.8 million of American Dollars.

The third element concerns costs due to reduced productivity and management of incapacity and support services (Agredo Zúñiga et al., 2013). Authors Cavuoto and Nussbaum (2014) have pointed out that obesity affects the muscle and psychomotor performance of individuals. They can suffer from reduced motion of the shoulder, lumbar spine, and knee, for example (Park, Ramachandran, Weisman, & Jung, 2010). Moreover Andreyeva, Luedicke, and Wang (2014), mentions that on obese individuals the probability of being injured at work increases from 25% to 68%. Among the main injuries are strains, sprains, or twists (Gu et al., 2014). Consequently, economic costs from medical incapacities and productivity loss, including absenteeism, increase notably for organizations. In accordance with Andreyeva et al. (2014), as far as absenteeism is concerned, obese participants are 1.7 more likely to be absent from work at some moment, since they reported seven or more work absences in the late six months compared with those non obese. From this perspective, economic losses from the full time working population in the United States of America have been estimated to 73.1 billions of dollars per year (Finkelstein, da Costa DiBonaventura, Burgess, & Hale, 2010).

About the fourth element when studying obesity, is the work environment, which contributes to increased overweight and obesity rates, although it may also help to prevent them. Among those main work environment factors are insecurity at work (Muenster, Rueger, Ochsmann, Letzel, & Toschke, 2011), low use of work skills and decision making (Han, Trinkoff, Storr, & Geiger-Brown, 2011), a hostile environment (Luckhaupt, Cohen, Li, & Calvert, 2014), high psychological demands (Hellerstedt & Jeffery, 1997), and a lack of support from supervisors (Blandina-Fernández & González-Jaimes, 2014). In addition, the lack of physical activity, which is frequently found in the new forms of sedentary work is affecting obesity (Ahola et al., 2012). While irregular work shifts (Eberly & Feldman, 2010) and long workdays (Han et al., 2011) also have an impact on weight gain. In fact, working extended hours, especially during night shifts, increases somnolence (Charles et al., 2009), which in turn affects the state of alert and increases probabilities of unhealthy food intake (Kivimaki et al., 2006). Therefore, the type of meals and food provided by companies to their employees also play an important role in obesity and overweight.

BURNOUT AND OBESITY IN MIDDLE AND SENIOR MANAGERS

Mexican companies experience a time of great changes: an accelerated pace of life, greater competition, and higher demand of specialization. Such situations have forced them to reformulate their goals and techniques for decision making, and even though top positions may seem purely beneficial, high salaries do come with implications. That is, senior and middle managers must be able to achieve specific goals and meet the objectives of the company, even if this implies being submerged in stressful situations. The decisions they make, sometimes under uncertainty, will always affect the conditions of the company and perhaps even the unemployment level of the country (Salgado & Mejía, 2008). Moreover, these leaders may cover work schedules of up to 36 consecutive hours (Montiel, Ramírez, Esparza, & Guerrero, 2014) and must strive to maintain the satisfaction of all employees for which they are responsible (Rivera Moya & Briseño Escobedo, 2013). Additionally, most of the stress felt by middle managers also derives from the fact that they are directly responsible when orders are followed or not. Thus, they usually are the most stressed people among the managerial group (Luque-Reca, Augusto-Landa, & Pulido-Martos, 2014).

The abovementioned conditions can therefore be possible sources of BS and its related diseases, such as obesity. Authors Luckhaupt et al. (2014) found out that positions and occupations related to office and administrative support, health care, and social assistance, as well as industries of public administration, architecture, engineering and social services were more prone to obesity. However, an excessive weight is gained by the sedentary characteristic of new jobs and, the inappropriate food intake. For instance, Casanueva, Pérez-Lizaur, Ripoll, Plazas, and Benito (2005) argued that senior managers tended to eat in places that unconsciously encouraged them to have an unhealthy diet of fat-rich meals and big-sized proportions. As for middle managers, authors stated that part of their weight gain was due to first ate in the company's facility but also had a full meal at home by the end of the day. Moreover, the same authors highlighted that, unfortunately, meals in these facilities did not favor a healthy diet. Therefore, in addition to taking preventive measures at work, it is also necessary to implement health programs that include more healthy meals, especially for the operative staff and for those employees who are constantly submerged in stress.

Methodology

Several factors were considered to define the sample of this research. First, needs mentioned in the literature of BS were taken into account. Then, a special concern over obesity in middle and senior managers was found, since they are the key to the development and performance of companies. Therefore, their physical and mental conditions are relevant. Additionally, the fact that BS symptoms and an inappropriate diet may lead to poor performance, serious accidents due to distractions, and the development of chronic diseases in this personnel will lead t incremented costs derived from productivity loss and medical expenses.

Data Collection

To carry out this study, first, authors took advantage of the monthly meeting of the committee of health and safety at the Health and Security Committee of the Ciudad Juárez Maquiladora Association (AMAC: Asociacion de Maquiladoras-Index Juarez, in Spanish).The committee is composed of physicians from different maquiladora companies of this city. The significance and objectives of the research were given to them, and members willing to participate provided a contact email address and phone number from the companies where they worked, so they could be reached. In total, 25 email addresses and phone numbers were collected, while merely six companies finally participated in the study. The Human Resources department authorized the administration of the questionnaires to middle and senior managers. Participants were organized into groups of 10 or 15 employees, and a different schedule was assigned to every group to take the survey. The sample was composed of group leaders, supervisors, technicians, and managers, as well as administrative staff from the areas and departments of production, human resources, maintenance, environment, quality, engineering, finances, and health, among others. The questionnaire was answered within a period of 15-20 minutes.

- **Survey Administration and Collection:** As previously stated, meetings were scheduled between authors of this research and the Human Resources department of every company for the questionnaire administration. The study relied on the following two instruments:
    - The Maslach Burnout Inventory General Survey (MBI-GS): it was used to analyze the different dimensions of BS. The version of the survey administered was the MBI-GS from C. Maslach, Jackson, and Leiter (1996) in its Spanish translation validated by Moreno-Jiménez et al. (2001). This instrument, allows to evaluating chronic stress in occupations that are not of assistance type, such as administrative jobs. It measures BS through 16 items divided into the three dimensions. That is, EE is composed of 5 items (1, 2, 3, 4, and 6), CYN also comprises five items (8, 9, 13, 14, and 15), and PE is formed of six items (5, 7, 10, 11, 12, and 16). Moreover, the questionnaire uses a seven-point scale to be responded: (1) never, (2), rarely along the year, (3) sometimes along the year, (4) often along the year, (5) frequently along the year, (6) al-

most every day and (7) every day. Finally, once the questionnaires were answered, methodology described by Guerrero and Vicente (2001) was followed to calculate the level of BS of every respondent.

- **Sociodemographic Information Sheet:** It included different types of questions that enabled to characterize the sample. Information demanded concerned the current job position, seniority in months in the company, the type of work contract, number of hours worked per week, academic degree, gender, marital status, number of children, and – in the case of women – whether they were pregnant. Similarly, weight (in kilograms, kg) and height (in meters, m) were requested in order to determine the BMI (Kg/m^2), which is obtained from the body mass, expressed in kilograms, divided by the square of the body height, expressed in meters. Both measures were reported according to their perception. In such situations, it is hence advised to subtract 2.5 centimeters Fernández, Marley, Noriega, and Ibarra (2010) in the height of every participant. Finally, BMI was classified based on criteria established by the WHO. Hence, for the analysis, the inclusion criterion of participants was having a BMI greater than 30 kg/m2.
- **Database Construction and Debugging:** Information gathered was captured by means of SPSS® v.20 software; however, before its analysis, missing and extreme values were detected. Afterwards, they were replaced by the arithmetic mean, in the case of nominal variables, and the median, for ordinal variables.
- **Descriptive Analysis of the Sample:** The descriptive analysis of the sample of middle and senior managers of the maquiladora industry was performed using SPSS v.20. To this end, descriptive statistical such as the range, mean, standard deviation of non-ordinal sociodemographic variables were used; including height, weight, age and seniority. These variables were properly plotted. Additionally, BS by level are described. Finally, BS levels and obesity according to some sociodemographic and work variables are presented. Among them are: age, type of work contract, seniority in months, academic degree, number of hours worked per week, department, current job position, gender and marital status.

RESULTS OF THE DESCRIPTIVE STUDY

This section describes results obtained from the survey administration to the sample with obesity.

Questionnaire Administration

This study was carried out at six maquiladora companies from Ciudad Juarez, Chihuahua, Mexico. The sample was non-probabilistic, since the survey was administered during a specific time determined by the Human Resources department of every organization. Table 2 shows the total number of companies surveyed, as well as their percentage and frequency of participation. Similarly, three manufacturing companies related to the automotive sector, two were concerned with electrical products, and one focused on diverse manufacturing. According to the inclusion criteria, only 34.4% of participants were considered in the sample corresponding to 124 participants.

Results of Burnout Syndrome in the Sample

Figure 2 shows BS levels found in the sample. It can be observed that 29.8% is exempt from BS, 10.5% has low level, 12.9% has a middle level, and 28.2% presents fairly level of BS and 18.5% an extreme level. Therefore, since the majority of the sample shows concerning levels of burnout, strong preventive measures must be pursued to reduce and prevent it.

According to (Apiquian, 2007), every stage of the burnout syndrome carries out different symptoms, which are described as follows:

- **Low Level:** The worker may develop vague and unspecific symptoms, such as headaches, backaches, and lumbago. They also become a bit less productive.
- **Medium, Moderated Level:** The person suffers from insomnia, attention deficit, and a lack of concentration. Similarly, they may self-medicate.
- **Fairly or High Level:** The worker miss work regularly, is reluctant to perform certain tasks, and show signs of cynicism.

Table 2. Total number of companies surveyed

Company	Frequency	Percentage
Company 1: Electrical products	41	11.4%
Company 2: Automotive products	42	11.6%
Company 3: Electrical products	53	14.7%
Company 4: Automotive products	100	27.7%
Company 5: Automotive products	103	28.5%
Company 6: Diverse products	22	6.1%
Total	361	100.0

Figure 2. Burnout Syndrome in the Sample

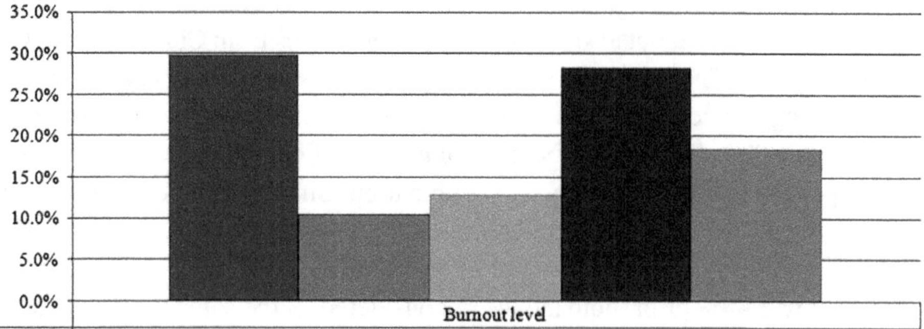

	Burnout level
None	29.8%
Low	10.5%
Middle	12.9%
Fairly	28.2%
Extreme	18.5%

- **Extreme Levels:** The person isolates and suffers from an existential crisis, chronic depression. Moreover, risk of committing suicide is high.

Results of the Analysis of Burnout and Obesity by Socio Demographical Variables

About the anthropometric measures of the sample of obesity, the height range of the sample is 1.435 - 1.875 meters (m), with a height mean of 1.672 m and a standard deviation of 0.092. The weight range of the sample is 70 - 115 kilograms (kgs), while the weight mean of sample is 92.71 kgs, and the standard deviation of 11.453. On the other hand, the age range of the sample is between 24-60 years old, the mean age is 40.2 years and a standard deviation of 7.71. The seniority range is 1-372 months, a seniority mean of 116.46 months and a standard deviation of 92.54.

Figure 3 describes the level of BS and obesity according the range of age of the sample. With respect, the none level of BS the highest percentage of participants is found in the range of age of 31-40 years old. With respect the low, middle, and fairlyly levels of BS the highest percentage of participants is found in the range of age of 41-50 years old. At the extreme level, the highest percentage of participants is found in the range of 31-40 years old. Moreover, regarding obesity, the highest percentage of participants of the sample is found in the range of age of 41-50 years old.

Figure 4, shows the levels of BS and obesity according the type of contract. With respect to BS, the none, low, middle, fairly and extreme level, the highest percentages are predominantly among those participants with a permanent contract compared

Figure 3. Age of Sample

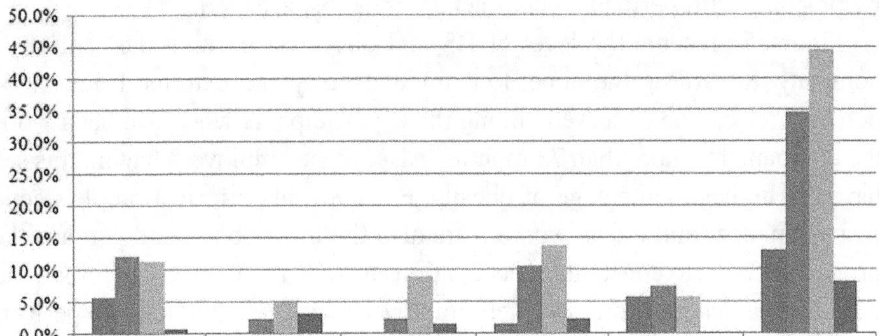

	None	Low	Middle	Fairly	Extreme	Obesity
<= 30 years old	5.6%	0.0%	0.0%	1.6%	5.6%	12.9%
31-40 years old	12.1%	2.4%	2.4%	10.5%	7.3%	34.7%
41-50 years old	11.3%	4.8%	8.9%	13.7%	5.6%	44.4%
>= 50 years old	0.8%	3.2%	1.6%	2.4%	0.0%	8.1%

Figure 4. Type of Contract of Sample

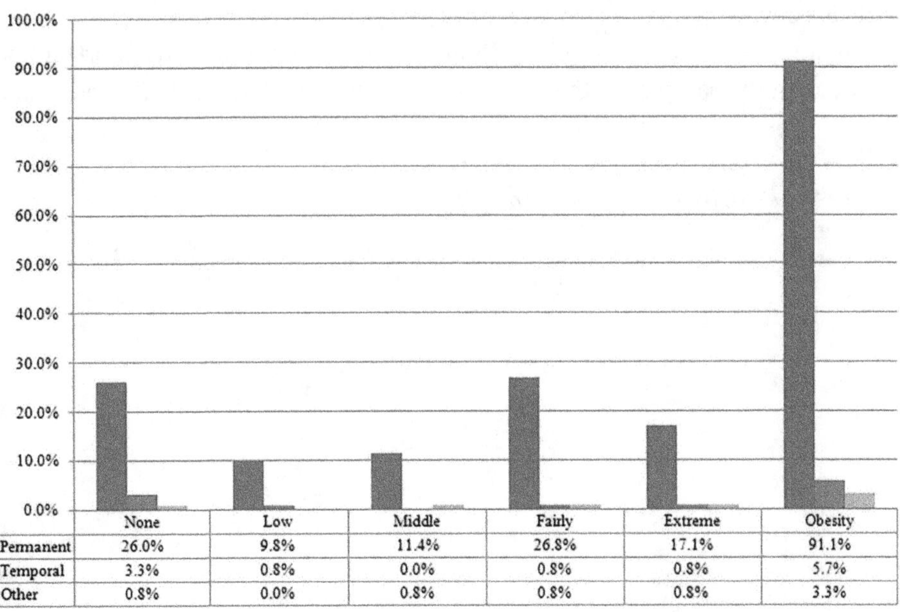

	None	Low	Middle	Fairly	Extreme	Obesity
Permanent	26.0%	9.8%	11.4%	26.8%	17.1%	91.1%
Temporal	3.3%	0.8%	0.0%	0.8%	0.8%	5.7%
Other	0.8%	0.0%	0.8%	0.8%	0.8%	3.3%

with participants with a temporary or another type of contract. About obesity, also participants with permanent contract are the most affected.

Figure 5 presents the level of BS and obesity according the seniority in the company. Regarding the none, low, middle, fairly and extreme level, the highest percentages can be observed among those participants who have been working in the company for more than 73 months. Also, those employees having this seniority have the highest percentage of obesity. From all this information, it is concluded that permanent and oldest workers are also the most obese, and perhaps the most prone to BS due to constant preoccupations to keep their work. Therefore, maquiladora companies must provide their employees with efficient tools to perform their works and tasks.

As for the roles of educational degree, Figure 6 shows the percentages of BS and obesity. With respect, the none and low level of BS, the highest percentage is found in participants with bachelor degree. At the middle level, the highest percentage is present in participants with high school. Meanwhile, the fairly and extreme level of BS, the highest percentage is concentrated in participants with bachelor degree. Regarding obesity, the highest percentage of participants are also those having a bachelor degree.

Figure 7 describes the level of BS and obesity according to the worked hours per week of the sample. With respect of the none, low, middle, fairly and extreme

Figure 5. Seniority in months of Sample

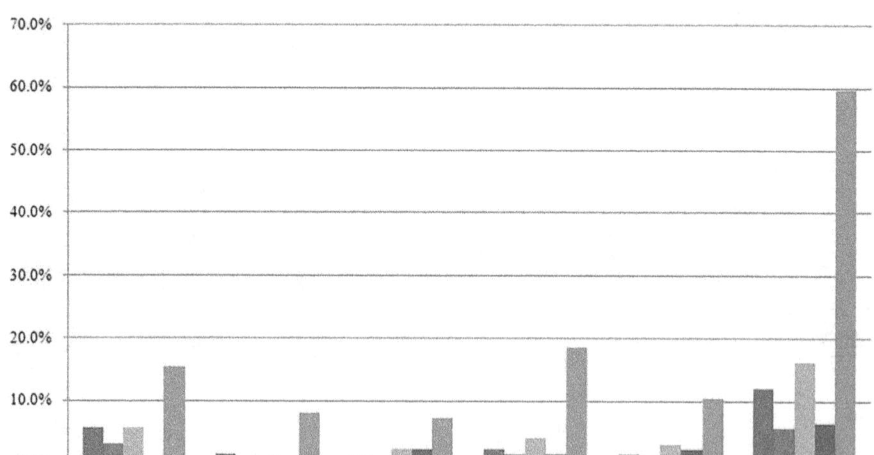

	None	Low	Middle	Fairly	Extreme	Obesity
<= 12 Months	5.6%	1.6%	0.8%	2.4%	1.6%	12.1%
13-24 Months	3.2%	0.0%	0.0%	1.6%	0.8%	5.6%
25-48 Months	5.6%	0.8%	2.4%	4.0%	3.2%	16.1%
49-72 Months	0.0%	0.0%	2.4%	1.6%	2.4%	6.5%
>73 Months	15.3%	8.1%	7.3%	18.5%	10.5%	59.7%

Figure 6. Academic degree of Sample

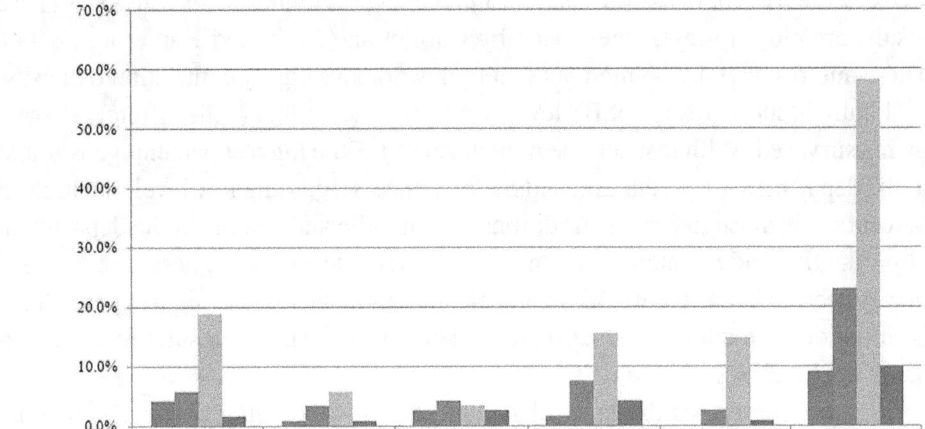

	None	Low	Middle	Fairly	Extreme	Obesity
Middle School	4.1%	0.8%	2.5%	1.6%	0.0%	9.0%
High School	5.7%	3.3%	4.1%	7.4%	2.5%	23.0%
Bachelor's degree	18.9%	5.7%	3.3%	15.6%	14.8%	58.2%
Master degree	1.6%	0.8%	2.5%	4.1%	0.8%	9.8%

Figure 7. Working Hours per Week of Sample

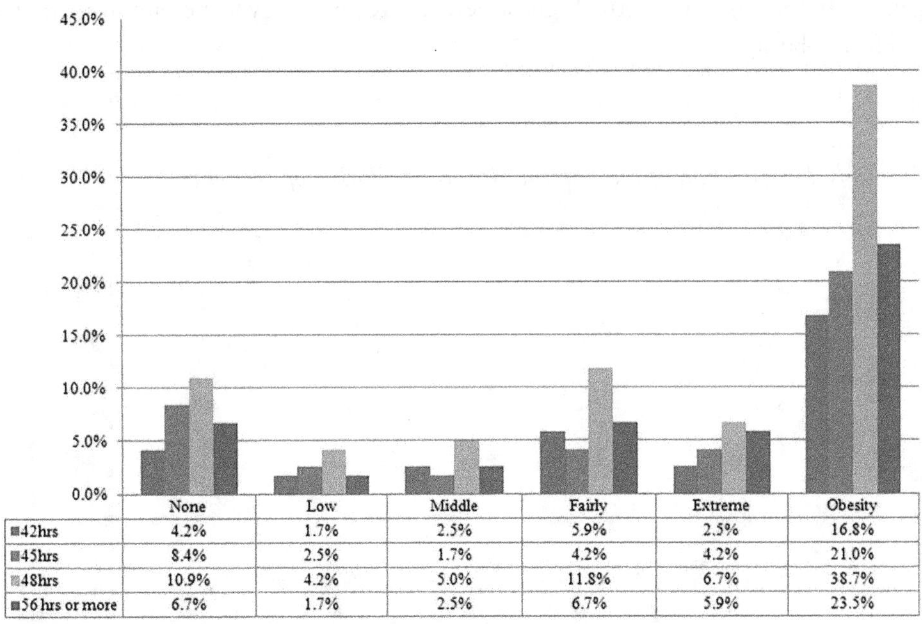

	None	Low	Middle	Fairly	Extreme	Obesity
42hrs	4.2%	1.7%	2.5%	5.9%	2.5%	16.8%
45hrs	8.4%	2.5%	1.7%	4.2%	4.2%	21.0%
48hrs	10.9%	4.2%	5.0%	11.8%	6.7%	38.7%
56 hrs or more	6.7%	1.7%	2.5%	6.7%	5.9%	23.5%

levels of BS, the highest percentages are found in participants working 48 hours per week. Similarly, for obesity, the highest percentage is found in this category. These results are close to researches made by Choi et al. (2010) and Han et al. (2011). These authors actually pointed out that long workdays highly contribute to obesity.

Figure 8, shows results of BS level and obesity according to the different departments surveyed. With respect, the none level of BS the highest percentage is found in the department of production and maintenance. Regarding low level, the highest percentage is in Engineering. Additionally, a middle and level is in the department of production and maintenance. Finally, as extreme level, the highest percentage is in engineering department. Taking in consideration obesity, the highest percentage is in the department of production and maintenance. Similar results found Luckhaupt et al. (2014).

Figure 9, describes the level of BS and obesity according the work position. With respect the none level of BS, the highest percentage is present is supervisors. Regarding low level, the highest percentages are in technicians and office administrators. Respects to middle and extreme level, the highest percentages are in supervisors. Moreover, this latter work position is who present also the highest percentage of obesity.

Figure 10 introduces results from the analysis of BS and obesity in relation to gender. In the case of BS, the highest percentages in all levels belong to men and too from obesity.

Figure 8. Distribution of the Sample Based on Work Departments

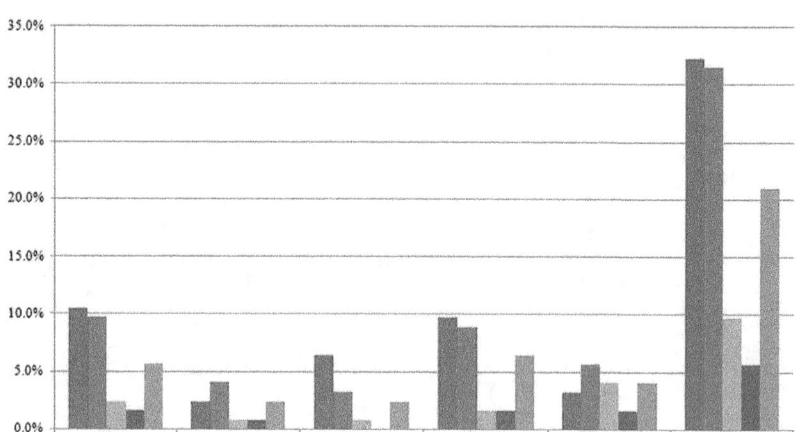

	None	Low	Middle	Fairly	Extreme	Obesity
Production and maintenance	10.5%	2.4%	6.5%	9.7%	3.2%	32.3%
Engineering	9.7%	4.0%	3.2%	8.9%	5.6%	31.5%
Materials	2.4%	0.8%	0.8%	1.6%	4.0%	9.7%
Safety and environment	1.6%	0.8%	0.0%	1.6%	1.6%	5.6%
Administrative staff	5.6%	2.4%	2.4%	6.5%	4.0%	21.0%

Figure 9. Distribution of the Sample Based on Work Positions

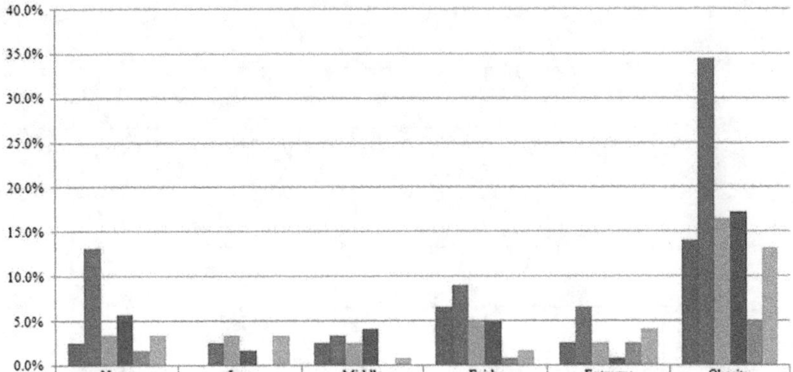

	None	Low	Middle	Fairly	Extreme	Obesity
Department managers	2.5%	0.0%	2.5%	6.6%	2.5%	13.9%
Supervisor	13.1%	2.5%	3.3%	9.0%	6.6%	34.4%
Technicians	3.3%	3.3%	2.5%	4.9%	2.5%	16.4%
Group leaders	5.7%	1.6%	4.1%	4.9%	0.8%	17.2%
Manufacturing administrators	1.6%	0.0%	0.0%	0.8%	2.5%	4.9%
Office administrators	3.3%	3.3%	0.8%	1.6%	4.1%	13.1%

Figure 10. Obesity Prevalence Based on Gender

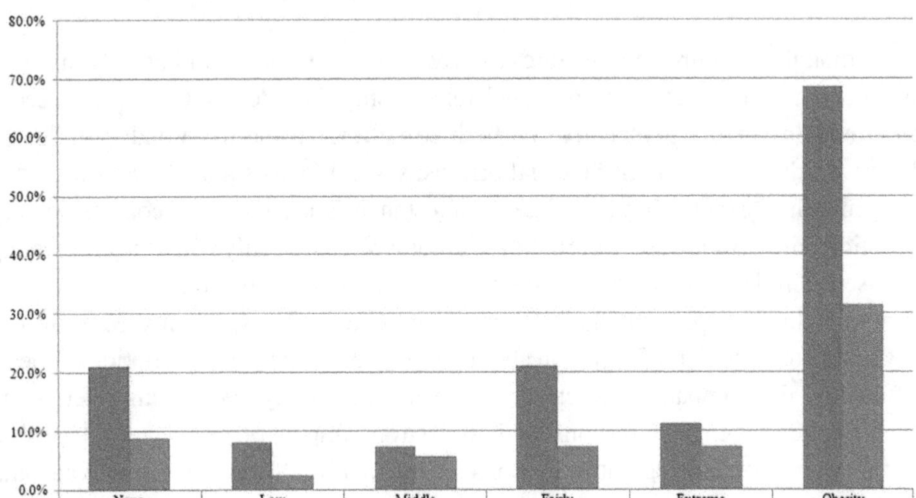

	None	Low	Middle	Fairly	Extreme	Obesity
Man	21.0%	8.1%	7.3%	21.0%	11.3%	68.5%
Woman	8.9%	2.4%	5.6%	7.3%	7.3%	31.5%

Finally, Figure 11 shows the percentages of BS and obesity according to marital status. With respect to BS, the highest percentages in all levels of BS are in married participants. Moreover, also the highest percentage of obesity is present in those participants.

Figure 11. Obesity Prevalence Based on Marital Status

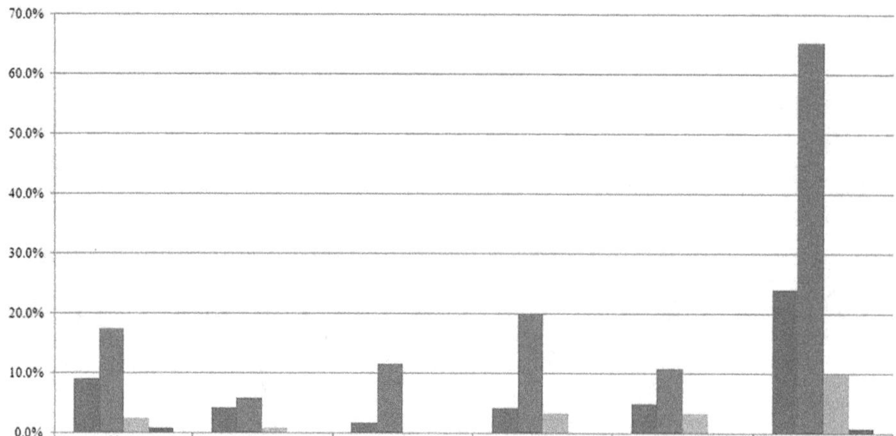

	None	Low	Middle	Fairly	Extreme	Obesity
Single	9.1%	4.1%	1.7%	4.1%	5.0%	24.0%
Married	17.4%	5.8%	11.6%	19.8%	10.7%	65.3%
Free Union	2.5%	0.8%	0.0%	3.3%	3.3%	9.9%
Widow (er)	0.8%	0.0%	0.0%	0.0%	0.0%	0.8%

FUTURE RESEARCH DIRECTIONS

Even though literature demonstrates a correlation between BS and obesity, it is still inconclusive in define the nature of such relationship. This descriptive research seeks to provide a general perspective on both conditions in the maquiladora industry. However, due to their multifactorial origins, several factors must be considered to determine how exactly they are related. For instance, is advised to use complementary questionnaires to analyze eating habits of employees, especially when they are feeling stressed. Similarly, know the coping techniques that they use to reduce stress. For example, do some physical activity, may help reduce BS and obesity. Moreover, it is suitable to consider information about the frequency in the consumption of meals offered by the companies' cafeteria facilities, since the type of meals offered and their frequency of consumption also have a strong impact on obesity development; in this way, effective regulatory actions for the quality of food taking into account the nutritional content are highly recommended.

In addition, BS levels found in the sample of this study demonstrate that it is crucial for maquiladora companies to take preventive measures in order to detect and reduce BS among their employees. It is suitable that workers are informed of the existence of BS as a condition, its symptoms, and consequences. Likewise, several leadership programs may be developed and implemented for senior and middle managers to train them in problem solving, self-control, and time management skills. This would enable them to prioritize tasks more effectively and optimize their time. Furthermore, organizations may consider dynamics to encourage the educational development of workers, foster hour flexibility and competitive salaries, clarify authority lines, and improve communication at all levels. Also, from a social perspective, companies are suggested to praise well-performed tasks, encourage challenges, etc.

CONCLUSION

Results obtained in this research provide maquiladora companies of Ciudad Juarez, researches, physicians and academics a perspective of the presence of burnout syndrome (BS) and obesity among key employees of the Mexican manufacturing industrial sector. It was demonstrated that BS is a prevalent condition among middle and senior managers. In addition, even though a definitive relationship between BS and obesity is not clear in literature and it was beyond the objectives of this chapter; obesity must be considered and studied in industries as a multifactorial condition that can be affected by BS and other elements, since it leads to severe consequences. Therefore, manufacturing industry in Ciudad Juarez and other similar industrial cities in emerging economies might be urged to take measures as a means to prevent obesity and BS. This would help them enhance productivity, work performance, quality of life at work as well as prevent BS or obesity-related diseases. Studies of work psychosocial aspects and their effects on human capital development in the industrial sector are scarce in developing countries, in this way; strategies must be done for the prevention and the effective handling of both diseases. Such strategies must encourage companies to take advantage of their human capital by means of professional advice of psychosocial and organizational culture, enhance healthier eating habits among their employees and a more effective manner to handle stressful situations at work.

REFERENCES

Agredo Zúñiga, R. A., García Ordoñez, E. S., Osorio, C., Escudero, N., López-Albán, C. A., & Ramírez-Vélez, R. (2013). Obesidad abdominal y ausentismo por causa médica en una empresa de la industria metalmecánica en Cali, Colombia. *Revista Peruana de Medicina Experimental y Salud Publica*, *30*, 251–255. PMID:23949511

Ahola, K., Pulkki-Råback, L., Kouvonen, A., Rossi, H., Aromaa, A., & Lönnqvist, J. (2012). Burnout and Behavior-Related Health Risk Factors: Results From the Population-Based Finnish Health 2000 Study. *Journal of Occupational and Environmental Medicine*, *54*(1), 17–22. doi:10.1097/JOM.0b013e31823ea9d9 PMID:22157806

Ahola, K., Vaananen, A., Koskinen, A., Kouvonen, A., & Shirom, A. (2010). Burnout as a predictor of all-cause mortality among industrial employees: A 10-year prospective register-linkage study. *Journal of Psychosomatic Research*, *69*(1), 51–57. doi:10.1016/j.jpsychores.2010.01.002 PMID:20630263

Alarcon, G. M. (2011). A meta-analysis of burnout with job demands, resources, and attitudes. *Journal of Vocational Behavior*, *79*(2), 549–562. doi:10.1016/j.jvb.2011.03.007

Andreyeva, T., Luedicke, J., & Wang, Y. C. (2014). State-Level Estimates of Obesity-Attributable Costs of Absenteeism. *Journal of Occupational and Environmental Medicine*, *56*(11), 1120–1127. doi:10.1097/JOM.0000000000000298 PMID:25376405

Apiquian, A. (2007). *El Síndrome del Burnout en las empresas*. Paper presented at the Tercer Congreso de Escuelas de Psicología de las Universidades Red Anáhuac., Mérida, Yucatán. Retrieved from https://www.ucm.es/data/cont/media/www/pag-28861/sindrome%20burnout.pdf

Aranda Beltrán, C., López Gónzalez, J. L., & Barraza Salas, J. H. (2013). Factores psicosociales y síndrome de burnout en trabajadores de la industria de la transformación de la masa, Tepic, México. *Revista Colombiana de Psiquiatría*, *42*(2), 167–172. doi:10.1016/S0034-7450(13)70003-9 PMID:26572811

Armon, G., Shirom, A., Berliner, S., Shapira, I., & Melamed, S. (2008). A prospective study of the association between obesity and burnout among apparently healthy men and women. *Journal of Occupational Health Psychology*, *13*(1), 43–57. doi:10.1037/1076-8998.13.1.43 PMID:18211168

Barattucci, Y. (2011). *Estrés y Alimentación*. Universidad Fasta, Argentina: Licenciatura en Nutrición.

Blandina-Fernández, J. A., & González-Jaimes, N. L. (2014). Factores psico-sociales-laborales asociados al IMC en trabajadores de la industria de manufactura textil. *Rev Mex Sal Trab*, *6*(15), 14–19.

Block, J. P., He, Y., Zaslavsky, A. M., Ding, L., & Ayanian, J. Z. (2009). Psychosocial stress and change in weight among US adults. *American Journal of Epidemiology*, *170*(2), 181–192. doi:10.1093/aje/kwp104 PMID:19465744

Borak, J. (2011). Obesity and the workplace. *Occupational Medicine (Oxford, England)*, *61*(4), 220–222. doi:10.1093/occmed/kqr030 PMID:21622907

Borritz, M., Christensen, K. B., Bültmann, U., Rugulies, R., Lund, T., Andersen, I., & Kristensen, T. S. et al.Prospective Results of the Danish PUMA Study Among Human Service Workers. (2010). Impact of burnout and psychosocial work characteristics on future long-term sickness absence. Prospective results of the Danish PUMA Study among human service workers. *Journal of Occupational and Environmental Medicine*, *52*(10), 964–970. doi:10.1097/JOM.0b013e3181f12f95 PMID:20881631

Bosqued, M. (2008). *Quemados: El síndrome del Burnout: ¿Qué es y cómo superarlo?* España: Paidós Ibérica.

Camacho-Alamilla, R., Maldonado-Macias, A., García-Alcaraz, J. L., & Hernández-Arellano, J. L. (2014). Determination of Burnout Syndrome among Middle and Senior Managment Personnel in Autootive Industry in Juarez City México. In C. Espejo-Guasco, E. De la Vega Bustillos, & E. Chacón Martínez (Eds.), Ergonomía Ocupacional. Investigaciones y aplicaciones. (Vol. 7, pp. 306-317). Sociedad de Ergonomistas de México, A.C.

Casanueva, E., Pérez-Lizaur, A., Ripoll, C., Plazas, M., & Benito, A. (2005). Un estudio sobre las condiciones de salud de los ejecutivos en la Ciudad de México. In M. Pérez Lizaur (Ed.), *Ejecutivos de alto nivel: ¿ Una èlite global?* Universidad Iberoamericana.

Cavuoto, L. A., & Nussbaum, M. A. (2014). The influences of obesity and age on functional performance during intermittent upper extremity tasks. *Journal of Occupational and Environmental Hygiene*, *11*(9), 583–590. doi:10.1080/15459624.2014.887848 PMID:24484265

Charles, L. E., Burchfiel, C. M., Gu, J. K., Andrew, M. E., Fekedulegn, D., & Violanti, J. M. (2009). Abstract: Sleep Duration and Biomarkers of Metabolic Function Among Police Officers. *Annals of Epidemiology*, *19*(9), 666. doi:10.1016/j.annepidem.2009.07.036

Choi, B., Schnall, P. L., Yang, H., Dobson, M., Landsbergis, P., Israel, L., & Baker, D. et al. (2010). Sedentary work, low physical job demand, and obesity in US workers. *American Journal of Industrial Medicine*, *53*(11), 1088–1101. doi:10.1002/ajim.20886 PMID:20737422

Dallman, M. F. (2010). Stress-induced obesity and the emotional nervous system. *Trends in Endocrinology and Metabolism*, *21*(3), 159–165. doi:10.1016/j.tem.2009.10.004 PMID:19926299

Dávila-Torres, J., González-Izquierdo, J. J., & Barrera-Cruz, A. (2015). Panorama de la obesidad en México. (Spanish). *Obesity in Mexico, 53*(2), 240. Retrieved from http://search.ebscohost.com/login.aspx?direct=true&db=edb&AN=101483297&lang=es&site=eds-live

Eberly, R., & Feldman, H. (2010). Obesity and shift work in the general population. *The Internet Journal of Allied Health and Nursing at Nova Southeastern University, 8.*

Epel, E., Lapidus, R., McEwen, B., & Brownell, K. (2001). Stress may add bite to appetite in women: A laboratory study of stress-induced cortisol and eating behavior. *Psychoneuroendocrinology*, *26*(1), 37–49. doi:10.1016/S0306-4530(00)00035-4 PMID:11070333

Fernández, J. E., Marley, R. J., Noriega, S., & Ibarra, G. (2010). *Ergonomía ocupacional: diseño y administración del trabajo. Ciudad Juárez, Chih.* Universidad Autónoma de Ciudad Juárez.

Finkelstein, E. A., daCosta DiBonaventura, M., Burgess, S. M., & Hale, B. C. (2010). The costs of obesity in the workplace. *Journal of Occupational and Environmental Medicine*, *52*(10), 971–976. doi:10.1097/JOM.0b013e3181f274d2 PMID:20881629

Foss, B., & Dyrstad, S. M. (2011). Stress in obesity: Cause or consequence? *Medical Hypotheses*, *77*(1), 7–10. doi:10.1016/j.mehy.2011.03.011 PMID:21444159

Franco, S. (2012). *USA: Organization for the Economic Cooperation and Development.* Retrieved from http://www.oecd.org/health/49716427.pdf

Freudenberguer, H. J. (1974). Staff Burnout. *The Journal of Social Issues*, *30*(1), 159–165. doi:10.1111/j.1540-4560.1974.tb00706.x

Gómez-Alcaina, B., Montero-Marín, J., Demarzo, M. M. P., Pereira, J. P., & García-Campayo, J. (2013). Utilidad de los marcadores biológicos en la detección precoz y prevención del Síndrome de Burnout. *Revista de Psicopatología y Psicología Clínica*, *18*(3), 245–253. doi:10.5944/rppc.vol.18.num.3.2013.12924

Gu, J. A. K., Charles, L. E., Ma, C. C., Hartley, T. A., Andrew, M. E., Violanti, J. M., & Burchfiel, C. M. (2014). Obesity and Work-Site Injury: The National Health Interview Survey (NHIS), 20042012. *Annals of Epidemiology*, *24*(9), 695. doi:10.1016/j.annepidem.2014.06.065

Guerrero, E., & Vicente, F. (2001). *Síndrome de "Burnout" o desgaste profesional y afrontamiento del estrés en el profesorado*. Cáceres: Universidad de Extremadura.

Han, K., Trinkoff, A. M., Storr, C. L., & Geiger-Brown, J. (2011). Job Stress and Work Schedules in Relation to Nurse Obesity. *The Journal of Nursing Administration, 41*(11), 488–495. doi:10.1097/NNA.0b013e3182346fff PMID:22033319

Hellerstedt, W. L., & Jeffery, R. W. (1997). The association of job strain and health behaviours in men and women. *International Journal of Epidemiology, 26*(3), 575–583. doi:10.1093/ije/26.3.575 PMID:9222783

Hudson. (2005). *Burnout Britain: Raising the Alarm for Employers*. Retrieved from www.hudson.com

Hunter, S. T. (2009). On committing corporate suicide. In T. Casserley & D. Megginson (Eds.), *Learning from Burnout*. Elsevier.

Isasi, C. R., Parrinello, C. M., Jung, M. M., Carnethon, M. R., Birnbaum-Weitzman, O., Espinoza, R. A., & Gallo, L. C. et al. (2015). Psychosocial stress is associated with obesity and diet quality in Hispanic/Latino adults. *Annals of Epidemiology, 25*(2), 84–89. doi:10.1016/j.annepidem.2014.11.002 PMID:25487969

Juárez-García, A., Idrovo, A. J., Camacho-Ávila, A., & Placencia-Reyes, O. (2014). Síndorme de burnout en población mexicana: Una revisión sistemática. *Salud Mental, 37*(2), 159–176. doi:10.17711/SM.0185-3325.2014.020

Kivimaki, M., Head, J., Ferrie, J. E., Shipley, M. J., Brunner, E., Vahtera, J., & Marmot, M. G. (2006). Work stress, weight gain and weight loss: Evidence for bidirectional effects of job strain on body mass index in the Whitehall II study. *International Journal of Obesity, 30*(6), 982–987. doi:10.1038/sj.ijo.0803229 PMID:16418750

Kyrou, I., & Tsigos, C. (2009). Stress hormones: Physiological stress and regulation of metabolism. *Current Opinion in Pharmacology, 9*(6), 787–793. doi:10.1016/j.coph.2009.08.007 PMID:19758844

Leiter, M. P., & Maslach, C. (2009). Nurse turnover: The mediating role of burnout. *Journal of Nursing Management, 17*(3), 331–339. doi:10.1111/j.1365-2834.2009.01004.x PMID:19426369

Llaneza, J. (2002). *Ergonomía y psicología aplicada: Manual para la formación del especialista*. Lex Nova.

Luckhaupt, S. E., Cohen, M. A., Li, J., & Calvert, G. M. (2014). Prevalence of obesity among U.S. workers and associations with occupational factors. *American Journal of Preventive Medicine, 46*(3), 237–248. doi:10.1016/j.amepre.2013.11.002 PMID:24512862

Luque-Reca, O., Augusto-Landa, J. M., & Pulido-Martos, M. (2014). La relación entre la inteligencia emocional percibida y la salud mental en directivos y mandos intermedios: El papel del estrés percibido como mediador. *Ansiedad y Estrés*, *20*(1), 61–73.

Maldonado-Macías, A., Camacho-Alamilla, R., Torres, S. G. V., Alcaraz, J. L. G., & Limón, J. (2015). Determination of Burnout Syndrome among Middle and Senior Managers in Manufacturing Industry in Ciudad Juarez. *Procedia Manufacturing*, *3*, 6459–6466. doi:10.1016/j.promfg.2015.07.927

Marchand, A., Juster, R.-P., Durand, P., & Lupien, S. J. (2014). Burnout symptom sub-types and cortisol profiles: Whats burning most? *Psychoneuroendocrinology*, *40*(0), 27–36. doi:10.1016/j.psyneuen.2013.10.011 PMID:24485473

Martínez, M. P. (2015, 5 Febrero). Estima la OIT estrés laboral en 40% de lo trabajadores mexicanos. *El Economista*. Retrieved from http://eleconomista.com.mx/industrias/2015/02/05/estima-oit-estres-laboral-40-trabajadores-mexicanos

Maslach, C. (2009). Comprendiendo el burnout. *Ciencia & Trabajo*, *11*, 37–43.

Maslach, C., & Jackson, S. E. (1981). The measurement of experienced burnout. *Journal of Organizational Behavior*, *2*(2), 99–113. doi:10.1002/job.4030020205

Maslach, C., Jackson, S. E., & Leiter, M. P. (1996). *MBI: The Maslach Burnout Inventory Manual* (3rd ed.). Palo Alto, CA: Consulting Psychologists Press.

McCormack, N., & Cotter, C. (2013). *Managing Burnout in the Workplace. A Guide for Information Professionals*. Oxford, UK: Chandos Publishing.

Montiel, O., Ramírez, A., Esparza, V. M., & Guerrero, A. (2014). Relatos de vida de gerentes de producción en la industria maquiladora de Cd.Juárez, México. *Global Conference on Business & Finance Proceedings*, *9*(1), 1700-1709.

Moreno-Jiménez, B., Rodríguez-Carvajal, R., & Escobar, E. (2001). La Evaluación del Burnout Profesional: Factorización del MBI-GS. Un análisis preliminar. *Ansiedad y Estrés*, *7*(1), 69–78.

Muenster, E., Rueger, H., Ochsmann, E., Letzel, S., & Toschke, A. M. (2011). Association between overweight, obesity and self-perceived job insecurity in German employees. *BMC Public Health*, *11*(1), 162. doi:10.1186/1471-2458-11-162 PMID:21401919

National-Institute-of-Statistics-Geography-and-Informatics. (2015). *Estadística Integral de Programa de la Industria Manufacturera, Maquiladora y Servicios de Exportación*. IMMEX.

Nevanpera, N. J., Hopsu, L., Kuosma, E., Ukkola, O., Uitti, J., & Laitinen, J. H. (2012). Occupational burnout, eating behavior, and weight among working women. *The American Journal of Clinical Nutrition*, *95*(4), 934–943. doi:10.3945/ajcn.111.014191 PMID:22378728

Newman, E., OConnor, D., & Conner, M. (2007). Daily hassles and eating behaviour: The role of cortisol reactivity status. *Psychoneuroendocrinology*, *32*(2), 125–132. doi:10.1016/j.psyneuen.2006.11.006 PMID:17198744

O`Connor, D. B., & Conner, M. (2011). Effects of Stress on Eating Behavior. In R. J. Contrada & A. Baum (Eds.), *The Handbook of Stress Science: Biology, Psychology, and Health*. Springer Publishing Company.

Park, W., Ramachandran, J., Weisman, P., & Jung, E. S. (2010). Obesity effect on male active joint range of motion. *Ergonomics*, *53*(1), 102–108. doi:10.1080/00140130903311617 PMID:20069486

Proper, K. I., Koppes, L. J., Meijer, S., & Bemelmans, J. E. (2013). The Association Between Body Mass Index Status and Sick Leave and the Role of Emotional Exhaustion—A Mediation Analysis Among a Representative Sample of Dutch Employees. *Journal of Occupational and Environmental Medicine*, *55*(10), 1213–1218. doi:10.1097/JOM.0b013e31829f2f5c PMID:24064779

Proper, K. I., Koppes, L. J., Van Zwieten, M. J., & Bemelmans, W. E. (2012). The prevalence of chronic psychological complaints and emotional exhaustion among overweight and obese workers. *International Archives of Occupational and Environmental Health*, *85*(5), 537–545. doi:10.1007/s00420-011-0703-y PMID:21947369

Raffo, E., Ráez, L., & Cachay, O. (2013). Riesgos psicosociales. *Revista de la Facultad de Ingenieria Industrial*, *16*(2), 70–79.

Rivera Moya, Y., & Briseño Escobedo, J. (2013). El estrés en las organizaciones. *Contribiciones a la Economía*. Retrieved from www.eumed.net/ce/2013/estres-organizaciones.html

Ross, E. (1993). Preventing Burnout Among Social Workers Employed in the Field of AIDS/HIV. *Social Work in Health Care*, *18*(2), 91–108. doi:10.1300/J010v18n02_06 PMID:8332942

Rubio, J. C. (2003). *Fuentes de estrés, Síndrome de Burnout y Actitudes disfuncionales en Orientadores de Instituto de Enseñanza Secundaria*. Universidad de la Extremadura, Badajoz.

Salgado, P. M., & Mejía, R. S. (2008). Estrés en ejecutivos de medianas y grandes empresas mexicanas: Un enfoque de desarrollo humano organizacional. *Estudios Gerenciales, 24*(108), 15–36. doi:10.1016/S0123-5923(08)70042-1

Schwartz, J. (2004, Septiembre 5). Always on the job: Employees pay with health. *The New York Times.*

Secretaría-de-Salud. (2010). *Acuerdo Nacional para la Salud Alimenentaria.* Retrieved from http://www.sep.gob.mx/work/models/sep1/Resource/635/1/images/programadeaccion_sept.pdf

Serrano, M., Alacreu-Crespo, A., Costa, R., Abad, D., & González-Bono, E. (2015). *Variables Psicobiológicas.* Madrid: Pearson Educación.

Serrano, M., & Salvador, A. (2015). *Psicobiología del Estrés.* Madrid: Pearson Educación.

Serrano, M., Salvador, A., & Costa, R. (2015). Concepto de estrés. In M. Serrano & A. Salvador (Eds.), Psicobiología del estrés. Madrid: Pearson Educación.

Shirom, A. (2003). Job-related burnout. In Q. J. C & L. E. Tetrick (Eds.), Handbook of occupational health psychology (pp. 245–265). Washington, DC: American Psychological Association.

The-World-Health-Organization. (2015). *Obesidad y sobrepeso.* Retrieved from http://www.who.int/mediacentre/factsheets/fs311/es/

Torres, S. J., & Nowson, C. A. (2007). Relationship between stress, eating behavior, and obesity. *Nutrition (Burbank, Los Angeles County, Calif.), 23*(11-12), 887–894. doi:10.1016/j.nut.2007.08.008 PMID:17869482

Van Bogaert, P., Clarke, S., Roelant, E., Meulemans, H., & Van de Heyning, P. (2010). Impacts of unit-level nurse practice environment and burnout on nurse-reported outcomes: A multilevel modelling approach. *Journal of Clinical Nursing, 19*(11-12), 1664–1674. doi:10.1111/j.1365-2702.2009.03128.x PMID:20579204

Zhang, Y., & Feng, X. (2011). The relationship between job satisfaction, burnout, and turnover intention among physicians from urban state-owned medical institutions in Hubei, China: A cross-sectional study. *BMC Health Services Research, 11*(1), 235. doi:10.1186/1472-6963-11-235 PMID:21943042

KEY TERMS AND DEFINITIONS

Administrative and Office Assistants or Staff: In the context of manufacturing companies, these are employees who provide support and assistance in the different departments.

Middle Manager (Supervisor): Supervisors must be able to communicate enthusiasm, and enthusiastic employees feel proud of their teams and speak proudly of their work. In addition, these managers must be fully familiar with their work and responsibilities. They ought to have instruction and leadership skills, as well as the ability to improve methods implemented.

Senior Manager (Top Manager): These managers are fully accountable for their work. They are characterized by an entrepreneurial spirit and the ability to manage changes and the flow of the organization. Similarly, they have specific cognitive qualities (decision making and analysis skills, and the ability to remember different kinds of information), as well as interpersonal, communication, leadership, motivation, and staff management skills. Also, they must have a competitive spirit, moral integrity, ethics, and the capacity for being critical and self-correcting, among others.

Chapter 11
Technological Advancements in Payments:
From Cash to Digital through Unified Payments Interface(UPI)

Ankit Dhamija
Amity University Gurgaon, India

Deepika Dhamija
Amity University Gurgaon, India

ABSTRACT

Mobile banking in India has witnessed a lot of changes with respect to technological and architectural changes. The continuous rise in the number of mobile banking users is due to this fact that the technological advancements that has restored the faith and boosted the trust of users towards mobile banking and payments. However, in a developing economy like India, where this number of mobile users is expected to grow exponentially, the complexity will also grow as the mobile users expect the mobile banking services to be fast, convenient and most importantly, more secure. There is a scope of improvement with the already existing thing and mobile banking is no different In this direction, the National Payments Corporation of India has initiated a system called Unified Payments Interface (UPI) that further eases the process of money transfer through smart phones and feature phones, thereby bringing this technology within everybody's reach. This chapter further puts insights into the implementation and feasibility aspects of UPI and how it is better than the systems prevailing today.

DOI: 10.4018/978-1-5225-1974-4.ch011

INTRODUCTION

Doing business in India is a challenging task as this country is mired in procedures. Organizations need easier ways of doing business that are less time consuming and more productive. The Information Technology has helped a lot in this direction and has given a whole new set of options for new types of businesses in web based businesses, mobile application based, on social media platforms, through television advertisements. All such kind of businesses cannot flourish without technology and they will need technological enhancements and innovations to grow further.

The most important area where information technology comes into picture is online payments and mobile banking. Like organizations, customers also need less complex ways of making payments. A recent development in this context was made with the launch of Unified Payment Interface (UPI) which aims to make money transfers easy, quick and hassle free. Payments through mobile phone is in trend and also quite successful, but simplifying it to an extent that it looks as easy as sending an SMS is the highlight of UPI.

As the India Prime Minister had recently launched the Digital India Campaign which focuses on aligning every aspect of the economy with technology and make it transparent, the launch of UPI will further boost the digital India campaign and bring the country's population in the formal financial sector and towards digital transactions, making India a cashless economy.

Developed by National Payments Corporation of India (NPCI) and launched by RBI Governor Raghu Ram Rajan, the UPI is all set to revolutionize the way online payments and money transfers take place in this country.

This chapter is further organized as follows: The background section Provide broad definitions and discussions of the topic and the literature review. The next section presents the issues and problems associated with the already existing payment mechanisms. Then, the next section will provide the solutions to the problems raised by author in the previous section. Finally, future research directions and the conclusion of the chapter will follow.

BACKGROUND

Before moving further, it is important to understand some terms that will be used very frequently in the chapter ahead:

KEY TERMS

- **Mobile Banking:** Mobile Banking in lay man terms means the using of a mobile phone to offer banking services. Banks have introduced two different products in mobile banking. One is a personal/retail banking product and the other is a product to promote financial inclusion. As a personal banking product it is offered to every savings/current account holder and provides anytime anywhere banking. The mobile banking initiatives were started by foreign and private banks followed by public sector banks. Mobile banking service is primarily available over SMS (Short Messaging Service) or through GPRS (General Packet Radio Service) or sometimes through USSD (Unstructured Supplementary Service Data). The services available are:
    - Funds transfer (intra and interbank)
    - Balance enquiry services/mini statements
    - Request services (cheque book)
    - Utility bill payments and credit card payments
    - Demat account services
    - Mobile top up
    - Merchant payment, life insurance premium
    - Stop payment instructions
- **RTGS:** The acronym 'RTGS' stands for Real Time Gross Settlement, which can be defined as the continuous (real-time) settlement of funds transfers individually on an order by order basis (without netting). 'Real Time' means the processing of instructions at the time they are received rather than at some later time; 'Gross Settlement' means the settlement of funds transfer instructions occurs individually (on an instruction by instruction basis). Considering that the funds settlement takes place in the books of the Reserve Bank of India, the payments are final and irrevocable.
- **NEFT:** NEFT stands for National Electronic Funds Transfer and is a payment system which facilitates one-to-one funds transfer.
- **IMPS:** Immediate Payment Service (IMPS) is an instant interbank electronic fund transfer service through mobile phones. It is also being extended through other channels such as ATM, Internet Banking, etc.

There are three types of payment systems that are prevailing in India: NEFT, RTGS and IMPS. Out of these three, NEFT and RTGS systems were introduced by RBI and IMPS was launched by National Payment Corporation in 2010. Till date, all three options are being provided by the banks on the customer's net banking account and on mobile apps also. Although, there are more than 900 million mobile users in India, the second largest smart phone market globally, is expected to witness a mani-fold growth in the number of smart phones to over 650 million in the next four years, a study by networking solutions giant Cisco said. This will surely have boosted the numbers of mobile banking users but despite this, there are only about 36 million mobile banking customers, according to a report by The Financial Express.

PROBLEMS AND ISSUES WITH EXISTING ONLINE PAYMENT MECHANISMS

Although the NEFT, RTGS and IMPS payment settlement systems are working fine, there are some problem areas in each one of them which are summarized below:

1. **Requirement of so Many Details:** The biggest problem in all these three methods is that these all are dependent on so many things. For them to function well, the user is supposed to provide so many details like beneficiary's account number, account type, branch details, IFSC code of the branch, account holder's name etc and so on.
2. **Excessive Transaction Processing Time:** There is a difference in the time taken by all three types of payment settlement. NEFT processes the transactions in batches which normally take 2-3 hours, RTGS processes them as they come i.e. on One to One basis and IMPS does it instantaneously. As this difference is not known to all the customers, they hesitate and get confused as to which option to use.
3. **Processing Fee:** There is a processing fee in all three types which depends on the amount that is being transferred and the users mostly remain unaware of the transactions processing fee which again acts as a hindrance in making a choice.
4. **Transaction Limits:** Each of the three methods have set a transaction limit that will be processed in a day which may also worry some people.

Figure 1. Mobile Banking Trends in India
Source: The Financial Express

TRENDS IN MOBILE BANKING

YEAR	NO. OF USERS (MILLION)	VOLUME (MILLION)	VALUE (₹ BILLION)
2011-12	12.96	25.56	18.21
2012-13	22.51 (73.69%)	53.31 (108.56%)	59.90 (228.94%)
2013-14	35.53 (57.84%)	94.71 (77.66%)	224.38 (274.59%)

5. **Dependent on Net banking:** All these three features require the use of internet and the user must be logged on to their net banking account for performing transactions.
6. **Other Technical Glitches:** These include problems like Funds Transferred but not credited to the destination Account etc and other technical issues may also arise.

THE SOLUTION: UNIFIED PAYMENT INTERFACE (UPI)

As we have seen in the above section, there are numerous problems associated with the existing payment methods and all of them are dependent on Net Banking and the Internet at all times to function properly.

In order to make the system more user friendly and more easy to use and to have a huge user base, a very new method called UPI has been proposed by National Payments Corporation of India (NPCI) which caters to the needs of most of the population and which will change the way payments are made in this country.

UPI may be defined as "A Payment interface to be used on a smart phone for making payments in a hassle free manner".

"It is a smart phone/feature phone based electronic payment mechanism that focuses on providing a secure architecture to propel easy and instant payments".

HOW UPI WORKS?

Basic Model

See Figure 2 for the basic model of UPI.

Figure 2. Basic model of UPI explained

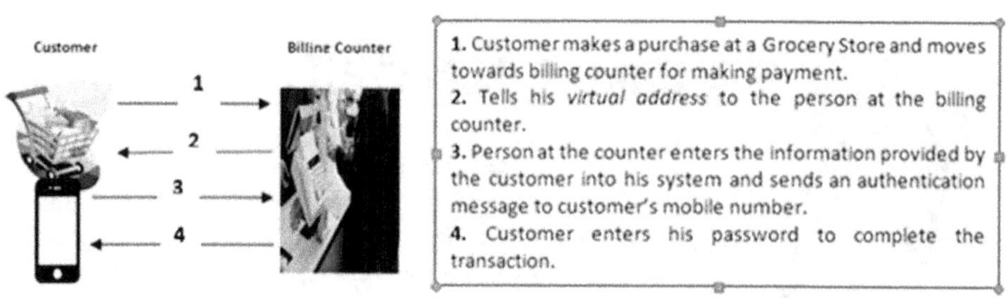

Technical Model

See Figure 3 for the technical model of UPI.

For UPI to work fine the following are the most important technical requirements that need to be set up:

1. **Mapping of Customer's Mobile Number and Bank Accounts:** The UPI system will be dependent on customer's mobile number as it will be used by the customer to authenticate the transactions. Thus, the user needs to get their mobile numbers and bank accounts mapped with their banks.
2. **Virtual Address Generation:** To initiate a transaction payment through UPI, the customer will need to enter their virtual addresses which will be generated when the customer register their mobile number with the bank. The customer may have multiple virtual addresses for multiple accounts in various banks.
3. **Single Click Multi-Factor Authentication:** The payment mechanism will be based on single click multi-factor authentication which involves a two-way process of authenticating the transaction by the end user. First, the user has to provide their 'virtual address' to the person at billing counter and second, the user has to enter their password/pin to finally authenticate the transaction. Only after completing these two steps, the transaction will be successful.

Figure 3. Technical Model of UPI
Source: NPCI

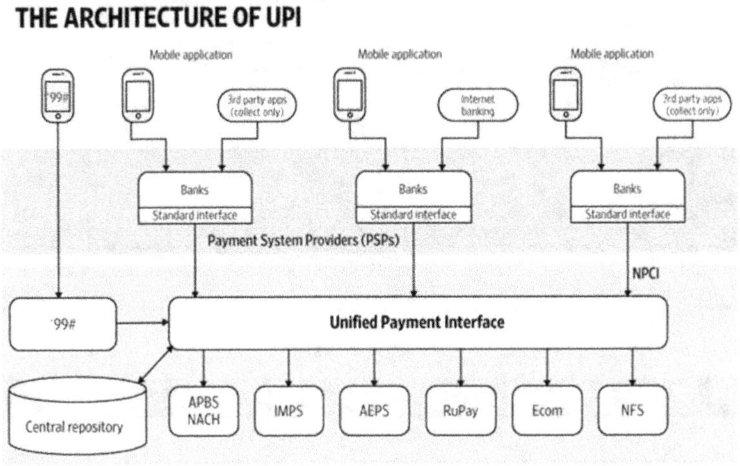

Working of the Technical Model

This technical model depicts UPI as a layer built on top of all other payment mechanisms including IMPS that gives an idea of the wide spectrum of UPI. The UPI system will be accessed by the users through mobile apps that the users will be required to install on their smart phones (those who want to use it on the move, through smart phones) and also through web platforms (those who want to use it on desktop/laptop machines). The users will initiate their transactions through any of the above said medium and banks act as a very important link in this system to function properly as linking of user's mobile number and bank accounts is a pre-requisite for this system to function. After this linking, each user is provided with a 'virtual address' which will act as a 'first factor' in transaction authentication. Then, the users are supposed to create their passwords/pin, which will act as 'second factor' authentication. Here, the role of payment Service Providers (PSP's) becomes important. The PSP's include various online merchants and organizations who are in ecommerce business and who are willing to collect money from their customers in an online mode. Presently, they are accepting payments through debit/credit cards, net banking, COD, mobile wallets, NEFT, IMPS, cash cards, gift vouchers etc. They need to modify their payment portal (on both mobile and web platform) and make provision for accepting payments through UPI. They can do so very easily by just giving UPI as a payment option along with all other existing options, as depicted in Figure 4.

Figure 4. Integration of UPI in merchant's payment portal

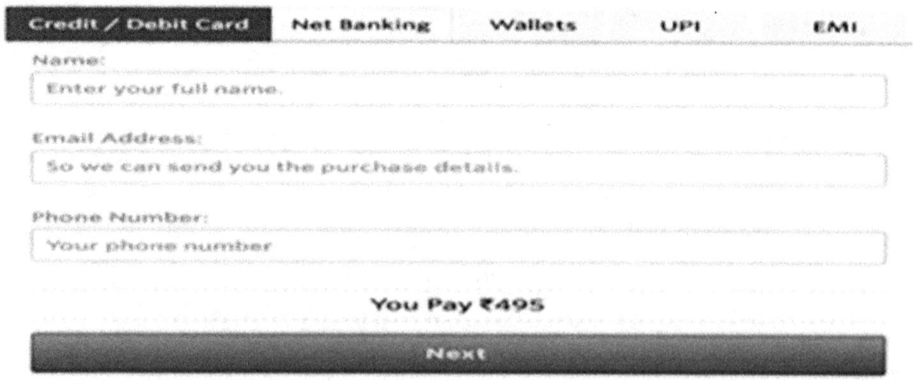

EXPECTED BENEFITS

The objective of introducing and implementing UPI is to provide a single platform to a large user base which offers seamless and uninterrupted service of making and accepting payments. With this objective in mind, UPI is expected to offer the following benefits:

- **Transaction Simplicity:** UPI is expected to make the procedure of making and receiving payments simple and more users friendly. The users won't need to go through a hassled system of registering a beneficiary and remembering complex bank account numbers and several pins. The users will be able to perform all these tasks by just single click on their mobile device or desktop/ laptops.
- **Revolutionary Idea:** The idea of implementing UPI is an revolutionary idea as it will function within the existing system and no major changes are required in the existing system and with some modifications at the end of banks and PSP's, this can be accommodated.
- **Scalable Option:** The whole objective of introducing UPI is to make our economy, a cashless one. The UPI must be scalable to a billion users and must be adopted by most of the people.
- **Interoperable:** The system is expected to be interoperable in the sense that it must work fine with different identifiers like mobile number, aadhaar number and other virtual addresses. Similarly, it must allow people without smart phone to use the features of the system and so on.
- **Data Security:** The system is designed in such a manner that the important data like users bank account details and other important information doesn't gets disclosed at any point. This is the reason why transactions are made to pass through a two way authentication process.

CONCLUSION

UPI is a great initiative taken by National payments Corporation of India which intends to bring our citizens into a formal payment model which is very simple to use and towards bringing us a digital and cashless economy which will further help our country grow further. However, for the system to be fully operational and functional, there are complexities like integrating bank accounts and mobile numbers, cooperation from banks, third parties and online merchants and vendors etc which needs to be resolved. Having said that, it is clear that UPI is a blessing and the much needed X factor to boost the digital customer base and it is hopeful that it will put a halt to the unaccounted money going around which is hindering this country's progress.

REFERENCES

Admin. (2014). *NEFT v/s RTGS v/s IMPS*. Retrieved May 04, 2016, from http://www.investologic.in/neft-vs-rtgs-vs-imps/

Admin. (2016). *Banking on technology- Indian banking industry*. Retrieved May 02, 2016, from http://www.ey.com/IN/en/Industries/Financial-Services/Banking---Capital Markets/EY-banking-on-technology-india-banking-industry

Reserve bank of India website. (2016). Retrieved May 04, 2016, from https://www.rbi.org.in/scripts/FAQView.aspx?Id=65

Sasi, A. (2015). *Smartphone usage drives up mobile banking numbers*. Retrieved May 04, 2016, from http://www.financialexpress.com/article/economy/smartphone-usage-drives-up-mobile-banking-numbers/31666/

Swain, S. (2016). *An Indian Fintech Entrepreneur's Views on UPI*. Retrieved May 5, 2016, from http://tech.economictimes.indiatimes.com/catalysts/an-indian-fintech-entrepreneur-s-views-on-upi/1455

Compilation of References

Abubakar, A., Kassim, S. H. J., & Yusoff, M. B. (2015). Financial development, human capital accumulation and economic growth: Empirical evidence from the Economic Community of West African States (ECOWAS). *Procedia: Social and Behavioral Sciences*, *172*, 96–103. doi:10.1016/j.sbspro.2015.01.341

Acemoglu, D., & Robinson, J. A. (2012). *Why nations fail: The origins of power, prosperity, and poverty*. New York, NY: The Crown Publishing Group.

Adenike, A. (2011, January). Organisational Climate as a Predictor of Employee Job Satisfaction. *Business Intelligence Journal*, *4*(1), 151–165.

Adhikari, R., & Regmī, D. (2001). *Anti-competitive practices in Nepal*. Discussion Paper. Kathmandu: South Asia Watch on Trade, Economic & Environment (SAWTEE) and Consumer Unity & Trust Society-Centre for International Trade, Economics & Environment (CUTS-CITEE).

Admin. (2014). *NEFT v/s RTGS v/s IMPS*. Retrieved May 04, 2016, from http://www.investologic.in/neft-vs-rtgs-vs-imps/

Admin. (2016). *Banking on technology- Indian banking industry*. Retrieved May 02, 2016, from http://www.ey.com/IN/en/Industries/Financial-Services/Banking---Capital Markets/EY-banking-on-technology-india-banking-industry

Afonso, O. (2010). Growth and wage inequality in a scale-independent model with R&D and human-capital accumulation. *The Manchester School*, *78*(2), 149–182. doi:10.1111/j.1467-9957.2009.02135.x

Agredo Zúñiga, R. A., García Ordoñez, E. S., Osorio, C., Escudero, N., López-Albán, C. A., & Ramírez-Vélez, R. (2013). Obesidad abdominal y ausentismo por causa médica en una empresa de la industria metalmecánica en Cali, Colombia. *Revista Peruana de Medicina Experimental y Salud Publica*, *30*, 251–255. PMID:23949511

Ahmad, N., Jaapar, A., Adnan, H., Bari, N. A. A., & Rashid, R. A. (2012). Important Qualities of Design Teams in Managing Clients Brief and their Impact on Delivering Quality Buildings. *Procedia: Social and Behavioral Sciences*, *35*, 728–738. doi:10.1016/j.sbspro.2012.02.143

Ahme, E. M., & Krishnasamy, G. (2013). Human capital investment to achieve knowledge-based economy in ASEAN5: DEA applications. *Journal of the Knowledge Economy*, *4*(4), 331–342. doi:10.1007/s13132-011-0059-2

Ahola, K., Pulkki-Råback, L., Kouvonen, A., Rossi, H., Aromaa, A., & Lönnqvist, J. (2012). Burnout and Behavior-Related Health Risk Factors: Results From the Population-Based Finnish Health 2000 Study. *Journal of Occupational and Environmental Medicine*, *54*(1), 17–22. doi:10.1097/JOM.0b013e31823ea9d9 PMID:22157806

Ahola, K., Vaananen, A., Koskinen, A., Kouvonen, A., & Shirom, A. (2010). Burnout as a predictor of all-cause mortality among industrial employees: A 10-year prospective register-linkage study. *Journal of Psychosomatic Research*, *69*(1), 51–57. doi:10.1016/j.jpsychores.2010.01.002 PMID:20630263

Ahrens, J. P., Landmann, A., & Woywode, M. (2015). Gender preferences in the CEO successions of family firms: Family characteristics and human capital of the successor. *Journal of Family Business Strategy*, *6*(2), 86–103. doi:10.1016/j.jfbs.2015.02.002

Åkerstedt, T., Fredlund, P., Gillberg, M., & Jansson, B. (2002). Work load and work hours in relation to disturbed sleep and fatigue in a large representative sample. *Journal of Psychosomatic Research*, *53*(1), 585–588. doi:10.1016/S0022-3999(02)00447-6 PMID:12127175

Aktaş, E., Çiçek, I., & Kıyak, M. (2011). The Effect Of Organizational Culture On Organizational Efficiency: The Moderating Role Of Organizational Environment and CEO Values. *Procedia: Social and Behavioral Sciences*, *24*, 1560–1573. doi:10.1016/j.sbspro.2011.09.092

Akter, T., & Simonovic, S. P. (2005). Aggregation of fuzzy views of a large number of stakeholders for multi-objective flood management decision-making. *Journal of Environmental Management*, *77*(2), 133–143. doi:10.1016/j.jenvman.2005.02.015 PMID:16046249

Alarcon, G. M. (2011). A meta-analysis of burnout with job demands, resources, and attitudes. *Journal of Vocational Behavior*, *79*(2), 549–562. doi:10.1016/j.jvb.2011.03.007

Alessandrini, D., Kosempel, S., & Stengos, T. (2015). The business cycle human capital accumulation nexus and its effect on hours worked volatility. *Journal of Economic Dynamics & Control*, *51*, 356–377. doi:10.1016/j.jedc.2014.11.004

Ali, A., Mujahid, N., Rashid, Y., & Shahbaz, M. (2015). Human capital outflow and economic misery: Fresh evidence for Pakistan. *Social Indicators Research*, *124*(3), 747–764. doi:10.1007/s11205-014-0821-5

Alniacik, U., Alniacik, E., & Genc, N. (2011). How corporate social responsibility information influences stakeholders intentions. *Corporate Social Responsibility and Environmental Management*, *18*(4), 234–245. doi:10.1002/csr.245

Amala. (2004). *History of Education*. Discovery Publishing House. Retrieved from https://books.google.co.in/books?isbn=8171418600

Anderson, C. L., & Bieniaszewska, R. L. (2005). The role of corporate social responsibility in an oil companys expansion into new territories. *Corporate Social Responsibility and Environmental Management, 12*(1), 1–9. doi:10.1002/csr.71

Anderson, D., Binder, M., & Krause, K. (2003). The Motherhood Wage Penalty Revisited: Experience, Heterogeneity, Work Effort, and Work-Schedule Flexibility. *ILR Review, 56*(2), 273–294. doi:10.1177/001979390305600204

Anderson, J. W. (1989). *Corporate social responsibility*. Westport, CT: Greenwood Press.

Andreyeva, T., Luedicke, J., & Wang, Y. C. (2014). State-Level Estimates of Obesity-Attributable Costs of Absenteeism. *Journal of Occupational and Environmental Medicine, 56*(11), 1120–1127. doi:10.1097/JOM.0000000000000298 PMID:25376405

Anju, M., Anjala, K., & Payal, P. (2012). *How Mobile Phones, Computers and the Internet can Catalyse Women's Entrepreneurship: India – A Case Study*. Cherie Blair Foundation. Retrieved from http://www.icrw.org/files/publications/Connectivity-how-mobile-phones-computers-and-the-internet-can-catalyze-womens-entrepreneurship.pdf

Anusha, S. (2012, October 28). Of Milk and Honey. *Business Today*. Retrieved November 18, 2015, from http://www.businesstoday.in/cover-story/bestb-schools-2012-mann-deshi-udyogini-curriculum/story/188847.html

Aoki, M. (1990). Toward an economic model of the Japanese firm. *Journal of Economic Literature*.

Apiquian, A. (2007). *El Síndrome del Burnout en las empresas*. Paper presented at the Tercer Congreso de Escuelas de Psicología de las Universidades Red Anáhuac., Mérida, Yucatán. Retrieved from https://www.ucm.es/data/cont/media/www/pag-28861/sindrome%20burnout.pdf

Aranda Beltrán, C., López Gónzalez, J. L., & Barraza Salas, J. H. (2013). Factores psicosociales y síndrome de burnout en trabajadores de la industria de la transformación de la masa, Tepic, México. *Revista Colombiana de Psiquiatría, 42*(2), 167–172. doi:10.1016/S0034-7450(13)70003-9 PMID:26572811

Armon, G., Shirom, A., Berliner, S., Shapira, I., & Melamed, S. (2008). A prospective study of the association between obesity and burnout among apparently healthy men and women. *Journal of Occupational Health Psychology, 13*(1), 43–57. doi:10.1037/1076-8998.13.1.43 PMID:18211168

Arquilla, J., & Ronfeldt, D. (1997). In Athena's Camp: Preparing for Conflict in the Information Age. California, USA: RAND.

Arthur, W. (1996). Increasing returns and the new world of business. *Harvard Business Review*, 100–109. PMID:10158472

Asher, J. J., & Sciarrino, J. A. (1974). Realistic work sample tests: A review. *Personnel Psychology, 27*(4), 519–533. doi:10.1111/j.1744-6570.1974.tb01173.x

Asif, M., Searcy, C., Santos, P. D., & Kensah, D. (2013). A review of Dutch corporate sustainable development reports. *Corporate Social Responsibility and Environmental Management*, *20*(6), 321–339. doi:10.1002/csr.1284

Asif, M., Searcy, C., Zutshi, A., & Fisscher, O. A. M. (2013). An integrated management systems approach to corporate social responsibility. *Journal of Cleaner Production*, *56*(1), 7–17. doi:10.1016/j.jclepro.2011.10.034

Åstbro, T., & Bernhardt, I. (2005). The winner's curse of human capital. *Small Business Economics*, *24*(1), 63–78. doi:10.1007/s11187-005-3097-y

Atalay, R. (2015). The education and the human capital to get rid of the middle-income trap and to provide the economic development. *Procedia: Social and Behavioral Sciences*, *174*, 969–976. doi:10.1016/j.sbspro.2015.01.720

Axtell, C. M., Holman, D. J., Unsworth, K. L., Wall, T. D., Waterson, P. E., & Harrington, E. (2000). Shopfloor innovation: Facilitating the suggestion and implementation of ideas. *Journal of Occupational and Organizational Psychology*, *73*(3), 265–285. doi:10.1348/096317900167029

Azarnert, L. V. (2012). Guest-worker migration, human capital and fertility. *Review of Development Economics*, *16*(2), 318–330. doi:10.1111/j.1467-9361.2012.00664.x

Backman, M. (2014). Human capital in firms and regions: Impact on firm productivity. *Papers in Regional Science*, *93*(3), 557–575. doi:10.1111/pirs.12005

Bain, J. S. (1968). *Industrial organization*. New York: Wiley.

Baker, D. P., Gustafson, S., Beaubien, J., Salas, E., & Barach, P. (2003). Medical teamwork and patient safety: The evidence-based relation. Washington, DC: American Institutes for Research. Retrieved from http://citeseerx.ist.psu.edu/viewdoc/download?doi=10.1.1.136.9246&rep=rep1&type=pdf

Baker, D. P., Day, R., & Salas, E. (2006). Teamwork as an essential component of high-reliability organizations. *Health Services Research*, *41*(4 Pt 2), 1576–1598. doi:10.1111/j.1475-6773.2006.00566.x PMID:16898980

Baker, W. E., & Faulkner, R. R. (1993). The social organization of conspiracy: Illegal networks in the heavy electrical equipment industry. *American Sociological Review*, *58*(6), 837–860. doi:10.2307/2095954

Barattucci, Y. (2011). *Estrés y Alimentación*. Universidad Fasta, Argentina: Licenciatura en Nutrición.

Barney, J. B. (1986). Strategic factor markets: Expectations, luck, and business strategy. *Management Science*, *32*(10), 1231–1241. doi:10.1287/mnsc.32.10.1231

Barney, J. B., & Wright, P. M. (1998). On becoming a strategic partner: The role of human resources in gaining competitive advantage. *Human Resource Management*, *37*(1), 31–46. doi:10.1002/(SICI)1099-050X(199821)37:1<31::AID-HRM4>3.0.CO;2-W

Baron, A., & Armstrong, M. (2007). *Human capital management: Achieving added value through people*. London, UK: Kogan Page.

Barrick, M. R., & Mount, M. K. (1991). The big five personality dimensions and job performance: A meta-analysis. *Personnel Psychology, 91*(1), 1–26. doi:10.1111/j.1744-6570.1991.tb00688.x

Barro, . (1991). Economic Growth in a Cross section of Countries. *The Quarterly Journal of Economics, 106*(2), 407. Retrieved from http://www.econ.nyu.edu/user/debraj/Courses/Readings/BarroGrowth.pdf doi:10.2307/2937943

Barzilai-Nahon, K. (2008). Toward a theory of network gatekeeping: A frame work for exploring information control. *Journal of the American Society for Information Science and Technology, 59*(9), 1493–1512. doi:10.1002/asi.20857

Basil, D. Z., & Weber, D. (2006). Values motivation and concern for appearances: The effect of personality traits on responses to corporate social responsibility. *International Journal of Nonprofit and Voluntary Sector Marketing, 11*(1), 61–72. doi:10.1002/nvsm.38

Basu, P. K., Hicks, J., Krivokapic-Skoko, B., & Sherley, C. (2015). Mining operations and corporate social responsibility: A case study of a large gold mine in regional Australia. *The Extractive Industries and Society, 2*(3), 531–539.

Batabyal, A. A., & Beladi, H. (2013). Human capital, knowledge spillovers, and one kind of semi-endogenous regional economic growth. *Letters in Spatial and Resource Sciences, 6*(3), 121–135. doi:10.1007/s12076-013-0092-9

Beaubien, J. M., & Baker, D. P. (2004). The use of simulation for training teamwork skills in health care: how low can you go? *Quality and Safety in Health Care, 13*(suppl 1), i51–i56. http://doi.org/<ALIGNMENT.qj></ALIGNMENT>10.1136/qshc.2004.009845

Becker. (2009). *Human Capital: A theoretical and Empirical Analysis, with Special reference to Education*. Retrieved from https://books.google.co.in/books?id=9t69iICmrZ0C&source=gbs_navlinks_s

Becker, G. S. (1993). *Human capital: A theoretical and empirical analysis, with special reference to education*. Chicago, IL: University of Chicago Press. doi:10.7208/chicago/9780226041223.001.0001

Becker, G. S. (2011). Forward. In A. Burton-Jones & J. Spender (Eds.), *The Oxford handbook of human capital* (pp. xiii–xvi). Oxford, UK: Oxford University Press.

Beckers, D. G. J., van der Linden, D., Smulders, P. G. W., Kompier, M. A. J., van Veldhoven, M., & van Yperen, N. (2004). Working Overtime Hours: Relations with Fatigue, Work Motivation, and the Quality of Work. *Journal of Occupational and Environmental Medicine, 46*(12), 1282–1289. PMID:15591981

Beevis, D., & Slade, I. M. (2003). Ergonomicscosts and benefits. *Applied Ergonomics, 34*(5), 413–418. doi:10.1016/S0003-6870(03)00061-9 PMID:12963327

Benabou, R., & Triole, J. (2010). Individual and corporate social responsibility. *Economica, 77*(305), 1–19. doi:10.1111/j.1468-0335.2009.00843.x

Bendjenna, H., Charre, P. J., & Zarour, N. E. (2012). Using multi-criteria analysis to prioritize stakeholders. *Journal of Systems and Information Technology, 14*(3), 264–280. doi:10.1108/13287261211255365

Bhatia, A. (2012). The corporate social responsibility report: The hybridization of a confused genre (20072011). *IEEE Transactions on Professional Communication, 55*(3), 221–238. doi:10.1109/TPC.2012.2205732

Bhattacharya, M., Doty, D. H., & Garavan, T. (2014). The organizational context and performance implications of human capital investment variability. *Human Resource Development Quarterly, 25*(1), 87–113. doi:10.1002/hrdq.21182

Blackburn, K., & Varvarigos, D. (2008). Human capital accumulation and output growth in a stochastic environment. *Economic Theory, 36*(3), 435–452. doi:10.1007/s00199-007-0280-1

Blakley, B. R., Quinones, M. S., Crawford, M. S., & Jago, I. A. (1994). The validity of isometric strength tests. *Personnel Psychology, 47*(2), 247–274. doi:10.1111/j.1744-6570.1994.tb01724.x

Blandina-Fernández, J. A., & González-Jaimes, N. L. (2014). Factores psico-sociales-laborales asociados al IMC en trabajadores de la industria de manufactura textil. *Rev Mex Sal Trab, 6*(15), 14–19.

Bligard, L.-O., & Osvalder, A. L. (2014). CCPE: Methodology for a Combined Evaluation and Physical Ergonomics in the Interaction between Human and Machine. *Human Factors and Ergonomics in Manufacturing, 24*(6), 685–711. doi:10.1002/hfm.20512

Block, J. P., He, Y., Zaslavsky, A. M., Ding, L., & Ayanian, J. Z. (2009). Psychosocial stress and change in weight among US adults. *American Journal of Epidemiology, 170*(2), 181–192. doi:10.1093/aje/kwp104 PMID:19465744

Blue Ocean Strategy. (n.d.). Retrieved from http://www.blueoceanstrategy.com

Bogdetsky, V., & Novikov, V. (2012). *Mining, development and environment in Central Asia: Case studies: A toolkit companion.* Joensuu, Finland: University of Eastern Finland.

Booth-Kewley, S., & Vickers, R.R., Jr. (1994). Associations between major domains of personality and health behavior. *Journal of personality, 62*(3), 281-298.

Borak, J. (2011). Obesity and the workplace. *Occupational Medicine (Oxford, England), 61*(4), 220–222. doi:10.1093/occmed/kqr030 PMID:21622907

Borca, C., & Baesu, V. (2014). A Possible Managerial Approach for Internal Organizational Communication Characterization. *Procedia: Social and Behavioral Sciences, 124*, 496–503. doi:10.1016/j.sbspro.2014.02.512

Bornay-Barrachina, M., de la Rosa-Navarro, D., López-Cabrales, A., & Valle-Cabrera, R. (2012). Employment relationships and firm innovation: The double role of human capital. *British Journal of Management*, *23*(2), 223–240. doi:10.1111/j.1467-8551.2010.00735.x

Borritz, M., Christensen, K. B., Bültmann, U., Rugulies, R., Lund, T., Andersen, I., & Kristensen, T. S. et al.Prospective Results of the Danish PUMA Study Among Human Service Workers. (2010). Impact of burnout and psychosocial work characteristics on future long-term sickness absence. Prospective results of the Danish PUMA Study among human service workers. *Journal of Occupational and Environmental Medicine*, *52*(10), 964–970. doi:10.1097/JOM.0b013e3181f12f95 PMID:20881631

Bosma, N., van Praag, M., Thurik, R., & de Wit, G. (2004). The value of human and social capital investment for the business performance of start-ups. *Small Business Economics*, *23*(3), 227–236. doi:10.1023/B:SBEJ.0000032032.21192.72

Bosqued, M. (2008). *Quemados: El síndrome del Burnout: ¿Qué es y cómo superarlo?* España: Paidós Ibérica.

Branco, M. C., & Rodrigues, L. L. (2007). Positioning stakeholder theory within the debate on corporate social responsibility. *Electronic Journal of Business Ethics and Organization Studies*, *12*(1), 5–15.

Brannick, M. T., & Levine, E. L. (2002). *Job analysis*. Thousand Oaks, CA: Sage.

Breaugh, J. A. (2009). Employee selection at the beginning of the 21st century[Editorial]. *Human Resource Management Review*, *19*(3), 167–168. doi:10.1016/j.hrmr.2009.03.009

Breaugh, J. A. (2009). The use of biodata for employee selection: Past research and future directions. *Human Resource Management Review*, *19*(3), 219–231. doi:10.1016/j.hrmr.2009.02.003

Breaugh, J. A., Macan, T. H., & Grambow, D. M. (2008). Employee Recruitment. *Current Knowledge and Directions for Future Research, International Review of Industrial and Organizational Psychology*, *23*, 45–82.

Breitbarth, T., & Harris, P. (2008). The role of corporate social responsibility in the football business: Towards the development of a conceptual model. *European Sport Management Quarterly*, *8*(2), 179–206. doi:10.1080/16184740802024484

Breton, T. R. (2015). Human capital and growth in Japan: Converging to the steady state in a 1% world. *Journal of the Japanese and International Economies*, *36*, 73–89. doi:10.1016/j.jjie.2015.03.001

Brian, U. (1999). Embeddedness in the Making of Financial Capital: How Social Relations and Networks Benefit Firms Seeking Financing. *American Sociological Review*, *64*. Retrieved from http://www.kellogg.northwestern.edu/faculty/uzzi/ftp/lending.pdf

Brody, W., & Powell, N. J. (1947). A new approach to oral testing. *Educational and Psychological Measurement*, *7*(2), 289–298. doi:10.1177/001316444700700206 PMID:20256563

Brown, S., & Taylor, K. (2005). Wage growth, human capital and financial investment. *The Manchester School*, *73*(6), 686–708. doi:10.1111/j.1467-9957.2005.00472.x

Burt, R. S. (1992). *Structural Holes: The Social Structure of Competition*. Cambridge, MA: Harvard University Press.

Cahan, S. F., Chen, C., Chen, L., & Nguyen, N. H. (2015). Corporate social responsibility and media coverage. *Journal of Banking & Finance*, *59*, 409–422. doi:10.1016/j.jbankfin.2015.07.004

Camacho-Alamilla, R., Maldonado-Macias, A., García-Alcaraz, J. L., & Hernández-Arellano, J. L. (2014). Determination of Burnout Syndrome among Middle and Senior Managment Personnel in Autootive Industry in Juarez City México. In C. Espejo-Guasco, E. De la Vega Bustillos, & E. Chacón Martínez (Eds.), Ergonomía Ocupacional. Investigaciones y aplicaciones. (Vol. 7, pp. 306-317). Sociedad de Ergonomistas de México, A.C.

Camara, W. J., & Schneider, D. L. (1994). Integrity tests: Facts and unresolved issues. *The American Psychologist*, *49*(2), 112–119. doi:10.1037/0003-066X.49.2.112

Campbell, B. (2012). Corporate social responsibility and development in Africa: Redefining the roles and responsibilities of public and private actors in the mining sector. *Resources Policy*, *37*(2), 138–143. doi:10.1016/j.resourpol.2011.05.002

Campiglio, L. (1995). Discussion about "Conspiracy among the many: the mafia in Legitimate industries". In G. Fiorentini & S. Peltzman (Eds.), *The economics of Organised Crime*. New York: Cambridge University Press.

Campion, M. A. (1983). Personnel selection for physically demanding jobs: Review and recommendations. *Personnel Psychology*, *36*(3), 527–550. doi:10.1111/j.1744-6570.1983.tb02234.x

Campion, M. A., Palmer, D. K., & Campion, J. E. (1997). A review of structure in the selection interview. *Personnel Psychology*, *50*(3), 655–702. doi:10.1111/j.1744-6570.1997.tb00709.x

Campion, M. A., Pursell, E. D., & Brown, B. K. (1988). Structured interviewing: Raising the psychometric properties of the employmentinterview. *Personnel Psychology*, *48*, 289–308.

Cappato, A., & Pennazio, V. (2006). *Corporate social responsibility in sport: Torino 2006 Olympic Winter Games*. Turin, Italy: University of Turin.

Carayon, P., Hundt, A., Karsh, B. T., Gurses, A. P., Alvarado, C. J., Smith, M., & Flatley Brennan, P. (2006). Work system design for patient safety: the SEIPS model. *Quality & Safety in Health Care, 15*(suppl 1), i50–8. http://doi.org/<ALIGNMENT.qj></ALIGNMENT>10.1136/qshc.2005.015842

Carayon, P., & Smith, M. J. (2000). Work organization and ergonomics. *Applied Ergonomics*, *31*(6), 649–662. doi:10.1016/S0003-6870(00)00040-5 PMID:11132049

Carayon, P., Wetterneck, T. B., Rivera-Rodriguez, A. J., Hundt, A., Hoonakker, P., Holden, R., & Gurses, A. P. (2014). Human factors systems approach to healthcare quality and patient safety. *Applied Ergonomics*, *45*(1), 14–25. doi:10.1016/j.apergo.2013.04.023 PMID:23845724

Carmeli, A., & Schaubroeck, J. (2005). How leveraging human resource capital with its competitive distinctiveness enhances the performance of commercial and public organizations. *Human Resource Management*, *44*(4), 391–412. doi:10.1002/hrm.20081

Caroly, S., Coutarel, F., Landry, A., & Mary-Cheray, I. (2010). Sustainable MSD prevention: Management for continuous improvement between prevention and production. Ergonomic intervention in two assembly line companies. *Applied Ergonomics*, *41*(4), 591–599. doi:10.1016/j.apergo.2009.12.016 PMID:20097327

Carpenter, M. A., Geletkanycz, M. A., & Sanders, W. G. (2004). Upper echelons research revisited: Antecedents, elements, and consequences of top management team composition. *Journal of Management*, *30*(6), 749–778. doi:10.1016/j.jm.2004.06.001

Carroll, A. B. (1991). The pyramid of corporate social responsibility: Towards the moral management of organizational stakeholders. *Business Horizons*, *34*(4), 39–48. doi:10.1016/0007-6813(91)90005-G

Carroll, R. J., Primo, D. M., & Richter, B. K. (2016). Using item response theory to improve measurement in strategic management research: An application to corporate social responsibility. *Strategic Management Journal*, *37*(1), 66–85. doi:10.1002/smj.2463

Casanueva, E., Pérez-Lizaur, A., Ripoll, C., Plazas, M., & Benito, A. (2005). Un estudio sobre las condiciones de salud de los ejecutivos en la Ciudad de México. In M. Pérez Lizaur (Ed.), *Ejecutivos de alto nivel: ¿ Una èlite global?* Universidad Iberoamericana.

Casta, P. T., & McCrae, R. R. (1992). NEO PI-R professional manual. Odessa, FL: Psychological Assessment Resources.

Castelló-Climent, A., & Doménech, R. (2008). Human capital inequality, life expectancy and economic growth. *The Economic Journal*, *118*(528), 653–677. doi:10.1111/j.1468-0297.2008.02136.x

Castells, M. (2011). A Network Theory of Power. *International Journal of Communication*, 5.

Castka, P., & Prajogo, D. (2013). The effect of pressure from secondary stakeholders on the internalization of ISO 14001. *Journal of Cleaner Production*, *47*, 245–252. doi:10.1016/j.jclepro.2012.12.034

Cattell, R. B., Eber, H. W., & Tatsuoka, M. M. (1970). *The handbook for the Sixteen Personality Factor Questionnaire*. Champaign, IL: Institute for Personality and Ability Testing.

Cavuoto, L. A., & Nussbaum, M. A. (2014). The influences of obesity and age on functional performance during intermittent upper extremity tasks. *Journal of Occupational and Environmental Hygiene*, *11*(9), 583–590. doi:10.1080/15459624.2014.887848 PMID:24484265

Cenfetelli, R. T., & Bassellier, G. (2009). Interpretation of Formative Measurement in Information Systems Research. *Management Information Systems Quarterly*, *33*(4), 689–707.

Cerrato, D., & Piva, M. (2012). The internationalization of small and medium-sized enterprises: The effect of family management, human capital and foreign ownership. *Journal of Management and Governance*, *16*(4), 617–644. doi:10.1007/s10997-010-9166-x

Chambers, D., & Krause, A. (2010). Is the relationship between inequality and growth affected by physical and human capital accumulation? *The Journal of Economic Inequality*, *8*(2), 153–172. doi:10.1007/s10888-009-9111-x

Chan, D., & Schmitt, N. (1997). Video-based versus chapter and pencil method of assessment in situational judgment tests: Subgroup differences in test performance and face validity perceptions. *The Journal of Applied Psychology*, *82*(1), 143–159. doi:10.1037/0021-9010.82.1.143 PMID:9119795

Chandrama, G., & Manisha, B. (2014). The Non-Farm Sector - Rural Non-Farm Employment in Assam: A Gender Based Analysis. *Space and Culture*, *2*(1). Retrieved from http://spaceand-culture.in/index.php/spaceandculture/article/view/38

Chandrasekhar, S. (2011). Macro-economic Overview. In D.M. Nachane (Ed.), *India Development Report* (pp. 26-38). New Delhi: Oxford University Press. Retrieved October 11, 2015, from http://www.igidr.ac.in/pdf/publication/IDR-2011.pdf

Chapple, W., & Moon, J. (2005). Corporate social responsibility (CSR) in Asia: A seven-country study of CSR website reporting. *Business & Society*, *44*(4), 415–441. doi:10.1177/0007650305281658

Charles, L. E., Burchfiel, C. M., Gu, J. K., Andrew, M. E., Fekedulegn, D., & Violanti, J. M. (2009). Abstract: Sleep Duration and Biomarkers of Metabolic Function Among Police Officers. *Annals of Epidemiology*, *19*(9), 666. doi:10.1016/j.annepidem.2009.07.036

Chava, S. (2014). Environmental externalities and cost of capital. *Management Science*, *60*(4), 2223–2247. doi:10.1287/mnsc.2013.1863

Chen, B. L., Chen, H. J., & Wang, P. (2011). Labor-market frictions, human capital accumulation, and long-run growth: Positive analysis and policy evaluation. *International Economic Review*, *52*(1), 131–160. doi:10.1111/j.1468-2354.2010.00622.x

Chen, C.-K., Shie, A.-J., & Yu, C.-H. (2012). A customer-oriented organisational diagnostic model based on data mining of customer-complaint databases. *Expert Systems with Applications*, *39*(1), 786–792. doi:10.1016/j.eswa.2011.07.074

Cheng, B., Ioannou, I., & Serafeim, G. (2014). Corporate social responsibility and access to finance. *Strategic Management Journal*, *35*(1), 1–23. doi:10.1002/smj.2131

Chen, H. J. (2012). Social status, human capital formation and the long-run effects of money. *Journal of Economics*, *105*(3), 225–246. doi:10.1007/s00712-011-0227-7

Choi, B., Schnall, P. L., Yang, H., Dobson, M., Landsbergis, P., Israel, L., & Baker, D. et al. (2010). Sedentary work, low physical job demand, and obesity in US workers. *American Journal of Industrial Medicine*, *53*(11), 1088–1101. doi:10.1002/ajim.20886 PMID:20737422

Choi, K. H., & Shin, S. (2015). Population aging, economic growth, and the social transmission of human capital: An analysis with an overlapping generations model. *Economic Modelling*, *50*, 138–147. doi:10.1016/j.econmod.2015.05.015

Choudhry, R. M., Fang, D., & Mohamed, S. (2007). The nature of safety culture: A survey of the state-of-the-art. *Safety Science*, *45*(10), 993–1012. doi:10.1016/j.ssci.2006.09.003

Chui, M. A., Mott, D. A., & Maxwell, L. (2012). A qualitative assessment of a community pharmacy cognitive pharmaceutical services program, using a work system approach. *Research in Social & Administrative Pharmacy : RSAP*, *8*(3), 206–216. doi:10.1016/j.sapharm.2011.06.001 PMID:21824822

Clary, E. G., Snyder, M., Ridge, R. G., Copeland, J., Stukas, A. A., Haugen, J., & Miene, P. (1998). Understanding and assessing the motivation of volunteers: A functional approach. *Journal of Personality and Social Psychology*, *74*(6), 1516–1530. doi:10.1037/0022-3514.74.6.1516 PMID:9654757

Claudia, G. (2014). *Human Capital.* Harvard University and NBER – Handbook of Cliometrics. Retrieved from http://scholar.harvard.edu/files/goldin/files/human_capital_handbook_of_cliometrics_0.pdf

Cleeve, E. A., Debrah, Y., & Yiheyis, Z. (2015). Human capital and FDI inflow: An assessment of the African case. *World Development*, *74*, 1–14. doi:10.1016/j.worlddev.2015.04.003

Coakes, S. J., & Steed, L. (2009). SPSS: Analysis Without Anguish Using Spss Version 14.0 for Windows. New York: John Wiley & Sons, Inc. Retrieved from http://dl.acm.org/citation.cfm?id=1804538

Coff, R. W. (1997). Human assets and management dilemmas: Coping with hazards on the road to resource-based theory. *Academy of Management Review*, *22*(2), 374–402.

Colledani, M., Tolio, T., Fischer, A., Iung, B., Lanza, G., Schmitt, R., & Váncza, J. (2014). Design and management of manufacturing systems for production quality. *CIRP Annals - Manufacturing Technology, 63*(2), 773–796. http://doi.org/<ALIGNMENT.qj></ALIGNMENT>10.1016/j.cirp.2014.05.002

Colombini, D., Occhipinti, E., Álvarez-Casado, E., Hernández-Soto, A., & Tello Sandoval, S. (2012). *El Método OCRA Checklist Revisado. Gestión y evaluación del riesgo por movimientos repetitivos de las extremidades superiores*. Editorial Human Factors Barcelona.

Conway, J. M., Jako, R. A., & Goodman, D. F. (1995). A meta-analysis of interrater and internal consistency reliability of selection interviews. *The Journal of Applied Psychology*, *80*(5), 565–579. doi:10.1037/0021-9010.80.5.565

Costa, P.T. &McCrae, R.R. (1985). Comparison of EPI and psychoticism scales with measures of the five-factor model of personality. *Personality and Individual Differences*, 6(5), 587- 597.

Costa, P. T. Jr, & McCrae, R. R. (1992). Four ways five factors are basic. *Personality and Individual Differences, 13*(6), 653–665. doi:10.1016/0191-8869(92)90236-I

Cramer, J. (2005). Experiences with structuring corporate social responsibility in Dutch industry. *Journal of Cleaner Production, 13*(6), 583–592. doi:10.1016/j.jclepro.2003.12.008

Cronbach, L. J. (1951). Coefficient alpha and the internal structure of tests. *Psychometrika, 16*(3), 297–334. doi:10.1007/BF02310555

Cuadrado-Ballesteros, B., Rodriguez-Ariza, L., & Garcia-Sanchez, I. M. (2015). The role of independent directors at family firms in relation to corporate social responsibility disclosures. *International Business Review, 24*(5), 890–901. doi:10.1016/j.ibusrev.2015.04.002

Dahlman & Utz. (2005). *India and the Knowledge Economy – Leveraging Strengths and Opportunities.* World Bank Institute. Retrieved from http://info.worldbank.org/etools/docs/library/145261/India_KE_Overview.pdf

Dahlsrud, A. (2008). How corporate social responsibility is defined: An analysis of 37 definitions. *Corporate Social Responsibility and Environmental Management, 15*(1), 1–13. doi:10.1002/csr.132

Dallman, M. F. (2010). Stress-induced obesity and the emotional nervous system. *Trends in Endocrinology and Metabolism, 21*(3), 159–165. doi:10.1016/j.tem.2009.10.004 PMID:19926299

Dalziel, T., Gentry, R. J., & Bowerman, M. (2011). An integrated agency-resource dependence view of the influence of director's human and relational capital on firms' R&D spending. *Journal of Management Studies, 48*(6), 1217–1242. doi:10.1111/j.1467-6486.2010.01003.x

Dam, L., & Scholtens, B. (2012). Does ownership type matter for corporate social responsibility? *Corporate Governance: An International Review, 20*(3), 233–252. doi:10.1111/j.1467-8683.2011.00907.x

Dashwood, H. S. (2007). Towards sustainable mining: The corporate role in the construction of global standards. *Multinational Business Review, 15*(1), 47–66. doi:10.1108/1525383X200700003

Davidson, E. J., & Tay, A. S. M. (2003). Studying teamwork in global IT support. In *36th Annual Hawaii International Conference on System Sciences, 2003. Proceedings of the* (p. 10 pp.). IEEE. http://doi.org/ doi:<ALIGNMENT.qj></ALIGNMENT>10.1109/HICSS.2003.1173663

Davidsson & Honig. (2003). The Role of Social and Human Capital Among Nascent Entrepreneurs. *Journal of Business Venturing.* Retrieved from http://eprints.qut.edu.au/5832/1/5832.pdf

Dávila-Torres, J., González-Izquierdo, J. J., & Barrera-Cruz, A. (2015). Panorama de la obesidad en México. (Spanish). *Obesity in Mexico, 53*(2), 240. Retrieved from http://search.ebscohost.com/login.aspx?direct=true&db=edb&AN=101483297&lang=es&site=eds-live

de Bakker, F. G. A. (2012). Exploring networks of activism on corporate social responsibility: Suggestions for a research agenda. *Creativity and Innovation Management, 21*(2), 212–223. doi:10.1111/j.1467-8691.2012.00641.x de Beer, E., & Rensburg, R. (2011). Towards a theoretical framework for the governing of stakeholder relationships: A perspective from South Africa. *Journal of Public Affairs, 11*(4), 208–225. doi:10.1002/pa.414

de Brucker, K., Macharis, C., & Verbeke, A. (2013). Multi-criteria analysis and the resolution of sustainable development dilemmas: A stakeholder management approach. *European Journal of Operational Research, 224*(1), 122–131. doi:10.1016/j.ejor.2012.02.021

de la Torre-Caldera, V., Hernandez-Arellano, J. L., García-Alcaraz, J. L., & Ibarra-Mejia, G. (2014). Workload Assessment in Industrial Settings: A Proposal Applying the Analytic Hierarchy Process. Proceedings of the XXVI Annual occupational Ergonomics and Safety Conference, El Paso, TX, USA (pp. 32–37).

de Villiers, C. (1999). Corporate social reporting in South Africa: Signs of a pygmy awakening? *Social and Environmental Accounting, 19*(2), 5–7. doi:10.1080/0969160X.1999.9651613

Deegan, C., & Rankin, M. (1996). Do Australian companies report environmental news objectively? An analysis of environmental disclosures by firms prosecuted successfully by the environmental protection authority. *Accounting, Auditing & Accountability Journal, 9*(2), 50–67. doi:10.1108/09513579610116358

Dess, G. G., & Robinson, R. B. (1984). Measuring organizational performance in the absence of objective measures: The case of the privately-held firm and conglomerate business unit. *Strategic Management Journal, 5*(3), 265–273. doi:10.1002/smj.4250050306

Detert, J. R., & Burris, E. R. (2007). Leadership behavior and employee voice: Is the door really open? *Academy of Management Journal, 50*(4), 869–884. doi:10.5465/AMJ.2007.26279183

Detomasi, D. A. (2008). The political roots of corporate social responsibility. *Journal of Business Ethics, 82*(4), 807–819. doi:10.1007/s10551-007-9594-y

Dev, S. (2013). What makes employees stay?: Exploring the dimensions in context of urban-centric business process outsourcing industry in India, Strategic Outsourcing. *International Journal (Toronto, Ont.), 6*(3), 258–276.

Dhaliwal, D. S., Radhakrishnan, S., Tsang, A., & Yang, Y. G. (2012). Nonfinancial disclosure and analyst forecast accuracy: International evidence on corporate social responsibility disclosure. *Accounting Review, 87*(3), 723–759. doi:10.2308/accr-10218

Dharwada, P., Sadasivan, S., Nickles, G., & Gramopadhye, A. (2006). Task Analytic Methodology for the Design of an Aircraft Inspection Training Program. In W. Karwowski (Ed.), International Encyclopedia of Ergonomics and Human factors (2nd ed., pp. 2366–2374). Taylor & Francis.

Di Fatta, D., Musotto, R., D'Aleo, V., Vesperi, W., Morabito, G., & Bue, S. L. (2016b). Weak Ties and Value of a Network in the New Internet Economy. Social Media Data Extraction and Content Analysis, 66.

Dobers, P. (2009). Corporate social responsibility: Management and methods. *Corporate Social Responsibility and Environmental Management, 16*(4), 185–191. doi:10.1002/csr.201

Dreze & Sen. (2002). *India Development and Participation*. Oxford University Press.

Duarte, F. (2010). Working with corporate social responsibility in Brazilian companies: The role of managers values in the maintenance of CSR cultures. *Journal of Business Ethics, 96*(3), 355–368. doi:10.1007/s10551-010-0470-9

Dul, J., & Neumann, W. P. (2009). Ergonomics contributions to company strategies. *Applied Ergonomics, 40*(4), 745–752. doi:10.1016/j.apergo.2008.07.001 PMID:18775532

Du, S., & Vieira, E. T. Jr. (2012). Striving for legitimacy through corporate social responsibility: Insights from oil companies. *Journal of Business Ethics, 110*(4), 413–427. doi:10.1007/s10551-012-1490-4

Dutta, N., & Osei-Yeboah, K. (2013). A new dimension to the relationship between foreign direct investment and human capital: The role of political and civil rights. *Journal of International Development, 25*(2), 160–179. doi:10.1002/jid.1739

Eberly, R., & Feldman, H. (2010). Obesity and shift work in the general population. *The Internet Journal of Allied Health and Nursing at Nova Southeastern University, 8.*

Eccles, R. G., & Crane, D. B. (1987). Managing through networks in investment banking. *California Management Review, 30*(1), 176–195. doi:10.2307/41165273

Eder, R. W., & Ferris, G. R. (Eds.). (1989). *The employment interview: Theory, research, and practice*. Newbury Park, CA: Sage Publishing.

Ejere. (2011). Human Capital Formation as Catalyst for National Development: Nigeria in Perspective. *International Business and Management, 2*(2). Retrieved from http://www.cscanada.net/index.php/ibm/article/view/j.ibm.1923842820110202.011

El Ghoul, S., Guedhami, O., Kwok, C., & Mishra, D. (2011). Does corporate social responsibility affect the cost of capital? *Journal of Banking & Finance, 35*(9), 2388–2406. doi:10.1016/j.jbankfin.2011.02.007

Elkington, J. (1997). *Cannibals with forks: The triple bottom line of 21st century business*. Gabriola Island, Canada: New Society Publishers.

Embrey, D. E. (1986). SHERPA: A systematic human error reduction and prediction approach. *Proceedings of the international topical meeting on advances in human factors in nuclear power systems* (pp. 184–193).

Epel, E., Lapidus, R., McEwen, B., & Brownell, K. (2001). Stress may add bite to appetite in women: A laboratory study of stress-induced cortisol and eating behavior. *Psychoneuroendocrinology, 26*(1), 37–49. doi:10.1016/S0306-4530(00)00035-4 PMID:11070333

Esteves, A. M., & Vanclay, F. (2009). Social development needs analysis as a tool for SIA to guide corporate-community investment: Applications in the minerals industry. *Environmental Impact Assessment Review*, *29*(2), 137–145. doi:10.1016/j.eiar.2008.08.004

Etgar, M. (2007). A descriptive model of the consumer co-production process. *Journal of the Academy of Marketing Science*, *36*(1), 97–108. doi:10.1007/s11747-007-0061-1

Evald, M. R., Klyver, K., & Christensen, P. R. (2011). The effect of human capital, social capital, and perceptual values on nascent entrepreneur's export intentions. *Journal of International Entrepreneurship*, *9*(1), 1–19. doi:10.1007/s10843-010-0069-3

Fagan, J., & Ployhart, R. E. (2015). The information processing foundations of human capital resources: Leveraging insights from information processing approaches to intelligence. *Human Resource Management Review*, *25*(1), 4–11. doi:10.1016/j.hrmr.2014.09.003

Fanger, P. O. (1973). *Thermal Comfort*. New York, NY: McGraw Hill.

Fan, L. (2009). Measuring interprovincial flows of human capital in China: 1995–2000. *Population Research and Policy Review*, *28*(3), 367–387. doi:10.1007/s11113-008-9103-8

Fatemi, A., Fooladi, I., & Tehranian, H. (2015). Valuation effects of corporate social responsibility. *Journal of Banking & Finance*, *59*, 182–192. doi:10.1016/j.jbankfin.2015.04.028

Fatta, D. D., Caputo, F., Evangelista, F., & Dominici, G. (2016a). Small world theory and the World Wide Web: Linking small world properties and website centrality. *International Journal of Markets and Business Systems*, *2*(2), 126–140.

Faust, K., and Wasserman, S. (1992). Blockmodels: Interpretation and evaluation. *Social networks*, *14*(1), 5-61. 15

Fernández, J. E., Marley, R. J., Noriega, S., & Ibarra, G. (2010). *Ergonomía ocupacional: diseño y administración del trabajo. Ciudad Juárez, Chih*. Universidad Autónoma de Ciudad Juárez.

Fieseler, C. (2011). On the corporate social responsibility perceptions of equity analysts. *Business Ethics (Oxford, England)*, *20*(2), 131–147. doi:10.1111/j.1467-8608.2011.01616.x

Finkelstein, E. A., daCosta DiBonaventura, M., Burgess, S. M., & Hale, B. C. (2010). The costs of obesity in the workplace. *Journal of Occupational and Environmental Medicine*, *52*(10), 971–976. doi:10.1097/JOM.0b013e3181f274d2 PMID:20881629

Fiorentini, G. (1999). Cartels Run by Criminal Organizations and Market Contestability. Proceedings of the IEA Conference Series (*Vol. 124)*. doi:10.1007/978-1-349-14540-9_3

Fiorentini, G., & Peltzman, S. (Eds.), *The economics of Organised Crime*. New York: Cambridge University Press. doi:10.1017/CBO9780511751882

Fitjar, R., Gielsvik, M., & Rodriguez-Pose, A. (2013). The combined impact of managerial and relational capabilities on innovation in firms. *Entrepreneurship & Regional Development: An International Journal*, *25*(5/6), 500–520. doi:10.1080/08985626.2013.798353

Foss, B., & Dyrstad, S. M. (2011). Stress in obesity: Cause or consequence? *Medical Hypotheses*, *77*(1), 7–10. doi:10.1016/j.mehy.2011.03.011 PMID:21444159

Fourati, H., & Affes, H. (2011). Financial constraints, human and social capital, and risk-taking attitude in the foundation of new firms. *Strategic Change*, *20*(5/6), 219–232. doi:10.1002/jsc.897

Franco, S. (2012). *USA: Organization for the Economic Cooperation and Development*. Retrieved from http://www.oecd.org/health/49716427.pdf

Freeman, E. E. (1984). *Strategic management: A stakeholder approach*. Boston, MA: Pitman Publishing.

Freeman, R. E., Wicks, A. C., & Parmar, B. (2004). Stakeholder theory and the corporate objective revisited. *Organization Science*, *15*(3), 364–369. doi:10.1287/orsc.1040.0066

Freudenberguer, H. J. (1974). Staff Burnout. *The Journal of Social Issues*, *30*(1), 159–165. doi:10.1111/j.1540-4560.1974.tb00706.x

Friebel, G., Leinyuy, J., & Seabright, P. (2015). The Schubert effect: When flourishing businesses crowd out human capital. *World Development*, *68*, 124–135. doi:10.1016/j.worlddev.2014.11.022

Frynas, J. G. (2005). The false developmental promise of corporate social responsibility: Evidence from multinational oil companies. *International Affairs*, *81*(3), 581–598. doi:10.1111/j.1468-2346.2005.00470.x

Futagami, K., & Yanagihara, M. (2008). Private and public education: Human capital accumulation under parental teaching. *The Japanese Economic Review*, *59*(3), 275–291. doi:10.1111/j.1468-5876.2008.00417.x

Gael, S. (Ed.). (1988). *The job analysis handbook for business, industry, and government* (Vol. 1 & 2). New York: Wiley.

Galbreath, J. (2010). How does corporate social responsibility benefit firms? Evidence from Australia. *European Business Review*, *22*(4), 411–431. doi:10.1108/09555341011056186

Gallardo-Vazquez, D., & Sanchez-Hernandez, M. I. (2014). Measuring corporate social responsibility for competitive success at a regional level. *Journal of Cleaner Production*, *72*, 14–22. doi:10.1016/j.jclepro.2014.02.051

Gallié, E. P., & Legros, D. (2012). Firm's human capital, R&D and innovation: A study on French firms. *Empirical Economics*, *43*(2), 581–596. doi:10.1007/s00181-011-0506-8

Gambetta, D. (1993). *The Sicilian Mafia: The Business of Private Protection*. Cambridge, MA: Harvard University Press.

Gambetta, D., & Reuter, P. (1995). Conspiracy among the many: the mafia in Legitimate industries. In G. Fiorentini & S. Peltzman (Eds.), *The economics of Organised Crime*. New York: Cambridge University Press. doi:10.1007/978-1-349-62853-7_5

Gangl, M. (2004). Welfare states and the scar effects of unemployment: A comparative analysis of the United States and West Germany. *American Journal of Sociology*, *109*(6), 1319–1364. doi:10.1086/381902

Ganotakis, P. (2012). Founder's human capital and the performance of UK new technology based firms. *Small Business Economics*, *39*(2), 495–515. doi:10.1007/s11187-010-9309-0

Gao, L., & Zhang, J. H. (2015). Firms earnings smoothing, corporate social responsibility, and valuation. *Journal of Corporate Finance*, *32*, 108–127. doi:10.1016/j.jcorpfin.2015.03.004

García-Acosta, G., & Lange-Morales, K. (2008). Macroergonomic study of food sector company distribution centres. *Applied Ergonomics*, *39*(4), 439–449. doi:10.1016/j.apergo.2008.02.004 PMID:18377868

García, J. L., Maldonado, A. A., Alvarado, A., & Rivera, D. G. (2014). Human critical success factors for kaizen and its impacts in industrial performance. *International Journal of Advanced Manufacturing Technology*, *70*(9-12), 2187–2198. doi:10.1007/s00170-013-5445-4

García-Rodríguez, F. J., García-Rodríguez, J. L., Castilla-Gutiérrez, C., & Major, S. A. (2013). Corporate social responsibility of oil companies in developing countries: From altruism to business strategy. *Corporate Social Responsibility and Environmental Management*, *20*(6), 371–384. doi:10.1002/csr.1320

Gatewood, R. D., Feild, H. S., & Barrick, M. (2008). *Human resource selection*. Mason, Ohio: Thompson South-Western.

Gaugler, B. B., Rosenthal, D. B., Thornton, G. C. III, & Bentson, C. (1987). Meta-analyses of assessment center validity. *The Journal of Applied Psychology*, *72*(3), 493–511. doi:10.1037/0021-9010.72.3.493

Gautam, S., & Sharma, V.K. (2014). A study of job stress among b.ed. teachers in relation to organizational climate. *Indian Streams Research Journal*, *3*(12).

Georgopoulos, P. G. (2011). *Red ocean vs blue ocean strategy*. MBA-TQM, University of Piraeus.

Gerald, M., Deary, I. J., & Whiteman, M. C. (1998). *Personality traits* (2nd ed.). Cambridge: Cambridge University Press.

Gibson, H. J. (1998). Sport tourism: A critical analysis of research. *Sport Management Review*, *1*(1), 45–76. doi:10.1016/S1441-3523(98)70099-3

Gifford, B., Kestler, A., & Anand, S. (2010). Building local legitimacy into corporate social responsibility: Gold mining firms in developing nations. *Journal of World Business*, *45*(3), 304–311. doi:10.1016/j.jwb.2009.09.007

Gil-Lafuente, A. M., & de Paula, L. B. (2013). Algorithm applied in the identification of stakeholders. *Kybernetes*, *42*(5), 674–685. doi:10.1108/K-04-2013-0073

Gille, V. (2015). Distribution of human capital and income: An empirical study on Indian States. *Journal of Macroeconomics*, *43*, 239–256. doi:10.1016/j.jmacro.2014.11.003

Gimmon, E., & Levie, J. (2010). Founder's human capital, external investment, and the survival of new high-technology ventures. *Research Policy*, *39*(9), 1214–1226. doi:10.1016/j.respol.2010.05.017

Giordano, A., & Pagano, A. (2013). Brazil in the transition towards knowledge economy: Between qualification and internationalization of human capital. *Transition Studies Review*, *20*(1), 19–31. doi:10.1007/s11300-013-0267-5

Giunta, A., Nifo, A., & Scalera, D. (2012). Subcontracting in Italian Industry: Labour Division, Firm Growth and the North–South Divide. *Regional Studies*, *46*(8), 1067–1083. doi:10.1080/00343404.2011.552492

Giziene, V., & Simanaviciene, Z. (2015). The impact of human capital on labour market: Lithuanian case. *Procedia: Social and Behavioral Sciences*, *191*, 2437–2442. doi:10.1016/j.sbspro.2015.04.331

Gjølberg, M. (2010). Varieties of corporate social responsibility (CSR): CSR meets the Nordic Model. *Regulation & Governance*, *4*(2), 203–229. doi:10.1111/j.1748-5991.2010.01080.x

Glover, W. J., Farris, J. A., Van Aken, E. M., & Doolen, T. L. (2011). Critical success factors for the sustainability of Kaizen event human resource outcomes: An empirical study. *International Journal of Production Economics*, *132*(2), 197–213. doi:10.1016/j.ijpe.2011.04.005

Goldberg, L. R., Grenier, R. M., Guion, L. B., Sechrest, L. B., & Wing, H. (1991). *Questions used in the prediction of trustworthiness in pre-employment selection decisions: An APA Task Force Report*. Washington, D.C.: American Psychological Association.

Gómez-Alcaina, B., Montero-Marín, J., Demarzo, M. M. P., Pereira, J. P., & García-Campayo, J. (2013). Utilidad de los marcadores biológicos en la detección precoz y prevención del Síndrome de Burnout. *Revista de Psicopatología y Psicología Clínica*, *18*(3), 245–253. doi:10.5944/rppc.vol.18.num.3.2013.12924

Gómez-Bull, K. G., Hernández-Arellano, J. L., & Ibarra-Mejía, G. (2015). A Proposed Methodology for Task Analysis in Ergonomic Evaluations. *Procedia Manufacturing*, *3*, 4756–4760. doi:10.1016/j.promfg.2015.07.573

Gonzalez-Benito, J., Lannelongue, G., & Queiruga, D. (2011). Stakeholders and environmental management systems: A synergistic influence on environmental imbalance. *Journal of Cleaner Production*, *19*(14), 1622–1630. doi:10.1016/j.jclepro.2011.05.013

Gonzalez, M. D., & Martinez, C. (2004). Fostering corporate social responsibility through public initiative: From the EU to the Spanish case. *Journal of Business Ethics*, *55*(3), 275–293. doi:10.1007/s10551-004-0994-y

Gonzalez-Rodriguez, M. R., Diaz-Fernandez, M. C., & Simonetti, B. (2015). The social, economic and environmental dimensions of corporate social responsibility: The role played by consumers and potential entrepreneurs. *International Business Review*, *24*(5), 836–848. doi:10.1016/j.ibusrev.2015.03.002

Gopal, S. (Ed.). (1983). *Jawaharlal's Nehru's Speech at the Constituent Assembly, New Delhi, 14th August 1947 reprinted in, Jawaharlal Nehru: An Anthology*. New Delhi: Oxford University Press.

Gordon, J., & Sohal, A. S. (2001). Assessing manufacturing plant competitiveness - An empirical field study. *International Journal of Operations & Production Management*, *21*(1/2), 233–253. doi:10.1108/01443570110358567

Gorostiaga, A., Hromcová, J., & López-García, M. (2013). Optimal taxation in the Uzawa–Lucas model with externality in human capital. *Journal of Economics*, *108*(2), 111–129. doi:10.1007/s00712-012-0285-5

Gossling, T., & Rutten, R. (2007). Innovation in regions. *European Planning Studies*, *15*(2), 253–270. doi:10.1080/09654310601078788

Gottredson, L. S. (Ed.). (1982). The g factor in employment. *Journal of Vocational Behavior*, *29*(3).

Government of India Planning Commission. (2014). *Preface to Report of the Expert Group to Review the Methodology for Measurement of Poverty*. Retrieved October 11, 2015, from http://planningcommission.nic.in/reports/genrep/pov_rep0707.pdf

Govindan, K., Kannan, D., & Shankar, K. M. (2014). Evaluating the drivers of corporate social responsibility in the mining industry with multi-criteria approach: A multi-stakeholder perspective. *Journal of Cleaner Production*, *84*(1), 214–232. doi:10.1016/j.jclepro.2013.12.065

Granovetter, M. S. (1973). The strength of weak ties. *American Journal of Sociology*, *78*(6), 1360–1380. doi:10.1086/225469

Greiner, A. (2012). Human capital formation, learning by doing and the government in the process of economic growth. *Scottish Journal of Political Economy*, *59*(1), 71–89. doi:10.1111/j.1467-9485.2011.0569.x

Grier, R. (2005). The interaction of human and physical capital accumulation: Evidence from Sub-Saharan Africa. *Kyklos*, *58*(2), 195–211. doi:10.1111/j.0023-5962.2005.285_1.x

Grootjen, M., Bierman, E.P.B., & Neerincx, M.A. (2006). Optimizing cognitive task load in naval ship control centers: Design of an adaptive interface. *Proceedings of the16th World Congress on Ergonomics.*

Grootjen, M., Neerincx, M.A., Stolk, K.D., van Weert, J.C.M., & Bierman, E.P.B. (2007). Design and user evaluation of an interface prototype that adapts to the operator's cognitive task load. In HFES/ACI Baltimore. Retrieved from http://www.researchgate.net/publication/228403104_Design_and_user_evaluation_of_an_interface_prototype_that_adapts_to_the_operator's_cognitive_task_load/file/9fcfd50e7648b88cf9.pdf

Guelaud, F., Beauchense, M. N., Gautrat, J., & Roustrang, G. (1977). *Pour une analyse des conditions du travail ouvrier dans l'entreprise* (Vol. 11). Paris: Espirit.

Guerrero, E., & Vicente, F. (2001). *Síndrome de "Burnout" o desgaste profesional y afrontamiento del estrés en el profesorado.* Cáceres: Universidad de Extremadura.

Gu, J. A. K., Charles, L. E., Ma, C. C., Hartley, T. A., Andrew, M. E., Violanti, J. M., & Burchfiel, C. M. (2014). Obesity and Work-Site Injury: The National Health Interview Survey (NHIS), 20042012. *Annals of Epidemiology, 24*(9), 695. doi:10.1016/j.annepidem.2014.06.065

Gulati, R., Nohria, N., & Zaheer, A. (2000). Strategic Networks. *Strategic Management Journal, 21*(3), 203–215. doi:10.1002/(SICI)1097-0266(200003)21:3<203::AID-SMJ102>3.0.CO;2-K

Gupta, S., Polonsky, M., Woodside, A., & Webster, C. M. (2010). The impact of external forces on cartel network dynamics: Direct research in the diamond industry. *Industrial Marketing Management, 39*(2), 202–210. doi:10.1016/j.indmarman.2008.11.009

Hahn, R. (2013). ISO 26000 and the standardization of strategic management processes for sustainability and corporate social responsibility. *Business Strategy and the Environment, 22*(7), 442–455. doi:10.1002/bse.1751

Hair, J. F., Black, W. C., Babin, B. J., & Anderson, R. (2010). *Multivariate Data Analysis: A Global Perspective* (7th ed.). Englewood Cliffs, NJ: Prentice Hall.

Hair, J. F., Black, W. C., Babin, B. J., Anderson, R., & Tatham, R. L. (2006). *Multivariate data analysis (6th ed.).* Upper Saddle River, NJ: Pearson Prentice Hall.

Hamann, R. (2004). Corporate social responsibility, partnerships, and institutional change: The case of mining companies in South Africa. *Natural Resources Forum, 28*(4), 278–290. doi:10.1111/j.1477-8947.2004.00101.x

Hammer, M. (1990). Reengineering work: Don't automate, obliterate. *Harvard Business Review, 68*(4), 104–112.

Han, J., Han, J., & Brass, D. J. (2014). Human capital diversity in the creation of social capital for team creativity. *Journal of Organizational Behavior, 35*(1), 54–71. doi:10.1002/job.1853

Han, K., Trinkoff, A. M., Storr, C. L., & Geiger-Brown, J. (2011). Job Stress and Work Schedules in Relation to Nurse Obesity. *The Journal of Nursing Administration, 41*(11), 488–495. doi:10.1097/NNA.0b013e3182346fff PMID:22033319

Haq. (1997). *Reflections on Human Development.* Delhi: Oxford University Press.

Haro, E., & Kleiner, B. M. (2008). Macroergonomics as an organizing process for systems safety. *Applied Ergonomics, 39*(4), 450–458. doi:10.1016/j.apergo.2008.02.018 PMID:18407244

Harris, C. M., Pattie, M. W., & McMahan, G. C. (2015). Advancement along a career path: The influence of human capital and performance. *Human Resource Management Journal, 25*(1), 102–115. doi:10.1111/1748-8583.12047

Hart, S. G., & Staveland, L. E. (1988). Development of NASA-TLX (Task Load Index): Results of empirical and theoretical research. *Advances in Psychology*, *52*, 139–183. doi:10.1016/S0166-4115(08)62386-9

Heikkurinen, P., & Ketola, T. (2012). Corporate responsibility and identity: From a stakeholder to an awareness approach. *Business Strategy and the Environment*, *21*(5), 326–337. doi:10.1002/bse.744

Hellerstedt, W. L., & Jeffery, R. W. (1997). The association of job strain and health behaviours in men and women. *International Journal of Epidemiology*, *26*(3), 575–583. doi:10.1093/ije/26.3.575 PMID:9222783

Hemingway, C. A., & Maclagan, P. W. (2004). Managers personal values as drivers of corporate social responsibility. *Journal of Business Ethics*, *50*(1), 33–44. doi:10.1023/B:BUSI.0000020964.80208.c9

Henderson, D. J., & Russell, R. R. (2005). Human capital and convergence: A production-frontier approach. *International Economic Review*, *46*(4), 1167–1205. doi:10.1111/j.1468-2354.2005.00364.x

Hendrick, H. W. (1987). Human Factors in Organizational Design and Management. In A. H. Peter (Ed.), *Advances in Psychology* (pp. 347–398). Amsterdam: North-Holland Publishing Co. doi:10.1016/S0166-4115(08)62313-4

Hendrick, H. W. (1998). Measuring the economic benefits of ergonomics. In P. A. Scott, R. S. Bridger, & J. Charteris (Eds.), *Global ergonomics*. Amsterdam: Elsevier. doi:10.1016/B978-008043334-9/50170-0

Hendrick, H. W. (2003). Determining the cost-benefits of ergonomics projects and factors that lead to their success. *Applied Ergonomics*, *34*(5), 419–427. doi:10.1016/S0003-6870(03)00062-0 PMID:12963328

Hendrick, H. W., & Kleiner, B. M. (2000). *Macroergonomics: An Introduction to Work System Design* (Vol. 2). Santa Monica, CA: Human Factors and Ergonomics Society.

Hernandez-Arellano, J. L., Ibarra-Mejía, G., Serratos-Pérez, J. N., Garcia-Alcaraz, J. L., & Brunette, M. J. (2012). Construction of a survey to assess workload and fatigue among AMT operators in Mexico. *Work (Reading, Mass.)*, *41*, 1790–1796. doi:10.3233/WOR-2012-0387-1790 PMID:22316973

Hewitt-Dundas, N. (2006). Resource and capability constraints to innovation in small and large plants. *Small Business Economics*, *26*(3), 257–277. doi:10.1007/s11187-005-2140-3

Hignett, S., & McAtamney, L. (2000). Rapid Entire Body Assessment (REBA). *Applied Ergonomics*, *31*(2), 201–205. doi:10.1016/S0003-6870(99)00039-3 PMID:10711982

Hill, W. (1988). Differentiation versus low cost or differentiation and low cost. *Academy of Management Review*, *13*(3), 401–412.

Hilson, G. (2012). Corporate social responsibility in the extractive industries: Experiences from developing countries. *Resources Policy*, *37*(2), 131–137. doi:10.1016/j.resourpol.2012.01.002

Hitt, M. A., Bierman, L., Shimizu, K., & Kochhar, R. (2001). Direct and moderating effects of human capital on strategy and performance in professional service firms: A resource-based perspective. *Academy of Management Journal*, *44*(1), 13–28. doi:10.2307/3069334

Hoegl, M., & Gemuenden, H. G. (2001). Teamwork Quality and the Success of Innovative Projects: A Theoretical Concept and Empirical Evidence. *Organization Science*, *12*(4), 435–449. doi:10.1287/orsc.12.4.435.10635

Hofheinz, P. (2009). EU 2020: Why skills are key for Europe's future. *Policy Brief*, *IV*(1), 1–23.

Hogan, J. (1991). Physical abilities. In M.D. Dunnette& L.M. Hough (Eds.), Handbook of industrial and organizational psychology (Vol. 2, pp. 753-831). Palo Alto, CA: Consulting Psychologists Press.

Holcomb, J. L., Upchurch, R. S., & Okumus, F. (2007). Corporate social responsibility: What are top hotel companies reporting? *International Journal of Contemporary Hospitality Management*, *19*(6), 461–475. doi:10.1108/09596110710775129

Honjo, Y., Kato, M., & Okamuro, H. (2014). R&D investment of start-up firms: Does founder's human capital matter? *Small Business Economics*, *42*(2), 207–220. doi:10.1007/s11187-013-9476-x

Hossain, G., & Yeasin, M. (2015). Effect of Ability-Demand Gap on Cognitive Dissonance and Overload. *IEEE Transactions on Autonomous Mental Development*, PP(99), 1. Doi:10.1109/TAMD.2015.2450681

Hosseini, H., Hamid, K., Azar, A., & Rostamy, A. (2003). The intervening role of innovative climate: A study of middle managers in manufacturing organisations in Iran. *Public Organization Review*, *3*(2), 151–170. doi:10.1023/A:1024288830211

Hough, L. M. (1984). Development and evaluation of the accomplishment record methods of selecting and promoting professionals. *The Journal of Applied Psychology*, *69*(1), 135–146. doi:10.1037/0021-9010.69.1.135

Hough, L. M., Keyes, M. A., & Dunnette, M. D. (1983). An evaluation of three alternative selection measures. *Personnel Psychology*, *36*(2), 261–276. doi:10.1111/j.1744-6570.1983.tb01436.x

Howard, O.J., & Howard, K.J.M. (1998). An introduction to five- factor model for personality for Human resource professionals.

Howard, A. (1983). Work samples and simulations in competency evaluation. *Professional Psychology, Research and Practice*, *14*(6), 780–796. doi:10.1037/0735-7028.14.6.780

Huang, F. H., Ye, Y. J., & Kao, C. H. (2015). Developing a novel intuitionistic fuzzy importance–performance analysis for evaluating corporate social responsibility in sport tourism event. *Expert Systems with Applications: An International Journal*, *42*(19), 6530–6538. doi:10.1016/j.eswa.2015.04.008

Hudson. (2005). *Burnout Britain: Raising the Alarm for Employers*. Retrieved from www.hudson.com

Huffcutt, A. I., & Arthur, W. Jr. (1994). Hunter and Hunter (1984) revisited: Interview validity for entry-level jobs. *The Journal of Applied Psychology*, *79*(2), 184–190. doi:10.1037/0021-9010.79.2.184

Huffcutt, A. I., & Woehr, D. J. (1999). Further analysis of employment interview validity: A quantitative evaluation of interviewer-related structuring methods. *Journal of Organizational Behavior*, *20*(4), 549–560. doi:10.1002/(SICI)1099-1379(199907)20:4<549::AID-JOB921>3.0.CO;2-Q

Humphrey, S. E., Nahrgang, J. D., & Morgeson, F. P. (2007). Integrating motivational, social, and contextual work design features: A meta-analytic summary and theoretical extension of the work design literature. *The Journal of Applied Psychology*, *92*(5), 1332–1356. doi:10.1037/0021-9010.92.5.1332 PMID:17845089

Hunnur, R.R., Bagli, M.M. (2014). A Study On Relationship Between Occupation Stress Index Dimensions And Demographic Variables Of Police Sub Inspectors And Asst. Sub Inspectors In Police Department. *International Journal of Business and Administration Research Review*, *1*(3), 161-175.

Hunter, J. (1986). Cognitive ability, cognitive aptitudes, job knowledge, and job performance. *Journal of Vocational Behavior*, *29*(3), 340–362. doi:10.1016/0001-8791(86)90013-8

Hunter, J., & Hunter, R. F. (1984). Validity and utility of alternative predictors of job performance. *Psychological Bulletin*, *96*(1), 72–98. doi:10.1037/0033-2909.96.1.72

Hunter, S. T. (2009). On committing corporate suicide. In T. Casserley & D. Megginson (Eds.), *Learning from Burnout*. Elsevier.

Huppe, G. A. (2011). *Alpha's tale: The economic value of CSR*. Paper presented at the 2011 PRI Academic Network Conference, Sigtuna, Sweden. doi:10.2139/ssrn.1969583

Ibrahim, N. A., & Angelidis, J. P. (1995). The corporate social responsiveness orientation of board members: Are there differences between inside and outside directors? *Journal of Business Ethics*, *14*(5), 405–419. doi:10.1007/BF00872102

ILO. (2008). *Conclusions on Skills for Improved Productivity, Employment Growth and Development*. International Labour Conference. Retrieved from http://www.ilo.org/wcmsp5/groups/public/---ed_emp/---ifp_skills/documents/publication/wcms_103457.pdf

Inoue, Y., & Kent, A. (2012). Investigating the role of corporate credibility in corporate social marketing: A case study of environmental initiatives by professional sport organizations. *Sport Management Review*, *15*(3), 330–344. doi:10.1016/j.smr.2011.12.002

Isasi, C. R., Parrinello, C. M., Jung, M. M., Carnethon, M. R., Birnbaum-Weitzman, O., Espinoza, R. A., & Gallo, L. C. et al. (2015). Psychosocial stress is associated with obesity and diet quality in Hispanic/Latino adults. *Annals of Epidemiology*, *25*(2), 84–89. doi:10.1016/j.annepidem.2014.11.002 PMID:25487969

Ismail, R. B. (2007). *Implementations Problems in Lean Manufacturing: A study in manufacturing industries*. Malaysia Technical University of Melaka.

Iwamoto, H., & Takahashi, M. (2015). A quantitative approach to human capital management. *Procedia: Social and Behavioral Sciences*, *172*, 112–119. doi:10.1016/j.sbspro.2015.01.343

Jacob, M. (1981). *Human Capital and Economic Growth*. Working Paper No. 803. National Bureau of Economic Research. Retrieved from http://www.nber.org/papers/w0803.pdf

Jacobs, B. (2005). Optimal income taxation with endogenous human capital. *Journal of Public Economic Theory*, *7*(2), 295–315. doi:10.1111/j.1467-9779.2005.00205.x

Jacobson, L. S., LaLonde, R. J., & Sullivan, D. G. (1993). Earnings losses of displaced workers. *The American Economic Review*, *83*(4), 685–709.

Jain, K., & Jain, P. (2013). Job Satisfaction: A Comparative Study of Public & Private Sector Banks. *International Journal of Organizational Behaviour and Management Perspectives*, *2*(1).

Jakiela, P., Miguel, E., & te Velde, V. L. (2015). You've earned it: Estimating the impact of human capital on social preferences. *Experimental Economics*, *18*(3), 385–407. doi:10.1007/s10683-014-9409-9

Jamali, D. R., El Dirani, A. M., & Harwood, I. A. (2015). Exploring human resource management roles in corporate social responsibility: The CSR-HRM co-creation model. *Business Ethics (Oxford, England)*, *24*(2), 125–143. doi:10.1111/beer.12085

Jamali, D., Safieddine, A. M., & Rabbath, M. (2008). Corporate governance and corporate social responsibility synergies and interrelationships. *Corporate Governance: An International Review*, *16*(5), 443–459. doi:10.1111/j.1467-8683.2008.00702.x

Jaradat, Y. M., & Sy, M. V. U. (2012). Organizational Communication Practices of Toc Glycol Company Ltd., Thailand. *Procedia: Social and Behavioral Sciences*, *40*, 122–127. doi:10.1016/j.sbspro.2012.03.170

Jenkins, H., & Yakovleva, N. (2006). Corporate social responsibility in the mining industry: Exploring trends in social and environmental disclosure. *Journal of Cleaner Production*, *14*(3/4), 271–284. doi:10.1016/j.jclepro.2004.10.004

Jones, G., & Schneider, W. J. (2006). Intelligence, human capital, and economic growth: A Bayesian Averaging of Classical Estimates (BACE) approach. *Journal of Economic Growth*, *11*(1), 71–93. doi:10.1007/s10887-006-7407-2

Juárez-García, A., Idrovo, A. J., Camacho-Ávila, A., & Placencia-Reyes, O. (2014). Síndorme de burnout en población mexicana: Una revisión sistemática. *Salud Mental*, *37*(2), 159–176. doi:10.17711/SM.0185-3325.2014.020

Judge, T. A., Higgins, C. A., & Cable, D. M. (2000). The employment interview: A review of recent research and recommendations for future research. *Human Resource Management Review*, *10*(4), 383–406. doi:10.1016/S1053-4822(00)00033-4

Julian, S. D., & Ofori-dankwa, J. C. (2013). Financial resource availability and corporate social responsibility expenditures in a Sub-Saharan economy: The institutional difference hypothesis. *Strategic Management Journal*, *34*(11), 1314–1330. doi:10.1002/smj.2070

Jung, H. S., & Jung, H.-S. (2001). Establishment of overall workload assessment technique for various tasks and workplaces. *International Journal of Industrial Ergonomics*, *28*(6), 341–353. doi:10.1016/S0169-8141(01)00040-3

Kapelus, P. (2002). Mining, corporate social responsibility and the community: The case of Rio Tinto, Richards Bay Minerals and the Mbonambi. *Journal of Business Ethics*, *39*(3), 275–296. doi:10.1023/A:1016570929359

Karampour, A., Sharifi, K., & Safabakhsh, Sh. (2012). *A model-based approach for evaluating the effects of components on export performance based on cost leadership strategy in non-metallic mineral industry*. Business Management.

Karhu, O., Kansi, P., & Kuorinka, I. (1977). Correcting working postures in industry: A practical method for analysis. *Applied Ergonomics*, *8*(4), 199–201. doi:10.1016/0003-6870(77)90164-8 PMID:15677243

Kar, S. (2013). Exploring the causal link between FDI and human capital development in India. *DECISION*, *40*(1), 3–13. doi:10.1007/s40622-013-0001-5

Karwowski, W. (2001). International Encyclopedia of Ergonomics and Human Factors (W. Karwowski, Ed.; 3rd ed.). New York: Taylor & Francis. Retrieved from https://books.google.com/books?hl=es&lr=&id=KeoMi5Y8Q_gC&pgis=1

Karwowski, W. (2000). Symvatology: The science of an artifact-human compatibility. *Theoretical Issues in Ergonomics Science*, *1*(1), 76–91. doi:10.1080/146392200308480

Kasemsap, K. (2013a). Practical framework: Creation of causal model of job involvement, career commitment, learning motivation, and learning transfer. *International Journal of the Computer, the Internet and Management, 21*(1), 29–35.

Kasemsap, K. (2013b). Innovative business management: A practical framework and causal model of participation in decision making, career adaptability, affective commitment, and turnover intention. Paper presented at the 2nd International Conference on Economics, Business Innovation (ICEBI 2013), Copenhagen, Denmark.

Kasemsap, K. (2014a). The role of social capital in higher education institutions. In N. Baporikar (Ed.), *Handbook of research on higher education in the MENA region: Policy and practice* (pp. 119–147). Hershey, PA, USA: IGI Global. doi:10.4018/978-1-4666-6198-1.ch007

Kasemsap, K. (2014b). The role of sports marketing in the global marketplace. In M. Dos Santos (Ed.), *Strategies in sports marketing: Technologies and emerging trends* (pp. 279–298). Hershey, PA: IGI Global. doi:10.4018/978-1-4666-5994-0.ch017

Kasemsap, K. (2014b). Unifying a framework of organizational culture, organizational climate, knowledge management, and job performance. In R. Perez-Castillo & M. Piattini (Eds.), *Uncovering essential software artifacts through business process archeology* (pp. 336–362). Hershey, PA, USA: IGI Global. doi:10.4018/978-1-4666-4667-4.ch013

Kasemsap, K. (2014c). The role of social media in the knowledge-based organizations. In I. Lee (Ed.), *Integrating social media into business practice, applications, management, and models* (pp. 254–275). Hershey, PA: IGI Global. doi:10.4018/978-1-4666-6182-0.ch013

Kasemsap, K. (2015a). The roles of cross-cultural perspectives in global marketing. In J. Alcántara-Pilar, S. del Barrio-García, E. Crespo-Almendros, & L. Porcu (Eds.), *Analyzing the cultural diversity of consumers in the global marketplace* (pp. 37–59). Hershey, PA: IGI Global. doi:10.4018/978-1-4666-8262-7.ch003

Kasemsap, K. (2015b). The roles of sports sponsorship and brand management in global sports marketing. In H. Leng & N. Hsu (Eds.), *Emerging trends and innovation in sports marketing and management in Asia* (pp. 1–21). Hershey, PA: IGI Global. doi:10.4018/978-1-4666-7527-8.ch001

Kasemsap, K. (2015c). The role of ethical leadership in ethical organizations: A literature review. In C. Anyansi-Archibong (Ed.), *Contemporary issues surrounding ethical research methods and practice* (pp. 135–168). Hershey, PA: IGI Global. doi:10.4018/978-1-4666-8562-8.ch006

Kasemsap, K. (2016a). Analyzing the roles of human capital and competency in global business. In S. Sen, A. Bhattacharya, & R. Sen (Eds.), *International perspectives on socio-economic development in the era of globalization* (pp. 1–29). Hershey, PA, USA: IGI Global. doi:10.4018/978-1-4666-9908-3.ch001

Kasemsap, K. (2016a). Encouraging corporate social responsibility and sustainable tourism development in global tourism. In L. Guliani & S. Rizwan (Eds.), *Corporate social responsibility in the hospitality and tourism industry* (pp. 197–224). Hershey, PA: IGI Global. doi:10.4018/978-1-4666-9902-1.ch016

Kasemsap, K. (2016b). The role of social entrepreneurship in the global business environments. In Z. Fields (Ed.), *Incorporating business models and strategies into social entrepreneurship* (pp. 177–201). Hershey, PA: IGI Global. doi:10.4018/978-1-4666-8748-6.ch011

Kasemsap, K. (2016b). The roles of knowledge management and organizational innovation in global business. In G. Jamil, J. Poças-Rascão, F. Ribeiro, & A. Malheiro da Silva (Eds.), *Handbook of research on information architecture and management in modern organizations* (pp. 130–153). Hershey, PA, USA: IGI Global. doi:10.4018/978-1-4666-8637-3.ch006

Kasemsap, K. (2016c). The role of knowledge sharing on organisational innovation: An integrated framework. In *Business intelligence: Concepts, methodologies, tools, and applications* (pp. 406–429). Hershey, PA, USA: IGI Global. doi:10.4018/978-1-4666-9562-7.ch022

Kasemsap, K. (2016d). Creating product innovation strategies through knowledge management in global business. In A. Goel & P. Singhal (Eds.), *Product innovation through knowledge management and social media strategies* (pp. 330–357). Hershey, PA, USA: IGI Global. doi:10.4018/978-1-4666-9607-5.ch015

Kasemsap, K. (2016e). Exploring the roles of entrepreneurship and internationalization in global business. In L. Carvalho (Ed.), *Handbook of research on entrepreneurial success and its impact on regional development* (pp. 481–512). Hershey, PA, USA: IGI Global. doi:10.4018/978-1-4666-9567-2.ch021

Kasemsap, K. (2016f). Advocating entrepreneurship education and knowledge management in global business. In N. Baporikar (Ed.), *Handbook of research on entrepreneurship in the contemporary knowledge-based global economy* (pp. 313–339). Hershey, PA, USA: IGI Global. doi:10.4018/978-1-4666-8798-1.ch014

Kasemsap, K. (2016g). Promoting leadership development and talent management in modern organizations. In U. Aung & P. Ordoñez de Pablos (Eds.), *Managerial strategies and practice in the Asian business sector* (pp. 238–266). Hershey, PA, USA: IGI Global. doi:10.4018/978-1-4666-9758-4.ch013

Kato, M., & Honjo, Y. (2015). Entrepreneurial human capital and the survival of new firms in high- and low-tech sectors. *Journal of Evolutionary Economics*, *25*(5), 925–957. doi:10.1007/s00191-015-0427-3

Kato, M., Okamuro, H., & Honjo, Y. (2015). Does founder's human capital matter for innovation? Evidence from Japanese start-ups. *Journal of Small Business Management*, *53*(1), 114–128. doi:10.1111/jsbm.12094

Kaufman, N. A., & Geroy, G. D. (2007). An energy model for viewing embodied human capital theory. *Performance Improvement Quarterly*, *20*(1), 37–47. doi:10.1111/j.1937-8327.2007.tb00430.x

Kerner, H. J. (1973). *Professionelles und organisiertes vercrechen. Versuch einer Bestandsaufnabme und Bericht unber neuere Entwicklunggstendenzen in der Bundesrepublik Deutschland und in des Niederlanden*. Wiesbaden: BKA.

Kerner, H. J., & Mack, J. A. (1975). *The crime industry*. Lexington Lexington Books.

Kim, W. C. M. (2005a). Blue ocean strategy: From theory to practice. *California Management Review*.

Kim, W. C. M. (2005b). Blue ocean strategy. Cambridge, MA: Harvard Business School Press.

Kim, W. C. M. (2005c). Blue ocean strategy: How to create uncontested Market Space and Make the competition Irrelevant. Boston: Harvard Business School Press.

Kim, W. C. M. R (2004). Blue Ocean strategy: How to create uncontested market space and make competition irrelevant. Boston: Harvard Business School Press.

Kim, J. B., Zhang, H., Li, L., & Tian, G. (2014). Press freedom, externally-generated transparency, and stock price informativeness: International evidence. *Journal of Banking & Finance*, *46*, 299–310. doi:10.1016/j.jbankfin.2014.05.023

Kim, J., & Park, J. (2013). Foreign direct investment and country-specific human capital. *Economic Inquiry*, *51*(1), 198–210. doi:10.1111/j.1465-7295.2012.00478.x

Kim, T. (2015). Impacts of learning interventions on organizational human capital and performance. *Performance Improvement Quarterly*, *27*(4), 7–28. doi:10.1002/piq.21180

Kim, W. C. M. (2005d). Value Innovation: A leap the blue ocean. *The Journal of Business Strategy*, *26*(4), 22–28. doi:10.1108/02756660510608521

Kim, Y. J., & Lee, J. W. (2011). Technological change, human capital structure, and multiple growth paths. *The Japanese Economic Review*, *62*(3), 305–330. doi:10.1111/j.1468-5876.2009.00507.x

Kim, Y., Park, M. S., & Wier, B. (2012). Is earnings quality associated with corporate social responsibility? *Accounting Review*, *87*(3), 761–796. doi:10.2308/accr-10209

Kirkman, B. L., & Shapiro, D. L. (2001). The impact of team members cultural values on productivity, cooperation, and empowerment in self-managing working teams. *Journal of Cross-Cultural Psychology*, *32*(5), 597–617. doi:10.1177/0022022101032005005

Kivimaki, M., Head, J., Ferrie, J. E., Shipley, M. J., Brunner, E., Vahtera, J., & Marmot, M. G. (2006). Work stress, weight gain and weight loss: Evidence for bidirectional effects of job strain on body mass index in the Whitehall II study. *International Journal of Obesity*, *30*(6), 982–987. doi:10.1038/sj.ijo.0803229 PMID:16418750

Klaus, D. (2003). *Land Policies for Growth and Poverty Reduction. A World Bank Policy Research Report*. World Bank and Oxford University Press. Retrieved from http://info.worldbank.org/etools/docs/library/34919/landpoliciesexecsummary.pdf

Kleiner, B. M. (1998). Macroergonomic analysis of formalization in a dynamic work system. *Applied Ergonomics*, *29*(4), 255–259. doi:10.1016/S0003-6870(97)00034-3 PMID:9701539

Kleiner, B. M. (2006). Macroergonomics: Analysis and design of work systems. *Applied Ergonomics*, *37*(1), 81–89. doi:10.1016/j.apergo.2005.07.006 PMID:16226212

Klomp, J., & de Haan, K. (2013). Political regime and human capital: A cross-country analysis. *Social Indicators Research*, *111*(1), 45–73. doi:10.1007/s11205-011-9983-6 PMID:23378681

Kolk, A., & Pinkse, J. (2010). The integration of corporate governance in corporate social responsibility disclosures. *Corporate Social Responsibility and Environmental Management*, *17*(1), 15–26.

Kolk, A., & van Tulder, R. (2010). International business, corporate social responsibility and sustainable development. *International Business Review*, *19*(1), 1119–1125.

Koroglu, B. A., & Eceral, T. O. (2015). Human capital and innovation capacity of firms in defense and aviation industry in Ankara. *Procedia: Social and Behavioral Sciences*, *195*, 1583–1592. doi:10.1016/j.sbspro.2015.06.196

Kor, Y. Y., & Leblebici, H. (2005). How do interdependencies among human-capital deployment, development, and diversification strategies affect firm's financial performance? *Strategic Management Journal*, *26*(10), 967–985. doi:10.1002/smj.485

Kotilainen, J., Prokhorova, E., Sairinen, R., & Tiainen, H. (2015). Corporate social responsibility of mining companies in Kyrgyzstan and Tajikistan. *Resources Policy*, *45*, 202–209. doi:10.1016/j.resourpol.2015.06.001

Krackhardt, D., & Hanson, J. R. (1993). Mapping employees relationships can help managers harness the real power in their organizations. *Harvard Business Review*, 16.

Krebs, V. E. (2001). Mapping Networks of Terrorist Cells. *Connections*, *24*, 43–52.

Kruger, P. (2014). Corporate goodness and shareholder wealth. *Journal of Financial Economics*, *115*(2), 304–329. doi:10.1016/j.jfineco.2014.09.008

Kucharcíková, A., Tokarcíková, E., & Blašková, M. (2015). Human capital management: Aspect of the human capital efficiency in university education. *Procedia: Social and Behavioral Sciences*, *177*, 48–60. doi:10.1016/j.sbspro.2015.02.332

Kumud, S. (2011, October). Small Loans, Big Dreams: Women and Microcredit in a Globalising Economy. *Economic and Political Weekly*, *46*(43). Retrieved from http://www.epw.in.iproxy.inflibnet.ac.in:2048/journal/2011/43/review-womens-studies-review-issues-specials/small-loans-big-dreams-women-and

Kwan, L. Y. Y., & Chiu, C. Y. (2015). Country variations in different innovation outputs: The interactive effect of institutional support and human capital. *Journal of Organizational Behavior*, *36*(7), 1050–1070. doi:10.1002/job.2017

Kwon, D.-B. (2009). Human capital and its measurement. Retrieved November 30, 2016, from http://www.oecd.org/site/progresskorea/44109779.pdf

Kyrou, I., & Tsigos, C. (2009). Stress hormones: Physiological stress and regulation of metabolism. *Current Opinion in Pharmacology*, *9*(6), 787–793. doi:10.1016/j.coph.2009.08.007 PMID:19758844

Lagacé, D., & Bourgault, M. (2003). Linking manufacturing improvement programs to the competitive priorities of Canadian SMEs. *Technovation*, *23*(8), 705–715. doi:10.1016/S0166-4972(02)00026-3

Lajili, K. (2015). Embedding human capital into governance design: A conceptual framework. *Journal of Management and Governance*, *19*(4), 741–762. doi:10.1007/s10997-014-9295-8

Lange-Morales, K., Röbig, S., & Bruder, R. (2011). Compatibility in multiplicity: towards a complex understanding of medical devices use. In S. Albolino, S. Bagnara, T. Bellandi, J. Llaneza, G. Rosal, & R. Tartaglia (Eds.), *Healthcare systems ergonomics and patient safety* (1st ed.; pp. 334–337). Taylor & Francis Group.

Lattemann, C., Fetscherin, M., Alon, I., Li, S., & Schneider, A. M. (2009). CSR communication intensity in Chinese and Indian multinational companies. *Corporate Governance: An International Review*, *17*(4), 426–442. doi:10.1111/j.1467-8683.2009.00758.x

Lau, R. S. M. (2002). Competitive factors and their relative importance in the US electronics and computer industries. *International Journal of Operations & Production Management*, *22*(1), 125–135. doi:10.1108/01443570210412105

Lavanya, T. (2010). *Women Empowerment through Entrepreneurship*. New Delhi: New Century Publications.

Lavezzi, A. M. (2008). Struttura economica e vulnerabilitá del crimine organizzato in Sicilia. La A. Spina (Eds.), I costi della illegalitá. Mafia ed estorsioni in Sicilia. Bologna, Italy: il Mulino.

le Roux, T. (2014). The description of South African corporate communication practitioners that contribute to organisational performance. *Public Relations Review*, *40*(2), 193–215. doi:10.1016/j.pubrev.2013.11.008

Lee, C. C., & Sirch, M. L. (1994). Counseling in an enlightened society: Values for a new millennium. *Counseling and Values*, *38*(2), 90–97. doi:10.1002/j.2161-007X.1994.tb00826.x

Lee, H., & Choi, B. (2003). Knowledge Management Enablers, Processes, and Organizational Performance: An Integrative View and Empirical Examination. *Journal of Management Information Systems*, *20*(1). Retrieved from http://www.tandfonline.com/doi/abs/10.1080/07421222.2003.11045756

Lee, J., & Maxfield, S. (2015). Doing well by reporting good: Reporting corporate responsibility and corporate performance. *Business and Society Review*, *120*(4), 577–606. doi:10.1111/basr.12075

Leeuwen. (2007). *Human Capital and Economic Growth in India, Indonesia and Japan: A Quantitative Analysis*. Retrieved from https://books.google.co.in/books?id=JAxpCWzpDuQC&dq=18.%09Bas+Van+Leeuwen.+().+Human+Capital+and+Economic+Growth&source=gbs_navlinks_s

Leiponen, A. (2005). Skills and innovation. *International Journal of Industrial Organization*, *23*(5/6), 303–323. doi:10.1016/j.ijindorg.2005.03.005

Leiter, M. P., & Maslach, C. (2009). Nurse turnover: The mediating role of burnout. *Journal of Nursing Management, 17*(3), 331–339. doi:10.1111/j.1365-2834.2009.01004.x PMID:19426369

Le, T., Gibson, J., & Oxley, L. (2006). A forward-looking measure of the stock of human capital in New Zealand. *The Manchester School, 74*(5), 593–609. doi:10.1111/j.1467-9957.2006.00511.x

Levenson, A., & Zoghi, C. (2010). Occupations, human capital and skills. *Journal of Labor Research, 31*(4), 365–386. doi:10.1007/s12122-010-9098-x

Levenstein, M. C., & Suslow, V. Y. (2006). What determines cartel success. *Journal of Economic Literature, 44*(1), 43–95. doi:10.1257/002205106776162681

Likert, R. (1932). A technique for the measurement of attitudes. *Archives de Psychologie*, 22.

Li, L. X. (2000). An analysis of sources of competitiveness and performance of Chinese manufacturers. *International Journal of Operations & Production Management, 20*(3), 299–315. doi:10.1108/01443570010294307

Lim, A. S. K., & Tang, K. K. (2008). Human capital inequality and the Kuznets curve. *The Developing Economies, 46*(1), 26–51. doi:10.1111/j.1746-1049.2007.00054.x

Lim, A., & Tsutsui, K. (2012). Globalization and commitment in corporate social responsibility: Cross-national analyses of institutional and political-economy effects. *American Sociological Review, 77*(1), 69–98. doi:10.1177/0003122411432701

Lin, K. J., Tan, J., Zhao, L., & Karim, K. (2015). In the name of charity: Political connections and strategic corporate social responsibility in a transition economy. *Journal of Corporate Finance, 32*, 327–346. doi:10.1016/j.jcorpfin.2014.10.007

Lin, R. J. (2013). Using fuzzy DEMATEL to evaluate the green supply chain management practices. *Journal of Cleaner Production, 40*, 32–39. doi:10.1016/j.jclepro.2011.06.010

Lin, S. C., Kim, D. H., & Wu, Y. C. (2013). Foreign direct investment and income inequality: Human capital matters. *Journal of Regional Science, 53*(5), 874–896. doi:10.1111/jors.12077

Lipscomb, J. A., Trinkoff, A. M., Geiger-Brown, J., & Brady, B. (2002). Work-schedule characteristics and reported musculoskeletal disorders of registered nurses. *Scandinavian Journal of Work, Environment & Health, 28*(6), 394–401. doi:10.5271/sjweh.691 PMID:12539799

Li, Q., Luo, W., Wang, Y., & Wu, L. (2013). Firm performance, corporate ownership, and corporate social responsibility disclosure in China. *Business Ethics (Oxford, England), 22*(2), 159–173. doi:10.1111/beer.12013

Li, Y., Wang, X., Westlund, H., & Liu, Y. (2015). Physical capital, human capital, and social capital: The changing roles in China's economic growth. *Growth and Change, 46*(1), 133–149. doi:10.1111/grow.12084

Llaneza, J. (2002). *Ergonomía y psicología aplicada: Manual para la formación del especialista*. Lex Nova.

Lorange, P. (2007). *Scott Morton*. Strategic Control.

Luckhaupt, S. E., Cohen, M. A., Li, J., & Calvert, G. M. (2014). Prevalence of obesity among U.S. workers and associations with occupational factors. *American Journal of Preventive Medicine*, *46*(3), 237–248. doi:10.1016/j.amepre.2013.11.002 PMID:24512862

Ludescher, J. C., Mahsud, R., & Prussia, G. E. (2012). We are the corporation: Dispersive CSR. *Business and Society Review*, *117*(1), 55–88. doi:10.1111/j.1467-8594.2011.00399.x

Luneburg, W. V., & Susman, T. M. (2005). *The Lobbying Manual: A Complete Guide to Federal Law Governing Lawyers and Lobbyists* (W. V. Luneburg & T. M. Susman, Eds.; 3th ed.). Chicago, IL: ABA Publishing. Retrieved from https://books.google.com/books?hl=es&lr=&id=DhL_4k4X5lEC&pgis=1

Luning, S. (2012). Corporate social responsibility (CSR) for exploration: Consultants, companies and communities in process of engagements. *Resources Policy*, *37*(2), 205–211. doi:10.1016/j.resourpol.2011.02.004

Luque-Reca, O., Augusto-Landa, J. M., & Pulido-Martos, M. (2014). La relación entre la inteligencia emocional percibida y la salud mental en directivos y mandos intermedios: El papel del estrés percibido como mediador. *Ansiedad y Estrés*, *20*(1), 61–73.

Luthans, F. (2005). *Organizational Behavior* (10th ed.). Boston: McGraw-Hill.

Luximon, A., & Goonetilleke, R.S. (2001). Simplified subjective workload assessment technique. *Ergonomics*, *44*(3), 229–243. Doi:10.1080/00140130121511

Macan, T. (2009). The employment interview: A review of current studies and directions for future research. *Human Resource Management Review*, *19*(3), 203–218. doi:10.1016/j.hrmr.2009.03.006

MacIntosh, E., & Doherty, A. (2007). Extending the Scope of Organisational Culture: The External Perception of an Internal Phenomenon. *Sport Management Review*, *10*(1), 45–64. doi:10.1016/S1441-3523(07)70003-7

MacLeod, I. S. (2003). Real-world effectiveness of Ergonomic methods. *Applied Ergonomics*, *34*(5), 465–477. doi:10.1016/S0003-6870(03)00066-8 PMID:12963332

Maister, D. H. (2012). *Managing The Professional Service Firm*. New York: Simon & Schuster UK. Retrieved from https://books.google.com/books?hl=es&lr=&id=2VpMK-uoJVMC&pgis=1

Majumdar, S. I., Rahman, M. S., & Rahman, M. M. (2014). Stakeholder prioritization in requirement engineering process: A case study on school management system. *Computing in Science & Engineering*, *4*(1), 17–27.

Maldonado, A., García, J. L., Alvarado, A., & Balderrama, C. O. (2013). A hierarchical fuzzy axiomatic design methodology for ergonomic compatibility evaluation of advanced manufacturing technology. *International Journal of Advanced Manufacturing Technology*, *66*(1-4), 171–186. doi:10.1007/s00170-012-4316-8

Maldonado-Macías, A., Camacho-Alamilla, R., Torres, S. G. V., Alcaraz, J. L. G., & Limón, J. (2015). Determination of Burnout Syndrome among Middle and Senior Managers in Manufacturing Industry in Ciudad Juarez. *Procedia Manufacturing*, *3*, 6459–6466. doi:10.1016/j.promfg.2015.07.927

Malsch, B. (2013). Politicizing the expertise of the accounting industry in the realm of corporate social responsibility. *Accounting, Organizations and Society*, *38*(2), 149–168. doi:10.1016/j.aos.2012.09.003

Mamuneas, T. P., Savvides, A., & Stengos, T. (2006). Economic development and the return to human capital: A smooth coefficient semiparametric approach. *Journal of Applied Econometrics*, *21*(1), 111–132. doi:10.1002/jae.813

Mane, K. M., & Waldorf, B. S. (2013). Human capital and wages: A comparison of Albanian and Italian immigrants. *The Annals of Regional Science*, *51*(1), 53–72. doi:10.1007/s00168-012-0532-2

Mann Deshi Foundation - Impact Report. (2013). Retrieved November 18, 2015, from http://www.thefundingnetwork.org.uk/wp-content/uploads/2013/07/Mann-Deshi-3-year-Impact-Report-Final.pdf

Marchand, A., Juster, R.-P., Durand, P., & Lupien, S. J. (2014). Burnout symptom sub-types and cortisol profiles: Whats burning most? *Psychoneuroendocrinology*, *40*(0), 27–36. doi:10.1016/j.psyneuen.2013.10.011 PMID:24485473

Marchionini, G. (1991). Technological trends and implications: Toward the new millennium. *School Library Media Annual*, *9*, 182–187.

Mark, G. (1983). The Strength of Weak Ties: A Network Theory Revisited. *Sociological Theory*, *1*. Retrieved from http://www.soc.ucsb.edu/faculty/friedkin/Syllabi/Soc148/Granovetter%20 1983.pdf

Martínez, M. P. (2015, 5 Febrero). Estima la OIT estrés laboral en 40% de lo trabajadores mexicanos. *El Economista*. Retrieved from http://eleconomista.com.mx/industrias/2015/02/05/estima-oit-estres-laboral-40-trabajadores-mexicanos

Marvel, M. R. (2013). Human capital and search-based discovery: A study of high-tech entrepreneurship. *Entrepreneurship Theory and Practice*, *37*(2), 403–419. doi:10.1111/j.1540-6520.2011.00465.x

Maslach, C. (2009). Comprendiendo el burnout. *Ciencia & Trabajo*, *11*, 37–43.

Maslach, C., & Jackson, S. E. (1981). The measurement of experienced burnout. *Journal of Organizational Behavior*, *2*(2), 99–113. doi:10.1002/job.4030020205

Maslach, C., Jackson, S. E., & Leiter, M. P. (1996). *MBI: The Maslach Burnout Inventory Manual* (3rd ed.). Palo Alto, CA: Consulting Psychologists Press.

Mason, E.S. (1939). Price and production policies of large-scale enterprises. *American Economic Review*, *29*, 61-74.

Mason, C., & Simmons, J. (2011). Forward looking or looking unaffordable? Utilising academic perspectives on corporate social responsibility to assess the factors influencing its adoption by business. *Business Ethics (Oxford, England)*, *20*(2), 159–176. doi:10.1111/j.1467-8608.2011.01614.x

Mason, C., & Simmons, J. (2014). Embedding corporate social responsibility in corporate governance: A stakeholder systems approach. *Journal of Business Ethics*, *119*(1), 77–86. doi:10.1007/s10551-012-1615-9

Mastrobuoni, G., & Patacchini, E. (2012). Organized crime networks: An application of network analysis techniques to the American mafia. *Review of Network Economics*, *11*(3).

Matos, S., & Silvestre, B. S. (2013). Managing stakeholder relations when developing sustainable business models: The case of the Brazilian energy sector. *Journal of Cleaner Production*, *45*, 61–73. doi:10.1016/j.jclepro.2012.04.023

Matten, D., Crane, A., & Chapple, W. (2003). Behind the mask: Revealing the true face of corporate citizenship. *Journal of Business Ethics*, *45*(1/2), 109–120. doi:10.1023/A:1024128730308

Mattingly, J. E., & Berman, S. L. (2006). Measurement of corporate social action: Discovering taxonomy in the Kinder Lydenburg Domini ratings data. *Business & Society*, *45*(1), 20–46. doi:10.1177/0007650305281939

Mazumdar & Ahmed. (2015). Empowerment of Rural Women Through Entrepreneurship: An Overview. *International Research Journal of Interdisciplinary and Multidisciplinary Studies*, *1*(1). Retrieved from http://www.researchinformation.org/files/Mrs.-Manashi-Mazumdar.pdf

McAdam, R., Moffett, S., Hazlett, S. A., & Shavlin, M. (2010). Developing a model of innovation implementation for UK SMEs: A path analysis and explanatory case analysis. *International Small Business Journal*, *28*(3), 195–214. doi:10.1177/0266242609360610

McAndrew, D. (1999). The structural analysis of criminal networks. In D. Canter & L. Alison (Eds.), *The Social Psychology of Crime: Groups* (Vol. 3). Aldershot, Dartmouth: Teams, and Networks, Offender Profiling Series.

Mcatamney, L., & Corlett, E. N. (1993). RULA: a survey method for the investigation of world-related upper limb disorders. Applied Ergonomics, *24*(2), 91–99. Doi:10.1016/0003-6870(93)90080-S

McCormack, N., & Cotter, C. (2013). *Managing Burnout in the Workplace. A Guide for Information Professionals*. Oxford, UK: Chandos Publishing.

McCrae, R. R., & Costa, P. T. J. R. (1980). Openness to experience and ego level in Loevingers sentence completion test: Dispositional contribution to developmental models of personality. *Journal of Personality and Social Psychology*, *39*(6), 1179–1190. doi:10.1037/h0077727

McGuirk, H., Lenihan, H., & Hart, M. (2015). Measuring the impact of innovative human capital on small firm's propensity to innovate. *Research Policy*, *44*(4), 965–976. doi:10.1016/j.respol.2014.11.008

Meiseberg, B., & Ehrmann, T. (2012). Lost in translation? The prevalence and performance impact of corporate social responsibility in franchising. *Journal of Small Business Management, 50*(4), 566–595. doi:10.1111/j.1540-627X.2012.00367.x

Melo, T., & Garrido-Morgado, A. (2012). Corporate reputation: A combination of social responsibility and industry. *Corporate Social Responsibility and Environmental Management, 19*(1), 11–31. doi:10.1002/csr.260

Merritt, H. (2015). The role of human capital in university-business cooperation: The case of Mexico. *Journal of the Knowledge Economy, 6*(3), 568–588. doi:10.1007/s13132-015-0258-3

Michailides, T. P., & Lipsett, M. G. (2013). Surveying employee attitudes on corporate social responsibility at the frontline level of an energy transportation company. *Corporate Social Responsibility and Environmental Management, 20*(5), 296–320. doi:10.1002/csr.1291

Michod, R. E. (1993). Biology and the origin of values. In M. Hechter, L. Nadel, & R. Michod (Eds.), *The origin of values* (pp. 261–271). New York, NY: Aldine de Gruyter.

Mihir, S., Rangu, R., & Shankar, V. P. S. (2007). Rural Credit in the 20th Century: An Overview of History and Perspectives. *Economic and Political Weekly*. Retrieved from https://www.researchgate.net/publication/239783568_Rural_Credit_in_20th_Century_India_An_Overview_of_History_and_Perspectives

Miles, R.E., Snow, C.C., Meyer, A.D., & Coleman, H.J. (1978). Organizational strategy, structure, and process. *Academy of Management Review, 3*(3), 546–562. PMID:10238389

Militello, L. G., & Hutton, R. J. (1998). Applied Cognitive Task Analysis (ACTA): A practitioners toolkit for understanding cognitive task demands. *Ergonomics, 41*(11), 1618–1641. doi:10.1080/001401398186108 PMID:9819578

Mitchell, C., & Quinn, N. (2005). Environmental reporting disclosure in South Africa: A comparative study of the expectations of selected groups of preparers and users. *Meditari Accountancy Research, 13*(2), 17–33. doi:10.1108/10222529200500010

Mitrofan, N., & Bulborea, A. (2013). The Role of Organizational Communication in Structuring Interpersonal Relationships. *Procedia: Social and Behavioral Sciences, 76*, 511–515. doi:10.1016/j.sbspro.2013.04.155

Miyake, S. (2001). Multivariate workload evaluation combining physiological and subjective measures. *International Journal of Psychophysiology, 40*(3), 233–238. doi:10.1016/S0167-8760(00)00191-4 PMID:11228350

Moav, O., & Neeman, Z. (2012). Saving rates and poverty: The role of conspicuous consumption and human capital. *The Economic Journal, 122*(563), 933–956. doi:10.1111/j.1468-0297.2012.02516.x

Mohr, L. A., Webb, D. J., & Harris, K. E. (2001). Do consumers expect companies to be socially responsible? The impact of corporate social responsibility on buying behavior. *The Journal of Consumer Affairs, 35*(1), 45–72. doi:10.1111/j.1745-6606.2001.tb00102.x

Möller, K., Gamerschlag, R., & Guenther, F. (2011). Determinants and effects of human capital reporting and controlling. *Journal of Management Control, 22*(3), 311–333. doi:10.1007/s00187-011-0138-3

Montiel, O., Ramírez, A., Esparza, V. M., & Guerrero, A. (2014). Relatos de vida de gerentes de producción en la industria maquiladora de Cd.Juárez, México. *Global Conference on Business & Finance Proceedings, 9*(1), 1700-1709.

Mooi-Reci, I., & Ganzeboom, H. B. (2015). Unemployment scarring by gender: Human capital depreciation or stigmatization? Longitudinal evidence from the Netherlands, 1980–2000. *Social Science Research, 52*, 642–658. doi:10.1016/j.ssresearch.2014.10.005 PMID:26004486

Moreno-Jiménez, B., Rodríguez-Carvajal, R., & Escobar, E. (2001). La Evaluación del Burnout Profesional: Factorización del MBI-GS. Un análisis preliminar. *Ansiedad y Estrés, 7*(1), 69–78.

Moretti, E. (2004). Human capital externalities in cities. In J. Henderson & J. Thisse (Eds.), *Handbook of regional and urban economics* (pp. 2243–2291). Amsterdam, The Netherlands: Elsevier.

Morgeson, F. P., & Humphrey, S. E. (2003). *Work Design Questionnaire (WDQ): Developing and validating a comprehensive measure of work design.* Paper presented at the 62nd Annual Meeting of the Academy of Management, Seattle, WA.

Morgeson, F. P., & Humphrey, S. E. (2006). The Work Design Questionnaire (WDQ): Developing and validating a comprehensive measure for assessing job design and the nature of work. *The Journal of Applied Psychology, 91*(6), 1321–1339. doi:10.1037/0021-9010.91.6.1321 PMID:17100487

Motowidlo, S. J., Dunnette, M. D., & Carter, G. (1990). An alternative selection procedure: A low fidelity simulation. *The Journal of Applied Psychology, 75*(6), 640–647. doi:10.1037/0021-9010.75.6.640

Muenster, E., Rueger, H., Ochsmann, E., Letzel, S., & Toschke, A. M. (2011). Association between overweight, obesity and self-perceived job insecurity in German employees. *BMC Public Health, 11*(1), 162. doi:10.1186/1471-2458-11-162 PMID:21401919

Munoz, M. J., Rivera, J. M., & Moneva, J. M. (2008). Evaluating sustainability in organisations with a fuzzy logic approach. *Industrial Management & Data Systems, 108*(6), 829–841. doi:10.1108/02635570810884030

Musakhani, M., Haghighi, M., & Torkzadeh, S. (2012). A model for customer loyalty using customer knowledge management in the banking industry private banks. *Business Management, 4*(12), 147–164.

Musotto, R. (2012). *Inefficient Institutions and Organised Crime.* Universitá degli Studi di Palermo.

Musotto, R. (2014). Criminalidad Organizada, Estado y Servicios Públicos: un Análisis Socioeconómico. In J.J. Martínez Bolaños (Ed.), *Criminalidad Organizada.* Spain: Estudios Internacionales. Criminologia y Justicia Editorial.

Mutti, D., Yakovleva, N., Vazquez-Brust, D., & di Marco, M. H. (2012). Corporate social responsibility in the mining industry: Perspectives from stakeholder groups in Argentina. *Resources Policy*, *37*(2), 212–222. doi:10.1016/j.resourpol.2011.05.001

Nachane, D. M. (2011). Two decades of structural reforms: A balance sheet. In D.M. Nachane (Ed.), *India Development Report* (pp. 1-21). New Delhi: Oxford University Press. Retrieved October 11, 2015, from http://www.igidr.ac.in/pdf/publication/IDR-2011.pdf

Nakata, A., Haratani, T., Takahashi, M., Kawakami, N., Arito, H., Kobayashi, F., & Araki, S. (2004). Job stress, social support, and prevalence of insomnia in a population of Japanese daytime workers. *Social Science & Medicine (1982)*, *59*(8), 1719–30. http://doi.org/<ALIGNMENT.qj></ALIGNMENT>10.1016/j.socscimed.2004.02.002

National-Institute-of-Statistics-Geography-and-Informatics. (2015). *Estadística Integral de Programa de la Industria Manufacturera, Maquiladora y Servicios de Exportación*. IMMEX.

Naveen, K. (2015). Poverty Reduction through Women's Entrepreneurial Activities in Rural Andhra Pradesh (Vol. 34). Ritsumeikan Journal of Asia Pacific Studies. Retrieved from http://www.apu.ac.jp/rcaps/uploads/fckeditor/publications/journal/RJAPS34_6_Kolloju.pdf

Ned, K. (2015). WarpPLS© 5.0 user manual. Laredo, TX: ScriptWarp SystemsTM.

Neerincx, M. A. (2003). Cognitive Task Load Analysis: allocation Tasks and Designing Support. In E. Hollnagel (Ed.), *Handbook of Cognitive Task Design* (pp. 283–305). Mahwah, NJ: Lawrence Erlbaum Associates; doi:10.1201/9781410607775.ch13

Nes, E. B., Solberg, C. A., & Silkoset, R. (2007). The impact of national culture and communication on exporter–distributor relations and on export performance. *International Business Review*, *16*(4), 405–424. doi:10.1016/j.ibusrev.2007.01.008

Nevanpera, N. J., Hopsu, L., Kuosma, E., Ukkola, O., Uitti, J., & Laitinen, J. H. (2012). Occupational burnout, eating behavior, and weight among working women. *The American Journal of Clinical Nutrition*, *95*(4), 934–943. doi:10.3945/ajcn.111.014191 PMID:22378728

Newman, E., OConnor, D., & Conner, M. (2007). Daily hassles and eating behaviour: The role of cortisol reactivity status. *Psychoneuroendocrinology*, *32*(2), 125–132. doi:10.1016/j.psyneuen.2006.11.006 PMID:17198744

Ng, T. W. H., & Feldman, D. C. (2010). Human capital and objective indicators of career success: The mediating effects of cognitive ability and conscientiousness. *Journal of Occupational and Organizational Psychology*, *83*(1), 207–235. doi:10.1348/096317909X414584

Nordin, S. M., Sivapalan, S., Bhattacharyya, E., Ahmad, H. H. W. F. W., & Abdullah, A. (2014). Organizational Communication Climate and Conflict Management: Communications Management in an Oil and Gas Company. *Procedia: Social and Behavioral Sciences*, *109*(8), 1046–1058. doi:10.1016/j.sbspro.2013.12.587

Norman, W., & MacDonald, C. (2004). Getting to the bottom of triple bottom line. *Business Ethics Quarterly*, *14*(2), 243–262. doi:10.5840/beq200414211

Ntim, C. G., & Soobaroyen, T. (2013). Corporate governance and performance in socially responsible corporations: New empirical insights from a neo-institutional framework. *Corporate Governance: An International Review*, *21*(5), 468–494. doi:10.1111/corg.12026

Nybakk, E., & Panwar, R. (2015). Understanding instrumental motivations for social responsibility engagement in a micro-firm context. *Business Ethics (Oxford, England)*, *24*(1), 18–33. doi:10.1111/beer.12064

O`Connor, D. B., & Conner, M. (2011). Effects of Stress on Eating Behavior. In R. J. Contrada & A. Baum (Eds.), *The Handbook of Stress Science: Biology, Psychology, and Health*. Springer Publishing Company.

O'Donnell, L., Kramar, R., & Dyball, M. C. (2009). Human capital reporting: Should it be industry specific? *Asia Pacific Journal of Human Resources*, *47*(3), 358–373. doi:10.1177/1038411108099293

OECD Centre for Educational Research and Development. (2001). *The Well Being of Nations – The Role of Human and Social Capital– Education and Skills.* Retrieved October 9, 2015, from http://www.oecd.org/site/worldforum/33703702.pdf

OECD. (2011). *Skills for innovation and research.* Paris, France: OECD Publishing.

Ogunade Adeyemi, O. (2011). *Human Capital Investment in the Developing World: An Analysis of Praxis.* Schmidt Labor Research Centre Seminar Series. Retrieved from http://www.uri.edu/research/lrc/research/papers/Ogunade_Workforce_Development.pdf

Ohyama, A. (2015). Entrepreneurship and job-relatedness of human capital. *Economica*, *82*(328), 740–768. doi:10.1111/ecca.12144

Okpara, J. O., & Wynn, P. M. (2012). Stakeholders perceptions about corporate social responsibility: Implications for poverty alleviation. *Thunderbird International Business Review*, *54*(1), 91–103. doi:10.1002/tie.21441

Olfert, M. R., Jelinski, M., Zikos, D., & Campbell, J. (2012). Human capital drift up the urban hierarchy: Veterinarians in Western Canada. *The Annals of Regional Science*, *49*(2), 551–570. doi:10.1007/s00168-011-0448-2

Oliva, E., & Palazzolo, S. (2006). *Bernardo Provenzano: il ragioniere di Cosa nostra*. Rubbettino Editore.

Ones, D. S., Viswesvaran, C., & Schmidt, F. L. (1993). Comprehensive meta-analysis of integrity test validities: Findings and implications for personnel selection and theories of job performance.[monograph]. *The Journal of Applied Psychology*, *78*(4), 531–537. doi:10.1037/0021-9010.78.4.679

Ooi, C. A., Hooy, C. W., & Som, A. P. M. (2015). Diversity in human and social capital: Empirical evidence from Asian tourism firms in corporate board composition. *Tourism Management*, *48*, 139–153. doi:10.1016/j.tourman.2014.11.002

Orlitzky, M., & Benjamin, J. D. (2001). Corporate social performance and firm risk: A meta-analytic review. *Business & Society*, *40*(4), 369–396. doi:10.1177/000765030104000402

Oxfam Hong Kong. (2010). *Corporate social responsibility survey of Hang Seng Index constituent companies 2009*. Hong Kong: Oxfam Hong Kong.

Oyedele, L. O., & Tham, K. W. (2007). Clients assessment of architects performance in building delivery process: Evidence from Nigeria. *Building and Environment*, *42*(5), 2090–2099. doi:10.1016/j.buildenv.2005.06.030

Palacios-Marques, D., Gil-Pechuán, I., & Lim, S. (2011). Improving human capital through knowledge management practices in knowledge-intensive business services. *Service Business*, *5*(2), 99–112. doi:10.1007/s11628-011-0104-z

Panda, P., & Bina, A. (2005). Marital Violence, Human Development and Womens Property Status in India. *World Development*, *33*(5), 823–850. doi:10.1016/j.worlddev.2005.01.009

Pangannavar Arjun Yallappa. (2012). *Self-help Groups and Women Empowerment in India*. New Delhi: New Century Publications.

Paoli, L. (2002). The paradoxes of organized crime. *Crime, law and social change*, *37*(1), 51-97. 17

Papantonopoulos, S., & Salvendy, G. (2008). Analytic Cognitive Task Allocation: A decision model for cognitive task allocation. *Theoretical Issues in Ergonomics Science*, *9*(2), 155–185. doi:10.1080/14639220600765386

Paralikas, A., & Lygeros, A. (2005). A multi-criteria and fuzzy logic based methodology for the relative ranking of the fire hazard of chemical substances and installations. *Process Safety and Environmental Protection*, *83*(2), 122–134. doi:10.1205/psep.04236

Park, W., Ramachandran, J., Weisman, P., & Jung, E. S. (2010). Obesity effect on male active joint range of motion. *Ergonomics*, *53*(1), 102–108. doi:10.1080/00140130903311617 PMID:20069486

Parzinger, M. J., Lemons, M. A., & McDaniel, K. (2012, Spring). The Impact Of Organizational Context On Turnover And Job Satisfaction: A Multi-Analysis Study Of Bank Employees. *International Journal of the Academic Business World*, *6*(1), 39–50.

Pearl, J. (2001). Direct and indirect effects. In Proceedings of the Seventeenth conference on Uncertainty in artificial intelligence (pp. 411–420). San Francisco, CA: Morgan Kaufmann Publishers Inc.; Retrieved from http://dl.acm.org/citation.cfm?id=2074022.2074073

Pelinescu, E. (2015). The impact of human capital on economic growth. *Procedia Economics and Finance*, *22*, 184–190. doi:10.1016/S2212-5671(15)00258-0

Peng, M. W., Sun, S. L., & Markóczy, L. (2015). Human capital and CEO compensation during institutional transitions. *Journal of Management Studies*, *52*(1), 117–147. doi:10.1111/joms.12106

Perera, L. C. R., & Chaminda, J. W. D. (2013). Corporate social responsibility and product evaluation: The moderating role of brand familiarity. *Corporate Social Responsibility and Environmental Management*, *20*(4), 245–256. doi:10.1002/csr.1297

Perera-Tallo, F. (2005). Missing markets for human capital and differences in growth. *Economica*, *72*(286), 241–265. doi:10.1111/j.0013-0427.2005.00413.x

Perna, L. W., Orosz, K., & Jumakulov, Z. (2015). Understanding the human capital benefits of a government-funded international scholarship program: An exploration of Kazakhstan's Bolashak program. *International Journal of Educational Development*, *40*, 85–97. doi:10.1016/j.ijedudev.2014.12.003

Pestonjee (1999). *Stress and Coping the Indian Experience*; Sage Publications, New Delhi.

Pestonjee, D. M. (1973). *Organization Structure and Job Attitudes*. Calcutta: The Minnerva Association.

Pestonjee, D. M. (1987). Executive Stress: Should it always be avoided? *Vikalpa*, *12*(1), 23–30.

Petter, S., Straub, D., & Rai, A. (2007). Specifying Formative Constructs in Information Systems Research. *Management Information Systems Quarterly*, *31*(4), 623–656. Retrieved from http://www.jstor.org/stable/25148814

Pharm, A., & Sritharan, R. (2013). Challenges for Rural Women Entrepreneurs: Problems Being faced by Women Entrepreneurs in Rural Areas. *International Journal of Engineering Science*, *2*(3). Retrieved from http://www.theijes.com/papers/v2-i3/I023052055.pdf

Piegorsch, K. M., Watkins, K. W., Piegorsch, W. W., Reininger, B., Corwin, S. J., & Valois, R. F. (2006). Ergonomic decision-making: A conceptual framework for experienced practitioners from backgrounds in industrial engineering and physical therapy. *Applied Ergonomics*, *37*(5), 587–598. doi:10.1016/j.apergo.2005.11.002 PMID:16386700

Pinto, H., Cruz, A. R., & Combe, C. (2015). Cooperation and the emergence of maritime clusters in the Atlantic: Analysis and implications of innovation and human capital for blue growth. *Marine Policy*, *57*, 167–177. doi:10.1016/j.marpol.2015.03.029

Pitcher, P., & Smith, A. D. (2001). Top management team heterogeneity: Personality, power, and proxies. *Organization Science*, *12*(1), 1–18. doi:10.1287/orsc.12.1.1.10120

Ployhart, R. E. (2006). Staffing in the 21st Century: New Challengesand Strategic Opportunities. *Journal of Management*, *32*(6), 868–897. doi:10.1177/0149206306293625

Ployhart, R. E., Schneider, B., & Schmitt, N. (2006). *Staffing organizations: Contemporary practice and theory* (3rd ed.). Mahwah, NJ: Lawrence Erlbaum.

Polo, M. (1995). Internal cohesion and competition among criminal organizations. In G. Fiorentini & S. Peltzman (Eds.), *The economics of Organised Crime*. New York: Cambridge University Press.

Poplawska, J., Labib, A., Reed, D. M., & Ishizaka, A. (2015). Stakeholder profile definition and salience measurement with fuzzy logic and visual analytics applied to corporate social responsibility case study. *Journal of Cleaner Production*, *105*, 103–115. doi:10.1016/j.jclepro.2014.10.095

Porter, M. E. (1996). What is strategy? *Harvard Business Review*, *74*, 61–78. PMID:10158474

Porter, M.E. (1980). *Competitive Strategy: Techniques for Analysing Industries and Competitors*. NY: The Free Press.

Porter, M.E. (1981). The contributions of industrial organization to strategic management. *Academy of Management Review*, *6*(4), 609–620.

Posthuma, R. A., Morgeson, F. P., & Campion, M. A. (2002). Beyond employment interview validity: A comprehensive narrative review of recent research and trends over time. *Personnel Psychology*, *55*(1), 1–81. doi:10.1111/j.1744-6570.2002.tb00103.x

Postonjee, D.M., & Singh, G.P. (1987). *Organizational behaviour issues for managers and systems analysis*. Indian institute of Managements, Ahmadabad.

Preziosi, R. C. (1980). Organisational Diagnosis Questionnaire (ODQ). In University Associates (Ed.), The 1980 annual handbook for group facilitators (pp. 112–120). Academic Press.

Prior, T., Giurco, D., Mudd, G., Mason, L., & Behrisch, J. (2012). Resource depletion, peak minerals and the implications for sustainable resource management. *Global Environmental Change*, *22*(3), 577–587. doi:10.1016/j.gloenvcha.2011.08.009

Proper, K. I., Koppes, L. J., Meijer, S., & Bemelmans, J. E. (2013). The Association Between Body Mass Index Status and Sick Leave and the Role of Emotional Exhaustion—A Mediation Analysis Among a Representative Sample of Dutch Employees. *Journal of Occupational and Environmental Medicine*, *55*(10), 1213–1218. doi:10.1097/JOM.0b013e31829f2f5c PMID:24064779

Proper, K. I., Koppes, L. J., Van Zwieten, M. J., & Bemelmans, W. E. (2012). The prevalence of chronic psychological complaints and emotional exhaustion among overweight and obese workers. *International Archives of Occupational and Environmental Health*, *85*(5), 537–545. doi:10.1007/s00420-011-0703-y PMID:21947369

Psacharopoulos, G., & Patrinos, H. A. (2004). Returns to investment in education: A further update. *Education Economics*, *12*(2), 111–134. doi:10.1080/0964529042000239140

Pulakos, E. D. (2005). *Selection Assessment Methods: a guide to implementing formal assessments to build high-quality workforce*. SHRM Foundation.

Raffo, E., Ráez, L., & Cachay, O. (2013). Riesgos psicosociales. *Revista de la Facultad de Ingenieria Industrial*, *16*(2), 70–79.

Raheem, . (2011). *Women Empowerment through Self-help Groups (SHGs)*. New Delhi: New Century Publications.

Ramasamy, B., Yeung, M. C. H., & Au, A. K. M. (2010). Consumer support for corporate social responsibility (CSR): The role of religion and values. *Journal of Business Ethics*, *91*(1), 61–72. doi:10.1007/s10551-010-0568-0

Ramlall, S. (2003). Organizational Application Managing Employee Retention as a Strategy for Increasing Organizational Competitiveness. *Applied H.R.M. Research*, *8*(2), 63–72.

Rauch, A., Frese, M., & Utsch, A. (2005). Effects of human capital and long-term human resources development and utilization on employment growth of small-scale businesses: A causal analysis. *Entrepreneurship Theory and Practice*, *29*(6), 681–698.

Rauch, A., & Rijsdijk, S. A. (2013). The effects of general and specific human capital on long-term growth and failure of newly founded businesses. *Entrepreneurship Theory and Practice*, *37*(4), 923–941. doi:10.1111/j.1540-6520.2011.00487.x

Raymark, M. J., Schmit, M. J., & Guion, R. M. (1997). Identifying potentially useful personality constructs for employee selection. *Personnel Psychology*, *50*(3), 723–736. doi:10.1111/j.1744-6570.1997.tb00712.x

Realyvásquez, A., Maldonado-Macías, A., García-Alcaraz, J., Cortés-Robles, G., & Blanco-Fernández, J. (2016). Structural Model for the Effects of Environmental Elements on the Psychological Characteristics and Performance of the Employees of Manufacturing Systems. *International Journal of Environmental Research and Public Health*, *13*(1), 1–21. doi:10.3390/ijerph13010104 PMID:26742054

Ree, M. J., Earles, J. A., & Teachout, M. S. (1994). Predicting job performance: Not much more than g. *The Journal of Applied Psychology*, *79*(4), 518–524. doi:10.1037/0021-9010.79.4.518

Reserve bank of India website. (2016). Retrieved May 04, 2016, from https://www.rbi.org.in/scripts/FAQView.aspx?Id=65

Resnick, H. (1994). Future of electronic technology in human service practice and education. Special topic: Electronic tools for social work practice and education: II. *Computers in Human Services*, *11*, 379–384.

Reuter, P. (1987). *Racketeering in Legitimate Industries: A Study in the Economics of Intimidation*. California: RAND.

Rey-Martí, A., Ribeiro-Soriano, D., & Palacios-Marqués, D. (2016). Entrepreneurial attributes of human capital and contingency factors in the culinary tourism. *The International Entrepreneurship and Management Journal*, *12*(1), 67–85. doi:10.1007/s11365-015-0375-2

Ringov, D., & Zollo, M. (2007). Corporate responsibility from a socio-institutional perspective. The impact of national culture on corporate social performance. *Corporate Governance*, *7*(4), 476–485. doi:10.1108/14720700710820551

Ring, P.S., & Van de Ven, A.H. (1992). Structuring Cooperative Relationships between Organizations. *Strategic Management Journal*, *13*(10).

Rivera Moya, Y., & Briseño Escobedo, J. (2013). El estrés en las organizaciones. *Contribiciones a la Economía*. Retrieved from www.eumed.net/ce/2013/estres-organizaciones.html

Robert, P. (1993). *The Prosperous Community: Social Capital and Public Life – The American Prospect*. Retrieved from http://prospect.org/article/prosperous-community-social-capital-and-public-life

Robert, P. (2008). *Skills and Productivity in the Informal Sector. International labour Office, Skills and employability Dept.* ILO Geneva. Employment Working Paper No. 5. Retrieved from http://www.ilo.org/wcmsp5/groups/public/---ed_emp/---ifp_skills/documents/publication/wcms_103983.pdf

Robson, P. J. A., Akuetteh, C. K., Westhead, P., & Wright, M. (2012). Innovative opportunity pursuit, human capital and business ownership experience in an emerging region: Evidence from Ghana. *Small Business Economics*, *39*(3), 603–625. doi:10.1007/s11187-011-9333-8

Rodgers, S. H. (2005). Muscle Fatigue Assessment: Functional Job Analysis Technique. In N. Stanton, A. Hedge, K. Brookhuis, E. Salas, & H. Hendrick (Eds.), *Handbook of Human Factors and Ergonomics Methods* (pp. 12–1–12–10). CRC Press.

Rokeach, M. (1973). *The nature of human values*. New York, NY: The Free Press.

Ross, A. (1992). Personality psychology (theories and processes) (trans. Siavashjamalfar). Besat publication institute.

Ross, A. (2002). A multi-dimensional empirical exploration of technology investment, coordination and firm performance. *International Journal of Physical Distribution & Logistics Management*, *32*(7), 591–609. doi:10.1108/09600030210442603

Ross, E. (1993). Preventing Burnout Among Social Workers Employed in the Field of AIDS/HIV. *Social Work in Health Care*, *18*(2), 91–108. doi:10.1300/J010v18n02_06 PMID:8332942

Royal, C., & O'Donnell, L. (2005). Embedding human capital analysis in the investment process: A human resources challenge. *Asia Pacific Journal of Human Resources*, *43*(1), 117–136. doi:10.1177/1038411105050308

Rubio, J. C. (2003). *Fuentes de estrés, Síndrome de Burnout y Actitudes disfuncionales en Orientadores de Instituto de Enseñanza Secundaria*. Universidad de la Extremadura, Badajoz.

Ruf, B. M., Muralidhar, K., Janney, J. J., & Paul, K. (2001). An empirical investigation of the relationship between change in corporate social performance and financial performance: A stakeholder theory perspective. *Journal of Business Ethics*, *32*(2), 143–156. doi:10.1023/A:1010786912118

Rumelt, R.P. (1974). *Strategy, structure and economic performance*. Boston: Harvard University Press.

Sabrina, Q. (2007). *How Empowering is Microcredit: A Look at Grameen Bank*. Sixth Congress of the U.S. Basic Income Guarantee Network. Retrieved from www.usbig.net/papers/173-Quaraishi-GrameenBank.doc

Sackett, P. R., & Wanek, J. E. (1996). New developments in the use of measures of honesty, integrity, conscientiousness, dependability, trustworthiness, and reliability for personnel selection. *Personnel Psychology*, *49*(4), 787–829. doi:10.1111/j.1744-6570.1996.tb02450.x

Saha & Banerjee. (2001) Women partners in development.Employment News, 25(49).

Saini, D. S. (2006, September). *Book review: Blue ocean strategy: how to create uncontested market space and make competition irrelevant*. Academic Press.

Salas, E., Cooke, N. J., & Rosen, M. A. (2008). On Teams, Teamwork, and Team Performance: Discoveries and Developments. *Human Factors: The Journal of the Human Factors and Ergonomics Society*, *50*(3), 540–547. doi:10.1518/001872008X288457 PMID:18689065

Salgado, J. F. (1999). Personnel selection methods. In C. L. Cooper & I. Robertson (Eds.), *International Review of Industrial and Organizational Psychology* (pp. 1–54). London, UK: Wiley.

Salgado, P. M., & Mejía, R. S. (2008). Estrés en ejecutivos de medianas y grandes empresas mexicanas: Un enfoque de desarrollo humano organizacional. *Estudios Gerenciales*, *24*(108), 15–36. doi:10.1016/S0123-5923(08)70042-1

Salmon, P., Stanton, N., Walker, G., & Green, D. (2006). Cognitive Task Analysis. In W. Karwowski (Ed.), *International Encyclopedia of Ergonomics and Human factors* (pp. 3044–3048). Taylor & Francis.

Samkin, G. (2012). Changes in sustainability reporting by an African defence contractor: A longitudinal analysis. *Meditari Accountancy Research*, *20*(2), 134–166. doi:10.1108/10222521211277834

Santarelli, E., & Tran, H. T. (2013). The interplay of human and social capital in shaping entrepreneurial performance: The case of Vietnam. *Small Business Economics*, *40*(2), 435–458. doi:10.1007/s11187-012-9427-y

Santos-Rodrigues, H., Dorrego, P. F., & Jardon, C. F. (2010). The influence of human capital on the innovativeness of firms. *International Business and Economics Research Journal*, *9*(9), 53–63.

Sardinha, I. D., Craveiro, D., & Milheiras, S. (2013). A sustainability framework for redevelopment of rural brownfields: Stakeholder participation at Sáo Domingos Mine, Portugal. *Journal of Cleaner Production*, *57*(1), 200–208. doi:10.1016/j.jclepro.2013.05.042

Saridakis, G., Mole, K., & Storey, D. J. (2008). New small firm survival in England. *Empirica*, *35*(1), 25–39. doi:10.1007/s10663-007-9049-9

Sasi, A. (2015). *Smartphone usage drives up mobile banking numbers*. Retrieved May 04, 2016, from http://www.financialexpress.com/article/economy/smartphone-usage-drives-up-mobile-banking-numbers/31666/

Scheer, A.-W., & Nüttgens, M. (2000). ARIS Architecture and Reference Models for Business Process Management. In W. van der Aalst, J. Desel, & A. Oberweis (Eds.), *Business Process Management* (Vol. 1806, pp. 376–389). Berlin: Springer Berlin Heidelberg; doi:10.1007/3-540-45594-9_24

Schein, E. H. (2006). Organizational Culture and Leadership (3rd ed.). John Wiley & Sons, Inc. Retrieved from https://books.google.com/books?hl=es&lr=&id=xhmezDokfnYC&pgis=1

Schein, E. H. (2010). Organizational culture and leadership (4th ed.). San Francisco, CA: John Wiley & Sons, Inc. Retrieved from https://books.google.com.mx/books?id=DlGhlT34jCUC

Schelling, T.C. (1971). What is the business of organized crime? *The American Scholar*, 40(4), 643–652.

Scherer, A. G., & Palazzo, G. (2011). The new political role of business in a globalized world: A review of a new perspective on CSR and its implications for the firm, governance, and democracy. *Journal of Management Studies*, *48*(4), 899–931. doi:10.1111/j.1467-6486.2010.00950.x

Scherer, F.M. (1980). *Industrial Market Structure and Economic Performance*. Chicago: Rand McNally.

Schlitte, F. (2012). Local human capital, segregation by skill, and skill-specific employment growth. *Papers in Regional Science*, *91*(1), 85–106. doi:10.1111/j.1435-5957.2011.00373.x

Schmidt, F. L., & Hunter, J. (2004). General mental ability in the world of work: Occupational attainment and job performance. *Journal of Personality and Social Psychology*, *86*(1), 162–173. doi:10.1037/0022-3514.86.1.162 PMID:14717634

Schneider, L., Günther, J., & Brandenburg, B. (2010). Innovation and skills from a sectoral perspective: A linked employer-employee analysis. *Economics of Innovation and New Technology*, *19*(2), 185–202. doi:10.1080/10438590902872887

Schuler, H. (2001). *International Encyclopedia of the Social & Behavioral Sciences*. Oxford: Pergamon Press.

Schuler, H., Farr, J. L., & Smith, M. (Eds.). (1993). *Personnel Selection and Assessment: Individual and Organizational Perspectives*. Hillsdale, NJ: Erlbaum.

Schulz, E., Chowdhury, S., & van de Voort, D. (2013). Firm productivity moderated link between human capital and compensation: The significance of task-specific human capital. *Human Resource Management*, *52*(3), 423–439. doi:10.1002/hrm.21537

Schwartz, J. (2004, Septiembre 5). Always on the job: Employees pay with health. *The New York Times*.

Schwartz, S. H. (1992). In M. Zanna (Ed.), *Universal in the content and structure of values: Theoretical advances and empirical tests in 20 countries* (pp. 1–65). Advances in experimental social psychologyNew York, NY: Academic Press.

Schwartz, S. H., & Bilsky, W. (1987). Toward a universal psychological structure of human values. *Journal of Personality and Social Psychology*, *53*(3), 550–562. doi:10.1037/0022-3514.53.3.550

Scicchitano, S. (2010). Complementarity between heterogeneous human capital and R&D: Can job-training avoid low development traps? *Empirica*, *37*(4), 361–380. doi:10.1007/s10663-009-9113-8

Secretaría-de-Salud. (2010). *Acuerdo Nacional para la Salud Alimenentaria.* Retrieved from http://www.sep.gob.mx/work/models/sep1/Resource/635/1/images/programadeaccion_sept.pdf

Seghers, A., Manigart, S., & Vanacker, T. (2012). The impact of human and social capital on entrepreneur's knowledge of finance alternatives. *Journal of Small Business Management*, *50*(1), 63–86. doi:10.1111/j.1540-627X.2011.00344.x

Serrano, M., & Salvador, A. (2015). *Psicobiología del Estrés.* Madrid: Pearson Educación.

Serrano, M., Alacreu-Crespo, A., Costa, R., Abad, D., & González-Bono, E. (2015). *Variables Psicobiológicas.* Madrid: Pearson Educación.

Serrano, M., Salvador, A., & Costa, R. (2015). Concepto de estrés. In M. Serrano & A. Salvador (Eds.), Psicobiología del estrés. Madrid: Pearson Educación.

Servaes, H., & Tamayo, A. (2013). The impact of corporate social responsibility on firm value: The role of customer awareness. *Management Science*, *59*(5), 1045–1061. doi:10.1287/mnsc.1120.1630

Setó-Pamies, D. (2015). The relationship between women directors and corporate social responsibility. *Corporate Social Responsibility and Environmental Management*, *22*(6), 334–345. doi:10.1002/csr.1349

Shah & Saurabh. (2015). Women Entrepreneurs in Developing Nations: Growth and Replication Strategies and Their Impact on Poverty Alleviation. *Technology Innovation Management Review*. Retrieved from http://timreview.ca/sites/default/files/article_PDF/ShahSaurabh_TIMReview_August2015.pdf

Shao, S., & Yang, L. (2014). Natural resource dependence, human capital accumulation, and economic growth: A combined explanation for the resource curse and the resource blessing. *Energy Policy*, *74*, 632–642. doi:10.1016/j.enpol.2014.07.007

Sharad, R. (2015, July 3). India is now a $2-trillion economy. *The Hindu*. Retrieved October 13, 2015, from http://www.thehindu.com/business/Economy/india-is-now-a-2trillion-economy-says-world-bank-data/article7380442.ece

Sharma, B., & Fisher, T. (1997). Functional strategies and competitiveness: An empirical analysis using data from Australian manufacturing. *Benchmarking for Quality Management & Technology*, *4*(4), 286–294. doi:10.1108/14635779710195122

Sherief. (1994). Entrepreneurship as an economic force in rural development. *Africa Economic Analysis*. Retrieved from http://www.africaeconomicanalysis.org/articles/gen/rural_entrepreneurship.html

Shirom, A. (2003). Job-related burnout. In Q. J. C & L. E. Tetrick (Eds.), Handbook of occupational health psychology (pp. 245–265). Washington, DC: American Psychological Association.

Shivambhare, M. (2010). *Empowering Men and Women through self-Help Group (SHG).* Jaipur: RBSA Publishers.

Shweta, D. (2013, May 17). MBAs for India's Rural Women. India Real Time. *The Wall Street Journal.* Retrieved from http://blogs.wsj.com/indiarealtime/2013/05/17/mbas-for-indias-rural-women/

Siegel, A. W., & Schraagen, J. M. C. (2014). Measuring Workload Weak Resilience Signals at a Rail Control Post. *IIE Transactions on Occupational Ergonomics and Human Factors*, *2*(3-4), 179–193. doi:10.1080/21577323.2014.958632

Siegel, A., & Schraagen, J. (2014). A Method to Reveal Workload Weak-Resilience-Signals at a Rail Control Post. In D. Harris (Ed.), *Engineering Psychology and Cognitive Ergonomics SE - 9* (Vol. 8532, pp. 82–93). Springer International Publishing; doi:10.1007/978-3-319-07515-0_9

Sierra-García, L., Zorio-Grima, A., & García-Benau, M. A. (2015). Stakeholder engagement, corporate social responsibility and integrated reporting: An exploratory study. *Corporate Social Responsibility and Environmental Management*, *22*(5), 286–304. doi:10.1002/csr.1345

Silos, P., & Smith, E. (2015). Human capital portfolios. *Review of Economic Dynamics*, *18*(3), 635–652. doi:10.1016/j.red.2014.09.001

Sirikrai, S. B., & Tang, J. C. S. (2006). Industrial competitiveness analysis: Using the analytic hierarchy process. *The Journal of High Technology Management Research*, *17*(1), 71–83. doi:10.1016/j.hitech.2006.05.005

Skaperdas, S. (2001). The political economy of organized crime: Providing protection when the state does not. *Economics of Governance*, *2*(3), 173–202. doi:10.1007/PL00011026

Skaperdas, S., & Syropoulos, C. (1995). Gangs as primitive states. In G. Fiorentini & S. Peltzman (Eds.), *The economics of Organised Crime*. New York: Cambridge University Press.

Skouloudis, A., Evangelinos, K., & Malesios, C. (2015). Priorities and perceptions for corporate social responsibility: An NGO perspective. *Corporate Social Responsibility and Environmental Management*, *22*(2), 95–112. doi:10.1002/csr.1332

Slaughter, S. A., Ang, S., & Boh, W. F. (2007). Firm-specific human capital and compensation organizational tenure profiles: An archival analysis of salary data for it. *Human Resource Management*, *46*(3), 373–394. doi:10.1002/hrm.20169

Smith. (1776). *An Inquiry into the Nature and Causes of the Wealth of Nations.* Retrieved from http://www.ifaarchive.com/pdf/smith_-_an_inquiry_into_the_nature_and_causes_of_the_wealth_of_nations%5B1%5D.pdf

Snook, S. H., & Ciriello, V. M. (1991). The design of manual handling tasks: Revised tables of maximum acceptable weights and forces. *Ergonomics*, *34*(9), 1197–1213. doi:10.1080/00140139108964855 PMID:1743178

Soboleva, I. (2010). Paradoxes of the measurement of human capital. *Problems of Economic Transition*, *52*(11), 43–70. doi:10.2753/PET1061-1991521103

Solow, . (1956). A Contribution to the Theory of Economic Growth. *The Quarterly Journal of Economics*, *70*(1), 65. Retrieved from http://faculty.smu.edu/tosang/pdf/Solow_1956.pdf doi:10.2307/1884513

Soltanpanah, H., & Karimi, M. (2011). Accumulation of human capital and FDI inflows in ASEAN-3 countries (Malaysia, Thailand, Indonesia). *African Journal of Business Management*, *7*(17), 1599–1605. doi:10.5897/AJBM11.1681

Sonne, M., Villalta, D. L., & Andrews, D. M. (2012). Development and evaluation of an office ergonomic risk checklist: ROSArapid office strain assessment. *Applied Ergonomics*, *43*(1), 98–108. doi:10.1016/j.apergo.2011.03.008 PMID:21529772

Sperry, R., & Jetter, A. J. (2012). *Fuzzy cognitive maps to implement corporate social responsibility in product planning: A novel approach*. Paper presented at the 2012 Technology Management for Emerging Technologies (PICMET 2012), Vancouver, Canada.

Stagner, R. (1957). Some problems in contemporary industrial psychology. *Bulletin of the Menninger Clinic*, *21*, 238–247. PMID:13472270

Stanton, N. (2006). Hierarchical task analysis: Developments, applications, and extensions. *Applied Ergonomics*, *37*(1), 55–79. Doi:10.1016/j.apergo.2005.06.003

Stanton, N. A., Ashleigh, M., & Cale, T. (2006). Design Issues: Action Research in Control Operations. In W. Karwowski (Ed.), International Encyclopedia of Ergonomics and Human factors (2nd ed., pp. 1403–1405). Taylor & Francis.

Stark, O., Hyll, W., & Wang, Y. (2012). Endogenous selection of comparison groups, human capital formation, and tax policy. *Economica*, *79*(313), 62–75. doi:10.1111/j.1468-0335.2010.00876.x

Stark, O., & Wang, Y. (2005). The intergenerational overlap and human capital formation. *Review of International Economics*, *13*(1), 45–58. doi:10.1111/j.1467-9396.2005.00491.x

Steven Moore, J., & Garg, A. (1995). The strain index: A proposed method to analyze jobs for risk of distal upper extremity disorders. *American Industrial Hygiene Association*, *56*(5), 443–458. doi:10.1080/15428119591016863 PMID:7754975

Stevens, A. H. (1997). Persistent effects of job displacement: The importance of multiple job losses. *Journal of Labor Economics*, *15*(1), 165–188. doi:10.1086/209851

Stigler, G. J. (1971). The Theory of Economic Regulation. *The Bell Journal of Economics and Management Science*, 2(1), 3-21.

Stokes, G. S. (1999). Introduction to special issue: The next one hundred years of biodata. *Human Resource Management Review*, *9*(2), 111–116. doi:10.1016/S1053-4822(99)00014-5

Storper, M., & Scott, A. J. (2009). Rethinking human capital, creativity and urban growth. *Journal of Economic Geography*, *9*(2), 147–167. doi:10.1093/jeg/lbn052

Story, J., & Neves, P. (2015). When corporate social responsibility (CSR) increases performance: Exploring the role of intrinsic and extrinsic CSR attribution. *Business Ethics (Oxford, England)*, *24*(2), 111–124. doi:10.1111/beer.12084

Streefkerk, J. W., Van Esch-Bussemakers, M. P., & Neerincx, M. A. (2006). Designing personal attentive user interfaces in the mobile public safety domain. *Computers in Human Behavior*, *22*(4), 749–770. doi:10.1016/j.chb.2005.12.006

Strulik, H. (2005). The role of human capital and population growth in R&D-based models of economic growth. *Review of International Economics*, *13*(1), 129–145. doi:10.1111/j.1467-9396.2005.00495.x

Suhonen, M., & Paasivaara, L. (2011). Shared human capital in project management: A systematic review of the literature. *Project Management Journal*, *42*(2), 4–16. doi:10.1002/pmj.20211

Sun, L., & Stuebs, M. (2013). Corporate social responsibility and firm productivity: Evidence from the chemical industry in the United States. *Journal of Business Ethics*, *118*(2), 251–263. doi:10.1007/s10551-012-1579-9

Susniene, D., & Purvinis, O. (2013). Empirical insights on understanding stakeholder influence. *Journal of Business Economics and Management*, *16*(4), 1–15.

Swain, S. (2016). *An Indian Fintech Entrepreneur's Views on UPI*. Retrieved May 5, 2016, from http://tech.economictimes.indiatimes.com/catalysts/an-indian-fintech-entrepreneur-s-views-on-upi/1455

Swanson, D. L. (1995). Addressing a theoretical problem by reorienting the corporate social performance model. *Academy of Management Review*, *20*(1), 43–64.

Tabassi, A. A., Ramli, M., & Bakar, A. H. A. (2012). Effects of training and motivation practices on teamwork improvement and task efficiency: The case of construction firms. *International Journal of Project Management*, *30*(2), 213–224. doi:10.1016/j.ijproman.2011.05.009

Taft, R. (1948). Use of the group situation observation method in the selection of trainee executives. *The Journal of Applied Psychology*, *32*(6), 587–594. doi:10.1037/h0061967

Tagesson, T., Blank, V., Broberg, P., & Collin, S. O. (2009). What explains the extent and content of social and environmental disclosures on corporate websites: A study of social and environmental reporting in Swedish listed corporations. *Corporate Social Responsibility and Environmental Management*, *16*(6), 352–364. doi:10.1002/csr.194

Tan, H. W., & Geeta, B. (1996). *Enterprise Training in Developing Countries: Overview of Incidence, Determinants and Productivity Outcomes*. The World Bank Private Sector Development Department. Occasional Paper 9. Retrieved from http://www.oecd.org/dev/2731650.pdf

Teixeira, A. A. C., & Tavares-Lehmann, A. T. (2014). Human capital intensity in technology-based firms located in Portugal: Does foreign ownership matter? *Research Policy*, *43*(4), 737–748. doi:10.1016/j.respol.2014.01.001

Tett, R. P., Jackson, D. N., & Rothstein, M. (1991). Personality measures as predictors of job performance: A meta-analytic review. *Personnel Psychology*, *44*(4), 703–742. doi:10.1111/j.1744-6570.1991.tb00696.x

Thangavelu, S. M., & Narjoko, D. (2014). Human capital, FTAs and foreign direct investment flows into ASEAN. *Journal of Asian Economics*, *35*, 65–76. doi:10.1016/j.asieco.2014.11.002

Theodore, S. (1961). Investment in Human Capital. *The American Economic Review*, *51*(1). Retrieved from http://www.ssc.wisc.edu/~walker/wp/wp-content/uploads/2012/04/schultz61.pdf

The-World-Health-Organization. (2015). *Obesidad y sobrepeso*. Retrieved from http://www.who.int/mediacentre/factsheets/fs311/es/

Thornton, G. C. III. (1992). *Assessment centers in human resources management*. Addison-Wesley.

Thornton, G. C. III, & Byham, W. C. (1982). *Assessment centers and managerial performance*. New York: Academic Press.

Thornton, G. C. III, & Gibbons, A. M. (2009). Validity of assessment centers for personnel selection. *Human Resource Management Review*, *19*(3), 169–187. doi:10.1016/j.hrmr.2009.02.002

Tian, J., Haleblian, J., & Rajagopalan, N. (2011). The effects of board human and social capital on investor reactions to new CEO selection. *Strategic Management Journal*, *32*(7), 731–747. doi:10.1002/smj.909

Tikkanen, J., & Halinen, A. (2003). Network approach to strategic management: Exploration to the emerging perspective. *Proceedings of the 19th IMP International Conference*, Lugano, Switzerland.

Toet, A. (2005). Integrated design of intelligent surveillance systems and their user interface. In *Proceedings of the 2005 International Conference on Artificial Intelligence IC-AI'05* (Vol. 1, pp. 17–23). Retrieved from http://h3b1jq.bay.livefilestore.com/y1pIgG86fKS56YPhVoAK_ROut-WU5Co0j2wx5YfYCTcsyj_LYfXFJr_lCeidb6243F1e10elmFrgqL3Oj7fPF030Kw/Toet2005b.pdf?download\n:\Library\Toet\Toet2005b.pdf

Tohidi, H., & Tarokh, M. J. (2006). Productivity outcomes of teamwork as an effect of information technology and team size. *International Journal of Production Economics*, *103*(2), 610–615. doi:10.1016/j.ijpe.2005.12.002

Toner, P. (2011). Workforce skills and innovation: An overview of major themes in the literature. Paris, France: OECD Directorate for Science, Technology and Industry (STI), Centre for Educational Research and Innovation (CERI).

Torres, S. J., & Nowson, C. A. (2007). Relationship between stress, eating behavior, and obesity. *Nutrition (Burbank, Los Angeles County, Calif.)*, *23*(11-12), 887–894. doi:10.1016/j.nut.2007.08.008 PMID:17869482

Tracey, M., Vonderembse, M. A., & Lim, J.-S. (1999). Manufacturing technology and strategy formulation: Keys to enhancing competitiveness and improving performance. *Journal of Operations Management*, *17*(4), 411–428. doi:10.1016/S0272-6963(98)00045-X

Trendafilova, S., Babiak, K., & Heinze, K. (2013). Corporate social responsibility and environmental sustainability: Why professional sport is greening the playing field. *Sport Management Review*, *16*(3), 298–313. doi:10.1016/j.smr.2012.12.006

Trinkoff, A. M., Le, R., Geiger-Brown, J., & Lipscomb, J. (2007). Work Schedule, Needle Use, and Needlestick Injuries Among Registered Nurses. *Infection Control and Hospital Epidemiology*, *28*(2), 156–164. doi:10.1086/510785 PMID:17265396

Tripathi. (2014). Women Entrepreneurship in Rural India and Sustainable Economic Development. *New Man International Journal of Multidisciplinary Studies*, *1*(12). Retrieved from http://www.newmanpublication.com/admin/issue/br/Untitled4.pdf

Ucbasaran, D., Westhead, P., & Wright, M. (2008). Opportunity identification and pursuit: Does an entrepreneur's human capital matter? *Small Business Economics*, *30*(2), 153–173. doi:10.1007/s11187-006-9020-3

UK Centre for the Measurement of Economic Activity. (2008). *Proposals for a Satellite Account on Human Capital Resource formation*. Retrieved October 10, 2015, from http://www.google.co.in/url?url=http://www.ons.gov.uk/ons/guide-method/ukcemga/ukcemga-publications/publications/archive/proposals-for-a-satellite-account-on-human-capital-resource-formation

UN Publication. (2007). *Economic and Social Survey of Asia and the Pacific 2007: Surging ahead in Uncertain Times*. UN.

UNDP. (1997). *Human Development Report*. New Delhi: Oxford University Press.

University of Michigan. (2012). 3DSSPP. Retrieved from http://c4e.engin.umich.edu/tools-services/3dsspp-software/

Van Bogaert, P., Clarke, S., Roelant, E., Meulemans, H., & Van de Heyning, P. (2010). Impacts of unit-level nurse practice environment and burnout on nurse-reported outcomes: A multilevel modelling approach. *Journal of Clinical Nursing*, *19*(11-12), 1664–1674. doi:10.1111/j.1365-2702.2009.03128.x PMID:20579204

Varese, F. (2011). *Mafias on the move: How organized crime conquers new territories*. Princeton University Press. doi:10.1515/9781400836727

Venkatraman, N., & Subramaniam, M. (2002). Theorizing the Future of Strategy: Questions for Shaping Strategy Research in the Knowledge Economy. In A. Pettigrew, H. Thomas, & R. Whittington (Eds.), *Handbook of Strategy and Management*. London: Sage Publications.

Verčič, A. T., Verčič, D., & Sriramesh, K. (2012). Internal communication: Definition, parameters, and the future. *Public Relations Review*, *38*(2), 223–230. doi:10.1016/j.pubrev.2011.12.019

Vindelyn, A. S., & Omar, M. (2005). FDI, international business and regulation: The behavior of UK multinational corporations. *European Business Review*, *17*(1), 69–82. doi:10.1108/09555340510576276

Viveros, H. (2016). Examining stakeholders perceptions of mining impacts and corporate social responsibility. *Corporate Social Responsibility and Environmental Management*, *23*(1), 50–64. doi:10.1002/csr.1363

Vogel, J. (2015). The two faces of R&D and human capital: Evidence from Western European regions. *Papers in Regional Science*, *94*(3), 525–551. doi:10.1111/pirs.12084

Vomberg, A., Homburg, C., & Bornemann, T. (2015). Talented people and strong brands: The contribution of human capital and brand equity to firm value. *Strategic Management Journal*, *36*(13), 2122–2131. doi:10.1002/smj.2328

Wagschal, P. H. (1994). Hey Bucky, can you spare a paradigm? reflections on synergistic education. *NASSP Bulletin*, *78*(560), 51–61. doi:10.1177/019263659407856008

Wahba, H. (2008). Exploring the moderating effect of financial performance on the relationship between corporate environmental responsibility and institutional investors: Some Egyptian evidence. *Corporate Social Responsibility and Environmental Management*, *15*(6), 361–371. doi:10.1002/csr.177

Walters, G., & Tacon, R. (2010). Corporate social responsibility in sport: Stakeholder management in the UK football industry. *Journal of Management & Organization*, *16*(4), 566–586. doi:10.1017/S1833367200001942

Wang, H., & Wong, K. F. E. (2012). The effect of managerial bias on employee's specific human capital investments. *Journal of Management Studies*, *49*(8), 1435–1458. doi:10.1111/j.1467-6486.2012.01053.x

Warhurst, A. (2001). Corporate citizenship and corporate social investment: Drivers of tri-sector partnerships. *Journal of Corporate Citizenship*, *1*(1), 57–73. doi:10.9774/GLEAF.4700.2001.sp.00008

Waters, T. R., Putz-Anderson, V., & Garg, A. (1994). *Applications manual for the revised NIOSH lifting equation*. Cincinnati, Ohio.

Webber, S. S. (2011). Dual organizational identification impacting client satisfaction and word of mouth loyalty. *Journal of Business Research*, *64*(2), 119–125. doi:10.1016/j.jbusres.2010.02.005

Weichmann, D., Schmitt, N., & Harvey, V. S. (2001). Incremental validity of situational judgment tests. *The Journal of Applied Psychology*, *86*(3), 410–417. doi:10.1037/0021-9010.86.3.410 PMID:11419801

Weisenfeld, U. (2012). Corporate social responsibility in innovation: Insights from two cases of Syngentas activities in genetically modified organisms. *Creativity and Innovation Management*, *21*(2), 199–211. doi:10.1111/j.1467-8691.2012.00643.x

Welford, R., Chan, C., & Man, M. (2008). Priorities for corporate social responsibility: A survey of businesses and their stakeholders. *Corporate Social Responsibility and Environmental Management*, *15*(1), 52–62. doi:10.1002/csr.166

Whetzel, D. L., & McDaniel, M. A. (2009). Situational judgment tests: An overview of current research. *Human Resource Management Review*, *19*(3), 188–202. doi:10.1016/j.hrmr.2009.03.007

White, R. E. (1986). Generic business strategies, organizational context and performance: An empirical investigation. *Strategic Management Journal*, *7*(3), 217–231. doi:10.1002/smj.4250070304

Wickens, C. D. (2014). Effort in Human Factors Performance and Decision Making. Human Factors. *The Journal of the Human Factors and Ergonomics Society*, *56*(8), 1329–1336. doi:10.1177/0018720814558419 PMID:25509817

Williams, P. (1998). The nature of drug-trafficking networks. *Current History (New York, N.Y.)*, *97*, 154–159.

Wilson, I. (2010). The Biggest Cock: Territoriality, Invulnerability and Honour amongst Jakarta's Gangsters. *Indonesian Studies Working Papers*, *13*, 1–19.

Wilson, J. R., & Carayon, P. (2014). Systems ergonomics: Looking into the future – Editorial for special issue on systems ergonomics/human factors. *Applied Ergonomics*, *45*(1), 3–4. doi:10.1016/j.apergo.2013.08.007 PMID:23684119

Wincent, J., Thorgren, S., & Anokhin, S. (2014). Entrepreneurial orientation and network board diversity in network organizations. *Journal of Business Venturing*, *29*(2), 327–344. doi:10.1016/j.jbusvent.2013.04.002

Wingard, H. C., & Vorster, Q. (2001). Financial performance of environmentally responsible South African listed companies. *Meditari Accountancy Research*, *9*(1), 313–332. doi:10.1108/10222529200100017

Witt, M. A., & Redding, G. (2011). The spirits of corporate social responsibility: Senior executive perceptions of the role of the firm in society in Germany, Hong Kong, Japan, South Korea and the USA. *Socio-economic Review*, *10*(1), 109–134. doi:10.1093/ser/mwr026

Wright, P. M., & McMahan, G. C. (2011). Exploring human capital: Putting "human" back into strategic human resource management. *Human Resource Management Journal*, *21*(2), 93–104. doi:10.1111/j.1748-8583.2010.00165.x

Wu, M., & Shen, C. (2013). Corporate social responsibility in the banking industry: Motives and financial performance. *Journal of Banking & Finance*, *37*(9), 3529–3547. doi:10.1016/j.jbankfin.2013.04.023

Wyatt, A., & Frick, H. (2010). Accounting for investments in human capital: A review. *Australian Accounting Review*, *20*(3), 199–220. doi:10.1111/j.1835-2561.2010.00104.x

Xu, J. J., & Chen, H. (2004). Fighting organized crimes: Using shortest-path algorithms to identify associations in criminal networks. *Decision Support Systems*, *38*(3), 473–487. doi:10.1016/S0167-9236(03)00117-9

Xu, J., & Chen, H. (2005). Criminal network analysis and visualization. *Communications of the ACM*, *48*(6), 100–107. doi:10.1145/1064830.1064834

Yahaya, A., Yahaya, N., Arshad, K., Ismail, J., Jaalam, S., & Zakariya, Z. (2009). Occupational Stress and its Effects towards the Organization Management. *Journal of Social Sciences*, *5*(4), 390-397.

Yamarik, S. (2011). Human capital and state-level economic growth: What is the contribution of schooling? *The Annals of Regional Science*, *47*(1), 195–211. doi:10.1007/s00168-010-0365-9

Yang, L.-R., Huang, C.-F., & Wu, K.-S. (2011). The association among project managers leadership style, teamwork and project success. *International Journal of Project Management*, *29*(3), 258–267. doi:10.1016/j.ijproman.2010.03.006

Yildiz, M. L., & Özcan, E. D. (2014). Organizational Climate as a moderator of the Relationship between Transformational Leadership and Creativity. *International Journal of Business and Management*, *2*(1), 76–87.

Young, S., & Marais, M. (2012). A multi-level perspective of CSR reporting: The implications of national institutions and industry risk characteristics. *Corporate Governance: An International Review*, *20*(5), 432–450. doi:10.1111/j.1467-8683.2012.00926.x

Zalaquett, C. P., Michael T. Turner (1997), Succeeding in the 21st Century: A qualitative analysis. *TCA Journal*, *25*(1), 331 – 340.

Zhang, Y., & Feng, X. (2011). The relationship between job satisfaction, burnout, and turnover intention among physicians from urban state-owned medical institutions in Hubei, China: A cross-sectional study. *BMC Health Services Research*, *11*(1), 235. doi:10.1186/1472-6963-11-235 PMID:21943042

Zhao, G., & Zhang, Z. (2010). Uncovering the relationship between FDI, human capital and technological progress in Chinese high-technology industries. *China & World Economy*, *18*(1), 82–98. doi:10.1111/j.1749-124X.2010.01182.x

Zhu, Q., & Zhang, Q. (2015). Evaluating practices and drivers of corporate social responsibility: The Chinese context. *Journal of Cleaner Production*, *100*, 315–324. doi:10.1016/j.jclepro.2015.03.053

Zlate, S., & Enache, C. (2015). The interdependence between human capital and organizational performance in higher education. *Procedia: Social and Behavioral Sciences*, *180*, 136–143. doi:10.1016/j.sbspro.2015.02.096

About the Contributors

Mohammad Abdolshah received his B.Sc. and M.Sc in Industrial Engineering from Amirkabir University of Technology, Tehran, Iran. Later, he obtained his Ph.D. from University of Putra Malaysia, Malaysia in Industrial Engineering. Dr. Mohammad Abdolshah's current research interests are Industrial Engineering, Quality Engineering, Control Project, and Project Management.

Minakshi Balkawade received her M.com (specialisation in Personnel Management and Industrial Relations, and Banking and Finance) and Bachelor of Education degree from the Savitribai Phule Pune University (formerly University of Pune). Later she cleared the State Eligibility Test (SET) and the National Eligibility Test) NET (UGC). She is currently working as a Lecturer in St. Mira's College for girls, Pune. She has teaching experience of 18 years at the under-graduate and post-graduate level and a visiting faculty for BBA course in the subject - Financial Management. She has to her credit four research papers published in International Journals. Currently she is pursuing her Ph.D at the Savitribai Phule Pune University in Finance.

Julio Blanco-Fernández studied Industrial Engineering and PhD studies in the University of the Basque Country (Spain). Currently he works in the Mechanical Engineering Department (Director of the grade on Mechanical Engineering). He has published more than 150 works (43 JCR works), 51 patents, has participated in more than 35 research projects and has been Director of Chair of Innovation, Technology and Knowledge Management of the La Rioja.

María del Rocío Camacho-Alamilla has a Bachelor Degree in Industrial Engineering. She is currently studying a Master's degree in Industrial Engineering with a concentration in ergonomics and psychosocial factors at the Autonomous University of Ciudad Juárez. Ms. Camacho also participated as speaker in the international congress of ergonomic (SEMAC) in 2014. Recently she has realized a research stay at the University of Valencia.

Vittorio D'Aleo is a Ph.D. Student in "Economics and Management" at Università degli Studi di Messina. After graduation in Political Science, achieved a master - MBA (Master of Business Administration) at Luiss Business School in Rome ,where during the MBA, he participated with success at the " International activities program " in Japan where he deepened studies in Business planning and Asian Public policy at the" Nagoya University of Commerce and Business.

Ankit Dhamija is a person from the technical as well as commerce background. Presently he is working as an Assistant Professor of Information Systems at Amity Business School, Amity University Haryana since Oct'2012. Before that, he has worked with several affiliated institutes of Guru Gobind Singh Indraprastha University, New Delhi and Maharishi Dayanand University, Rohtak. He is a double post graduate in MCA and M.Tech(IT) and a graduate with B.Com (H). Currently he is enrolled as a Ph.D research scholar in Computer Science & Engineering Department at Amity School of Engineering & Technology, Amity University Gurgaon. His areas of interests are Cloud computing security issues, network security and ecommerce payment systems security, Management Information Systems, Ecommerce and Mcommerce and software engineering. During his teaching experience of almost eight years, he has published and presented research papers and articles in various International Journals and national & International conferences of repute. His next immediate goal is to produce a quality research in his chosen research area.

Deepika Dhamija is working as an Assistant Professor at Amity College of Commerce, Amity University Gurgaon. She has more than seven years of teaching experience at both undergraduate and postgraduate level. Her areas of interest are Management Information Systems, e-commerce, Mobile Banking and Software Testing.

Davide Di Fatta is a PhD Student in economics. Research Fields marketing, web marketing, advances in e-marketing, Internet of things, Smart technologies and mobile marketing, Customer participation and value co-creation, Service marketing, Consumer ethnography and netnography, Consumer behaviour Customer relationship management, Social media marketing.

Fateme Eshragh is an MBA Student at Semnan University.

Nahid Farazmand is an MBA Master at Semnan University.

Jorge Luis Garcia-Alcaraz is a full time researcher of the Department of Industrial Engineering at the Autonomous University of Ciudad Juarez. He received a PhD in Industrial Engineering from Ciudad Juarez Technology Institute (Mexico). His research areas are related to Multicriteria decision making applied to manufacturing, production process modeling and statistical inference. He is founding member of the Mexican Society of Operation Research and active member in the Mexican Academy of Industrial Engineering. Currently, Dr. Garcia is a National Researcher recognized by the National Council of Science & Technology of México and have more than 60 papers in journals and more that 100 papers in international conferences.

Juan Luis Hernandez Arellano is a researcher and full-time teacher of the Design Department at the Autonomous University of Ciudad Juarez, Mexico. Dr. Hernandez Arellano obtained his PhD in Science and Engineering at the Universidad Autonoma de Ciudad Juarez. His research interest is about industrial ergonomics, ergonomic product design, statistics applied to research ergonomics, and biomechanics. Dr. Hernandez has published several articles and book chapters in international and prestigious journals.

Kijpokin Kasemsap received his BEng degree in Mechanical Engineering from King Mongkut's University of Technology, Thonburi, his MBA degree from Ramkhamhaeng University, and his DBA degree in Human Resource Management from Suan Sunandha Rajabhat University. He is a Special Lecturer in the Faculty of Management Sciences, Suan Sunandha Rajabhat University, based in Bangkok, Thailand. He is a Member of the International Association of Engineers (IAENG), the International Association of Engineers and Scientists (IAEST), the International Economics Development and Research Center (IEDRC), the International Association of Computer Science and Information Technology (IACSIT), the International Foundation for Research and Development (IFRD), and the International Innovative Scientific and Research Organization (IISRO). He also serves on the International Advisory Committee (IAC) for International Association of Academicians and Researchers (INAAR). He has had numerous original research articles in top international journals, conference proceedings, and books on the topics of business management, human resource management, and knowledge management, published internationally.

Jorge Limón Romero is a professor of industrial engineering in the Faculty of Engineering, Architecture and Design at the Autonomous University of Baja California, Mexico. He is member of the research group Quality and Productivity which has the highest recognition in Mexico and he has published several scientific papers and participated in several research projects. Dr. Limón is also a member of the National System of Researchers of the National Council of Science and Technology in Mexico. His research interests include topics related to Six Sigma Methodology and applied statistics for process improvement.

Aide Aracely Maldonado Macías completed her Bachelor Degree in Industrial Engineering, the MSc in Industrial Engineering by the Technological Institute of Ciudad Juárez and Ph. D. in Sciences in Industrial Engineering by the same Institute. She is currently a full-time Professor-Investigator at the Autonomous University of Ciudad Juárez (UACJ).Her research interests are the evaluation and ergonomic design, anthropometric studies and work-related stress studies, Multicriteria and Multi-attribute decision-making with fuzzy logic and axiomatic design applications, as well as the ergonomic evaluation for the selection of technology of advanced manufacturing (AMT) and Structural Equation Models. She has published in indexed journals in English and Spanish; such as International Journal of Industrial Engineering and International Journal of Advanced Manufacturing Technology, Expert Systems with Applications, Work a Journal of Prevention, Assessment & Rehabilitation, Journal of Accounting and Management, Journal of Educational Research among others. She has also collaborated with book chapters for Springer and IGI Global.

Giacomo Morabito is a PhD student at University of Messina (Italy).

Roberto Musotto is a Ph.D. Student at University of Messina; Research Assistant at University of Palermo; Barrister.

Arturo Realyvásquez has researched on Ergonomics. He has developed expert systems for evaluation of ergonomic compatibility of advanced manufacturing systems. He has published several chapters and papers. Currently he is a Doctorate student, and he is working to find an index to measure macroergonomic compatibility of manufacturing systems.

J. Serratos-Perez is a Chemical Engineer. Ergonomics MSc. PhD in Production Engineering (Occupational Ergonomics). Full Time Professor and Head of Department.

Shashi Singh is a management professional with Human Resource specialization. She has pursued her Ph.D from Uttarakhand Technical University, Dehradun. She has worked with Rajasthan Foundation, Kolkata Chapter which is an autonomous body instituted by Govt. of Rajasthan. Dr. Shashi has presented many papers in national and International Seminars and conferences. She has also more than fifteen publications in national and international journals and edited books. Presently she is working as assistant professor in Sunbeam College for Women, Bhagwanpur, and Varanasi. She is also specialized in organising quality circle workshops.

Walter Vesperi is a PhD student in Economics and Management at the University of Messina. He is teaching assistant in human resource management and organization behavior. His research focuses on the management of entrepreneurship, spinoffs and knowledge management. Also he is a member of several scientific community: ASSIOA and AIDP (Italian Association of personnel managers). He is author and co-author of scientific article for international conferences and journals. Walter is reviewer for international journals.

Index

U

W

www.ingramcontent.com/pod-product-compliance
Lightning Source LLC
LaVergne TN
LVHW061549290926
849162LV00004B/957